THE
BROKEN
BOUGH

Books by Edward M. Keating

THE BROKEN BOUGH (1975)
FREE HUEY! (1970)
THE SCANDAL OF SILENCE (1965)

Edward M. Keating

THE
BROKEN
BOUGH

*The Solution to
the Riddle of Man*

ATHENEUM

New York

1975

To Bonnie,

WHO SUSTAINED ME DURING
THE LONG NIGHT OF SILENCE

CONTENTS

Introduction   1

ALPHA   3
THE ARBOREAL/TERRESTRIAL CONFLICT
   THESIS   14

PART I THE LABYRINTH

BEFORE THE FALL   19
AFTER THE FALL   31
TOOLS, ERGO MAN   41
THE GREAT WALL OF MORTAR   74
FIGHTING ICE WITH FIRE   88
THE GREAT HUNT   95
THE TRUMPET SOUNDS   108
THE COCOON   117

Interlude   125

The Crouching Bison   127

PART II   THE CRADLE

THE MOTHER-TREE   137
BREAKING THE BOUGH   151
OEDIPUS IN THE VIENNA WOODS   172

PART III   THE GALLERY

THE WARRIOR   185
THE OBJECT   209
THE CHEAT   245
THE PRISONER   272
THE DREAMER   306
THE HUNTER   339

PART IV   JANUS

A PHOENIX RISING OUT OF MORTAR   367
REVOLUTION . . .   377
. . AND COUNTERREVOLUTION   394
THE FATE OF THE PHOENIX   409
TOWARD MERE EXISTENCE   419

Bibliography   458
Index   464

Introduction

ALPHA

NOTHING arouses man's curiosity more than himself. From the dawn of history to this very moment he has addressed himself to two basic questions of human existence: What are man's origins? What is his destiny? The answers are sought, not so much for their own sake, but for the possibility that they might serve as reference points from which to turn in toward the central question of human existence: What is man?

The idea is quite simple. Perhaps, it goes, if we could learn about the beginnings of the species and how, more or less, it got from there to here, we might better understand man's nature and thereby how to solve so many of the problems that afflict him. Unfortunately, man has never found a satisfying—and abiding—answer. Before the scientific age, he resorted to philosophy in an effort to seek out an answer. As a consequence he subsisted on pure speculation. There was no proof of anything beyond Descartes's dictum, *Cogito, ergo sum,* which upon even a moment's reflection means relatively little. It doesn't even qualify as a philosophical witticism. As for helping man to understand himself it contributes nothing, not even a starting point for speculation for the critical reason that Descartes begins where he should leave off: with man thinking.

Unable to determine beginnings, man has sought to discover endings, not so much to explain man and his sufferings, but to justify them. Since he cannot discover the cause of his afflictions and therefore cannot eliminate them, he tries to give them some utilitarian function. This idea is also quite simple. It states that suffering must have significance, even if not in terms of this life. Religion has spent thousands of years seeking the answer. In default of finding one, it has found many: Christianity, Buddhism, Islam, Hinduism, Judaism, etc., etc., etc. All agree on the fact of suffering, no two agree on its significance, and by differing on this, they thereby differ on the nature of man.

With the beginning of the scientific age, man began his earthly explorations into the matter. Something very commonsensical told him that if man had origins, they would be found somewhere in this world. Possibly not on the earth itself, but at least in this world. As for the question of destiny, for almost all of the scientific age, scientists have left the matter to others, for once feeling themselves inadequate to probe into something that had not yet come into existence.

Of course, Darwin shocked everyone by insisting that man was literally descended from the apes and that at one time his ancestors (remote! remote! it must be insisted!) actually lived in trees. While scientists and possibly a few amused atheists rallied around Darwin's cause, the rest of the world simply turned away from him, the way one turns away from an unpleasant odor.

With Darwin it could be said that at last man had discovered his origins, thereby providing him with an important reference point from which to commence the long journey to modern man, thus permitting him to understand his nature, solve his problems, and free himself from suffering. However, it was not to be. Something within man refused to admit to animal ancestry. Man was, after all, *Man*. He my have *come* from apelike creatures many millions of years ago, but anyone could see that man was unique in all of nature. This is not to say, the argument goes on, that we moderns continue to believe in the special creation theory propounded by the religionists, but still, what if Darwin were proved wrong after all? Everyone knows that it's just a theory. What facts are there actually? A few fossils scattered about, and on this scanty evidence you are going to suggest that man is an animal? What of man's sublime brain? His civilizations? His art, his music, his poetry? What of man's soul? Surely these are not descended from the apes!

We might restate the proposition this way: While man's ancestors may well have been one thing, man himself is something altogether different. We might even go so far as to say that man *evolved* from apelike creatures, and that at a certain point along the line of this long evolutionary process, a qualitative change took place that, when joined with all the previous quantitative changes, produced the unique creature called man.

In truth, it can be said that Darwin has been dismissed from current affairs. He may well have been right about man's ancestors living in trees, but that is the extent of it. Too much has happened to man living on earth to attach much significance to his origins in the trees. That sort of thing is best left to paleontologists; man needs the scrutiny of psychologists, sociologists, and cultural anthropologists if he is to understand his problems.

And thus the circle is completed. Having gone back to origins and having found little of value there, man has returned to his modern world where he sits upon the ground and worries about the future, the past having been put in its proper place: the past.

The future, of course, has its starting point in the present. We begin with man as he is and go on from there. This, then, confronts us with the nature of man, and the conclusion is drawn that man is a unique combination of instincts and learned responses. To safeguard the future, we must suppress man's destructive instincts (or could it be that they are learned responses?) and reinforce his socially acceptable behavior patterns (yet, is it possible they are instinctive?), thereby assuring man of a peaceful and socially prosperous future.

The difficulty with this view is its premise. What if man is not the unique combination they assert? Suppose that instead of man's destructive actions being instinctive, they are a response to certain external factors that comprise an integral and inescapable part of his earthly environment? What if there is a fundamental part of man that is not subject to social reinforcement? These questions alone raise critical doubts about the validity of the premise and thus, once again, we are confronted with the question of man's nature.

On the one hand there is man with his art, his music, his poetry, his ability to love, his great civilizations, his art of medicine, his sense of justice, and everything else he holds so dear. These good things are part of man and they are to be preserved; it is only the bad things man wants to be rid of: killing, oppression, aggression, suffering, and everything else that he holds in low esteem. It is as if man could be cleft in two; as if, because the good and the bad proceed from separate and distinct sources, man could exist with the good without being burdened by the bad. It is because man wants the good without the bad that he proceeds as he does to reinforce the one while seeking to eradicate the other. But can he? Thousands of years of history indicate that the good and the bad are so much a part of man that as long as man exists he will be comforted by one and plagued by the other. Thus, again, we complete a circle. Man cannot go into the future without taking with him everything that is within him, because he cannot be cleft in two. Man, is after all, man. Or is he?

The great complaint about man is that he kills other men. It is within most of us to accept man's killing of prey in order to eat. And yet it disturbs us. If prey is to be killed for food, let others do it—and out of our sight. We delight in roast beef, but we'd rather not see the slaughterhouse. It is the same when man kills other men. We want the fruits of war, but we don't want to do the actual killing. We cheer the victory, but prefer that others attain it for us. We can't stand the sight of blood.

In contrast, we lavish affection on man's creative talents. From our mother we derive life itself; from the artist, the life of the soul. We rejoice in the birth of a barnyard animal and the sprouting of the planted seed. All these are within man's province, and they are, in some miraculous way, the purest reflection of nature's world.

What is remarkable about man is that he refuses to accept the fact that he kills, while he accepts, and with enormous pleasure, the fact that he can actively participate in the creation of life. This is not something restricted to the biological reproduction of the species; that is common to all of nature. Man's uniqueness is in his ability to take the separate elements provided by nature and combine them into new life. This is really a most extraordinary accomplishment. It far surpasses that of killing. Other creatures kill. They do so primarily to eat. Yet not one of them can create life the way man can. Not one of them can take living elements from nature and combine them so as to provide food for themselves. This, I believe, is man's most astounding accomplishment. And yet, it is scarcely touched upon in attempting to understand him.

There is something else that man can do that no other creature can. He can take nonliving elements produced by nature and combine them into machines, and then take other nonliving elements of nature and feed them to machines as fuels. In other words, man can control the elements of nature in such a way as to produce energy: food energy for himself and his animals, and fuel energy for his machinery. No other creatures can do that. All they can do is take directly from nature that particular form of energy that will sustain their own lives.

So, man can create life and he can destroy it; he can produce energy for himself, and he can produce it for his machinery. He can do all this because he is man. What then is man that he can do all these things?

No matter what context we place the question in, we always come upon a circular path that finally reduces itself to the statement that man is man. And yet, is he?

Man has sought himself in his origins, in his present state, and in his future. Like a compulsive lecturegoer, he has seen dozens of slide shows—fossils, artifacts, psychological profiles,

microscopic scenes, battlefield vistas, and a thousand other bits
of evidence—and he has heard dozens of narrators telling the
story of man. The problem is that while the pictures at the
lectures are all the same, the story varies from lecture hall to
lecture hall. There is, in brief, a serious contradiction.

There is an explanation given. It is that man is an extremely
complex creature, whether we are talking of the object of our
scrutiny or whether we are talking of our storyteller. This complexity, it seems, explains the variations. It is a matter of emphasis. After all, everyone is agreed nowadays on two essential
facts: that the journey to man was begun by a very ancient
apelike creature living in trees; and that man exists today as
proof that the journey was successfully completed. As for the
path taken, it must be remembered that there is more than one
path to God. Similarly, there is ample room for many paths in
the journey from the trees to modern man.

Within this explanation is an inner core of dogged insistence
that the only important thing is that man has survived the
journey.

Implicit in this type of thinking is the notion that man is the
measure of all things. When he looks back at the landscape between himself and the barely discernible trees, he sees ever-
decreasing reflections of himself until a critical osmotic moment
when, quite mysteriously, man is no more; in his place is the
primordial ape.

The discerning reader will notice that I have practiced a
small, though critical, deception. I have gone backwards from
man in search of the original apelike creature. The evidence, as
it were, has all been projected on the screen, but in precisely
the reverse order. I began with man, rather than ending with
him. I was, in my demonstration, very much like Descartes, who
established *Cogito, ergo sum* as the premise of his speculations
on man. Yes, man thinks, but what of that distant ancestor in
the trees of Africa? Did it think as Descartes's man thinks?

The perspective which sets man as the standard has caused
all of the efforts at understanding to fail. Man is not the meas-

ure of all things; he is the conclusion. He is not the beginning; he is the ending. He is not the Alpha; he is the Omega.

To say that man thinks is to state a conclusion. To say that man is a killer, that he is a creator—in short, to say anything about man—is to talk about conclusions. Man is not the premise of his existence; he is the conclusion of another's existence.

This confusion between Alpha and Omega has had man living in a crazy world of mirrors. Everything is backward. Cause becomes effect, the child bears the parent, and the finish line becomes the starting point.

The same thing is true of man's great contemporary problems. If we have man as the premise of our considerations, say, of such things as his lethal practices and his creative practices, we run the serious risk of concluding that they are part of man's nature. If man actually possesses a killer instinct, there is nothing that can be done except to place him in confinement, which is a subtle way of saying that man should be put out of his misery. What is most fascinating—and it seems to have occurred to no one—is that man, if he possesses the killer instinct, should not be disturbed by the fact. Does the lion fret over its killer instinct? That man suffers over the fact he kills is, to me, important evidence that he in fact does not possess a killer instinct, but instead has an instinct at variance with that of the killer.

When we turn to man's creative practices, we see the reflection of the problem posed by his lethal practices. Man must produce his own food if he is to survive. Yet we know that millions all over the world get little or nothing to eat while a very small percentage of the world's population overstuffs itself. It is obvious that man has no instinct in such matters. To eat is instinctive, but to create food is not.

What is true of food is also true of fuel. Today the world faces a fuel crisis of monumental proportions. Man's logical processes have informed him over the years that there is only so much fuel in the world. Yet he is consuming it at a rate that will soon leave him without any. It would be easy to blame man's stupidity, his selfishness, or whatever for this critical energy situation, yet man is the victim, not the causal agent. There is nothing within man to guide him in these matters. It is the difference between habit and instinct. Man has no instinct in these matters; whatever regulatory abilities he has are the result of induced habit. The problems we face today stem from habit's attempting to control instinct. It simply won't work—especially when habit operates in ignorance of instinct.

For example, public officials are presently seeking to change "driving habits" so as to conserve fuel. This is a worthy objective. But what does this change of habit run into? The answer is suggested by one of the objections to restricted automobile driving: "I've got to drive to work every day." This, of course, is true. And why does the driver of the automobile go to work? To provide the money to buy the food he needs to live. To eat is instinctive. How are we going to get people to do the things that threaten (or appear to threaten) so basic a need as food? You might as well threaten to cut off the air he breathes.

And yet, that is precisely what is happening. Pollution also threatens modern man. Every logical process within man warns against polluting the air, the water, and the earth—the three things man needs most in order to survive. Yet man continues to pollute, and at an ever-increasing rate. Is this not insane? What is it inside of man that allows him to "soil the nest" in which he lives? Surely that is suicidal. The fact is that it isn't something within man that allows him to pollute the world. It is, in reality, the *absence* of something within man that is producing this problem.

In 1971 Geoffrey H. Bourne published *The Ape People: Our Nearest Relatives Reveal Man's Secrets and Similarities.*[1] Bourne was amply qualified to bring such a book together. He had studied apes—chimpanzees, gorillas, and orangutans—for many years and was at the time of the book the director of the Yerkes Primate Research Center of Emory University in

---

1. New York: G. P. Putnam's Sons. (The subtitle is very misleading. There were interesting comparisons, but no significant connections made.)

Atlanta, Georgia, then the only research center in the world which specialized in working with the great apes. Notwithstanding a lifetime of observation and research, Bourne, on one of the very earliest pages, made the following observation:

> The difficulty in toilet training highly intelligent animals as the primates is surprising, especially in view of the extraordinary toilet instincts of some of the felines.

While this may seem, at first blush, to be an exceedingly minor point, in reality it is tremendously important. It reveals that the authoritative author didn't really understand the nature of the beast he was studying—and writing about.

Why should it be so difficult to toilet-train a primate,[2] while felines don't even need to be trained, enjoying, as Bourne expressed it, "extraordinary toilet instincts"? The answer is obvious, yet Bourne never saw it. Felines have an *instinct* against soiling the nest which includes regulating elimination processes so as not to soil the nest. The primate, on the other hand, is an arboreal creature—that is, it lives in the trees—so there is no need for an instinct against soiling a nest (which it doesn't have anyway). The arboreal primate can allow urine, feces, and food to drop to the ground under the tree. In no way is the cleanliness or health of the primate affected by its careless disposal of its waste products. The feline, on the other hand, lives on the ground and bears and nurtures its offspring in secluded places. Survival demands a clean nest. Hence, the instinct. Survival doesn't make such a demand on the primate. Hence, the absence of such an instinct.

All this being true, what if an arboreal primate became confined to the ground? At best, and with patient training, it might

---

2. W. C. Osman Hill, in *Evolutionary Biology of the Primates* (New York: Academic Press, 1972), p. 1, defines primates as "Unguiculate, claviculate placental mammals, with orbits encircled by bone; three kinds of teeth, at least at one time of life; brain always with a posterior lobe and a calcarine fissure; the innermost digit of at least one pair of extremities opposable; hallux with a flat nail, or none; a well-developed caecum; penis pendulous, testes scrotal; always two pectoral mammae."

be able to develop a habit of tidiness. Yet what would happen if this painfully acquired habit conflicted with something instinctual? Habit would give way very quickly.

War, resources, pollution—to name but three of the most pressing and obvious problems—weigh heavily on man. They threaten his existence, in fact. If man continues to approach these problems as he has in the past and as he is doing today, he will never begin to solve them. And by failing to solve them, man will soon become extinct. It is either solve the problems or be swamped by them. It is that simple. But to get at the root of man's problems, we must get at the root of man.

If we are to understand man, we must begin where man began: in the trees where his distant ancestors lived the life of ordinary arboreal primates. It is there we will find the answer to the question, What is man? We will discover that man is an arboreal primate. Once we have grasped this essential fact, we can proceed to explore what has happened to this primate that he should suffer so today in a world to which he was not born.

This book is that exploration and, I am convinced, the explanation of man's suffering—and his accomplishments—is contained in its pages.

As the reader will shortly see, my thesis is really quite simple.

Part I, "The Labyrinth," is an exploration of the processes by which the human species came to be fashioned out of the base stock of the arboreal primate.

Part II, "The Cradle," is an explanation of the processes by which the adult of today is fashioned out of the base stock of the arboreal infant.

Part III, "The Gallery," consists of six sketches that reveal the principal facets of man, the descendant primate. "The Warrior" deals with man and war; "The Object" concerns the social-sexual subordination of women; "The Cheat" shows how man attempts to escape from terrestrial suffering; "The Prisoner" explores the conflict between man's arboreal and terrestrial minds; "The Dreamer" explains man's religious impulse; and

"The Hunter" describes man's efforts to construct neo-arborea.

Part IV, "Janus," reflects on man's journey to his present survival crisis, and contemplates man's future.

The purpose of Parts I and II is to establish the Arboreal/Terrestrial Conflict Thesis as it has affected the species and as it affects the life of the individual. The purpose of Part III is to show how this conflict manifests itself in the major facets of human existence. It is not enough that man's remote ancestors were arboreal primates. The importance of my thesis lies in the fact that modern man is being rent by the conflict between his arboreal nature and the demands of terrestrial living. Whether we are talking of war or sex, religion or psychology, crime or motherhood, this great conflict is always present, significantly affecting everything man does.

Man has never ceased to be an arboreal primate. Nothing in all his terrestrial experience has changed his original nature. It is because he remains an arboreal primate while being obliged to live in the terrestrial mode of existence that he suffers from the Arboreal/Terrestrial Conflict. This is my major theme.

Part IV brings together all the major strands of the Arboreal/Terrestrial Conflict Thesis in the form of an analysis of man's present situation, which is a major survival crisis brought about by this conflict within him. I close with a discussion of man's future, offering what I believe to be man's best hope of overcoming his ultimate terrestrial crisis.

If my thesis is right, then with this new-found truth finally possessed, man can set about the business of salvaging a future out of an impossible present that has as its premise a most improbable past that began with an arboreal primate climbing about the trees of Africa millions of years ago.

THE ARBOREAL
TERRESTRIAL
CONFLICT
THESIS

M<small>Y THESIS</small> is quite simple. There was a time—quite
some millions of years ago—when there was an apelike
creature living in the tropical forests of central Africa. Also,
there was a time—only a few thousand years ago—when there
appeared on the earth a creature called *Homo sapiens:* man.
The basic factor of my thesis is that the apelike creature that
once lived in the African forests was the remote, but direct,
ancestor of modern man. This basic factor is not a new notion.
Every reputable anthropologist today agrees with it. The evidence in its support is overwhelming, and it is not controverted
by a scintilla of supportable evidence.

The second step in my thesis is this: Modern man is, in respect to his essential nature, precisely the same arboreal primate
he once was while living in the African forests. While there
have occurred very obvious changes in physical form, the essential nature of both the original arboreal ancestor and modern
man are identical. This assertion, unlike the first, has not, as

far as I know, been made before. Yet I believe it is the most important fact about man; it explains the very essence of what is today known as "the human condition."

For several thousand years man has sought to explain himself. He has sought out the truth in philosophy, religion, psychology, and sociology. And in none of these has he found the answer to David's question to the Lord: "What is man that you should be mindful of him?" My reply to David would be that man is an arboreal primate living in a terrestrial mode of existence. Because the essential nature of the original primate persists to this day in modern man, I would extend my answer to say that man seeks to return to the arboreal environment.

The assertion that man is an arboreal primate means that man's instincts are arboreal. This being the case, something other than instinct has made it possible for men to survive in the terrestrial mode. His cultivated habituations to terrestrial living have been his means of survival.

Because of his arboreal nature and his arboreal instincts, man seeks to return to arborea in order to reduce the unbearable stress on his body occasioned by existence in terrestria. But because of certain physical changes, man cannot leave his terrestrial environment. He is confined to terrestria. Since he cannot go back to arborea, he seeks to establish within the confines of terrestria a neo-arborea in the hope of accomplishing what a direct return to arborea would accomplish.

In summary, my thesis is contained in three dichotomies. They are:

1) Man's origins were arboreal; his circumstances are terrestrial.

2) Man's instincts are arboreal; his habituations are terrestrial.

3) Man is confined to the terrestrial mode of existence; he aspires to return to arborea.

Within these three dichotomies is contained the essence of everything to be presented in this work. They explain man's origins and his present circumstances; they explain man's nature and the basis for the distortions of that nature; and they explain the ultimate purpose of terrestrialized man: the return to his natural habitat, and thus to his natural state. (In default of an ability to do this directly man seeks indirectly to do this by establishing neo-arborea within the confines of the terrestrial mode.)

Man is by nature arboreal; by circumstance he is terrestrial. As a consequence there exists in man what I call the Arboreal/ Terrestrial Conflict. This is my thesis.

PART ONE

The Labyrinth

Humpty Dumpty sat on a wall,
Humpty Dumpty had a great fall;
All the king's horses
And all the king's men
Couldn't put Humpty Dumpty together again.

BEFORE THE
FALL

O N C E , many millions of years ago, in the tropical forests of Africa there was, among a variety of arboreal primates, one that eventually had a descendant known as man. I think it is necessary to put it this way rather than to say that man's remote ancestor was an arboreal primate. The reason for this is the matter of perspective, something I believe that has seriously hampered all previous efforts at understanding man and his origins.

If, in our exploration into man's origins, we try to roll time backward, we will very shortly become lost in the shadows behind Sumer. But more important, we will see the whole process in reverse. We will, by this method, fail to see the dynamics of the process by which an arboreal primate was obliged to leave its arboreal world and descend, much against its will, into the terrestrial world. Also, if we look backward we will begin with man and end with an arboreal primate, whereas in reality man is the conclusion and the arboreal primate is the premise. By going backward in time we would perceive the entire process from the perspective of man. By going forward in time we can perceive the process from the perspective of the arboreal primate. And it is from this perspective that we can observe the

unfolding of the events that several million years later led
to man.

Accepting the arboreal premise, what are its implications?
Before saying what the affirmative implications are, we might
best begin by commenting on the negative implications. Briefly,
there is no language, there are no civilizations, there is no art,
there are not even clothes. There is nothing of man—except for
his aboreal premise. There is only a creature living in the trees.

To begin with, the original primate we are investigating was
naturally adapted to the arboreal environment, the end result
of a process that had begun millions of years earlier when the
original insectivore began its slow ascent into the arboreal
world where there was more food less competitively sought
after and where the little creature would be safe from terrestrial
predators.

An animal that lives in a tree, rather than merely visiting it,
must find its food there. Also, it must be able to find a place in
which to perch and in which to sleep. Further, it must be able
to reproduce and provide a place of nurture for dependent offspring. In other words, the processes of life, of reproduction,
and of nurture must all take place in the tree before it can be
said that adaptation is complete.

The first requirement is that of being able to get about in the
tree. It is one thing to walk around on the ground as the original insectivore did; it is something else to dash through the
trees, up, down, around, and up again. What is needed for any
but the smallest tree animals, such as the squirrel, are limbs
that can grasp the branches so as to be able to swing between
them. It is because of this grasping need that the primates developed the opposing thumb.

Because of the complexity and irregularity of the arboreal
world, as well as its three-dimensional nature, agile primates
have to be capable of a wide range of limb movements. Because
the arboreal world is precarious—falling is the greatest hazard
—limbs must do more than provide locomotion. Primates have
to free their forelimbs from functioning solely for locomotion

and support and use them also as exploratory devices. This freeing of the forelimbs, combined with the ability to grasp, also means that they can be used for gathering food and bringing it to their mouths, thus eliminating the need for a long snout.

Nutritional factors more than any other environmental factor direct the course of evolution, and the very origin of primates can be attributed to the fact of an abundant arboreal food supply which was largely herbivorous. Aside from Old World monkeys, the basic structure of the alimentary canal of all primates scarcely differs from that of the original insectivore. As a result of their relatively unspecialized teeth and digestive systems, arboreal primates are largely restricted to a diet of succulent fruits, tender leaves, young shoots, and buds that are obtainable only in a climate moist and warm enough to support abundant and tender vegetation during the entire year. This diet—a nutritionally complete one—is found in the trees of Africa's tropical forest, and was available in the remote past, on even a greater scale than today.

The arboreal world is not one of smells, as was the terrestrial world from which the insectivore came. As a consequence, the olfactory system atrophied and the long mammalian snout slowly diminished in size. In contrast, visual acuity is enormously important. It is the dominant sense in all primates. This can be seen in the size of the eyes, their position at the front of the head, and the differentiation of the retina. The eyes of ordinary mammals are entirely lateral, and there is no overlap of visual fields. In primates the optical axes are more or less parallel, thus granting them stereoptical vision, a distinct advantage when traveling rapidly from branch to branch and leaping from tree to tree. Further, the development of color vision has been important in aiding primates to discover various-colored foods. Interestingly, color vision began in fishes, but was lost in all intervening land types before the primates. Vision on land is far less important than smell; hence the rise of the olfactory system and the diminution of the visual—that is, until the primates. I mention this to show that in the adaptive process there is a substantive reason for everything; thus far we have seen the reason why primates developed the hand with the opposing thumb, why their digestive and dental systems developed the way they did, and why the primates' peculiar color-stereoptic vision developed. As can be readily appreciated, these primate attributes are also those of man.

As has been already suggested, the arboreal world is a hazardous world. A step, a miscalculation, and death or serious bodily injury can meet the careless or inadequate on the remote floor of the tropical forest. While it is true that for the original insectivore and for all those that evolved from this base stock, the arboreal world was one of abundant food and a welcome refuge from virtually all possible predators, it was nevertheless an extremely dangerous world for the ill-equipped. Awareness of the many and varied aspects of the arboreal environment is absolutely essential for survival. This demanded in the developmental period a greatly increased elaboration of the sense organs and, as can be anticipated, there has been among primates progressive development of those parts of the cerebral cortex concerned with sensory representation. Also, since in such a precarious environment firm control of movements and balance are required, the cortical areas of motor control and the cerebellum became elaborated. As a result of the need of primates to adapt to a hazardous tree-world or perish, selective pressures worked toward increasing complexity of the brain and its allied systems. The result is the primate's relatively large brain.

While there were various other adaptive developments of the primate, there is only one more we need examine here, and that relates to the number of offspring. The problems of the newborn infant are great in the arboreal world, and more offspring can be raised successfully if they are born in small numbers at a time. This reduces intrauterine competition for sustenance, and it increases postparturition nurturing prospects by the mother for each offspring. Primates tend to give birth to no more than two, and generally only one, infant at a time. Also, it is characteristic of primates that the prematuration period is extended and that infants are dependent on maternal care for a relatively long period of time. (It is interesting to note that a tree habitat is one of the few in which a reduction of litter size carries an increased overall reproductive fitness. And, of course, in arborea there is less danger to the young from predators so there is less need for large litters.)

We have, in summary, a network of adaptive developments that began with the terrestrial insectivore and ended with the fully evolved and adapted arboreal primate. As to the dynamics of the process, we might think of the environment as having a certain profile. Genetic action of a species seeks to conform the species to that profile at all times. Failure to maintain contact will doom a species to extinction. Success in maintaining contact leads to survival. As an environment changes its profile, genetic change must keep pace or contact will be lost and extinction will follow. With the primates, the change of environment from the terrestrial world to the arboreal was made by the original insectivore in exceedingly slow stages, so that contact between species and environment was always maintained, but—and this is critical—in the course of maintaining contact, the original insectivore evolved into the tree shrew and the tree shrew into what is known as the prosimian, the basic stock of the primate, an evolutionary process that took over fifty million years. But when the process was over there existed a variety of primates that maintained a species profile in contact with the profile of the arboreal environment, and survived. More, they flourished for tens of millions of years.

In the order of primates that so evolved were the ancestors of the modern chimpanzee, the gorilla, and the orangutan. Also in the order were the arboreal ancestors of man.

Adaptation is not merely a matter of anatomy. It is also a social process. And if we are to understand subsequent man, we must first understand the social dimension of primate adaptation to the arboreal environment.

The society of primates is dictated by a combination of their environment and their physical attributes. For example, there is the central matter of infant dependency. Although not as long as modern man's, that of primate infants is relatively protracted. It is not just a matter of purely physical dependence; it is also a matter of the infant's brain not being completely developed at birth. The infant must be taught all those things not provided by instinct. It is because the infant is so dependent for such a long time that a social system is necessary to protect its nurture.

If dependent offspring and their nurturing mothers were left to their own devices—and at their most vulnerable period— while the adult males went their own way, predators long ago would have driven primates to extinction, especially those who had to come to the ground rather frequently. To safeguard the survival of the species, a social system evolved, at the center of which were the dependent offspring and at the periphery of which were the adult males who guarded the affinity group.[1]

Probably the prime advantage of the primate social system is the facilitation of learning by the young. Infants could learn from their mothers only, without the existence of the affinity group. However, within social groups the amount of learning transmitted to the young can be increased and broadened beyond that provided by the individual mother alone. The affinity group maintains a pool of experience greater than that possessed by an individual, and this pooled experience is passed on by each generational group to the next. The identification of edible and inedible food, the recognition of competitors and predators, the lessons of dominance and territory, as well as of sex, are all essential knowledge and can often be gained secondhand from others without the need for personal experiences.

The second major advantage of the primate social system is that of mutual defense. The primate affinity group tends to be centered on the females and infants (through juveniles). The

---

1. Primates live in groups variously called troops, packs, and so on. I have chosen the term *affinity group* because a special affinity among the members is the basis for the existence of the group.

peripheral adult males are equipped by size and strength to defend the group from most dangers save those from large predators, against which primates have perfected a guarding and signaling system that allows the group to escape to the trees if they are on the ground, or to the highest branches if already in the trees.

Within the affinity group, there is a dominance hierarchy based on strength, agility, and personality. After the period of play conflict among the young, the dominance structure is maintained by threat, display, and actual physical attack. However, physical attacks are nonlethal, being those assertive actions necessary to maintain the hierarchical system. In brief, dominance and order are maintained by "adaptive aggressions." [2] This type of conduct is critically adaptive, since it avoids the risks of wounds, disease, and even death arising from open conflict within the group. Conflict, usually in the harmless form of display, is very important in maintaining proper relations with other species. Territory is maintained by threat, and for defense against enemies, sufficiently threatening gestures and sounds by adult males will usually scare off intruders—except, of course, major predators.

These, then, are the essential characteristics of primate society—the parent of man's society.

I must, at this juncture, anticipate a possible objection that would more or less insist that, while fossil evidence may reveal anatomy, no human was around those millions of years ago to witness the functioning of primate society. This is entirely true. For an analysis of behavior we must rely entirely on the observation of contemporary primates, but when we do, when we observe them all, from the obscure lemur to the most advanced

2. The subject of aggression, whether human or what is here described as "adaptive aggressions," is both complex and, unfortunately, emotionally loaded. A discussion intended to clear the air as much as possible is set forth in "The Warrior," *infra.* Unless specified otherwise, any future use of the word *aggression* is intended to refer to human aggression and not to "adaptive aggression" above described.

anthropoid apes, we see the very features just described. If these features are evident today, they must have had their origins in the past.

This, then, leads us to a summary of arboreal life. As we approach it, we must keep in mind that what I am about to describe was once the way of life for man's arboreal ancestors. Indeed, it was the foundation on which the descendants of these creatures built their later way of life. It is, in fact, this arboreal way of life that forms the premise of man: what I have previously referred to as man's arboreal premise.

When we consider the common elements of arboreal existence that are shared by the great majority of primates—especially the anthropoid apes, those primates most closely related to man—we discover six essential features. As we consider them, we should keep in mind the fact that the foundation of behavior is rooted in genetic composition. It is not happenstance that determines primate life. Primate behavior, like all creature behavior, is determined by the species/environment equation, and the species side of the equation is genetically molded.

With this in mind, let us now observe the six essential features that comprise a summary of primate existence in the arboreal world.

1. The eating of food is a casual, noncompetitive, noncooperative activity in which all members of the affinity group (after the infant dependency period) satisfy their sustenance needs on their own and without help from another member of the group. Further, eating is a direct transaction in that by use of its own limbs and faculties each is able to satisfy its sustenance needs. While modern observations show that chimpanzees, alone of the anthropoid apes, occasionally will eat meat, the central, sustaining diet is herbivorous.

2. There is sexual promiscuity. When a female comes into season, the adult males copulate with her, and she in turn sexually accepts all adult males. This is so even in the presence of dominant males. No primate infant knows its father, and no

adult male knows what infants have been sired by him. As a consequence, there is no such thing as paternity or paternal solicitude, or paternal nurturing. The relationship between an adult male and an infant is that between the protector of the affinity group and a member of that group. All nurturing of infants is done by their mothers.[3]

3. There is no need to control, as to time and place, the processes of elimination, as urine and feces fall to the ground. Thus there is no instinct against "soiling the nest," an instinct otherwise constant among mammals. Similarly, food picked but not eaten is allowed to drop to the forest floor, without soiling the nest.

4. Sleeping is casual, all but dependent infants tending to sleep (both during the day and at night) wherever they happen to be at the time. Generally, members of the affinity group sleep close to each other, often with the males slightly segregated from the females. Dependent infants sleep with their mothers. If very young, they sleep on their mothers; if older, next to their mothers. When preparing to sleep at night, adults fashion a temporary nest of vines and branches, and nothing more. The next night, wherever they may be, they fashion another temporary nest. Most infrequently will the same brief nest be used more than once.

5. Protection against predators is provided by a social system of leadership and warning. Because of primates' remarkable ability to move about in trees, there are few serious predators.

6. Intraspecies order is maintained by a dominance system which, in turn, is maintained by display and other forms of adaptive aggression. There is no lethal activity between members of the same species. Very rarely, when protecting the group, adult males may kill a predator, but this is essentially a defensive action. With the exceptions noted here and in No. 1,

---

3. The single exception to this general system is the modern gibbon "family," which consists of male, female, and dependent offspring. Factors beyond the scope of the present discussion militate strongly against the gibbon "family" being a precursor of the human family.

it can be said that primates do not kill for food or for other reasons.

These, then, are the six essential features that comprise a summary of existence in the arboreal world. Logically—inescapably—these were the essential features of arboreal life when man's hominid ancestors lived in arborea. They were essential if the species was to maintain its species profile in contact with the profile of the environment. Failure of any one of these features, with the possible exception of sleeping and elimination habits, would have meant extinction.

The reason for this is found in the fact that they concern the very essentials of existence, not merely those of arboreal primates.

Sustenance and sex are two essential elements in the existence of the individual and of the species. While it is true that on an individual level sex—at least its overt expression—may not be an essential element of existence, in the cumulative sense it is, for if enough individuals do not engage in sexual activity, the future of the species will be endangered.

Sustenance, in brief, is necessary for the survival of the individual; sex, for the survival of the species. Therefore, in order of priority, sustenance is anterior to sex; the individual must sustain itself at least to the point of maturity so that it can reproduce. Then, naturally, in the order of priority, comes sex.

However, for there to be sustenance and sex, there is actually a prior necessity: the individual must be able to protect itself from predation so that, seriatim, it can gain sustenance and engage in sexual activity.

Thus, when we view the entire sequence, we see three essential elements in the existence of both the individual and the species. They are, in order of priority, protection against predation, sustenance, and sex.

Under the social system that evolved as a result of species adaptation to the arboreal environment, these three essential elements were constantly present during the period when man's hominid ancestors lived in arborea. And they were constantly present in the form set forth here, because only in this form could the species have survived the strict demands of the arboreal environment.

In terms of protection against predators, the primate lacked "tooth and claw" with which to be able to defend effectively against predators possessing the necessary "tooth and claw." Therefore, they had to use an escape system. But this could only work if there was a warning system and if the adult males guarded the affinity group, since neither the females, either pregnant or nurturing, nor the infants were able to render that service.

As for sustenance, on the basis of the nature of the environment and of the food supply, each had to fend for itself. Indeed, each was able to fend for itself.

As for sex, promiscuity was essential to prevent the possibility of too much inbreeding, to allow as much as possible the principle of natural selection to operate, and to improve prospects of impregnation.

Lethality was not necessary to procure food. Attempts at lethality in an effort to protect the affinity group, in view of the fact that their predators were carnivorous mammals and snakes, would have been futile, guaranteeing quick extinction.

A final observation that must be made about arboreal life (though to a large extent it is also true of other animal life) concerns the role of the female. In arborea, as elsewhere in nature, the female is the protagonist. She perpetuates the species. Therefore, her well-being and protection has the highest priority. It is the function of the male to impregnate; it is the function of the female to procreate. Further, it is the female who nurtures and largely trains her offspring for life in the affinity group. It is the female, then, who shapes the society. The male, lacking a nurturing function, leads a peripheral existence, and this quite literally. It is he who protects the group, not by "tooth and claw," but by diligence in observing the surrounding prem-

ises for predators—and warning when necessary so that the
more vulnerable members of the group can move to safety. The
point is to preserve the reproductive capabilities of the species,
even if in the process some of the males are actually killed. Only
in emergencies does the male become the protagonist. Then he
commands and directs, and all else stops as he provides for the
flight to safety. At all other times, notwithstanding the formal
fact of male dominance, the true protagonist of the species is
the female. What is true of the modern primate was true of the
primate ancestor of man. The consequences of this fact have
proven of enormous importance to the development of man in
the terrestrial mode and form one of the principal ingredients
in the entire process.

In this way, then, man's arboreal ancestors existed in the
tropical forests of Africa for tens of millions of years.

In the midst of this seemingly endless existence there appeared a catastrophe, but of the most subtle nature. The rains,
so necessary for life in the arboreal world, slowly ceased. Some
twenty to twenty-five million years ago, a very slow aridation
began. As a consequence, there began the slow contraction of
the great expanse of tropical forest that at one time encom-
passed virtually all of the African continent. As the contraction
set in, a retreat began that saw, some several million years ago,
the final event transpire in central Africa. It was not a precipitous event, but it was one of monumental importance—at
least for man. The forests became so shrunken as a result of
the long period of aridation that man's hominid ancestors,
along with other types of arboreal primates, were forced out of
the trees by superior primates and were obliged to take up existence in the terrestrial environment. However, just as the
aridation process was of long duration and of subtle effect, so
too the terrestrialization process was of long duration and of
subtle effect. But it was a resolute process with no turning back.
In the end, it produced man.

AFTER THE
FALL

CIVILIZATION began at Sumer. All that occurred before was a prelude. In its way, the prelude was to Sumer what the insectivore had been to the order of primates. It led to the climb from prehistory to history; it led to the climb from transient man to fully settled man. It also led the species out of a most confounding and epoch-making labyrinth that saw an arboreal primate enter and modern man emerge. If we are fully to appreciate the extraordinary events that took place in the labyrinth and that took this arboreal primate and fashioned it into man, we must first study the emerged creature as closely as we have studied the creature that entered it, for only this way will we be able to grasp the significance of the transformation.

It was not tentative or transitional man that created Sumer. It was fully developed man. When we discover Sumerian man, we discover mankind and see the once-free arboreal primate of central Africa fully confined in its terrestrial prison.

Sumer, was not, of course, man's first permanent settlement. If we go behind the looming shadow of Sumer, we find such fascinating places as Jericho, Jarmo, and Çatal Hüyük, with their evidence of remarkable architectural achievement and social development. But when we do we find only extrinsic evidence of their lives. We have no way of knowing what they thought, for none before Sumer had a written language. Sumer, with its cuneiform writing, presented to us the first recorded thoughts of man. It tells us something most remarkable: that Sumerian man, in his thoughts, was modern man.

In its institutions Sumer was virtually indistinguishable from subsequent civilizations. There was a highly developed religion; the state was fully evolved, and under a system of kings; the law, written and promulgated, was extremely sophisticated; farming and animal husbandry were firmly established and supplied the economic basis of society; wars were fought, slavery enforced; medicine practiced, and education promoted. Thus Sumer was a complete system of human society.

Samuel Noah Kramer presents in *The Sumerians* what is probably the fullest description of Sumerian life:

> The basic unit of Sumerian society was . . . the family, whose members were knit closely together by love, respect, and mutual obligations. Marriage was arranged by the parents and the betrothal was legally recognized as soon as the groom presented a bridal gift to the father. The betrothal was often consummated with a contract inscribed on a tablet. While marriage was thus reduced to a practical arrangement, there is some evidence to show that surreptitious premarital love-making was not altogether unknown. A woman in Sumer had certain important legal rights: she could hold property, engage in business, and qualify as a witness. But her husband could divorce her on relatively light grounds, and if she had no children, he could marry a second wife. Children were under the absolute authority of their parents, who could disinherit them or even sell them into slavery. But in the normal course of events they were dearly loved and cherished and at the parents' death inherited all their property.[1]

---

1. Chicago: University of Chicago Press, 1963, pp. 78–79.

Kramer, who spent a lifetime as a Sumerologist, listed in another book, *From the Tablets of Sumer*, a large number of "firsts" that are attributable to Sumer: the first schools, the first bicameral congress, the first legal precedent, the first moral ideals, the first Biblical parallels, the first tale of resurrection, and the first love song. From this, and all the evidence Kramer marshals concerning Sumerian civilization, we can get a detailed picture of the life and times of Sumer as they stretched out over a period of three thousand years, commencing approximately 5000 B.C. It is in his brief summary of family life, however, that we can perceive the essential condition of man, a condition that with few exceptions endures to this day. But— and this is the point—when we perceive in this summary the condition of man, what we must appreciate is the fact that this condition is also the condition of a once-arboreal primate caught in the prison of terrestrial existence.

Once we have set aside the externals of Sumerian life, notwithstanding their great importance in other regards, we can focus our attention on Kramer's observation about family life. And when we do, what should command our astonished attention is the fact of family life itself.

It will be remembered that in arborea the female was the protagonist. Here, in Sumer, we see the male in the role of protagonist. He was, in every way, the *paterfamilias*: The female, though possessing several rights, was subject to the male. And, if she failed to bear *him* children (a most remarkable concept!), he could take a second wife.

Again, what is most revealing is the fact that the male was incorporated into the family situation. In arborea the female and dependent offspring were the only "family"; the male led a peripheral existence, one that had as its justification the impregnation of females and the protection of the affinity group from predators (as well as maintaining a hierarchical order within the group). In Sumer there existed a one-to-one relationship between a male and a female under a system that gave the male absolute authority over both the female and any offspring they might have—even to the extent of being able to set aside the female and deliver the offspring into slavery.

What was established by the time of Sumer was the principle of monogamy, even if only serial monogamy. And yet, most interesting is Kramer's remark to the effect that despite the contractual nature of marriage, thus revealing its essentially transactional nature, "there is some evidence to show that surreptitious premarital love-making was not altogether unknown." Although later I will go into detail on this point, it is enough to suggest here that this sexual activity reveals traces of the arboreal period in which sexual promiscuity was practiced.

There was, for example, the charming tale of Inanna, the Sumerian Venus, also known as the "Queen of Heaven," and Dumuzi, the shepherd god. It begins with Inanna recalling the previous night when "the heaven was shining bright," and Dumuzi met her.

> He met me, he met me,
> The Lord Kuli-Anna [Dumuzi] met me,
> The lord put his hand into my hand,
> Ushumgal-Anna [Dumuzi] embraced me.

Inanna pleads:

> Come [?] now [?] set me free, I must go home,
> Kuli-Enlil [Dumuzi] set me free, I must go home,
> What can I say to deceive my mother!
> What can I say to deceive my mother, Ningal!

Dumuzi replies:

> I will tell you, I will tell you,
> Inanna, most beautiful of women, I will tell you,
> [Say] "My girl friend, she took me with her to the public
>   square,
> There a player [?] entertained [?] us with dancing,
> His chant, the sweet, he sang for us,
> In sweet rejoicing he whiled away the time for us;"
> Thus deceitfully stand up to your mother,

While we by the moonlight take our fill of love,
I will prepare [?] for you a bed, pure, sweet, and noble,
The sweet day will bring you joyful fulfillment.[2]

What is significant here is the fully developed duality of sexual relationships that existed at the time—and that continue
today. While it is clear that Inanna was as amorous as Dumuzi,
it was nevertheless Dumuzi who was the sexual aggressor. It was
he who not only concocted an excuse with which to deceive
Inanna's mother (note: Inanna asked for an excuse) but also
prepared the bed of pleasure. Yet there is an implicit assurance
that Inanna would join him on the bed. Also, it is significant
that, unlike arborea where sex was an instinctual activity, here
in Sumer it was under control of the conscious mind.

There is in this whole matter of sexual relationships a second
duality, that between practicality and passion. The foundation
of sexual relationships was marriage which, in turn, was based
on an economic relationship between the man and the woman.
If love were present, generally it was as a bystander to the more
serious business of ordering the younger generation in such a
way as to ensure the future, both of economics and of offspring.
(And yet, what is love, what is passion to an arboreal primate?)

Another feature of Sumerian life pointed out by Kramer relates to property. In arborea there was no such thing as property.
No individual laid claim to anything as his own. The tropical
forest was there in all its abundance; it provided food, a place
to sleep, and a place of refuge from predators. In brief, the natural forest provided for all the needs of the individual without
the necessity of the individual making special provision for its
needs by accumulating or hoarding necessities.

In Sumer there was a complex network of relationships, not
only within a family, but also within the confines of the affinity
group, or what here might better be called society. There were
no "trees to be plucked" for the satisfaction of sustenance
needs. In Sumer, as elsewhere, sustenance was provided not by a
direct transaction, as in arborea, but by an indirect transaction

2. Ibid., p. 251.

by which the individual was obliged to participate in indirect activities, such as the use of his labor or the use of acquired property, in order to satisfy his sustenance needs.

The full ramifications of this can be seen in the relationships between the sexes. If it can be said that the satisfaction of sustenance needs was an indirect transaction for the male, how much more so was the satisfaction of such needs for the female. While it is true that the female could engage in business and hold property, she was very restricted in both activities. Sumer, and subsequent civilizations, placed woman in a dependent status by which she had to look to the man—first the father, then the husband—for every morsel of life from food, to protection, sex, and even her right to existence itself. She was, as were dependent children, under the authoritarian, and often, absolute, control of the paterfamilias. She had no independent existence of her own. This, then, placed her in a situation where she had to engage in doubly indirect transactions to satisfy her basic need of sustenance. She could not reach out, as it were, and "pluck the fruit from the trees" as she once had been able to do in arborea. In terrestria, her life was totally dependent upon her husband (or father). If he was a good provider, she could lead a good life; if he was a failure, she suffered accordingly. And, of course, what was true of the female was equally true of offspring.

Because modern man has been for so long obliged to engage in indirect transactions in order to obtain sustenance, and because in virtually all societies the woman is dependent on the male for the terms of her existence, there is a danger in our recapitulation of human characteristics of assuming this to be the normal state of affairs. While it is true that for humans it has been so for thousands of years, it is not so for the rest of mammalian life. Only man is obliged to use indirect means to satisfy the most basic need of life, sustenance. All other mammals satisfy this need by direct transactions. Also, while it is true that human females have been dependent on males, this is not true in other forms of animal life. After the usual infant dependency stage, all adult animals, including arboreal primates, both male and female, are capable of satisfying their sustenance needs by direct transactions, and thus are independent.

In all but man there is a genetic profile maintaining direct contact with the profile of the environment. All other creatures obtain sustenance by *natural* means. Only man requires *unnatural* means to obtain sustenance. In terrestria man must employ artificial intermediaries in order to feed himself. While it is true that in rare instances in certain parts of the world the individual can literally "pluck fruit from the trees" to feed himself, for the most part man can seldom satisfy his sustenance needs so directly. He grows fruits and vegetables; he raises animals. From these two occupations he derives food.

If we were to view this entire matter from the perspective of the arboreal primate existing in the distant past, we would have to shake our heads. Being herbivorous, we would anticipate that a primate, even in the terrestrial mode, might gather in fruits, roots, vines, berries, and so on. We ourselves, as arboreal primates, have been doing that from time immemorial. But how, we would have to ask ourselves, could an herbivorous primate end up a meat-eater? And even allowing for such an extraordinary eventuality, how could this same primate kill prey, in view of the fact that it utterly lacked the necessary "tooth and claw"?

As improbable as it may seem, the arboreal primate we now know as man has become the hunter of prey and the eater of meat and has in the process acquired the necessary "tooth and claw" to do so. This is the great fact of human history. Indeed, without it there could have been no human history at all.

But what makes this the fantastic improbability it is, is the fact that man the hunter, man the predator, derives from an arboreal primate that neither ate meat nor practiced predation, nor practiced lethality in any form.

Yet this is not the end of the matter. When we arrive at Sumer (not by going backward in time, but by going forward from arborea) we discover not only all that I have so far described, but two other bizarre features of life as well, two features we take so much for granted that, unless we are exceptionally observant, we might completely ignore. What should startle us is the fact that Sumerian man possessed the faculty of speech and had invented writing.

No other creature has either. No other creature needs them. It is true that arboreal primates have a system of verbal communication, but that is instinctual verbalization. Man's speech, in contrast, is a conscious activity. (Man, too, engages in instinctual verbalizations, as when he cries out in surprise, sighs, and so on, but that is not speech.) As for writing, it is uniquely human.

If we perceive all this from the perspective of an arboreal primate scrutinizing a distant descendant of ours, we inevitably come to the colossal question: Why? We don't have to rely on indirect transactions, we don't have a system of female dependency, we don't practice monogamy, we don't have speech, and we don't have writing. What happened between us and them, our distant descendants, that they should have the need for all these things? What went wrong that they had so drastically to change themselves from what they once were into what they are now?

Before replying to the questions posed by the original primate, we might first summarize the essential features of man, using as our base the six essential features of arboreal existence.

1. Man satisfies his sustenance needs by indirect transactions. Lacking a natural form of "tooth and claw," he has had to use artificial means to be able to procure food. These artificial means are tools (weapons).

2. There is sexual pairing, or monogamy. In this connection, paternal nurture and filialness toward the father were developed.

3. Elimination must be controlled as to time and place.

4. Sleeping is confined as to time and place.

5. Protection against predators is provided by a system of lethal practices.

6. Intraspecies order is maintained by a dominance system which, in turn, is maintained by the use of, or the threat to use, lethal means.

Now we may address ourselves directly to the questions raised by the ancient primate.

The answers to these great questions are locked away in the labyrinth of time that separates the primordial primate from modern man. It has been the misfortune of paleontologists to have to enter this vast and lonely labyrinth in their efforts to unravel the mystery of man. Once in the labyrinth, it is very difficult to find one's way out. One becomes quickly lost, and in this distraught condition all sorts of wraiths and shadows are raised as proof of the path taken by man's hominid ancestors in their ancient trek from the heart of the forest to the frontier of civilization.

Once in the labyrinth, there is an irresistible temptation to argue over every suggestion of evidence. The history of physical anthropology is an unending and acrimonious debate over whether a fragmentary mandible belonged to this or that creature, whether another bit found—a humerus will do—came from a creature later or earlier than another, or whether the period of the Australopithecines was a million or two million years in duration.

I have, I must add, enormous respect for the scholars who have attempted to sort out all the slivers of evidence they have managed to come across while slaving in the labyrinth. These are men and women who have dedicated their lives to the entire matter with a singlemindedness of devotion that would do justice to any group of scholars. But trying to follow them in their wanderings from chamber to chamber produces a confusion bordering on vertigo. Fortunately the contents of the labyrinth are not our major concern, nor are they the principal object of this work.

It is entirely possible that no one will ever be able to retrace the exact path taken by man's ancestors in their journey through the labyrinth. But that should not prevent us from examining three critical turns in the journey. The first decisive turn was that of tools; the second, that of fire; the third, that of speech. With them, the species was able to make it through the labyrinth. If any one of these critical turns had not been taken, man would not exist today. Indeed, other primates entered the labyrinth when man's ancestors did, but they failed for one reason or another to make all three of the critical turns. As a result they became extinct.

To grasp the full significance of these three great turns, we must place them in a certain sequence: At Point A, Arborea, there is an arboreal primate, sans tools, sans fire, sans speech. At Point T, Terrestria, there is man, with tools, with fire, with speech. If the arboreal premise is correct—and every reputable paleontologist says it is—then something occurred in the labyrinth that obliged the arboreal primate to take up tools, fire, and speech. Our task is to find out what it was that made them so necessary.

Our first difficulty lies in seeing the full problem for what it is. In terms of function there is nothing left of the original primate to see. Not a single essential feature of the arboreal primate is manifested in the life of man. It is as if in studying them we are studying two entirely separate and distinct forms of life. It is not merely a question of physical form and place of residence of each. Everything each does is different from what the other does. One is herbivorous and nonlethal; the other is heavily carnivorous and lethal. One is sexually promiscuous, the other is monogamous. One eats by means of a direct transaction, the other by indirect transactions. And so it goes, through every aspect of existence, even including matters of elimination and sleep.

And yet, notwithstanding all this, primate and man in all essential respects are identical to each other. The reason: tools, fire, and speech, have enabled man to so alter the external terms of his existence that at all times he has preserved his original arboreal nature.

TOOLS, ERGO MAN

W HY MAN? This is undoubtedly the most fascinating question in the universe. I put it in these exalted terms because the emergence of man involved such concatenation of extraordinary and unpredictable events as virtually to preclude their duplication anywhere else in the universe. I am not denying such a possibility; when we are dealing with such huge statistics as those that seek to account for extraterrestrial creatures of intelligence, almost anything is possible. But until a creature from outer space actually drops in on planet earth—and appears live on television—man, *Homo sapiens*, must stand as the most remarkable anomaly in the universe of creation.

Man can only be understood in terms of the circumstances attending his descent from arborea. The issue is this: If the original hominids voluntarily left the arboreal world for a more promising terrestrial world, and if entry into that world was accomplished by natural means, then it can be concluded that the species made a full adaptation to the terrestrial mode of existence. In that event, a particular sort of creature would come into existence. On the other hand, if the original hominids were forced to leave arborea and if neither they nor their descendants effected a natural adaptation but survived in terrestria solely as a result of compensatory and protective factors of a nongenetic nature, then we have an entirely different sort of emergent creature. In brief, then, everything turns on the terms of descent.

One would think that in a matter of such great importance, anthropologists and paleontologists would focus their attention on the terms of hominid descent. Yet for the most part they haven't. In fact, there are a large number who simply ignore the entire matter. They are the taxonomists who concentrate their efforts on sorting out the collected pile of fossil remains so as to construct a developmental sequence of body forms from, say, *Propliopithecus* to *Homo erectus*. In essence, these investigators use the former (via *Proconsul*) to get man's ancestors into the trees, and the latter (via *Australopithecus*) to show that man's ancestors got out of the trees. How or why, no one seems to ask.

There is a second group of researchers which very much turns its attention to the terms of descent. It may be divided into two subgroups. One, represented by the irrepressible and popular Robert Ardrey, follows the aridation theory with singleminded devotion in order to force the reluctant primate out of the trees and deposit it on the ground where, upon divesting itself of its apelike costume, it turns out to be, much to everyone's embarrassment, a most rapacious terrestrial killer named *Homo sapiens*. The net effect of such a theory is to make the forces working to bring about the descent completely irrelevant. It is as if there had been no arboreal period at all.

The second subgroup of theorists does not acknowledge a pushing force, but emphasizes a pulling force originating from the appeal of terrestrial living. Probably the most flamboyant theory of the pull school is Björn Kurtin's in *Not From the Apes*: ". . . the hominids came down from the trees because they had reached a stage where a lucrative new mode of life was available on the ground, one which was at least as good as the old life in the trees. . . . They were no dismal exiles from a vanishing Garden of Eden; on the contrary, they were pioneers conquering a new zone of life." [1]

---

1. New York: Random House, 1972, pp. 90–91.

Of the same general persuasion is Bernard Campbell. He advises us not to think of the descent as precipitous, as he should. Then he goes on to show that semibrachiation is pre-adaptive to bipedalism and that bipedalism is preadaptive to plains living, which may very well be true. But then he adds the following thought to his sequence: ". . . our hominid ancestors had some startling advantages for plains life, in terms of their sensory acuity, powers of prediction and manipulative ability. The opportunistic nature of the evolutionary process allowed the exploitation of an ecological situation with great possibilities." [2] In reading this sort of an opinion one can only wonder why hominids (and others) didn't flock to the ground at a much earlier date in order to take advantage of the Eden-like world awaiting them below. That there were countervailing and overwhelming obstacles to such a gentle descent simply escapes Kurtin's and Campbell's attention.

Compatible with such thinking is that of the popular zoologist Desmond Morris who, in *The Naked Ape*, views the aridation as opportunity—with every push there is a pull. He puts it this way: "We know that the climate began to work against them [the early apes] and that . . . their forest strongholds had become seriously reduced in size. Unlike the ancestors of the chimpanzees, gorillas, gibbons, and orangs which stayed put in the trees, the ancestors of man . . . struck out, left the forests, and threw themselves into competition with the already efficiently adapted ground-dwellers. It was a risky business, but in terms of evolutionary success it paid dividends." [3]

Ashley Montagu, in his *Introduction to Physical Anthropology*, sets the scene in Africa, suggests the aridation theory, describes the shrinking of the forests, and then observes, "Such environmental changes shifted the zone of adaptation from a life in the forest to one on the open savanna. Forest dwelling animals if they are to survive on the savanna must become adapted to the demands of an environment altogether different

2. *Human Evolution* (Chicago: Aldine, 1966), p. 335.
3. New York: McGraw-Hill, 1967, p. 19.

from that afforded by the forest." [4] Thereupon, in a cursory and summary fashion, Montagu assures us that man's hominid ancestors became properly adapted to terrestrial living.

But none of the foregoing really digs into the subject of descent. For them it is an *inter alia* transaction. Sherwood Washburn, one of the country's leading physical anthropologists, does specifically concern himself with the subject, but, curiously enough, for other reasons. Washburn gives very serious attention to hominid descent because, from his perspective, the traditional explanation would appear to interfere with his knuckle-walking theory. If one reads Washburn loosely, the aridation theory would seem to be overruled, but upon close reading it turns out that his knuckle-walking theory in no way pertains to, or interferes with, the aridation theory. What causes the apparent difficulty is the meaning Washburn gives to the word "descent."

To understand Washburn in this matter, and to understand the overall process at work, we must distinguish between two very separate and distinct steps in the terrestrialization process. And when we do, Washburn's knuckle-walking theory not only makes sense, it goes very far in actually explaining the descent of man's hominid ancestors. In addition, and most significantly, it helps to explain why Africa, of necessity, had to be the place of man's origins. (Paradoxically, Washburn perceives neither of these results.)

We may begin by distinguishing between *coming to the ground*, something an arboreal primate may do while still utilizing the arboreal world, and *descent* as generally used to describe the ending of all arboreal living and the beginning of existence exclusively in the terrestrial mode. In brief, were it not for the prior coming to the ground by a variety of very early apes ancestral to the modern chimpanzee, gorilla, and man, there could never have occurred the famous descent that had *Homo sapiens* as its end-product. It was this coming to the ground, in the

---

4. Springfield, Ill.: Charles C. Thomas, 1960, p. 296.

fashion of the modern chimpanzee which still retains access to the trees, that preadapted the ancestors of the African apes and man to the consequences flowing from the later aridation problem.

Also, there is another preliminary point that must be made before tracing Washburn's thoughts on the separate subjects of coming to the ground and descent. It invariably happens that in reflecting on the notion that superior primates drove inferior primates out of the shrinking forests of Africa, one *assumes* that a type of apelike creature proved to be superior to the apelike ancestor of man. However, this is not so. If Washburn is correct, and there is a gemlike quality to his logic in all this, it was not an apelike creature that caused all the difficulty; it was the monkey. This, it now appears, is the most significant fact in the entire matter of hominid descent into terrestria. It explains the descent, and what is more, it explains why it took place in Africa and nowhere else. It can be put even more strongly: It explains why the descent could only have occurred in Africa and nowhere else.

Here, as with the nature of the superior primate, there has existed another assumption. It goes somewhat like this: Man *might* have originated almost anywhere; Asian and African conditions (of both flora and fauna) made them the most likely sites; in a seesaw evolutionary contest Africa won out. Implicit in this assumption is the prospect that possible future finds in Asia might swing the race in Asia's favor, and future paleontologists would be able to correct the earlier error that had Africa as the original site. And, of course, even later finds could show that actually *Africa* was the right answer after all. If this assumption were to hold up, it could lead to the dreadful prospect of other finds proving that, at last, Asia is the winner. Such being the case, may all digging cease forthwith!

In reality, there is only one possible site for the descent: Africa. It all has to do with those superior primates, the African monkeys.

Now it is time to examine the evidence. We can begin by

reconstructing Washburn's theory of knuckle-walking, and
when we do, we must ask the opening question: Why did a
primate such as that ancestral to the chimpanzee, the gorilla,
or man have to forego a method of locomotion that had been
eminently successful for tens of millions of years and take up a
new one not nearly as adaptive?

The question goes to the essential nature of adaptation, a
subject I have discussed earlier in terms of the species/environ-
ment equation. In the evolutionary process that saw the development of the prosimians, the primates became, in Washburn's
words, "separated from the insectivores as a result of their
adaptation to climbing with grasping hands and feet." [5] This
system of locomotion, so necessary to successful mobility in the
trees, was one of the most critical—and universal—sectors of
the species side of the equation. It determined the form of all
arboreal primates.

During the Oligocene period, some thirty to forty million
years ago, monkeys evolved. According to all the evidence, during this period man's ancestors had been quadrupedal for some
twenty million years before the ape pattern of locomotion
evolved. With the evolution of the apes (Pongidae) there began to develop a new system of locomotion: *brachiation* (swinging by the arms from branch to branch), a method exclusively
possessed by apes (both modern and ancestral) and by the
arboreal ancestor of man after it broke off from the monkey
line. (Some New World monkeys also brachiate.) After we
account for the various separations of suborders and species,
we arrive at this summary situation: ". . . the similarities that
man shares with the gibbon and the orangutan are due to common arboreal ancestry, to life in the trees and to the locomotor
pattern called brachiation. The greater similarity that man
shares with the gorilla and chimpanzee is due to a common

5. Sherwood Washburn and R. S. Harding, "Evolution of Primate
Behavior," *The Neurosciences: Second Study Program*, F. O. Schmitt,
Editor-in-Chief (New York: Rockefeller University Press, 1970), p. 42.

knuckle-walking ancestry and a late separation—occurring after this behavioral stage had evolved." [6]

Why and when did knuckle-walking come about? Or, put differently, what happened to change the environmental profile so that the apes had to adjust their species profile to the changed profile presented to it? The answer lies with the Old World monkeys (Cercopithecidae). Washburn says, ". . . the fossil record shows that the monkeys have displaced all the smaller African apes. Small apes were numerous in the Miocene, but now only the large ones can compete in the African forests, and they are rare and most unsuccessful compared with the monkeys of the *Cercopithecus, Cercocebus,* and *Papio* groups." [7] Elsewhere,[8] Washburn explains the reason for the abundance of small apes in the Miocene: the highly successful *Cercopithecus, Cercocebus,* and *Papio* groups had not yet evolved. In other words, once the Cercopithecidae make their appearance, late in or after the Miocene, the African apes are in direct competition with superior primates and are obliged to make a partial withdrawal from arborea. This they accomplish by the evolution of knuckle-walking, and thus begins the coming to the ground of a once totally arboreal primate. According to Washburn this evolutionary development took place not when the forests were shrunken, but when they were fully expanded: "The larger the forests, the greater the extent of the forest floor and the forest edge, and the more habitat for knuckle-walkers; the fossils of *Ramapithecus* (including *Kenyapithecus*) suggest a form with a range extending from Africa well into Asia, when the habitat was suitable for a tree-living form." [9] It is clear that knuckle-walkers weren't *excluded* from arborea at this time, but that they were beginning to falter in

6. "Speculations on the Problem of Man's Coming to the Ground," in *Changing Perspectives of Man,* edited by Ben Rothblatt (Chicago: University of Chicago Press, 1968), p. 199.
7. "Evolution," p. 43.
8. "Speculations," p. 199.
9. "Behavior and the Origin of Man," in *Rockefeller University Review,* Vol. 6, No. 1 (January–February 1968), pp. 13–14.

the competition with monkeys.[10]

It was this knuckle-walking capability that preadapted hominids for terrestrial living, a preadaptation that was necessary
once the competition between African monkeys and apes (including hominids) reached a crisis situation brought about by
the shrinking forests.

What, then, of Asia? Asia, if anything, is proof that Africa
was the site of man's origins. The pivotal difference between
the situation in Africa and that of Asia lay in the fact that the
Colobinae of Asia were occupying the ecological niche occupied
by the Cercopithecinae in Africa. And the Colobinae were not,
and are not, in competition with the small apes of Asia: the
gibbon. Whereas the Cercopithecinae eat virtually the same diet
as the apes (largely fruit), the Colobinae are leaf-eaters. In fact,
80 percent of their diet is leaf and only 20 percent fruit, nuts,
etc. In contrast, the gibbons' diet is about 90 percent fruit,
nuts, etc., and only about 10 percent leaf. Because there was no
competition between monkeys and small apes in Asia, there
was no pressure seeking to force the apes to the ground. Washburn argues the point even further, observing that the Colobinae appear to be less aggressive than the African monkeys,
that the Asian macaques are primarily ground-living forms, offering less direct competition than African monkeys, and that
it is probable that the macaques evolved in Africa in the Pliocene and are late arrivals in Asia.

Consequently, today the gibbon is a totally arboreal primate.
So is the orangutan, the only other extant Asian ape. Asia could

---

10. Vincent Sarich suggests the same process, observing that "the adaptive radiation leading to the African apes and man began as a result of
competition in the trees by the evolving Cercopithecines (today the macaques, baboons, mangabeys, and guenons). . . . The reasons for their
recent evolutionary success are not yet clear (cf. Washburn, *supra*), but
there is every reason to think that it was this success that, in effect, chased
the African apes out of the trees into varying degrees of terrestrial adaptations made by the common ancestor of man, chimp, and gorilla. . . ."
(from "A Molecular Approach to the Questions of Human Origins," in
Background for Man, edited by Phyllis Dolhinov and Vincent M. Sarich
[Boston: Little, Brown, 1971], p. 79).

never have been the site of human origins because no Asian ape ever came to the ground, either partly or completely. Hence, there was no base stock from which a terrestrial hominid could develop.

In Africa, however, it was different. Indeed, not only were the apes obliged to go to the ground for much of their lives, so too were certain monkeys: ". . . at least four different kinds of Old World monkeys [elsewhere Washburn suggests they might be the patas, gelada, baboon-macaque, and entellas] have become primarily ground-living and this appears to be an adaptation to new areas to avoid competition with closely related forms." [11] Not only did certain monkeys and apes have to go to the ground because of competitive pressures, but others not preadapted to ground-living and who experienced this competitive pressure became extinct: "If the evolution of the apes is viewed with an understanding of the behavior of contemporary monkeys, it appears probable that the many small apes known to have lived in the African Miocene became extinct through competition with African arboreal monkeys." [12]

What saved the surviving apes, and the hominid ancestors of man, was their knuckle-walking ability derived from a competitive situation with monkeys in which grounding was the avenue to survival. When push came to shove during the late Pliocene, those so preadapted survived. Those lacking this preadaptation became extinct. It was the hominid's good fortune to have entered this knuckle-walking period. We have proof of this in the oldest known human hand found by Louis S. B. Leakey at Olduvai: It possesses many of the features of a knuckle-walker.

As for South America, not one primate has adapted to life on the ground: "When New World forests became smaller, there was less area available for primates and many forms became extinct. In the New World, at least, reduction in forests led to the extinction of primates and not to their spending

---

11. Washburn, "Behavior," p. 14.
12. Ibid., p. 14.

more time on the ground." [13]

Thus we can conclude that only Africa could have been the site of human origins, that knuckle-walking preadapted hominids for eventual terrestrial living, and that competition from superior primates, on an increasing basis, forced these hominids from the arboreal world to the terrestrial world where at one point all entry into arborea was denied them.

There is no way to establish the circumstances of the descent from the trees other than that it was the result of a severe and prolonged drought that pretty much occupied the ten-million-year Pliocene Epoch. Karl W. Butzer, in *Environment and Archeology*, writes of the aridation:

> There is abundant evidence for late Tertiary and early Pliocene climatic change in southern Africa. . . . Fluvial erosion under savannah-type climate sculptured the surface of much of southern Africa during mid-Tertiary times, but during the time of the Upper Miocene–Lower Pliocene arid conditions accompanied the deposition of the Kalahari System, found between the Vaal River and the lower Congo basin. . . . Entomological studies have demonstrated forest expansion in the Miocene with marked recession in the Pliocene, leaving residual forests in a ring around the central Congo basin and in East Africa, and with a certain amount of expansion in the Pleistocene.[14]

The best estimate of paleontologists is that somewhere around two to three million years ago, man's hominid ancestors began life in the terrestrial mode. They did so slowly, reluctantly. As the trees gradually became less and less accessible, and as the food sources in them decreased, superior primates occupied a correspondingly larger percentage of the forests, thereby driving out inferior primates who either became ex-

---

13. Washburn, "Speculations," p. 195.
14. Chicago: Aldine, 1964, p. 354.

tinct because they could not adapt to their new environment, or survived because they could adapt.

The process actually involved four major steps. In the first, hominids, probably as knuckle-walkers, lived at the base of the trees, seeking as best they could to preserve close contact with their original environment. This was not excessively difficult, since life at the base of the trees was not very dissimilar from life in the trees themselves. It must not be thought that expulsion was a single and irreversible sweep. Access to the trees continued on a fluctuating basis for a long period of time, certainly for many millennia. But as population pressures mounted and the superior primates took increasing command, hominids were able to spend less and less time in the trees. Undoubtedly, toward the end of this period the only entry into the trees was of a darting or surreptitious nature that lasted possibly only long enough to seek out some morsel of food or to escape some particularly pressing predator. During this transitional period, it should be noted, the major arboreal characteristics of the species were preserved almost intact. The trees still supplied 90 percent of their food supply and offered sanctuary from predators and a safe place to sleep at night, thus allowing hominids an opportunity to live quite normally.

Finally, however, hominids were denied all access to the trees. This condition, it appears, arose when continuing population pressures (resulting from continuing aridation) drove other primates to the base of the trees, thereby forcing the hominids out toward the fringes of the forest areas, where they were obliged to live between the forests and the great developing savannas. In this second phase of terrestrialization hominids were effectively denied 90 percent of their traditional food supply. In order to survive, they had to supplement their diet. To this end, they began to eat tubers and other terrestrial foods of at best marginal nutritional value. Adequate protein was essential. Hence, the slow change to eating large insects, rodents, small animals—all as a supplement to an otherwise inadequate diet.

Along with the critical problem of food, there arose an even greater threat to their survival. Without access to the trees, without "tooth and claw," the very early hominids were virtually defenseless against the predators that roamed the savannas and hunted the forest floors.

It must have been a most precarious existence, one literally on the borderline of extinction. Nevertheless, despite everything, they survived and progressed to a third phase of terrestrialization. Under continued population pressures from the forests, the early hominids were gradually pushed out entirely onto the savannas where, in a critical resolution of the problem of terrestrialization, they became successful hunters of prey. What is so remarkable about this phase of the process was that by becoming successful hunters they solved both the problem of sustenance and the problem of predators by a single act.

The fourth stage of terrestrialization—and the final one—occurred when hominids, actually early man, learned through the use of fire and clothes, to control their environment entirely. They then left the savannas of Africa and in time occupied the entire world.

I am now obliged to discuss *Australopithecus africanus*. I would prefer not to, for to wander into the labyrinth for more than a brief moment—say, to pick up a pebble tool—involves the risk of becoming hopelessly lost in the many corridors and chambers and in the vortex of the swirling arguments among paleontologists. But there is no choice. We must take a rather close look at *Australopithecus* because everything we know about man's earliest known terrestrial ancestor is contained in this small and controversial creature.

Raymond Dart, of the University of Witwatersrand in Johannesburg, discovered *Australopithecus*. Actually, he didn't discover it. A miner at the limestone quarry near Taung, a small village on the edge of the Kalahari Desert, came across the fossil material. Eventually it got to Dart, who, after weeks of carefully separating matrix from fossil, and after even more time in analyzing his "Taung baby," came to the conclusion that the skull was "ultrasimian and prehuman stock," that is, a manlike ape. Hence the name *Australopithicus* ("Southern Ape"), to which, for greater geographical identity, he added the postscript *africanus*. So if we are to properly name Dart's baby girl we must call her *Australopithecus africanus*.

Dart, of course, was guilty of a monstrous anthropological faux pas. He contradicted his betters by suggesting that man's origins were in Africa and not in Asia, where everyone of anthropological quality knew them to be—even though no substantial evidence existed for the assertion.

And then, too, there was Dart's indiscretion about the matter of brain size. Anyone who was anyone at that time knew that it was a large brain that made it possible for man's ancestors to climb down out of the trees and cope with terrestrial conditions. *Australopithecus africanus* had a brain much too small to be ancestral to *Homo sapiens*.

In short, Dart had it all backward. *Brains*, then terrestrialization, went the great weight of respected opinion. And why large brains first? Because man's ancestral hominids needed large brains to be able to make tools. What Dart's contemporaries were saying, *sub rosa*, was that to be man one had to have a large brain. And *sub sub rosa*, they were saying that for any creature even to think of becoming man, he had, first, to possess a very large brain. The end before the beginning! What makes the whole thing marvelously mad is the fact that Piltdown man—he of large brain and heavy jaw, he whose existence so completely proved the theory of the large brain first and then all the rest—had not yet been exposed for the fraud it was.

It took a Broom, if I may be forgiven an outrageous pun, to clear the cobwebs out of anthropological thinking, not so much by way of supporting Dart's slender but impudent evidence, but by the discovery of so many friends and relations of Dart's baby girl that the totality of clear evidence could no longer be ignored. I am, of course, referring to the discoveries of the Scotsman Robert Broom who, beginning in 1936, uncovered so many variations on Dart's theme that finally everyone accepted A. *a.* as at least a relative of man—a cousin, some would say; a begetter of *Homo*, others would say.

Australopithecus was a fully terrestrialized primate. Pelvic and foot evidence, in addition to other anatomical details, make this point clear beyond any doubt. It was bipedal—it walked—though not as upright as modern man. But that is to be expected; *Australopithecus* was the earliest bipedalist we know of. It was also the first known meat-eater and the first to practice cannibalism.

There is a curious imbalance of perspective toward *Australopithecus*. Some authorities, like Leakey, seem overly insistent in excluding the creature from man's ancestral line. On the other hand, men like Sir Wilfred LeGros Clark say it was the "earliest known, unequivocal hominid."

The real objection to its inclusion into the hominid enclave is the matter of its brain size. Its cranial capacity was below the lowest extremes allowable for a hominid and well within the upper limits allowable for apes. It was principally on these grounds that Leakey excluded it from the hominid line. However, we mustn't make too much of a small cranial capacity, lest we suffer the Piltdown Syndrome mentioned earlier. The fact is, erect posture and bipedalism came before a large brain.

I mention this controversy, not so as to be able to take sides, but to observe the interesting fact that as a result of the dispute over *Australopithecus* there is a tendency on the part of many paleontologists to treat man's hominid ancestor as something of a shadowy figure in the proximity of *Australopithecus*, never seen exactly, but somehow felt and thus accounted for. There is really no factual, or evidentiary, basis for conjuring a shadowy figure close by *Australopithecus* and labeling it as man's hominid ancestor, just as there is no plausible objection to constituting *Australopithecus* as man's hominid ancestor.

The difficulty turns, as I have just said, over the matter of brain size. And this is nothing but prejudice on the part of those who, despite the evidence before them, have a hard time believing what they see: tools in the possession of this small-brained creature.[15]

Sonia Cole, in writing of hominid fossils found in Bed I of Olduvai (Leakey's famous digs), calls a bone tool that was worked and polished at one end ". . . an incredible achievement for these early hominids and one that revolutionizes our ideas of their capabilities." [16]

Mary Leakey once commented about the discovery of tools at Olduvai, "At first the tools were a great shock to us and we had a hard time believing it. After this, it should be easy to believe anything." [17]

I have already cautioned against approaching the subject of man's origins, nature, and so on from the perspective of modern man looking back, the danger being that everything will be seen from man's perspective, rather than from the arboreal primate's point of view. Nothing reinforces this caution more than the classic definition of man which says that man is the maker of tools.[18] Since—so this line of reasoning goes—all men at all times have had tools, it is clear that man is the maker of tools. Or, *man, ergo tools.*

There is only one thing wrong with this definition. It is backward. The very opposite is true: *Tools are the maker of man.* To say that man is the maker of tools is to confuse cause and effect. Everyone sees man possessing tools, hence the traditional conclusion. Yet what they see *is* the conclusion. They see the end of the process, and inevitably, they see it in reverse.

When we proceed forward in the matter, we see an entirely

---

15. While Dart was the first to discover *Australopithecus*, it was Leakey who in 1959 uncovered the earliest form of *Australopithecus*, although with anthropological obstinacy he insisted on giving it the name *Zinjanthropus* ("East African Man"). And, of course, tools were found with it.

16. *The Prehistory of East Africa* (New York: Macmillan, 1963), p. 121.

17. Cited in John E. Pfeiffer, *The Emergence of Man* (New York: Harper & Row, 1964), p. 79.

18. Though recent events have obliged a revision of the definition so that it now says that man is the maker of tools on a regular pattern—or that he makes tools to make tools.

different sequence. We see tools making man. Or, *tools, ergo man.*

In order to understand this, it is necessary to review several salient points about man's hominid ancestors. Hominids, while still in the arboreal environment, were fully adapted to the arboreal environment. This adaptation to arboreal life determined the form and function of the primate. For example, the development of the limbs was such as to produce the opposable thumb and the prehensile foot, both necessary for locomotion and the procurement of food in the trees. Since the food available in the trees was such as could be taken by grasping forelimbs and since locomotion also required grasping limbs, the primate developed accordingly and achieved an eminently successful species profile in these regards.

Most students of primates, for whatever reason, describe primates as nonspecialized, or generalized, creatures. In a sense this is true, in that primates lack such individualized specialties as claw, hide, speed, and so forth. But just because primates lack individual specialties does not militate against their having a cluster of characteristics, each of a general nature, but which when combined into a cluster, produce a high degree of specialization.

Man's hominid ancestors, in their adaptation to the arboreal environment, produced no single physical specialization, but the cluster of generalized characteristics became itself a highly specialized feature of the hominid. In fact, the cluster produced such a high degree of specialization that, in the event the environment changed, or in the event the species left the arboreal environment for a significantly different one, extinction would be inevitable.

Earlier I described the adaptation of the forelimbs and prehensile feet to the arboreal profile so that, as evolved, they served both locomotive and eating needs. Because of the nature of the food, there was no need for lethal devices such as claws, great teeth, or powerful jaw muscles. When we add to this the acuity of sight and the atrophy of the olfactory system, we can

begin to perceive the outlines of a very highly specialized creature—a creature who, in fact, could exist in only one environment: arborea.

There is another aspect to this specialization. Primates protect themselves against predators, not by "tooth and claw," but
by intelligence: They perceive danger, warn the group, and flee
to the tops of the trees. They cannot confront a predator in
combat and win. In arborea, the primate is safe; on the ground
it is so vulnerable as to be doomed. Finally, there is the matter
of reproductive practices. In arborea, for reasons mentioned
earlier, survival is aided by the females giving birth to, as a rule,
a single offspring at a time. This system works to maintain a
good population balance because of the safety of arborea from
predators. However, if this almost defenseless creature were
obliged to live on the ground, thus subjecting it to intensified
predation, the primate reproductive practices would fail to
maintain an adequate population and very shortly the species
would be extinct.

All factors considered, when man's hominid ancestors were
forced out of the trees, they faced extinction. All factors considered, they were so well-adapted to the arboreal environment
and so ill-adapted to the terrestrial environment that there was
no possibility of survival. And yet, they did survive. The proof
is modern man.

For the hominid to exist elsewhere than in arborea, it would
have to adjust its species profile to fit that of the new environment. Just as the species profile slowly shifted as the insectivore
ascended into the trees, so too the species profile of the hominid
could slowly shift as it descended to the ground. In this case,
just as the insectivore changed into the tree shrew and the tree
shrew, after many intermediary stages, changed into the fully
evolved primate from which man's ancestors derived, so too the
hominid in its descent could have changed slowly into a series
of evolving creatures, each step being slowly and carefully taken
so as to maintain species contact with the changing environment. This could have been done, and done on the basis of

genetic change, and the final terrestrial creature would have created, by natural means, a species profile conforming to the profile of the terrestrial environment.

This is not a wholly fanciful notion. Aquatic mammals are good examples of this process. Possibly as long as a hundred million years ago, small air-breathing mammals slowly slipped into the water. They have lived there ever since. Notwithstanding the great difficulties—the need of aquatic mammals to rise to the surface at regular intervals to breathe, and the problems of nursing the infant whale at sea—aquatic mammals have survived. They have been able to do so because of a constant supply of appropriate food.

It would seem, then, that if mammals—air-breathing terrestrial creatures—could adapt to such a radically different and hostile environment as the water, arboreal hominids could have traveled to a relatively less hostile environment, and could have done so on the basis of genetic change. Surely if a land mammal could go into the water, an arboreal mammal could go to the ground.

It might have been possible, except for one thing: The food that sustained hominid life in the trees was not available on the ground. When the hominid was denied access to the trees it was denied access to 90 percent of its food supply. And while ground food was scarce, predators were plentiful. In order to survive, hominids had to solve both problems. Solving only one would do no good. It was both—or extinction.

As the long aridation of Africa continued, the once continent-wide forest shrank enormously. As this happened, grasses came in, eventually invading the now sparse forest areas. Unfortunately, the digestive system of primates won't accept grass. That left roots, tubers, seeds, and possibly an occasional egg from a ground-nesting bird. This was, at best, an emergency diet, providing less than the minimum needed protein. Somehow, hominids had to add to their protein intake. And at the same time hominids had to solve the problem of predators.

If hominids had attempted to evolve naturally into a terrestrial creature, from the very beginning their grasping, non-lethal forelimbs would have been hopelessly inadequate. Possibly they would have served to provide food—assuming there was an adequate source available. However, there was still the matter of predators. *That* could not be solved by grasping forelimbs. In order to solve the predation problem, hominids would somehow have to convert their grasping, nonlethal forelimbs into striking, lethal forelimbs. There was no way this could be done by natural means. There was nothing in the gene pool of the species that could produce naturally lethal forelimbs. As much as 75 to 100 million years of genetic buildup had been in precisely the opposite direction, in order to adapt to the arboreal environment. There simply were no genetic reserves that could be called upon to provide the hominid with lethal forelimbs.

Since natural means were denied hominids, there remained but one alternative: artificial means. The solution, of course, was the tool-weapon. By means of the tool-weapon, hominids were able to create the artificial extensions of the forelimbs so necessary to convert grasping, nonlethal forelimbs into striking, lethal forelimbs. As a result, they were able to kill their predators and, in a most extraordinary example of serendipity, convert their enemies into their food.

Again I must pause and issue a caution. What I have just described was the *solution* to the double problem. It in no way establishes how the first terrestrialized hominid went from the problem to the final solution. Nor does it resolve the problem of terminology and perspective.

Taking terminology first, the word *tool* to the modern person means anything from a hammer to an automated assembly-line. These were not the tools of the earliest terrestrial hominids. What they had at first was what nature provided. We don't know what tools came first. In all likelihood they were sticks and pieces of bone used for a variety of purposes. Whatever they were, they disappeared long before modern man began looking for them. What have been found are pebble tools:

small, hand-sized pebbles fashioned by nature in such a way as to provide a rough but effective cutting edge. These pebble tools were found in Bed I of Olduvai in conjunction with the earliest known example of *Australopithecus.*

Turning to the matter of perspective, we must again resist the temptation to look back from the modern vantage point and conclude how remarkably successful *Australopithecus* was in solving the double problem of predation and sustenance. To do so would be to honor the beneficiary of a process rather than the protagonist. The vital work had already been done by the time *Australopithecus* made an appearance. The proof of this is seen in the fact that *Australopithecus* was a fully bipedal, erect hominid. It did not get that way in order to be able to use tools. It got that way because prior successful use of tools by an earlier hominid had carried the species through the first crisis and to a point of stabilized existence in the terrestrial mode. Without this prior period of successful tool-use one of two results would have occurred. Either hominids would have become extinct, a fate experienced by collateral primates who sought to live in the terrestrial mode without tools, or they would have survived somehow, but less adapted, with the result that *Australopithecus* would have been considerably less erect and bipedal. The very fact that *Australopithecus* was bipedal is clear evidence of prior successful tool-use by an earlier terrestrialized primate. This means, then, that in the very early period of terrestrialization there was a slow buildup of tool-use leading to that of the fully erect *Australopithecus.*

Jane B. Lancaster makes an intriguing suggestion in this regard, holding that "casual, unskilled tool-use might have been typical of many species of apes during the Pliocene." [19] If Lancaster is right, it was tool-use by early arboreal hominids that preadapted them for terrestrial existence. This sort of tool-use by arboreal primates is illustrated today in the incident made

---

19. "On the Evolution of Tool-Using Behavior," in *Background for Man,* edited by Phyllis Dolhinov and Vincent M. Sarich (Boston: Little, Brown, 1971), p. 354.

famous by Jane Goodall, in which she witnessed chimpanzees using sticks to fish for termites. But tools are not essential to chimpanzee survival. I would suggest that hominid tool-use, at least during the arboreal period, was also not essential. It became essential, however, once hominids were forced into a terrestrial existence.

It is clear that man's hominid ancestors, regardless of how primitive and tentative their original tool-use was, slowly but surely became more and more adept at it. The significance of this is enormous. The hominid that began the use of tools was, for all practical purposes, anatomically just like any other arboreal primate. It was not much different from a modern chimpanzee. But increasing tool-use slowly, insistently demanded more erectness and more bipedalism. Thus there began a feedback system in which more bipedalism made for more tool-use which, in turn, led to more bipedalism, which then led to more tool-use, and so on. Had there not been tool-use there would have been no pressure for bipedalism, and without bipedalism there never would have developed a line of hominids culminating in man. It was, in the final analysis, tools that led to man. *Tools, ergo man!*

The proposition can be put another way. Were it not for tools, man's hominid ancestors could not have come into existence. Without tools, the same inoffensive creature forced out of the trees would have perished because of its inability to procure adequate food and its inability to protect itself from predators. There is ample evidence that other contemporary primates similarly driven from the trees remained herbivorous, failed to develop tools, and quickly became extinct.

Nothing in all the history of man is as important as the fact of tools. They, in effect, converted grasping, nonlethal forelimbs into striking, lethal forelimbs. By doing this they converted an arboreal primate into a terrestrial primate. By doing this they made man possible.

What happens when we take this creature's tools away? We are left with an arboreal primate, totally incapable of existing in the terrestrial mode. It cannot procure food, it cannot protect itself against predators. There is only one realm in which such a creature could survive, and that is arborea. What was true of early hominids is true today. The proof is in the reader's hands. Look at them. Are they any different from the hands of any other arboreal primate? Without artificial extensions of the forelimbs—from a gun to an automated production-line—modern man could not survive, except in those very rare situations in which men live on secluded islands possessing abundant tropical foods and free from predators.

It was tools that made man possible in the first instance; it is tools that permit man today to survive in the terrestrial mode of existence.

Tools, yes. But for what? Again, when we look backward and survey all that is between us and, say, *Australopithecus*, what do we see? We see hominids eating meat. As a result, we take the fact of meat-eating for granted. But if we proceed forward in time with the descending hominid, we gain an entirely different perspective.

We see a small, inoffensive, nonlethal herbivorous primate seeking to survive in the terrestrial mode. In size it was about four feet tall, weighing less than ninety pounds. It lacked both defensive and offensive capabilities, especially in relation to terrestrial predators. Most important, this small creature was anatomically and functionally constituted to eat herbivorously. With all this information, could anyone *in advance* have guessed that this creature would become a hunter and meateater? The very thought seems preposterous. Yes, it would be possible for such a creature to use tools—for digging up roots, pounding them to soften them up for eating—even for protection against predators. *But to use them to kill prey and eat them? Never! And yet that is precisely what happened!*

The descending primate lacked two requisites for becoming a predator. It lacked the physical attributes, such as great teeth and powerful jaws or deadly claws. And it lacked the instincts of the predator. Millions of generations of selective pressures working to preserve species contact with the arboreal environment had produced a gatherer, not a hunter. These same millions of generations had produced a body and brain appropriate to the gatherer's existence. Everything, from the grasping forelimbs to stereoptical color vision and a herbivorous digestive system, were perfected with this end in mind. Nothing in all the evolutionary development of the primate prepared it for the predator's life. There is only one conclusion that can be drawn from this: *A primate cannot be a true predator.*

Yet we know that starting with the earliest known terrestrial hominid and concluding with modern man, predation has been the central factor of life. How can this be?

The answer is contained in something I said earlier. The early hominids had to solve two problems: finding food and warding off predators. The element that met these two needs was the tool-weapon—an artificial extension of the forelimbs that could be used both to protect them from predators and to kill prey. In the first instance the weapon may well have been a single implement—say, a club, that would serve both to beat off a predator and to kill prey. Sometimes the slain predator might also have served as a source of meat, but more often than not they were the pursuers of predators, the early hominids were pursued by them. The more likely prospects for prey were the docile, nonpredator animals that lived in large groups. Regardless which became prey, the factor that both reduced the threat of predators and increased the food sources was the tool-weapon.

Still, there remains the critical question of how an herbivorous, nonpredatory arboreal primate reached the point of being capable of fighting off predators and killing prey. To answer the question fully, we must begin with the fact that all this was accomplished not by a form of aggression but by a form of defense.

We can begin to get a glimpse of the process employed by observing contemporary anthropoids, especially chimpanzees and gorillas. Field observations show that among primates there is very little object-manipulation except that connected with feeding activity. In feeding they will turn over rocks, probe fingers into holes, and pull off bark or shells in search of food. Chimpanzees are the only ones to make and use tools, at least in their natural habitat. Thus, when we look to the anthropoids for suggestions about tool-use in feeding activities, we find virtually nothing to help us. What object-manipulation there is, seems to be confined to doing those things that assist in perpetuating already established eating habits. It offers no clues that relate to changing from a herbivorous to a carnivorous diet.

However, when we examine display activities of both the chimpanzee and the gorilla we get a first hint of what might have happened several million years ago. The display of the gorilla is highly stereotyped sequential behavior that usually includes the throwing of vegetation just before a running charge. Many of the same elements, including this throwing of vegetation prior to a charge, constitute the basic elements of chimpanzee display. What is interesting is the matter of throwing things. The grasping forelimbs transform themselves into thrusting and thus, at least potentially, lethal forelimbs.

We must now look at modern chimpanzees to study cases of actual predation. Our only witness to this unusual phenomenon is Jane Goodall, who in *In the Shadow of Man* points out that only twice in many years of observing chimpanzees in the Gombe Stream Reserve has she seen actual kills.[20] The first one, that of a red colobus monkey, she describes as follows:

> . . . we were watching four red colobus monkeys that were evidently separated from their troop. Suddenly one adolescent male chimpanzee climbed cautiously up the tree next to the monkeys and moved slowly along a branch. There he sat down. After a moment, three of the monkeys

---

20. She has seen, and her husband has photographed, chimpanzees eating meat quite a number of times.

jumped away—quite calmly, it appeared. The fourth remained, his head turned toward the chimp. A second later
another adolescent male chimp climbed out of the thick
vegetation surrounding the tree, rushed along the branch
on which the last monkey was sitting, and grabbed it.
Instantly several other chimps climbed up into the tree
and, screaming and barking in excitement, tore their victim into several pieces. It was all over within a minute
from the time of capture.[21]

Four years later Goodall witnessed the killing of a baboon.
She describes the event in both *In the Shadow of Man* and an
earlier book, *My Friends the Wild Chimpanzees*. For some reason there are discrepancies between the two accounts. Because
it is less cluttered, I will present the earlier account:

> At 8:40 in the morning, on hearing a sudden commotion
> just down the slope from the camp, I had rushed out in
> time to see Rudolf, our largest male chimpanzee, in the act
> of killing a young baboon—holding it by one leg and bash-
> ing its head against the ground.
>   . . . the ape, his hair on end, flung the body in front of
> him, his face awful in its ferocity. Three other chimpanzees
> with him screamed loudly and threw their arms around one
> another, so intensely agitated that they seemed no more
> than a black, hairy tangle of bodies, arms, and legs.[22]

Natural predators, except those working in packs and hound-
ing their running prey, do not scream and make loud noises.
Frenzy would best describe the emotional content of both killings observed by Goodall. It might be said that the descriptions
of the killings, especially that of the baboon, with its greater detail, were descriptions of fierce displays that involved the almost
incidental element of a killing.

---

21. New York: Houghton Mifflin, 1971, p. 83.
22. Washington, D.C.: The National Geographic Society, 1967, p. 65.

We can contrast the foregoing with Goodall's description of another incident between chimpanzees and baboons. Apparently a baboon had been an intended victim and had escaped, making a lot of noise:

> . . . in response to its calls the whole baboon troop had rushed some hundred yards to the scene, and the chimps and baboons had engaged in a fierce conflict. Despite the fact that they had leaped at each other and called loudly, so far as we could see no physical damage had been inflicted on members of either side . . .[23]

Here we have an excellent example of display, but without an incidental killing. Although other field observers such as Vernon Reynolds, Helmut Albrecht, and Sinclair Dunnett have never observed directly (by sight) or indirectly (by study of feces) the killing and eating of meat by chimpanzees, Goodall's observations are irrefutable and are worthy of appraisal, not so much as to the killing and eating of prey but as to the dynamics of the various transactions.

But before going on, I must first set aside the inference that if chimpanzees kill and eat meat today, their remote ancestors, and thus by implication man's remote ancestors, were both predators and meat eaters. All evidence indicates that modern predaceous practices by chimpanzees are very rare and in no way form a significant behavioral pattern. While Goodall suggests at various times a sort of systematic hunting procedure among the chimpanzees, her evidence is slim. The entire matter of meat-eating and hunting by chimpanzees should remain open until such time as new and independent evidence is forthcoming. This would require the establishment of a new site for observation, Goodall having injudiciously interfered with the natural circumstances of her chimpanzees by setting up a feeding station for them. There is no way of knowing what, if

---

23. *In the Shadow of Man*, p. 204.

any, effect this has had on the lives of her chimpanzees. But if we are to determine once and for all whether chimpanzees eat meat and hunt in their natural habitat, we must observe them as they are and not as they are modified by an artificial factor such as a feeding station. Notwithstanding this point, Goodall's observations are an excellent point from which to view a primate killing and eating its victim—and even engaging in hunting—when *in extremis*. It reveals the essential capability of the chimpanzee to take those steps necessary to survival.

Evolution is not static, it is ongoing. It is hardly conceivable that a modern peripheral and adventitious activity as meat-eating was also present in comparably tentative form millions of years ago. In fact, we can go further and conclude that if meat-eating in the distant past had existed among chimpanzee ancestors to the small degree that it appears to exist today, the nutritional impact of meat-eating would have been such that over the millions of intervening years, the evolving chimpanzee would have become increasingly carnivorous so that today, instead of meat-eating being incidental and sporadic, it would have become the heart of chimpanzee diet—as it has become for man.

But evolving with the ancestor of the chimpanzee was the ancestor of man. *That* creature took up meat-eating, but not while still arboreal. Only when deprived of its arboreal source of food (something the ancestor of the chimpanzee never had to suffer) did it have to resort to extreme measures.

Display, with its throwing of objects, may well lie at the base of hominid weapon-activity. But we must search more deeply for the source of psychic energy that could impel hominids to go beyond display activity to actual predation. I believe the modern chimpanzee gives us a hint of what it might have been.

Frenzy, fear, even terror seem to be the emotional states of both killers and chimpanzee observers of the killings. It's almost as if the chimpanzees were dredging up a reserve system in order to kill. This reserve system, I believe, is that of self-defense *in extremis*.

Dr. Walter B. Cannon, in his famous *The Wisdom of the Body*, writes:

> In considering the homeo-stasis of blood sugar, oxygen supply, acid-base reactions and temperature certain adaptive reactions [keep] the body on an even course in spite of conditions which might [be] very disturbing. It is remarkable that most of these reactions occur as the accompaniment of the powerful emotions of rage and fear. Respiration deepens, the heart beats more rapidly, the arterial pressure rises, the blood is shifted . . . to the heart and central nervous system and the muscles, the processes of the alimentary canal cease, sugar is freed from the reserves in the liver, the spleen contracts and discharges its content of concentrated corpuscles, and adrenin is secreted from the adrenal medulla. The key to these marvelous transformations in the body is found in relating them to the natural accompaniments of fear and rage—running away in order to escape from danger, and attacking in order to be dominant. Whichever the action a life-or-death struggle may ensue.
>
> The emotional responses just listed may reasonably be regarded as preparatory for struggle. . . . The secreted adrenin cooperates with sympathetic nerve impulses in calling for the stored glycogen from the liver, thus flooding the blood with sugar for the use of laboring muscles; it helps in distributing the blood in abundance to the heart, the brain, and the limbs. . . . The increased respiration, the redistributed blood at high pressure, and the more numerous red corpuscles set free from the spleen provide for essential oxygen and for riddance of acid waste, and make a setting for instantaneous and supreme action. In short, all these changes are directly serviceable in rendering the organism more effective in the violent display of energy which fear or rage may involve.[24]

---

24. New York: W. W. Norton, 1932, pp. 213–214.

Chimpanzee "hunting" and meat-eating are not planned but appear to be the result of spontaneous situations, such as an isolated monkey or a single baboon, or other animal, such as the bushbuck or the bushpig, all of which Goodall reports comprise the chimpanzee's prey. There appears to be no nutritional pressure to change the status of "hunting" and meat-eating. Thus, it appears that killing prey is not a normal or natural activity. Display is natural; killing is not. *Killing, I believe, is an extension of display and requires the arousal of the one state that even a nonlethal, herbivorous primate possesses and that is the state of the body system when the organism is in danger.*

Fortunately, in most instances of approaching danger, the primate group warning system is so perfected that, upon signal, everyone on the ground can quickly dash into the sanctuary of the trees. In these instances, while the body system is activated for escape, it is not required to go to those extremes demanded when escape is prevented. It is when the organism is *in extremis* that all of its bodily forces must be marshaled. It is at such times that display will employ, not aggressive principles, but defensive principles that will manifest themselves by loud noises, bristling hair, charges, and the throwing of objects. The prime purpose of this activity is to drive the other creature away, it is not to kill.

Unlike the modern chimpanzee, early hominids were subjected to very powerful nutritional pressures. The arboreal source of foods was denied them, and the normal herbivorous foods available on the ground were inadequate. Meat is a superb source of protein. It is concentrated, and in a few minutes a meat-eater can consume all the needed protein, while a herbivorous primate must take up to eight hours to get the same nutritional results. Hence, there was nutritional pressure pushing the hominid to an alternative food source, with a nutritional pull created by the nutritional economy of meat.

The problem became acute when hominids, under pressures of other descending primates leaving the continuously shrinking forests, had to ease away from the margins of the forests and begin to penetrate the savannas.

It was in this emerging situation that the display with the throwing of objects had to achieve refinement of aim. No longer could hominids rely on chance encounters with small forest creatures. It is one thing in a frenzy sporadically to kill and enjoy the benefits of the kill; it is another thing to develop the process into a systematized way of life. Selective pressures, always operative, saw to it that those types that could best use tools and weapons would survive. We know that because *Australopithecus* is a significant way-station in the struggle of the hominid to survive.

There is one other aspect to the hominid's conversion from a casually tool-using, herbivorous, arboreal primate into a systematically tool-using, carnivorous, terrestrial primate. It has to do with intraspecies killing.

The hominid, including modern man, is the only animal that regularly kills and eats its own kind. There is a dogged determination by most anthropologists to turn away from the fact of cannibalism, as if somehow it has never really occurred, except ritually and then only in small out-of-the-way corners of the world. The truth is that from the very earliest time hominids were terrestrialized, they have been eating each other.

While this may seem to be an unpleasant fact, there is no avoiding it. Man eats man, just as man eats beast. Diet is not a matter of sensibilities but a matter of survival. When hominids began to enter the terrestrial mode, they faced the monumental—and apparently insoluble—task of finding a new food source. As we know, they found it in meat. To eat meat, they had to kill. Therefore, on two counts they violated their genetic nature. It was an easy thing to take the next unnatural step and, in emergencies, eat their own kind. This is shocking to moderns, who view man as a creature totally distinct from other animals, but it must be remembered that when all this began, hominids were indistinguishable from other primates and were, in fact, so integral a part of nature that they could share water holes with other wild animals.

Man's ancestors became predators in order to survive. In the manner just now outlined they became unnatural predators, and in so becoming they also became predators of other hominids.

True predators have a built-in system to protect the species against self-predation. Of all forms of animal life, a predator needs the most protection against self-destruction. For this reason, predators have a genetically based system of self-protection.

But man became an unnatural predator, i.e., an artificial predator, with no built-in system against self-predation. While this absence in any creature would be bad enough, it is especially bad in the case of man.

Evolution created the arboreal primate, not by design, but as a fact. In becoming adapted to the arboreal environment, the primate slowly developed all those systems of behavior that would work in that environment. One of these systems was that of display. Genetically, the arboreal primate is a nonlethal displayer, a creature who protects the affinity group and the dominance hierarchy by great noise and gesture and terrible threats, but not by actual physical violence. In regulating relationships within the affinity group and between the affinity group and other groups of the same species, nonlethal displays are employed. Because they are nonlethal, these displays can take on enormous proportions. They can be outrageous, monstrously noisy, and overwhelming in their threatening appearance because, in the final analysis, they are not even very violent physically, to say nothing of their being lethal.

What then if you place deadly weapons in the hands of such a displayer? Emotional extravagance is tolerable in someone who is harmless; it is intolerable in someone capable of great harm. The dilemma of man stems from the fact that genetically he is nonlethal, while functionally he is very lethal. Natural evolution has made him nonlethal; artifice has made him lethal. According to his genes man is nonlethal; according to the artificial extensions of his forelimbs, he is lethal.

Therefore, display is very dangerous. When man acts in accordance with his genes and displays extravagantly, instead of mere threat and bluff, there is killing. Man cannot control his instinct of display and so we have a vicious circle. Display is a primate's method of self-defense, and defense of the affinity group, and is founded on genetic composition. Man, acting on that instinct, displays and kills. If he were to rid himself of the artificial extensions of his forelimbs—weapons and tools—he would cease being lethal, but in the process he would so have lost contact with his environment's profile during the great hunt era that he would have become extinct.

Thus the hominid, from the earliest times of its terrestrial exile until today, has killed members of its own species. The next step, that of cannibalism, has been inevitable. Throughout hominid terrestrial history, whenever a food emergency has arisen, the solution has almost always been cannibalism. That is, whenever there has been no other food available—when neither meat nor other edible is to be had—man has turned to other men as a source of emergency food. Cannibalism occurs today and it occurred in the past. Most especially did it occur in the remote past when, new to the terrestrial mode and in desperate straits, the early hominids faced a totally inadequate food supply system. Conversion to meat was imperative. But they were little creatures and around them were larger, more powerful, natural predators. They lacked the weapons either to attack predators or to defend themselves against them. There really was little choice; during this early and critical period when for all practical purposes large potential prey were denied them, and when they were unable, in emergencies, to secure small prey or other edible food, there remained only other primates and their own species. *Australopithecus* killed and ate baboons; *Australopithecus* also killed and ate his own species.

Dart, after examining the fossil evidence presented by certain Australopithecine skulls and those of baboons, concluded that the peculiar but similar holes in them came from being frontally attacked and struck by double-ridged bones. The purpose was to get at the brains. He writes:

Australopithecus lived a grim life. He ruthlessly killed fellow Australopithecines and fed upon them as he would upon any other beast, young or old.[25]

As I have mentioned, the earliest terrestrial hominids were indistinguishable from other comparable primates. They were, in fact, like any other animal in nature. They may have had a "grim" existence, in that survival was for a long time an unsettled question, but they were not confronted by what modern man would call moral decisions. They had neither the consciousness to perceive such possibilities nor the circumstances in which to choose between possibilities. It was, in those difficult times, solely a question of eat or be eaten, live or perish. Instinct drove the early hominids toward survival, circumstance drove them to meat-eating, and occasional necessity drove them to eating their own kind. When we view it in that perspective, what significant difference is there between eating a hominid and eating a chimpanzee or a baboon? Man has been eating them all for millions of years.

---

25. Raymond A. Dart, *Adventures with the Missing Link* (New York: Harper & Row, 1959), p. 191.

THE GREAT
WALL OF
MORTAR

I N   O R D E R to prepare for what is undoubtedly the most important fact about the human species, it is necessary first to pursue an apparent side-issue.

Let us suppose, for sake of contrast, that hominids had descended from the trees in the same manner that had been used to get them in the trees many millions of years earlier—classic evolutionary progression. The same evolutionary process might conceivably have occurred in the descent. If it had, the original primate, forced out of the trees, would have crept down to the ground at a pace that would allow it to preserve the species/environment equation. It might have pursued the path taken by the baboon which, while originally from totally arboreal stock, went to the ground along a path that allowed it to maintain the species/environment equation. When it did so, the once insignificant olfactory system became critical and the baboon's peculiar snout evolved. The result is a baboon that is very well adapted to the terrestrial world (even though it most often has easy access to trees—and where there are no trees there is invariably a cliff, a cave or other sanctuary in which to sleep or escape predators) and which can, by virtue of the great canines of the adult males and the strict hierarchical system of the troop, protect itself from almost all predators.

If man's hominid ancestors had made this sort of descent, a series of genetic changes would have occurred to preserve the species/environment equation, and a fully terrestrialized creature would have come into existence. It might very well have been similar to the baboon. In any event, such a terrestrial creature would have developed a natural defense system to protect itself against terrestrial predators. Also, it would have been able to engage in direct transactions to meet its sustenance needs. If this had occurred, there would never have begun the process that had man as its end. There would have been, as with the baboon, another descendant of the arboreal stock living on the ground, a completely natural creature that had, as so many before, gone from one environment to another. The history of life is replete with this sort of process: from the sea to the land, from the land to the trees, and from the trees back to the land. And as has been noted, there have been those, such as the ancestors of whale, who left the land and slipped back into the water again millions of years ago.

What, then, makes man different? What was it in the descent to the ground that prevented normal evolution from taking place? We can never know for certain the condition of the primate when it began its descent. But once the terrestrialization process began the creature possessed tools, even if as primitive and tentative as the stick modern chimpanzees use to fish for termites. However, it was enough to begin a process that continues to this day. It was a process that made man, and it has been a process that has served to perpetuate the original arboreal primate in man. *Not only is man man, he is also the same primate that lived in arborea several million years ago.*

The proposition is basically very simple. Unaided, alone, and ill-equipped by natural evolution for life in the terrestrial mode, the original hominid could not have survived on the ground. We know that man's hominid ancestors did not become terrestrialized by means of genetic change. We also know that had these hominids not had artificial means to use for this purpose, they quickly would have become extinct. Therefore, we must conclude that it was these artificial means that permitted hominids to survive in the terrestrial mode.

The problem, by way of restatement, centers around the need of any species to present a species profile that will match the profile of the environment. Unaided, the early hominids simply couldn't have created a species profile to match that of the terrestrial environment. Hominids had, as it were, to fill in the gaps of their genetically created profile with artificial elements. These artificial fillers in the species profile I call *mortar*. Take away this mortar and the species profile could not have matched that of the terrestrial environment. The result would have been extinction.

If anything can prove that man is not in his natural habitat when in the terrestrial mode of existence, it is the fact that without this mortar, i.e., without the aid of artificial means in the quest for sustenance and protection against predators, he would perish. No other creature in nature has ever faced that predicament. All other creatures are able to present, on the basis of genetic composition, a species profile to match that of the environment in which they live. Loss of any significant element of that species profile has always meant extinction of the species. The only exception in all of nature is man. And he is the exception only because he has been, from the days of the earliest terrestrialized hominid, the creator of mortar.

In the beginning of the terrestrialization process the amount of mortar necessary to complete the species profile was extremely limited. It is possible that it was no more than the equivalent of the modern chimpanzee's stick with which it fishes for termites. But as hominids were slowly but inexorably pressured away from the base of the trees and eventually onto the full savanna and across the world, the amount of mortar, with appropriate slowness and inexorability, also increased.

From this we can extract a basic principle of human existence: *The closer man exists to his arboreal habitat, the less mortar is needed for survival; conversely, the farther he exists from his arboreal habitat, the more mortar is needed for survival.*

Mortar, then, serves to compensate for the genetic deficiencies of man existing in the terrestrial mode. The more terrestrialized he is, the more mortar he needs. The less terrestrialized, the less mortar is needed. Whether we are talking of the most primitive pebble-tool or of a modern industrial society, we are talking of mortar. It is the universal factor of human exi~tence. Without it man could not exist today; without it his earliest terrestrialized ancestors could not have survived.

From this basic principle flows another, equally basic and equally universal: *While mortar serves to complete the species profile so that it can match that of the environment, mortar also serves, as a result of its compensatory effect, to perpetuate those very genes that made the species profile deficient in the first instance.*

Genetic deficiencies in the first place obliged hominids to create mortar in order to survive in terrestria. Mortar, then, acted as a compensatory element in the species/environment equation. However, by being compensatory, it allowed for the genetic deficiencies to be perpetuated. Therefore, behind the wall of mortar the same primate who began the descent exists in modern man today, for always during the terrestrial period the species has perpetuated compensatory mortar. If man were ever to stop making mortar he would quickly become extinct, because he would be the original primate without "artificial extensions of the forelimbs." Again I refer the reader to his hands. With them alone how could he construct civilization? Hunt for food? Protect himself against predators? Or even make something as simple as a stool to sit on?

The reason for mortar is obvious. It permits an arboreal primate to survive in the terrestrial mode of existence. Thus, in a very literal sense, man is an arboreal primate living in the terrestrial environment. Or, in the idiom of my thesis, we can now advance the first two dichotomies:

Man's origins were arboreal; his circumstances are terrestrial.

Man's instincts are arboreal; his habituations are terrestrial.

We may now take the third step.

The terrestrialization process, while it was possible because of mortar, did not leave the original hominid unchanged. We can see that in the rather extreme differences in the appearance of man and other arboreal primates today. But the changes brought about by terrestrialization involved more than appearances: They involved significant structural changes. These structural changes have occurred as a result of genetic changes.

These pertain to an upright stance and bipedalism, affecting the feet, the pelvic structure, modification of the wrist, a shift in the position of the foramen magnum, the structure of the face, and dentition—to name the major changes. In addition, there were the important genetic changes relating to hand and eye coordination.

I mention this last by way of illustrating the thrust of genetic change. If mortar was the *sine qua non* of survival—and it clearly was—then everything possible had to be done to create it and perpetuate it. In the very beginning, when mortar was minimal, the structural changes of the hominid were similarly minimal. But as mortar increased, so too did structural changes increase, to be able constantly to improve the ability of the species to create mortar. As a result, significant genetic changes occurred only in relation to mortar, thus violating a basic evolutionary principle which says that genetic change occurs to allow a species better to adapt to the environment. In man, however, genetic change has concerned itself by and large with mortar and not with environment. Aside from the critical genetic changes just mentioned—all of which relate to mortar —there have been a considerable number of genetic changes that actually relate to environment. But these, though extensive, are not critical to the central theme of terrestrialization. For example, skin pigmentation generally varies due to variations in climate and sun exposure; Eskimos are short and compact for warmth; equatorial peoples are often tall and thin for coolness; and so forth. As can be seen, these genetic variations relate to environment, but they are peripheral and relate to special environmental conditions. All of the diverse peoples, notwithstanding variations, have in common a very ancient history that saw them go through the stages of the critical genetic changes which relate to mortar. Upright stance, bipedalism, feet, pelvic structure, modification of the wrist, shift in the position of the foramen magnum, structure of the face, and dentition all are common to man. These genetic changes were the very changes that produced terrestrialized man. Without them, there would be no human species, and there would be no human species without mortar.

The significance of this violation of evolutionary principles is great. In brief, man's development, even allowing for local variations in detail, has been in the direction of reinforcing mortar. This is so in the matter of genetic change and in the matter of social change.

Thus did man break with nature. It began with the very first pebble tool and expanded to the point where, not too many years ago, the break became so total that man by a fantastic sweep incorporated all of nature into his mortar.

Man has proceeded along lines not found in natural evolution. Instead, he has turned in on himself and his mortar and has proceeded to "evolve" in relation to his mortar. Man in the terrestrial mode has so broken with nature that he has stepped outside the realm of natural evolution.

Man, having stepped outside the realm of natural evolution, of necessity has had to create his own evolutionary processes in order that he might preserve and perpetuate mortar. I call this *involuted evolution*. This being the case, how did he—how could he—go about his involuted evolution? He did so by means of his brain. In effect, man—from the earliest hominid on—created increasing mortar by the operation of his ever-growing brain. As both brain and mortar grew, so too did the genetic changes occur, including the genetic changes of the brain.

From this can be seen the problem of paleontologists of the past when, proceeding from the perspective of modern man looking back, they saw the need for a big brain before tools. It was, in fact, the other way around. There was, first, the tool, possessed by a small-brained primate. As tool-use increased because of pressures forcing the earliest hominids away from the base of the trees, brain size increased. It had to, for it was the brain that made the tool (mortar) possible. Failure of the brain to grow and thus to provide better tools (mortar) undoubtedly explains the eventual extinction of *Australopithecus* which probably did not make its tools. It could *use* them, but it could not make them. This would restrict the creature to that environment which gratuitously supplied the tools, especially pebble tools. But nature is not sufficiently thoughtful as to leave pebble tools lying everywhere, and the time inevitably came when hominids had to leave their original homeland and wander elsewhere. When this happened, natural tools were both too rare and too inadequate to the new circumstances. As an erect, bipedal, terrestrialized creature, *Australopithecus* could not return to the trees, and lacking the ability to create tools (mortar) because of its inadequate brain, it became extinct.

What was true of *Australopithecus* is true of modern man. He has broken with nature and has produced an involuted evolution, the result of which has been mortar, around which all of his major genetic changes have clustered. As a consequence, man is forever confined to the terrestrial mode of existence.

There is one particularly interesting genetic change about which there has been a great deal of speculation. Somewhere in the deepest shadows of the labyrinth hominids ceased being recognizable primates and began to assume the proportions of man. As this was occurring, the primate that was to become *Homo sapiens* began to lose its great coat of hair.

Desmond Morris has written of man as the "naked ape." Anthropologists and others have sought to explain this phenomenon. Strictly speaking, of course, man is not a naked ape; he has the same number of hair roots, only the hair that grows is almost invisible over most of the body.

All sorts of ingenious explanations have been offered for the loss of body hair. Some relate it to sex, others to hunting efficiency, and still others to temperature-regulation. I would suggest another reason. In previous explanations it has been assumed that the coat of hair of a primate exists for the benefit of the primate inside the coat of hair. It seems to me that the coat of hair actually serves to benefit dependent offspring. Viewed from this perspective, hair exists so that dependent offspring have something to cling to from birth on. The very young cannot grasp the mother's flesh; their hands are not strong enough. They cannot embrace the mother's body; they are too small. However, their very small hands and feet can intertwine with the mother's hair, thereby linking them firmly with the mother.

Life in the trees demands that dependent offspring be attached to the mother, hence the hair. However, when the hominids were forced to the ground and obliged to habituate themselves to terrestrial living, one of the features of the new life was the camp. While undoubtedly very crude, it was nevertheless adequate.[1] Mothers with dependent offspring could now put them down somewhere. There was no danger of falling out of the tree; there was no need to carry the infant around, as is the case with such terrestrial primates as the baboon. Under these circumstances the hair was no longer necessary to the safety of the infant. Hence, its gradual disappearance.

Yet hair serves a secondary purpose: providing warmth. With

---

1. One of the earliest bits of evidence of a living site is in Bed I at Olduvai, in which a rough piling of stones has been interpreted as a windbreak.

the loss of hair by hominids, their need for warmth was met by the development of subcutaneous fat. Man is the only primate with such a protective layer. But then, man is the only naked primate. He is naked, I believe, because he no longer needs a network of hair to which offspring must cling, something all other primates need, even the very terrestrial baboon. Baboon mothers must carry their dependent offspring during the day; they must carry them at night, even in the remote caves that some use for safety. In contrast, man's efforts at survival, depending as they did on mortar, were better served by the abandonment of the unnecessary (hair) and the accumulation of the necessaries of terrestrial existence. This involved what I have referred to as involuted evolution.

Another manifestation of involuted evolution can be seen in the unity of the human species. Under ordinary circumstances, natural evolution functions in such a way as to adapt a given species to its environment. Should a species radiate into contiguous environments that are significantly different from the original one, speciation takes place and new species come into existence. However, this has not happened to *Homo sapiens*. Notwithstanding the immense variations in environments—from the deserts to the Arctic circle, from wet to dry, and from sea level to the highest plateau, and from habitations where raw meat is virtually the only form of sustenance to those where the diet is almost totally herbivorous—man remains but one species. What has preserved that unity has been mortar. And yet, there are the peripheral variations mentioned a moment ago and these relate to environment. It is these variations that produce the various races. However, common to all, and thus preserving a single species, are the critical genetic changes that relate specifically to mortar.[2]

---

2. Where does such an activity as running fit in? In the first instance, bipedalism arose from hominid need for mortar. With bipedalism comes the development of walking upright and eventually running. Running, as well as walking, developed as a result of species dependence on mortar. Hence, in this sense running is related to mortar. However, physical variations such as those that exist between a hunting people of the Kalahari and a hunting people of the Arctic, relate to environment.

Theodosius Dobzhansky makes an interesting observation applicable here: "Culture [what I call *mortar*] is an adaptive instrument which permits the human species to evolve by fitting its environment to its genes more often than by changing the genes to fit its environment." [3]

For hundreds of thousands of years, man has possessed enough mortar to fill in the gaps of the species profile so as to match any environmental profile. By means of tools, fire, and speech he has been able to carry his original subtropical environment wherever he has gone. If he ranges to the Arctic, he dresses, houses, and heats himself to that degree necessary to sustain himself. In effect, he raises the temperature immediately surrounding his body so as to duplicate his original environment. If he seeks to live in the desert, he uses mortar to reduce the temperature surrounding him. (It has been observed that all man has to do is maintain an appropriate artificial climate within one sixteenth of an inch of his body in order to survive.) As for food, although the digestive system of man is essentially constructed for herbivorous food, it can readily accommodate and process meat diets. Eskimos, for example, get all the vitamins and minerals they need from raw meat. Thus they lack nothing for good health. What makes all this work is mortar.

Such being the case, when in the long trek of time did hominids reach the level of development that would allow for radiation without further speciation? We can't be certain, but Washburn offers an interesting possibility. If he is correct, then it was with *Homo erectus* (Java and Peking man) that this occurred, and the time would have been about 600,000 years ago:

> *Homo erectus* is thought to have evolved from one of the species of *Australopithecus* and the origin of much of what we think of as human appears to have been in this last period of time, long after the appearance of stone tools and the separation of man and ape. . . . With the transi-

3. "Genetic Entities and Hominid Evolution," in *Classification and Human Evolution*, edited by Sherwood Washburn (Chicago: Aldine, 1963), p. 359.

tion to *Homo erectus* the brain doubled in size, the bipedal adaptation was completed, and human skills showed themselves in complex tools . . . , killing many large animals, fire, and the occupation of the whole temperate and tropical Old World by a single species. It is with *Homo erectus* that man became so adaptable and effective that there is no further evidence of speciation, and this was probably the result of greatly improved intelligence and technology.[4]

Mortar, of course, has hastened man's radiation throughout the world. If he had ever attempted to move—say, to the cold regions—without mortar, he could not have done it in the short time actually employed. Theoretically, such a move might be accomplished if enough time—at least several hundred thousand years would be necessary for every significantly different environment—were available in which the species/environment equation was maintained so as to support existence, while at the same time selective pressures were able to effect a breakthrough into a new environment without breaking the equation. In that event, there would be no need for mortar.

But man is a creature of mortar; it is what fashioned him out of the base hominid stock, and it is what preserves his existence in every corner of the modern world. It is, finally, the factor that preserves the unity of the species.

The brain that created mortar is the brain of consciousness. While this conscious brain created mortar, it also created awareness of self—what we call self-consciousness. And when it did this it produced what I call *time-anxiety*.

The central factor in human existence has been the hunt. It has been the principal element in mortar and the nub of all human institutions. The hunt, however, is not natural to man, as he is a nonlethal primate by nature. The hunt has been

---

4. Washburn and Judith Shirek, "Human Evolution," in *Behavior-Genetic Analysis*, ed. Jerry Hirsch (New York: McGraw-Hill, 1967) p. 19.

made possible only through the use of tools-weapons which, as we have seen, are part of mortar. As part of mortar, they are the creations of the conscious mind. As a result of these factors, the hunt has been both dangerous and demanding, as well as uncertain, yet life itself has depended on it. Thus it can be seen that life itself has been precarious, primarily because of the artificial means that have had to be employed in order to obtain sustenance.

In this predicament, then, we can imagine an early female (woman?) with, say, a suckling offspring and possibly several dependent offspring of various ages. Let us assume that the female is pregnant. In our scenario the males (men?) of the affinity group are out on the hunt. Sometime along the continuum of time consciousness rises to the point where a number of questions arise in the female's mind: When will the hunters return? Will they bring back enough meat? Will they all return? Will my hunter return?

Dependency on an uncertainty produces anxiety. This is particularly true of the female who for most of the terrestrial period has been dependent on the unknown and unknowable results of a distant hunt. This uncertainty, of course, is heightened for the female not only because her survival is dependent on the success of the hunt, but because of the life within her, the life suckling her, and the lives of those dependent on her for nurture. The female, in this instance, is anxious for herself and for those dependent upon her. When consciousness rose to the point where there evolved an awareness of time, anxiety —once an inchoate state—became concrete in its causal relationship to specific events, and since these specific events such as the hunt extended themselves in duration, we have time-anxiety. This condition has been with man ever since. It is one of the bases of neurosis.

Man, in his attempt to reduce time-anxiety, set out almost from the inception of the condition to reduce or eliminate time-anxiety in two ways, first by the control of the elements of the hunt so as to reduce the uncertainty of the entire process. He has done this through the process of science and civilization. The second way man has sought a reduction of time-anxiety has been through attempting to return to that state in which there was no uncertainty as to a food supply and no conscious awareness of death. The state I am referring to is arborea.

What has been true of the conscious mind which experiences time-anxiety, has also been true of the body which experiences stress as a consequence of the time-lag between an experienced body-need and the satisfaction of that need. The greater the time-lag, the greater the body stress. In arborea there was no appreciable time-lag; in terrestria there almost always is. Thus, the creation of quasi-arboreal conditions will reduce this body stress. When, in order to relieve time-anxiety, the mind of man seeks to create quasi-arboreal conditions, this search is reinforced by the body: The closer man comes to reproducing arboreal conditions, the less stress is felt by the body. Needless to say, the corollary is true: The farther man goes from arborea, thus increasing his time-anxiety, the greater his body stress.

All this being the case, we can now approach the third set of dichotomies that form the Arboreal/Terrestrial Conflict Thesis.

Man is confined to the terrestrial mode of existence; he aspires to return to Arborea.

We are seeing in this discussion the transformation of the species from a fully arboreal primate to terrestrial man. What, then, of man's nature? Is he still essentially an arboreal primate, or is he becoming significantly different? The answer lies in the compensatory effect of mortar which serves both to allow man to exist in terrestria and to preserve his arboreal nature. Yet, as we have seen, significant genetic changes, both critical and peripheral, have taken place. What, then, is left of the original primate? The answer lies in man's "essential genes," the genes that determine species-protective, sustenance, and sexual behavior, the three essentials of survival.

In essence, man seeks to act in accord with his essential genes. Thus, he seeks to protect himself in the manner of the primate, he seeks to meet his sustenance needs in the primate manner, i.e., by direct transactions; and he seeks sexual activity based on the primate model. Unfortunately, man has become so imbedded in mortar that it is extremely difficult for him to function in any but terrestrial ways.

Such being the case, how can we know that man remains an arboreal primate? We see the manifestation of his arboreal nature whenever the demands of terrestrial living are reduced or removed. In addition, we can perceive man's arboreal nature when he breaks or ignores certain terrestrial rules of behavior.

In subsequent chapters these matters will be discussed at length. Here a brief statement—at most an offer of proof—must suffice. As to the matter of protection, man must be trained and motivated to fight wars; with the advent of neo-arboreal conditions, there is an accompanying manifestation of his nonlethal nature. This is seen most vividly in rising world peace and nonviolent movements. (See "The Warrior," *infra*, pages 201 to 204, and "Revolution . . . ," *infra*, pages 389 to 392.) Man's sexual promiscuity expresses itself in such practices as prostitution, divorce, and nonmarital sex; in addition, when under the influence of certain drugs, such as alcohol, man's sexual promiscuity becomes amply displayed. (See "The Object," *infra*, pages 243 to 244; also, "The Cheat," *infra*, pages 263 to 265.) Finally, wherever possible man bypasses indirect transactions such as work to secure food and engages in direct transactions such as stealing or gambling to satisfy his needs.

As can be seen, there is a serious conflict between man's arboreal nature and his terrestrial circumstances. His body seeks to function on its arboreal premise; his conscious—terrestrial—mind seeks to regulate the body on a terrestrial premise. Hence the conflict which, to varying degrees, afflicts everyone.[5]

---

5. See "The Prisoner" for details.

FIGHTING ICE
WITH FIRE

THE STORY of man is largely the story of his mortar. In the early period, one that may have lasted for a million years or more, his only mortar consisted of stone, bone, and wood tools. Out of these he fashioned sufficient artificial extensions of the forelimbs to protect himself from predators and to secure food. In this way he survived—and for a very long and very stagnant time. Nothing much changed except that the few stone tools he possessed improved from those made of chance pebbles to hand axes expressly fashioned out of stone. We know almost nothing more. There was in this great period of time a very, very slow drift.

There was a reason for this. Nothing obliged a change. Man's mortar was sufficient for his needs. He was living in eastern and southern Africa; the weather was moderate and the sources of food were constant, both in terms of prey and vegetation. What more could any creature want? The essentials were provided for: He was safe from predators and he was able to feed himself. As for sex, it may be presumed because of the survival of the species.[1] Nothing more was needed. With an absolute minimum of mortar the species/environment

---

1. Important changes in sexual behavior were occasioned by existence in the terrestrial mode, something that will be discussed later.

equation was preserved because in many respects the species was existing on terms very similar to those that pertained in arborea.

Then disaster struck.

Beginning about a million and a half years ago, and only ending ten thousand years ago, there occurred the most extraordinary geologic event in the history of the earth, the Pleistocene Epoch which, more than anything else, shaped the face of the northern continents. The central events of the Pleistocene were four incredible glacial periods that, geologically speaking, came and went with ferocious speed. Across much of North America and Europe there rose and fell great sheets of ice, sometimes as thick as ten thousand feet. Contrary to common belief, these changes were not slow shiftings of climate. In each instance, less than two hundred years were required to raise the water out of the sea and deposit it on the northern continents as icecaps.[2] With equal rapidity, they melted.

There were, as I said, four great glacials. The first one began about 1,500,000 years ago. It lasted about 125,000 years and was called the Gunz Glacial.[3] Then there was what is termed an *interglacial*—warm—period that lasted for 170,000 years. This was followed by the second glacial, the Mindel Glacial, which lasted about 145,000 years. Then came a very long interglacial that lasted some 640,000 years. Next was the Riss Glacial, 80,000 years long. The next interglacial lasted 225,000 years and was followed by the Würm Glacial that lasted for 104,000 years. The earth emerged from the Würm Glacial 10,-000 years ago. (This raises the question, which cannot be answered, of whether we are in a postglacial era or in an interglacial period.) [4]

---

2. For details, see *The Deep and the Past*, David B. Ericson and Gösta Wollin, (New York: Alfred A. Knopf, 1964), p. 136.

3. I will here only list the European glacials, not the North American, which occurred at the same time but were given different names.

4. Ericson, op. cit., p. 209.

The enormity of the climatic changes is almost impossible to grasp. Mountains were leveled and new ones raised. Rivers and lakes were gouged out of the earth. The edges of continents were raised as incalculable weights of ice bore down on the continental masses.

Harmut Bastian describes the scene this way:

> The advance of the ice must indeed have been a terrifying phenomenon. The solid sheets of rain descending, the storms of sand obscuring the sun, the crushing, irresistible power of the slowly encroaching glaciers which sent out before them their own icy zones fatal to flora and fauna —they must have induced an actual end-of-the-world atmosphere . . . [A]n average human lifetime would have been sufficient to discern definite changes in the world around and to sense unmistakably the approach of the ice.[5]

Four times the great glacials built up, and four times they broke down. When this happened the once frozen tundra of the North became warm, almost subtropical. Fauna from the southern regions migrated north to the awaiting food sources. Then again, when the ice returned, the great migrations south took place. And so it went for three migrations north and four migrations south.

It has been estimated that thousands of species of flora and fauna perished in this violent age because of their inability to adapt or to migrate. Only one species of fauna flourished in the midst of this natural cataclysm: man. It is no exaggeration to say that protoman entered the Pleistocene Epoch carrying a pebble tool and ten thousand years ago *Homo sapiens* emerged carrying aloft a bronze sword, symbol of his sovereignty over all earthly life.

What transpired during that million-and-a-half-year period to affect so enormous a transformation from the rudimentary *Australopithecus* to the fully evolved *Homo sapiens?*

---

5. *And Then Came Man* (New York: Viking Press, 1964), pp. 278–279.

The eye of the answer is man's brain and its revolutionary growth, but to understand the eye we must appreciate the violent storm swirling around it. It was the violence of the Pleistocene storm that trebled the size of man's brain.

The Pleistocene, with its climatic shifts of such monumental proportions, produced such an extraordinary series of environment profiles that only a nimble and adaptive brain could produce the mortar necessary to complete the genetically deficient species, profile and thus maintain contact with the environment. Many species failed to maintain that contact; many hominid forms failed, too, and became extinct.

When the Pleistocene began, hominids were confined to southern and eastern Africa. But then the great migrations of beasts began, driven south by the onslaught of the first glacial. When the northern continents began to warm up 125,000 years later, there began a drift north of beasts seeking the developing temperate and even subtropical vegetation beginning there. By this time these beasts comprised the core of hominid diet and as the beasts began to drift north, so too did man's ancestors. In this way they began to leave Africa and settle throughout the Old World.

They had to migrate north because their source of food was migrating. And this faced man with his second great terrestrial crisis. How could a subtropical creature survive the cold of the north? The problem was this: Somehow man would have to find a way of carrying his warm African climate with him as he trekked north in pursuit of prey. Possibly the first step in the problem's solution was some sort of crude clothing, probably the skins of animals. But the big breakthrough came when man domesticated fire, for fire would produce warmth, it would (eventually) provide a means of cooking food and, significantly, it would keep wild animals at bay. And in this latter regard, fire could almost be considered the final cleaving factor between man and nature.

Undoubtedly, in the earliest period of fire-use, it was captured where it was found. Later, it was domesticated. I want to suggest, by the terminology used, that fire was like a wild animal—and still is in many ways. Fire is the natural enemy of all animals. Its bite is one of the most painful experiences possible. It can eat out a whole habitat and leave nothing but ashes. Worst of all, it can kill. Furthermore, once unleashed, fire cannot be checked until it has devoured everything within its reach. Therefore, when it is said that man made use of fire, something most unnatural and unexpected is being asserted.[6]

Only the most extraordinary necessity could have forced early man to affect a *modus vivendi* no other animal would risk. The necessity was survival in a world plunged into climatic madness by the Pleistocene Epoch.

The first evidence we have of fire is in the now-famous Choukoutien caves near Peking where, 600,000 years ago, Peking man (*Homo erectus*) lived. The cold regions around Peking must have produced food crises of serious proportion, for not only are the caves filled with the remnants of a wide variety of prey, but there is also unmistakable evidence of cannibalism.

By domesticating fire, man enlarged the mortar sector of the species profile considerably and by doing so presented himself with increasingly divergent choices of habitat, ranging from Africa to eastern Asia and western Europe.

Man's solution to the climate crisis seems almost as impossible as that of the first great crisis, that of surviving in terrestria while being denied access to the trees where 90 percent of its food sources were to be found. Speaking in parallel terms, the crisis presented by the drifting herds was that of losing 100 percent of his diet.

We can only appreciate the full measure of the crisis—that of survival itself—when we realize the means used to resolve it. Fire is like water: It must be 100 percent controlled;

---

6. In the following pages the term *fire* is intended to include all methods, such as clothing, shelter, etc., used by man to modify the climate and protect himself from the cold.

99 percent won't do, as water will slip away and fire will continue to eat away. Therefore, the fire solution required total control or nothing at all.

And yet, in each crisis faced by man's ancestors, that of diet and that of climate control, the extreme and dangerous solutions chosen provided them with stupendous occasions of serendipity. When hominids turned to animals, thus reducing predators as well as finding food, they turned to a far more efficient source of protein. When *Homo erectus* used fire for climate control he (possibly inadvertently) conceived the idea of cooking his food—and thus stumbled across an extraordinary bonus.

Man's digestive system, then as now, was very much apelike.[7] It was not anywhere near as well adapted to a meat diet as that of, say, the lion whose evolutionary line had been carnivorous for many millions of years. Cooking breaks down the complex molecules of proteins and fats, rendering meat more digestible and thus more nutritious, producing more calories per pound. The same is also true of certain vegetables, especially roots, whose carbohydrates are made more available when the tough cell walls are broken down by heat.

Man solved the great food and climate crises by artificial means. He did so reluctantly and only because survival demanded it. In both crises he was driven to solutions—he was not attracted to what lay beyond the solutions. He did not choose to become a meat-eater; he was denied his arboreal world and its food. He did not choose to domesticate fire; he had to leave his natural climate. In both situations, he sought to retain contact with the most natural environment available, thereby to preserve as much as possible the natural species/environment equation. Only when survival itself was at stake did he let go of the more natural environment and enter an unnatural one made possible solely by means of mortar. Without these two elements of mortar, tools and fire,

---

7. LeGros Clark, in *The Antecedents of Man*, goes into this very thoroughly.

man's early terrestrial ancestors would never have survived. If the first crisis, that of food, had been successfully overcome, but not the later one of environment control, the line leading to man would have been snapped during the early stages of *Homo erectus*. As it was, mortar preserved the line.

THE GREAT
HUNT

THE INFURIATING part of the labyrinth is the fact that the entire terrestrialization process took place in its deepest shadows. While there are such tangibles as stone tools, an occasional fossil of creatures like *Australopithecus* and *Homo erectus*, and evidence of fire-use that can be picked up and examined, when we come to such intangibles as the development of man's social systems or his sexual practices, there is absolutely nothing to go on. All we really know is that an arboreal primate entered the labyrinth and man exited. However, this means, even if we can't directly observe the terrestrialization process itself, that we can draw the logical conclusion that the process took place within the labyrinth for the obvious reason that when we come to Sumerian man we come upon modern man. As to what happened in all that long period, we can only conjecture.

We might begin by addressing ourselves to the fascinating question of what made the brain grow between the time of the tool-maker and that of the fire-domesticator. This is a period perhaps as long as a million years. It is clear that the situation of hominids was such that enormous and rapid brain growth was taking place, yet there is no evidence of tool progression worth noting. For all practical purposes, the tools and weapons of Peking man were not much advanced over those used by *Australopithecus*. The explanation for this rapid brain growth, I believe, lies not in externals but in internal factors of the terrestrialization process.

While it is true that we can only speculate on the social dimension of the terrestrialization process, we can begin our speculations on a most solid premise, that of the hunt.

Washburn and C. S. Lancaster establish our premise:

Human hunting is made possible by tools, but it is far more than a technique or even a variety of techniques. It is a way of life, and the success of this adaptation (in its total social, technical, and psychological dimensions) has dominated the course of human evolution for hundreds of thousands of years. In a very real sense our intellect, interests, emotions, and the basic social life—all are evolutionary products of the success of the hunting adaptation. When anthropologists speak of the unity of mankind, they are stating that the selection pressures of the hunting and gathering way of life were so similar and the result so successful that populations of *Homo sapiens* are still fundamentally the same everywhere. . . .

Perhaps the importance of the hunting way of life in producing man is best shown by the length of time hunting has dominated human history. The genus *Homo* [including Peking man] has existed for some 600,000 years, and agriculture has been important only during the last few thousand years . . . and the entire evolution of man from the earliest populations of *Homo erectus* to the existing races took place during the period in which man was a hunter.[1]

---

1. Sherwood Washburn and C. S. Lancaster, "The Evolution of Hunting," in *Man the Hunter*, edited by Richard B. Lee and Irven DeVore (Chicago: Aldine, 1968), p. 293.

Washburn and Lancaster, in their use of the phrase "our intellect, interest, emotions and the basic social life—all are evolutionary products of the success of the hunting adaptation," must not be understood to mean genetic evolution or genetic adaptation. They mean *cultural evolution*. Also, their "adaptation" is closer to my "habituation," since the success of the adaptation rested almost exclusively on the success of what I call involuted evolution.

Possibly it would be advisable, at this point, to relate the term *culture* as it is generally used by sociologists, and the term *mortar* as I use it here. In many ways they are identical, in that they describe that which permits man to exist in the terrestrial mode. The only possible difference would lie in the notion that culture is something that is passed on from generation to generation not by genes but by the individuals, while mortar, in this connection, would be the means by which they transmit that culture. I say this because, strictly speaking, mortar consists of means, while culture can be thought of as ends. For example, tools are a means to an end, and are part of mortar. The same is true of fire. Added up, however, they comprise, along with other elements, culture. However, in all that follows, unless otherwise stipulated, mortar and culture may be considered interchangeable terms.

The problem we must now address is that of the imposition of this culture on both arboreal genes and the base social system established in arborea.

The social system of arboreal primates is predicated on their genetic adaptation to the arboreal environment. Literally, it is not a matter of one following the other; they interplay on a feedback basis. But it is the physical relationship between primate and arboreal environment that demands a certain social system. As has been previously observed, the lack of "tooth and claw" determines the primate system of protection against predators. Also, the grasping forelimbs make it possible for the individual to feed itself and to do so in a direct transaction. And in the matter of reproduction, single births with a long dependency period allow for adequate nurture and social development. In any of these three essential elements—protection, sustenance, and sex—if the primate seeks to act in any way significantly different from the way its environment requires it to act, it will become extinct. To explain the phenomenon of the primate social system, we have recourse to the explanation that "the primate is acting in accord with its nature." Indeed, it cannot do otherwise; it cannot act against its nature. Or, it cannot act against its genetically founded nature.

The contradictions between the nature of hominids and their terrestrial circumstances are such as to demand that a new social system be superimposed on that created for life in the trees. This is a matter not just of changing habits but of seeking to alter radically a genetically based system. Quite simply, it is like an attempt to get, say, a chimpanzee to act like a human being.

We have already seen that tool-use tended toward bipedalism and that all the important anatomical changes experienced by the species during the terrestrialization process were clustered around tool-use ability. That is, anatomical changes occurred in direct relation to mortar. What we want to look at now is the central element around which all social changes took place.

As Washburn and Lancaster have said, "our intellect, interests, emotions, and the basic social life" derive from the central and controlling element in man's terrestrial existence: the hunt.

From the modern perspective it might be concluded that had man not chosen to hunt, he might have chosen to obtain sustenance some other way, for example, by being a gatherer of herbivorous foods. But it was not choice that made man a hunter, it was necessity. The hunt, in this circumstance, becomes the central component of mortar. And just as anatomical changes clustered around the creation of mortar, so too all social changes clustered around the central component of that mortar: the hunt.

Every human institution and practice revolves around the

hunt; every human institution and practice is subordinate to the hunt.[2] This is the basic rule of human existence. It is one that cannot be violated if man is to survive. In fact, we can go further and say that this rule made man possible; without this rule his earliest terrestrial ancestors would have perished at the very first moment of terrestrialization. The hunt was the great unifying factor in the development of man. Washburn and Lancaster consider the hunt so important a unifying factor that they say of it that "the selection pressures of the hunting . . . way of life were so similar and the result so successful that populations of *Homo sapiens* are still fundamentally the same everywhere." (It will be seen that I omitted the phrase "and gathering." I did so because the gathering of fruits, vegetables, nuts, and so forth were really a continuation of arboreal practices. What was uniquely terrestrial was the hunting activities.) In other words, hunting, and all the derivations from that practice, made *Homo sapiens* one species. Or we can say, *Hunting, ergo man.*

When we know what went in and who came out of the labyrinth, and when we further know the core element of that hidden existence, we can with reasonable certainty reconstruct what actually took place. As to *when* certain transformations took place, I would suggest that the great social developments took place during the formative period of *Homo erectus*, for in this way, I believe, we can account for the remarkably rapid growth of the brain during a period when there were no significant tool-developments to account for it. It should be recalled also that this rapid growth took place during the Pleistocene Epoch which continually made exceptional demands on the species, demands that could find adequate responses only in the form of a series of remarkable social changes.

---

2. This formula persists in the modern, post-hunt era where it is repeated, but with the term *economic activity* replacing *the hunt*. The patterns established during the long period of the hunt (99 percent of man's terrestrial period) became so ingrained they have persisted to this day with very little modification. See "Toward Mere Existence," *infra*, for details.

With the hunt as the commanding fact of human development, let us begin our reconstructive efforts with an examination of that fact.

The hunt, in its full development, was exclusively a male activity. From start to finish it was hazardous. In the very early period, at least to and possibly through the time of the Australopithecines, the small hominid was as often the prey as it was the hunter. With the aid of its weapons, however, it held its own, though undoubtedly the species suffered enormous loss of life. In time, as its skills increased, the hunter began to turn the tide and gain dominance. But hunting was a precarious matter in terms not only of success but also of survival.

Because of the terms of the hunt and of maternity, females could not become hunters. They were obliged to be gatherers —of berries, roots, rodents, and so forth. Neither could they travel with the males on the hunt. They had to remain in a more or less fixed place where they could safely tend to the needs of dependent offspring. This latter situation, with the passage of time, became aggravated.

Actually, the problem began in arborea and is common to all the anthropoid apes of today. The dependency period of offspring is longer for apes than for any other mammal but man, whose dependency period is the longest of all creatures. Dependency inhibits the activity of the mother. This is seen among modern chimpanzees as well as among humans. However, when forced into the terrestrial mode, the situation became even more aggravated. With the growth of the brain and the accompanying growth of the skull, parturition had to take place earlier and earlier during the development of the fetus, since the pelvic structure of the mother did not grow rapidly enough to keep pace with the growing fetal skull. As a result, the period of infant dependency increased considerably, thus further restricting the mobility of the mother.[3]

3. This is a fascinating—and compelling—bit of evidence that anatomical changes related to mortar. The brain's rapid growth, so essential

Thus, for a variety of reasons, there came about a division of labor along sexual lines. Males became hunters; females became gatherers and the keepers of the "camp." This, in turn, made the female dependent on the male for her food—something that did not occur in the arboreal mode. Thus began, for the first time, food-sharing, something utterly alien to primates.

The hunt produced another situation of great novelty and one fraught with enormous implications. Because hunting with tools was not instinctual, it was of necessity a cultural activity, requiring among other things the making and using of tools. (This is not to say that the seeking of food was not instinctive, but that the hominid method was.) As a consequence, the techniques of hunting, as well as those attendant to weapon and tool making, had to be taught. Older males had to teach younger males. Thus, for the first time, a special relationship between adult males and adolescent males came into being.

The result of the hominid hunting system was a complex network of relationships. Females and all offspring weaned from the breast were dependent on adult males. Thus, everyone depended on the adult male for survival. However, in time old age and incapacity would overtake the adult female and male and they would become dependent on the now-mature young male adult. So there developed a cycle of dependency. What created complications was the fact that a close relationship had to be constructed between the adult male and the subadult male—something never required in the arboreal world. Further, this close relationship had as its focal point the unnatural business of killing and training to kill.

Generally in nature it is the mother predator who introduces her offspring to killing. It is part of the weaning process, both in terms of terminating actual feeding off the mother and in

---

for mortar, and hence survival, outdistanced the growth of the female's pelvic system which was relatively less essential than that of the brain. The result was the above-mentioned problem of increasingly earlier births, and the accompanying longer dependency period.

terms of equipping the offspring to secure their own food.

It was the misfortune of hominids that they were not natural predators and that the adult male had to be the one to teach the subadult male how to become a hunter. These two factors combined to produce a volatile situation and formed the basis of the deep conflict between fathers and sons. There were no species mechanisms to safeguard the males caught in this highly charged circumstance and thus whatever control existed to prevent intraspecies killing was culturally self-imposed and subject to frequent breakdowns.

There existed, then, a constellation of factors affecting the basic relationships between the various individuals within any particular affinity group. The factor that coalesced all these factors into a finally determined set of special relationships was the inability of the hunter to supply more than minimal amounts of meat.

In arborea, everyone above the dependency age fended for itself. Thus, depending on the social system of various species, there could be a disproportionate ratio of females to males. In all events, the male-female ratio was unimportant, as was the ratio of adults to subadults, since all fed themselves. In terrestria this couldn't work. The ratio of females to males had to stabilize in order that the males within the affinity group could provide sufficient meat for everyone, including offspring. Thus, because of a limited food supply and the artificial means required to provide it, a new male-female relationship had to be created. The solution was a pair-bond system in which a specific female would have a special relationship with a specific male, under the terms of which the male would provide meat for the female and any offspring of the female, in return for which the female would prepare the food and distribute the food. In return for food security, and to assure its future, the female would train the offspring up to a certain age, at which time she would hand over the subadult male to the adult male for training in the hunt, while preserving the training of the subadult female for herself. This latter was a more natural sort of training, being, as it were, a nonlethal process and more in keeping with the sort of training other primate mothers provided their offspring, except that the female offspring would have to be culturally prepared (as distinct from being genetically adapted) for the dependency status.[4]

One of the major social inventions to emerge from existence in the terrestrial mode was that of fatherhood. Nowhere else in all of nature is there anything like it. True, in some other species there is lifelong monogamy and the existence of a "family," but in none is there the unique element of fatherhood, in which there is not only a fixed relationship between an adult male and an adult female but a requirement that the father, of absolute necessity, train his male offspring in the essentials of food-procurement. In all other forms of life, the procurement of food is an instinct; in man it is the consequence of consciously inculcated culture. All this, it need hardly be pointed out, was, and remains today, in total contradiction to the way of life in arborea.

Concomitant with fatherhood was filialness, something else that never existed in arborea, where the relationship between adult males and subadults was not direct or personal. Whatever relationship existed derived from the fact that subadults were members of the affinity group and thus subject to male dominance as well as to male protection. While it is true that adult males among modern apes will occasionally play with and be very tolerant of infants and juveniles, it is not play or tolerance based on a parent-child relationship.

Viewed in its entirety, the function of the affinity group in the arboreal mode of existence is to provide a social system that will preserve the integrity of the group so that dependent offspring can reach maturity, here meaning sexual maturity, so as to be able to perpetuate the species. The only real division of labor along sexual lines has the females bearing and rearing offspring and the males, aside from impregnating the females,

---

4. It must be remembered that genetically the female is no less capable of solving her sustenance problems than is the male.

protecting the affinity group from encroachment and predation. There is no special relationship between males and females and between adults and subadults, except for the specific one-to-one relationship between a mother and a dependent
offspring.[5]

All this was shattered on the ground. Early man could not
by natural means solve the most basic need of all life, that of
food-procurement. Instead, he had to create artificial, nongenetic extensions of the forelimbs in order to eat. To preserve
and to perpetuate the mortar without which he could not live,
early man had to completely reorganize the social system that
had been so successful in arborea but which could lead only
to extinction on the ground. Thus we come to the inescapable
conclusion that the system of monogamy, fatherhood, and
filialness exists solely in order to provide and perpetuate the
mortar necessary to preserve contact between the species profile and the environment profile. This mortar, this artificial
extension of the forelimbs, this culture, was fashioned by the
mind.

In addition to the social problems created by terrestrialization, there were also functional ones relating to soiling the nest
and sleep. Arboreal primates, for example, wake up in the
morning, sit on the edges of their brief nests, and eliminate
before beginning the day's activities. Their treatment of food
is similarly casual. They waste more than they eat and what
they waste they let drop to the forest floor, where it rots. Such
profligacy could not be tolerated on the ground. Not only
was food scarce, but the practice of just letting everything
drop on the spot could not be allowed. Aside from the matter
of simple tidiness was the problem of disease. Yet, notwithstanding the seriousness of the matter, because there was (and
is) no instinct against soiling the nest, this problem was never
adequately solved. Hominids have spent several million years

---

5. This general rule is modified in the case of the chimpanzee where,
long after the end of the dependency period, offspring still preserve a
relationship with the mother.

trying to establish a "tidiness" habit but have failed lamentably. In a way, this has been a boon to the paleontologist who, once he has discovered a living site, needs only to dig straight down through the site to trace man's history. This is precisely what the Leakeys did for so many years in Olduvai Gorge. Bones, refuse, tools, offal—everything was allowed to fall where, undisturbed by any sense of tidiness, it has lain until uncovered by paleontologists.

As for the casualness of arboreal sleeping arrangements, not much needs to be said other than that an ancient instinct had to be stifled by the needs of terrestrial living. Casualness simply had to go and everyone, from infants to adults, had to sleep in more or less a fixed camp and more or less at specific times.

It can be seen from this brief reconstruction that the essential form of primate existence was severely wrenched into something totally different by the terrestrialization process. Old, genetically based processes had to be suppressed and new, culturally created processes had to be invented.

What stands out above everything else is the conversion of the adult male from a peripheral protective individual into a providing figure who becomes the protagonist of human history. In arborea and elsewhere in nature it is the female who is the protagonist; among humans it is the male. This more than anything else has shaped human history. Whereas the female is genetically endowed for bearing and nurturing offspring, the male is not genetically endowed for anything but impregnating females and then assuming a peripheral position in the affinity group. There is in the male no natural basis for his being a hunter-predator, a father, or a teacher. Because he lacks any "predator instinct" and because he lacks any "paternal instinct," he has had to be constituted a hunter and father (who teaches) by artificial methods. Lacking the necessary "instincts," the male lacks those predator and paternal parameters ordinarily provided by nature and therefore is capable, depending on cultural influences, of enormous variations, ranging from apathy to insatiable appetite for killing and paternal authority. In other words, there is nothing within the male urging him even to minimal predation or paternity, and there is nothing within him to restrain him from tremendous excesses in either. Because of this men go to war and can be unmitigated tyrants in their families and in their social groups.

A second dominant feature of the new society formed by terrestrialization pressures was the loss of individuality. Adults in an arboreal affinity group were individuals living an existence based on individual independence within the social frame of the group. Upon terrestrialization, relationships of very specific sorts came into being, and the basis of those relationships was the utilitarian value of the members. A male had value as a hunter; the female, as a producer of offspring and caretaker of the camp; offspring, as potential hunters or mothers and caretakers. And it is here in the matter of utilitarian value that we have the problem of infanticide, particularly female infanticide in those hunting cultures where hunters were needed far more than mothers and caretakers who did not directly contribute to the hunt.

A third and extremely important feature of terrestrial life was the abandonment of sexual promiscuity and the imposition of sexual restraint. In arborea there was no one-to-one sexual relationship, on the part of either the female or the male. At the right moment of the female's estrus cycle, the males perceived the signs and copulation took place, not between that female and a designated male, but between that female and all adult males in the affinity group. In terrestria, however, when the male perceived signs of sexual receptivity in a female with whom he lacked a designated relationship he had to repress his instinct and forego copulation. Similarly, when the female felt sexually receptive, she had to reject all sexual advances except those of a designated male.

What resulted from all of these new forms of behavior can readily be predicted: increased time-anxiety and body stress. The former resulted from the uncertainty of mortar; the latter, from the inability of the body to function on the basis of its original genetic nature. Because modern man's essential genes are exactly the same as those of his remote arboreal ancestors, the time-anxiety and body stress experienced by his terrestrial hominid ancestors in their efforts to survive in the novel terrestrial situation is experienced in undiminished severity today by each individual. However, the precise degree of severity depends on the cultural conditions of the individual's particular society. Thus, in a society that manufactures a great deal of mortar, the tendency will be toward heightened time-anxiety and body stress; in one that requires less mortar, time-anxiety and body stress tend to be less.

THE TRUMPET
SOUNDS

A L L the transformations necessary to adjust an arboreal primate to terrestrial living took place within the dim corridors of the labyrinth. These transformations were not, however, transformations in the essential nature of the beast, as so many authorities seem to imply, but rather transformations in the species-profile as it sought constantly to maintain contact with that of the changing environment. This, as we have seen, was accomplished by means of mortar. As we have also seen, this life-supporting mortar had the secondary effect of perpetuating the genetic composition of the species that made mortar necessary in the first place.

The first and undoubtedly most important mortar was the tool-weapon by which access to terrestrial food sources, largely animal, was made possible. Without this first mortar, the early hominids which sought to live in terrestria would have become extinct. It was this mortar that, in time, gave man dominion over all other animals. It was the mortar of survival.

The second and next most critical mortar was fire (and clothing, etc.) that allowed man to travel out of tropical Africa and eventually find living accommodations everywhere in the world. Had man not domesticated fire and found other methods of controlling his environment, he would have been obliged to remain in his original habitat. In that event, those who were able to survive on at best a marginal subsistence once the migration of beasts began, would have remained locked in a dead-end passageway of the labyrinth. Man as we know him would not have developed. The recurring crises in the terrestrialization process occasioned by the stern demands of the Pleistocene epoch would not have affected these creatures. Thus the brain would not have grown as remarkably as it did. As it was, it was the endless challenges to the species as it sought to cope with the Pleistocene that produced the great brain of man.[1]

However, we can only begin fully to understand the terrestrialization process when we realize that tools and fire were only physical aspects of the process. They were the mortar that made it possible for an arboreal primate to survive in the terrestrial mode. They were, in fact, the mortar that made possible the central element of mortar, the hunt. It was the hunt that obliged the species to superimpose on the original arboreal social system a wholly new one that could both fit into the social terms required by the nature of the hunt and also act to preserve and perpetuate the hunt. This, then, required a whole complex of new relationships and functions, totally novel to an arboreal primate. They were provided by the new brain created during the terrestrialization process and superimposed on the original primate brain.

As more and more mortar was created by an ever-increasing terrestrial brain, man began to face his third great crisis. It arose over the need to transmit this mortar from individual to individual.

All relationships and functions of the original primate in its arboreal environment were regulated by its arboreal brain. The "content" of this brain, i.e., its ability to regulate the organism in its environment, was passed on from generation to generation by means of genes. Mortar, however, cannot be trans-

---

1. Because the subject of man's terrestrial brain is so important, it will be discussed in "The Prisoner," *infra*, pp. 272 to 305.

mitted by genetic means because it is the product of the terrestrial brain and its principal attribute, the conscious mind.
It can only be passed on by some transmission system of the
conscious mind. But how? Being human, we know the answer:
speech. It was the one thing that could link everyone together
in their efforts to create and perpetuate mortar.

We can see an example of the original problem in the developing child. While it is very young it needs no actual language. Sounds that are very directly related to animal verbalizations are enough to create a functioning bond with an infant.
Even as the infant enters early childhood little conversation
is actually needed, either between adult and child or between
two children. Everyone can function and relate under these
circumstances because at this stage of child development there
is no need for the child to participate in mortar production.
However, there comes a day when speech is necessary. This
day arrives when the child must prepare for the eventual time
when he will be obliged to contribute to mortar, when he
will have to go to school; mothers prepare their children for
school by helping them develop speech. Were it not necessary
to produce mortar there would be no need for speech.

We mustn't look at this remarkable talent of man from
modern man's point of view. In the modern era, it would appear that the child seems to *grow* into speech. At birth there
is the potential of later speech; we know this because babies
grow into children who speak.

This was not the case with speech in the first instance. If
we proceed not backward from modern man's perspective but
forward from the perspective of developing man, we discover
that he was not, as is the modern child, born with the potential for speech. For speech to be invented—and it was invented
in the same way as all other forms of mortar were invented—
two critical preconditions had to exist. The first and decisive
precondition was the *need* for speech. A crisis had to exist that
would require a novel solution in the same manner that the
first two crises required their own novel solutions. The second

precondition was the genetic breakthrough that would make possible the meeting of this need. Because the origins of human speech are hopelessly lost in the depths of the labyrinth, there is no way to know for certain whether it was a mutation or selective pressures that met this important precondition. All we know is that somewhere in the labyrinth man began to speak.

Primate vocalization is a function of the "old" brain; the speech of man is a function of the "new" brain. In 1967 Bryan W. Robinson reported on an experiment involving the electrical stimulation of 5,880 loci in the unanesthetized *Macaca mulatta*, a monkey. He was seeking the site of primate vocalization. He concluded his report this way:

> The data does indicate that primate vocalization is principally imbedded in the limbic system since the evoked vocalization closely resembled corresponding sounds given under field conditions. . . . There is no evidence that the neocortex participates in the production or organization of such sounds. . . . In the present study, several hundred neocortical sites were stimulated without the production of any type of sound. . . . Primate vocalization is used principally in situations bearing some emotional valence such as threat, aggression, fear, pain, pleasure, feeding and separation. The limbic system, which appears to mediate this type of emotional response is an appropriate matrix for vocalization.
>
> Human speech, by contrast, appears to depend primarily on neocortical structures. . . . We may suspect that limbic vocalization is still present in man and is manifested during emotional stress as cries, exclamations, etc.[2]

Primate vocalization is part of the brain system dealing directly with the reception of stimuli through the senses. Man's

---

2. "Vocalization Evoked in Forebrain in Macaca Mulatta," *Physiology and Behavior* 2 (1967): 353.

speech is not. Man's speech is part of the brain system created during his terrestrial existence.

By tools, man has been able to procure food. By fire (and clothing, etc.) man has been able to control his environment. To exist and be perpetuated, tools and fire each require a "reproductive" system whereby they can be transmitted from generation to generation and from individual to individual. This is where speech comes in. Speech is the reproductive system of the conscious mind and thus the perpetuator of culture. Idiomatically, speech is the mortar of mortar.[3]

Observation and imitation are reeds too slender on which to base survival. Just as the bird relies on genes to guide it in its nest-making, man needed something to guide him in his tool-making. The need was enormous; the preconditions and pre-adaptations were present. The result was speech—the tool that could make a tool that could make a tool. So we return to the hunt where, not unexpectedly, we discover the origin of speech.

Human speech began as a request for action. There are, in the simplest form, three types of sentences. They may be exemplified as follows:

1) Look!

2) George runs.

3) George is fast.

The first sentence, consisting solely of a verb, is a request for action. It is addressed to a second person, a hearer. The second sentence, consisting of a verb and a subject noun (or pronoun), is a statement, present in all languages. The third sentence is a descriptive statement, consisting of three terms,

---

3. What is true of speech is true of writing, with one significant exception. For speech to serve as the reproductive system of the conscious mind it must employ at least two people in direct communication. Writing, on the other hand, exists independently of human instrumentalities and therefore can bypass individuals and even entire generations without losing its effectiveness. Because writing originated outside the labyrinth it is not discussed here. Also, many cultures and individuals have become fully terrestrialized without the use of writing, so—strictly speaking—it is not an essential ingredient of the process.

a noun and a verb, plus an adjective. In these three sentences we can observe a sequential buildup, beginning with the simplest, a verb alone; then a noun and a verb; and then noun, verb, and adjective. We will consider only the first, since it is the earliest form of human speech.

As A. S. Diamond has expressed it, "the first [type of sentence] alone performs directly the basic function of all language—namely, that by it man in society, through the person addressed, wields and gains control over his environment." [4]

Diamond describes the nature of a request-for-action sentence (a single verb in the second person singular of the imperative mood) as follows:

> The request for action is the simplest form of mental process. It is the expression of a desire: the nearest thing in language to the operation of instinct. The minimum features of instinctive action are a *feeling* (the affective element), a striving (the conative element) and the resulting action. In the request for action there is the affective element . . . and the conative element; but now, instead of a direct striving, the speaker seeks by his *word* to bring about the action of another. . . . By tools man has extended his power of action, of influencing his environment. By the social tool of speech he seeks to bring about the action of his fellow. If the request for action is completed, it is completed by the action of the hearer, which it procures [italics in original] . . .[5]

I have already suggested that speech came into being only when it was needed. This being so, can we speculate as to when the need—the imperative need—arose?

We can eliminate certain situations. Speech was not needed by members of the family, or pair-bond plus offspring within the family situation. Especially does mating not require speech.

---

4. *The History and Origin of Language* (New York: Philosophical Society, 1959), p. 19.
5. Ibid., pp. 19–20.

The same is true of the situation between adults and offspring. A look, a gesture, a warning cry is all that is needed to raise them. These basic relationships may involve vocalizations, but clearly they stem from the limbic system, precisely the source of arboreal primate vocalizations. This is so because when man's ancestors were obliged to become terrestrial, like refugees, they took with them the social system of their original home. Speech was not needed for gathering berries, nuts, roots, and other vegetation. This system of food procurement existed in arborea. There is, then, but one area left where speech—a request for action in the second person singular of the imperative mood—would be needed: the hunt.

Diamond writes, ". . . the fundamental use of speech, and (over the ages) the commonest use of speech, and the original use of speech, is the request for action addressed to one person." [6] He points out that in those few families of languages (such as the Semitic and Hamitic) which make a distinction by gender, the verb-root is the masculine imperative. On this basis he concludes that the original addressees of a request for action were males, and that the original speakers were male. This is most logical in view of the fact that females were the gatherers, and thus not in a situation requiring speech.

Diamond concludes his theory of the origin of speech by saying:

The origin of language that we have arrived at, based, as it is, upon the common features of languages, may be explained by supposing that, among the innumerable sounds uttered by members of [an early community], there is a predominant usage of sounds of a distinct kind for this purpose—namely, as requests for action—and this usage ultimately defined and fixed in the mind the sounds of this character as having this meaning. For what type or types of action, then, would a request be . . . most commonly and urgently made? . . . No doubt the circum-

6. Ibid., p. 144.

stances of the requests would be innumerable, but among all others one circumstance, in particular, would be recurrent—namely, *that the asker was not strong enough to do the act for himself.* Accordingly, we may conjecture that the actions suggested were actions requiring the maximum of bodily effort—requests to smash, break, cut, crush, kill, destroy. Break it! Kill it! The common feature of all these is the act of striking with maximum effort, and a breaking or cutting. [Italics added] [7]

We can complete our speculation by looking at an inventory of animals eaten by Peking man (*Homo erectus*) while occupying the caves at Choukoutien. Of the remnants, 70 percent are of deer. The rest include antelope, sheep, saber-toothed cats, horses, hyenas, roebucks, rhinoceroses, camel, bear, and pigs. I call the reader's attention to the presence of carnivores such as the saber-toothed cats, hyenas, and bears, as well as such large animals as horses, rhinoceroses, and camels. In all probability, a single male could not bring down or trap such animals alone; he would need help from another male. And when we add to this the fact that *Homo erectus* stood possibly only as much as five feet tall—that is, not much bigger than *Australopithecus*—and that he had but the crudest of hardware, it can be seen how another tool, the social tool mentioned by Diamond, would be absolutely essential.

I would like to add a brief footnote to this speculative discussion on the origin of speech. It has to do with instinctive sounds such as cries and exclamations. As Robinson has pointed out, speech originates in the "new" brain, while vocalizations such as cries and exclamations originate in the "old" brain. What is significant is not so much the lack of relation between the two systems, but the fact that the old system, that of the limbic vocalizations, persists to this day.

---

7. Ibid., p. 145. What is extraordinary is that Diamond never connected this request for action with hunting!

The origin of these limbic vocalizations is the "old" brain —the arboreal brain which forms the basis of man's special brain. The presence of these limbic vocalizations in modern man is clear evidence that he still has an arboreal brain. Nothing in all the millions of years of terrestrial living has happened to silence this arboreal brain with its genetically based vocalizations. This is so because the genes of the original primate still exist in man.

THE COCOON

WITH speech, the terrestrialization process was completed. Man now had all the mortar he needed in order to survive in an alien and hostile environment. He had a means, albeit artificial, of obtaining sustenance as well as protecting himself from predators; he had a means, albeit artificial, of controlling his environment, thereby allowing him to move anywhere on earth; and he had speech, also artificial, the reproductive system of the conscious mind that enabled him to produce mortar within a generation and to perpetuate it from generation to generation. In short, man the arboreal primate lives in the terrestrial mode by virtue of mortar that preserves the species/environment equation.

Man emerged from the labyrinth, the dominant creature of the world. But even as he was emerging he prepared a testament for all future men to study and reflect upon. Just inside the labyrinth's exit, artists of unsurpassed genius executed the most remarkable collection of paintings the world has ever seen. I am referring to the great cave paintings of western Europe, done some fifteen thousand years ago. The question that has haunted scholars ever since their discovery has been this: What were the artists about?

To answer this perplexing question, we must see the paintings as the culmination of a process begun hundreds of thousands of years earlier. In all that vast time, from *Homo erectus* through Neanderthal to eventual *Homo sapiens,* man lived the life of a hunter. In all those hundreds of thousands of years, nothing changed. Man drifted with the great herds of beasts that provided his sustenance, his clothing, and much of his tools, and he drifted with the tides of climate caused by the Pleistocene glaciers. In this entire period, his material culture scarcely changed at all. The reason for this lay in the balance between the species and its environment. Between tools and fire, as protected by speech, man had sufficient mortar to satisfy his sustenance and protective needs. He had no other need besides that of reproducing the species, something accomplished within the framework of acquired terrestrial social practices. What more was needed? Nothing. What more is needed today? Nothing. The only difference between the drifting men of the late labyrinth period and modern man is the means by which these needs are met.

It was because there was a balance between needs and their satisfaction under then-existing conditions that there was this seemingly endless drift. Mortar certainly didn't need significant modification. Man had exactly what was needed, no less and no more. He had the elements of survival that, combined, created a species profile that matched that of the environment. Animals, the key feature of the environment profile, were in great abundance; all man had to do was stay near them, follow them as they slowly migrated, and slay what was needed for food, clothing, and tools. In this way man led a complete existence.

In achieving balance, man was obeying a rule established from the very beginning of his terrestrial exile: to remain as close to origins as possible. The closer to origins, the less need for mortar; the less mortar, the more natural man's existence; the more natural man's existence, the less time-anxiety and body stress. Hence, it was only survival crises that forced man to relinquish elements of naturalness and take on increments of mortar. When in the course of his efforts to survive, man entered the balanced relation between artifice and naturalness that secured his needs, he drifted with this balance, seemingly forever.

To give some sense of the extent of man's great prehistoric drift, we might note that there have been approximately one hundred generations since the beginning of the Christian era. The period I am here talking about lasted for over thirty thousand generations! And in all those generations not even the faintest ticking of time's clock could be heard.

Yet, even as man lived in his balanced drift, circumstances were conspiring to confront him with his fourth crisis—one that has retained its effect on man to this day.

The roots of man's fourth crisis lay in his arboreal nature, which prevented him from becoming a natural predator. He lacked the instincts of a true predator (as well as the "tooth and claw") who, in order to secure the future of the species, practices restrained predation. Man, in his efforts to secure minimum subsistence, used maximum means. He practiced, to use a modern term, overkill. He set fires to stampede herds, he drove them over cliffs, he herded them into swamps. He destroyed great numbers but could only use a few. This overkill went on for hundreds of thousands of years. It could not go on forever. It did not.

There was a second, conspiring circumstance. Its roots were shallow, going only as deep as the Würm Glacier. Just before man emerged from the labyrinth, and at the time he began his great cave paintings, the last of the four great glaciers was still at its height. What is significant, though, is the mixture of temperate, subarctic, and even subtropical animals in the cave paintings. Clearly, this was a transitional time. While the glacier was still well extended, it would not be very long before it would begin retreating to the North, leaving most of Europe on the threshold of a new and vastly different era. When the glacier finally did retreat, it left behind a great forest, extending over the larger part of the European mass, that put an end to a hunting tradition that had lasted for hundreds of thousands of years. The new and burgeoning forests were too thick to allow the flow of the great herds of animals on which man subsisted. Henceforth, man would have to find a new source of food and new ways of procuring it.

It is, I believe, most significant that just a short time after this period, and only a step or two outside the labyrinth's exit, man began the domestication of animals and grain. This is known as the Neolithic Revolution. What produced it was the Paleolithic Crisis in which man faced, for a fourth and culminating time, the loss of his source of food.

Until domestication, which guaranteed man's source of food, man had been totally dependent on what had appeared to be the endless cornucopia of nature. Man, however, was in partnership with nature because of the species/environment equation. This was so whether he appreciated the fact or not. By his profligacy, arising from his being an artificial predator, man had significantly altered the profile of the environment, especially that part of it represented by the great herds of animals. In addition to man's destruction of this significant sector of the environment's profile, nature itself, upon the retreat of the last glacier, changed its profile further.

What made the crisis so great was the fact that man's terrestrialization had followed a course in which every anatomical and social modification was centered around the key element of mortar, the hunt. What, then, of man if the central element of his mortar were taken away? Everything else would collapse, because everything else was designed to support, protect, and perpetuate the hunt.

When the species was first forced into the terrestrial mode, it might have found a different solution to its sustenance problem, some niche where the species, marginal at best, could exist and eventually make an accommodation with terrestrial demands—say, along the lines of a herbivorous groundling primate not much different from the baboon. In such an event, all anatomical and social modifications would have centered around that type of terrestrial existence. The point is to suggest that at the very beginning there was room for some variation because of the generalized form of the species. But as of thirty to forty thousand years ago, man had reached a point of no return. He was shaped around his special mortar so completely that he possessed no option but to retain it. He could not dissolve what he had and construct a radically different mortar. His body, bent around the mortar he had built up over the countless millennia, could not be straightened out and then reshaped around different mortar. Because of the form of his mortar, man's original arboreal primate genes were still locked inside him. Without mortar, his genetic deficiencies would have quickly doomed him in the terrestrial world. In brief, then, man had no options in the great crisis he now faced. He had to retain his mortar, notwithstanding the fact that the environment profile had altered significantly. How, in this critical situation, could man cure a defect in the environment profile? The question is enormous. It means that man somehow had to assume the power of nature and in some way reconstitute the environment's profile so that it might match that of man's mortar. Clearly, it was the greatest reversal in the history of existence. The solution by which man corrected nature's deficiency set the course of all future human development, for it encased man in a cocoon from which he will never be able to escape. And it is for this reason that man can never return to arborea.

Until the Paleolithic Crisis, man had but one major concern: to preserve contact with the source of his food. With the solution to the crisis, as exemplified by the Neolithic Revolution, man had to assume a second responsibility, that of producing his food. Because man has been doing this ever since, it is quite easy to accept such a proposition as natural. It is not. While certain insects may be said to produce their food (something they do by instinct), no mammal has had such a burden placed on it, except for man. To compound the problem, man has no more instinct for producing his food than he has for hunting it.

With the loss of nature's provision, man had to begin to

provide his own food in order that he might be able to consume it. Thus, he entered a cocoon divorced from nature and in which he began the production-consumption process that is the core of his present existence.

Once man had entered his cocoon, the hunt was over. With incredible speed—only a few thousand years—he ceased his migratory life and entered a settled existence. The settled existence we know as civilization began with Sumer and continues to this day.

It would seem that with the domestication of animals and grain man's greatest terrestrial problem would be solved. By controlling the production of food and also the consumption of food, man could lead an existence independent of nature. But that is not how it has turned out. The practices begun during the Neolithic Revolution, while limited in scope, set a pattern that man has followed ever since. By entering his cocoon, man no longer needed to project a complete species profile to match that of the environment. In the beginning, man incorporated part of nature—animals and grain—into his cocoon. As time went by he incorporated more and more of nature, finally reaching the point in the modern era of incorporating all of nature into his cocoon. As a result, nature exists at the sufferance of man.

But man lacks any instinct to regulate his utilization of nature. Just as man has always lacked the characteristics of the natural predator so that he could not practice restrained predation, so too he lacks the ability to practice restrained production. This problem is apparent in graphic terms today. Man has incorporated elements of nature, such as metals and fuels, at such a rate that within a foreseeably short time nature will have run out of those elements man needs in order to exist in his cocoon. What then of man?

It was possible for paleolithic man to solve his sustenance problem by incorporating something of nature into a cocoon. In this way a crisis was overcome. But since then man has increasingly incorporated other elements of nature into his cocoon in order to be able to produce those things which provide the basis for human consumption. What of man's next problem when there is no more of nature to incorporate? How then will man be able to produce the elements that permit existence within the cocoon? He can't break up the cocoon, for to do so would shatter his mortar, the only substance that can sustain human existence.

Thus, while the Neolithic Revolution solved the immediate crisis posed by the paleolithic situation, it set in motion those forces that today face man with his fifth and final crisis. If man doesn't solve the present energy-production crisis he will become extinct, for when he entered his cocoon he entered a state of existence that had no exit. Man today is completely bounded by his mortar. And his mortar is beginning to crumble.

Possibly man's predicament today can best be understood in terms of the problem of the species that began with the loss of arborea. Essentially it is a matter of man's relationship to nature. In the very first instance, while the species still lived in the trees, there was no distance between species and environment. There was a direct relationship between them, just as there is with all other forms of life. The problems man faces today had their origins when the species was obliged to leave arborea and enter the terrestrial mode of existence. This entry was into the labyrinth, and as protoman entered he carried a pebble tool; when he emerged, he did so as man wrapped in a cocoon.

The dilemma is clear. Whenever man has faced a survival crisis such as those examined in the discussions of tools, fire, and speech, he has always resolved those crises in favor of immediate terrestrial need. Every crisis has had to be resolved in favor of survival, and in every case this has meant terrestrial survival. Yet each decision for terrestrial survival has removed man that much further from nature, from his natural habitat, and from his natural self. The dilemma has been heightened by the fact that every decision in favor of terrestrial accommodation has resulted in more mortar and more species vulnerability created by that mortar.

The great problem that has always faced man has been that of time-anxiety and body stress. In the three great crises resolved by tools, fire, and speech, the resolution was in favor of immediate terrestrial survival, but in finding such a resolution—the alternative was extinction—man thereby increased both time-anxiety and body stress. In other words, he chose survival, but at a higher and higher price.

With the Paleolithic Crisis and its neolithic solution, man turned the final corner in his search for survival. By entering his cocoon he made time-anxiety and body stress an inescapable condition of human existence, for he had totally broken with nature, he had ended forever any chance of a return to his natural habitat, and he had encased his natural self inside an almost impenetrable swaddling of mortar. Unfortunately, this mortar is man-made, thereby heightening man's already extreme time-anxiety and body stress—today, almost to the breaking point.

The conscious mind which produces mortar established from the beginning its authority to dominate the arboreal body of man. With each new resolution of each new crisis, this authority has extended that much more over the arboreal body, thus tending on an increasing basis to stifle the naturalness of the body. Given sufficient mortar, the body will cease to function at all. It will have been stifled by mortar.

This has been the progression made by the terrestrialization process. Mortar, however, is now beginning to crumble. On the one hand man is threatened by extinction from the functioning of mortar; on the other, he is threatened by the disappearance of mortar. This is very much like the Paleolithic Crisis in which the profile of the natural environment was crumbling, thus forcing man to turn to himself for a solution. Today there is nowhere for man to look for the solution to his present crisis other than to himself.

Interlude

THE
CROUCHING
BISON

FOR a long time after their discovery in the last century, the great cave paintings of western Europe were considered by almost everyone to be remarkable forgeries. It was simply impossible that Stone Age men could have executed such masterpieces. But then, the truth of their origin was settled on and ever since they have been seriously regarded. As to their meaning or why men set about to paint them, everyone has had a personal opinion. First, however, even for those of the modern era of acceptance, there has been a certain response to them, typified by the observation of the noted prehistorian, Jacquetta Hawkes:

The flowering of the visual arts among the Paleolithic hunting peoples of Europe has a high claim to be recognized as the most improbable event in human history. After a million years during which development, in so far as we can observe it, was so slow that hundreds of generations might live and die without making the smallest change in their culture, men began to create works of art which can rival anything that has been achieved in the

last ten thousand years. . . . [T]hat true imaginative expression . . . should have appeared so soon, that truly is
astonishing.[1]

What should astonish us is not the early date of art's emergence but the phenomenon of art itself. The problem, I suspect, arises over the fact that art, like tools and speech, is so
integral a part of modern human life that we tend to forget
that there actually was a time before art, a time when man
lived, ignorant that such a thing as art was conceivable—the
way ancient horsemen were ignorant of the airplane.

Why did man invent art? To answer this question—if there
is an answer—we must discern the function of art.

Abbé Henri Breuil, the great investigator and expositor of
cave art, writes:

All the Arts of classical and mediaeval Antiquity, owed
their existence and development to the fact that Art put
itself at the service of the prevailing ideas of those times,
the cult of the dead in Egypt, that of the Gods on Olym-
pus, and the Christian ideal in the West. Art had to be
grafted onto these predominating social anxieties, giving
them an expression, and, as it were a language, which allowed the artist to exist and develop. . . .

Now, at the season of big game hunting, the daily pursuit of game and its multiplication by Nature, or the success of hunting expeditions, were the principal anxieties.[2]

If we add to Breuil's thought that of Aristotle, who said
that drama is the imitation of an action, I believe we can
compose an explanation for the great cave paintings of western
Europe.

---

1. Jacquetta Hawkes and Sir Leonard Woolley, *Prehistory and the
Beginnings of Civilization* (New York: Harper & Row, 1963), p. 186.
Hawkes's reference to "a million years" was based on the old estimate
of the length of the Pleistocene Epoch.

2. *Four Hundred Centuries of Cave Art* (Montignoi, France: Centre
d'études et de documentation préhistoriques, 1952), p. 23.

We can begin with the notion that an artist seeks to imitate nature—or, in his personal way, to reproduce nature, or even better, to represent it in some way. It would appear that some deep force within the artist impels him to respond to the world in which he lives, but his response is unique in that he seeks to communicate his response to others.

Yet, if art is to have meaning to the beholder, it must have something to say about predominating social anxieties. Art must touch upon something of vital concern. Perhaps vital *uncertainty* would better describe the condition.

If this be true, what was of such vital uncertainty that it impelled man to invent art? The answer is supplied by Breuil himself: the hunt. Man was being confronted by his fourth and culminating crisis. In what way could art resolve this vital crisis?

In the great cave galleries of Altamira (Spain), Font-de-Gaume, Les Combarelles, Lascaux, Niaux, and Les Trois Frères (all in France) are painted, engraved, and sculpted hundreds and hundreds of great beasts: wild horses, mammoths, reindeer, rhinoceroses, aurochs, stags, hinds, wild cattle, ibex, elephants, bears, lions, wolves, and most of all, the great bison.

The paintings reveal that their creators were fully evolved and modern *Homo sapiens*. They reveal heightened imagination, consummate skill, a remarkable sense of color, strong powers of observation, a sense of the dramatic, and most important of all, a profound sense of mystery.

The paintings in the deep recesses of caves could have been executed only by modern man. They express man's anxiety, his almost unbearable sense of alienation, and his greatest yearning: union with nature. I don't mean to invest the scene with sentimentality. When I say that man yearned for a union with nature I mean that man, in the greatest crisis of his terrestrial existence, saw his survival exclusively in terms of reunion with nature. His problem arose over his efforts to bring nature, in the form of the animals, into his cultivated world. He sensed his inability to return to the primordial period when man (in the form of his hominid ancestors) was *in* nature; he sought to end this alienation which so jeopardized his survival, by incorporating nature into his culture. Not long after the period of these paintings, that is exactly what man did.

The cave paintings represent the birth of modern man. What is so extraordinary about them is that they are artistic masterpieces, not tentative or unrealized efforts at artistic expression. Their fullness of being is very similar to the fullness of being of civilization when it bursts forth at Sumer not more than five thousand years after the latest of the paintings. There is nothing primitive or groping about Sumer; there is nothing primitive or groping about the cave paintings of paleolithic man.

There are two features of this great body of work that warrant examination. The first is the location of the cave galleries. Almost without exception, they are remote and isolated. They are not directly connected with living quarters and in almost all cases they are far removed from cave entrances and natural light. Some of them reach hundreds of yards into mountains where, almost inaccessible because of underground streams, sudden drops, and crevices almost too narrow to penetrate, prehistoric men chose to paint their masterpieces with no more light than could be gained from a flickering oil lamp.

Why were these galleries so inaccessible? The answer lies in the fact that painting, a form of communication, requires attendance. To travel to the back of deep caves, to stumble over underground streams, to wriggle through tight crevices, to creep past the drying bones of long-dead cave-bears and other creatures—and to do all this in great darkness—was to participate in a profound psychological process.

Going far back into the remoteness of the cave was the equivalent of going backward in time, in two distinct ways: a return to the individual's uterine life and a return to the species's origins. Incorporated in both returns was the dimness of perception where, at best, only faint phyletic memories could light the distant past.

At the end of the backward journey, in the flickering light of oil lamps, those to be instructed, those to be influenced, those to be initiated into the new ways, could focus on but one thing: the great beasts towering over them. Emergence from the gallery was emergence into the present, as if reborn.

There is a second unusual feature to the cave paintings. When these artists painted animals, they did so with great intensity and naturalness. When they painted men they painted them as stick figures. It is not a question of inability; the animals are proof of that. It's almost as if in the artist's mind the only real thing was the animal, that man somehow was not real or natural. Could these ancient artists somehow have felt this way? We can't know for sure, but one thing stands out. In those few instances where the artists painted a mixed figure—half man, half beast—they drew the human elements of the figures with the same naturalness with which they drew the animal elements. The most famous of these figures is "The Sorcerer" of Les Trois Frères.

Breuil describes the figure this way:

He is 75 cms high and 50 cms wide, he is entirely engraved, but the painting is unequally distributed; on the head there are only a few traces, on the eyes, nose, forehead and the right ear. The head is full face with round eyes with pupils; between the eyes runs a line for a nose, ending in a little arch. The pricked ears are those of a stag. From a black painted band across the forehead rise two big thick antlers with no frontal tines but with a single short tine, fairly high above the base of each branch, bending outwards and dividing again to the right or to the left. The figure has no mouth, but a very long beard cut in lines and falling to the chest. The fore-arms, which are raised and joined horizontally, end in two hands close

together, the shorter fingers outstretched; they are color-
less and almost invisible. A wide black band outlines the
whole body, growing narrower at the lumbar region, and
spreading out round the legs which are bent. A spot
marks the left knee-joint. The feet and big toes are rather
carefully made and show a movement similar to steps in
a "Cakewalk" dance. The male sex, emphasized but not
erect, pointing backwards but well developed, is inserted
under the bushy tail of a Wolf or Horse, with a little tuft
at the end.[3]

The figure is compelling. Its eyes stare at the viewer. Its
body is a symbiosis of man and animal. The danger is to read
oneself into the painting. Breuil, a religious, saw the sorcerer
as a "God, . . . the Spirit controlling the multiplication of
game and hunting expeditions." This is curious. There is
nothing in the painting or in the setting to suggest such a
proposition. But he advanced the proposition at a very early
stage, and it has stuck.

It would seem more reasonable to take the figure for what
it is, a blending of man and beast. It is interesting to note
that no other figures in which man and beast are joined are
typified as "sorcerers" or "gods." Possibly Breuil came to his
conclusion on the basis of the penetrating eyes. They are looking right at you. You are being stared at by a man in beast's
clothing. Or is it part man, part beast? Or is it "beastliness"
out of which man once emerged? Or a "beastliness" into
which man is turning? Whichever it is, there is at most one
man and several beasts. What is the figure trying to say? It
is, regardless of one's interpretations, a mute inquiry. It almost
forces a response. Breuil—and others—see it as a magico-reli-
gious figure, which it may be. It could just as well be the artist's
concept of the nature of man. When we contrast the naturalness of the figures that combine human and animal features
with those unnatural representations of man alone, we can-

---

3. Breuil, op. cit., p. 176.

not escape the possibility that the artists throughout the period considered man natural only when viewed as an animal-man creature. Man alone has no vital form or presence. Man as animal has enormously vital form and presence.

It would almost seem that the great works of art assembled in western Europe's caves—when viewed as a whole—are rather like an artist's rendering of the tale of Noah and the Ark. Only these great beasts, rather than being led by man into the dawn of the world's second beginning, are being led to their final slaughter, not by intention or desire on the part of man but because of man's inability to penetrate the mystery of life and thereby to discover his identity. Hence the "sorcerer," hence the penetrating mute question staring at us from the figure.

There is something uniquely compelling about a certain crouching bison in the cave at Altamira. It is as if one artist at last had penetrated the mystery of man. A polychrome painting of haunting beauty shows a great bison crouching, legs brought up under it, its powerful back arched to protect its head which is turned to face some great approaching menace. There is an aura of solemn resignation about the magnificent beast. Its eyes are open, unblinking, as it stares at its fate, as if it were waiting for some annihilating blow to be struck. But it doesn't cower, nor does it exhibit fear. It awaits its fate in beastly majesty. Yet there is another feeling about the painting, as if the artist were telling us something very important about man. Could the crouching bison be an allegory of man? I sometimes think so. Especially do I feel the allegory when I contemplate the superb beast and share its expectations of an annihilating blow.

I think of the annihilating blows that have fallen on man during his monumental struggle for existence in a hostile world. All man has had with which to fend off each mortal blow has been his brain. Blow after blow has fallen on man and yet—somehow he has prevailed. But at what a price!

Man, the arboreal primate, confined to his terrestrial prison;

man, the creature with harmless forelimbs who had to convert them to lethal forelimbs by artificial means to eat; man who had to confront and kill natural predators in order to survive; man who had to domesticate his mortal enemy, fire, to survive the cold; man who had to wander over the face of the earth to maintain contact with his migrating food source; man who had to endure the rigors of the merciless Pleistocene Epoch; man who had to survive in the terrestrial mode; man who never lost his desire to return to his ancestral home. What a price! What a beast! But—how many more blows can he withstand?

That seems to be the message of the crouching bison as it awaits its own destruction. The link is there: Man's survival is linked with the bison. Destroy the bison and what will happen to man?

The bison is natural man, the hidden primate suffocating in mortar. If you destroy everything that is natural in man, you destroy man. That is why the bison is so vital.

The end is not yet here. The bison, even though crouching, still lives. As does man. But it seems abundantly clear that man must overcome his present and final crisis by the reincorporation of nature into his cocoon. I am not talking here of outside nature—the elements, the products of nature—I am talking of the nature within man that in deep silence has endured the endless generations that span the incalculable distance between arborea and terrestria. Man is not by nature a terrestrial creature. He is terrestrial solely by circumstance. This fact must be respected, not so much by observers of man but by man himself. He must recognize the bison within him, for it is the bison within man that is the great missing link. Neither man nor the crouching bison within him can survive another annihilating blow—and another blow is about to strike.

PART TWO

The Cradle

Rock-a-bye baby, on the tree top,
When the wind blows the cradle will rock,
When the bough breaks the cradle will fall,
Down will come baby, cradle and all.

THE
MOTHER-TREE

E very *newborn infant is totally arboreal. It is the function of the mother and the rest of society to convert the
arboreal infant into a terrestrial adult.*

What I am saying by this is that just as the species began
as an arboreal primate, so does each child. And just as the
species was forced out of the arboreal environment, so too is
the newborn infant denied its arboreal niche. Finally, just as
the species was obliged to adapt to the terrestrial mode of
existence, so too is each newborn infant obliged to adapt to
the terrestrial mode. Thus each newborn infant is destined
to repeat the experience of the species. Hence, each member
of the species, in the process of development and growth, personally experiences the Arboreal/Terrestrial Conflict. This is
true whether the infants are born into a modern industrial
society or the most primitive tribe. There are no exceptions.

Let us look at the newborn child for evidence of its arboreality. To begin with, every infant is born with a clinging reflex,
once so necessary in arborea, where survival depended on the
ability of the infant to cling to its mother. This was required
because locomotor and eating needs of the mother frequently
prevented her from being able to hold her infant. Failure in

this regard—from birth on—would plunge the infant to its death on the distant forest floor.

Actually, two reflexes are involved: the palmar reflex of the hands and the plantar reflex of the feet. Healthy normal newborns always show the palmar reflex, and a great majority show the plantar. Both tend to diminish (because of millions of years of disuse) in time and generally disappear somewhere between four and eight months. It has been observed that, if anything, the palmar reflex of the premature infant is even stronger than that of the full-term baby.

Also reflective of arboreal demands in the newborn is what is known as the "falling" or Moro reflex. When the baby experiences a sudden change in position, such as in falling, that causes its head to drop suddenly, it startles, throws out its arms and legs, extends its neck, cries briefly, and then rapidly brings its arms together and flexes its body as if to grasp the branch of a tree or its mother as it falls. Two actions are present: first, to create as large a target as possible by extending its limbs as much as possible; second, to take action by bringing the arms together so as to latch onto something, either a tree branch or the mother. (If an infant chimpanzee is placed on its back, it responds by a large, sweeping motion of its arms, with its hands open. When an object is contacted, it is grasped and drawn toward the belly. Vernon Reynolds, British primatologist and author of *The Apes* [New York: E. P. Dutton, 1967], has reported seeing a falling adult chimpanzee assume the same extended posture. It crashed into the earth some distance away and when Reynolds got to the site the chimpanzee was gone, evidently unhurt.)

The next reflex necessary to survival once the infant has attached itself to the mother is that which propels the newborn, no matter how awkwardly, from the lower ventral surface of the mother to the breast area, where the nipples are to be found.[1] This reflex is extremely important because most

---

1. This reflex may go back to the amphibian phase of evolution, as the body exhibits a rhythmic extension and flexion of the legs and arms, accompanied by a swinging of the trunk from side to side.

arboreal primate mothers do not assist the newborn in any way to find the nipples. It is essential that the infant combine its cling reflex with its crawling reflex in order to "climb" its tree where, higher up (in the branches), nourishment is to be found.

Upon the infant's arrival at the nipple we see two more reflexes in operation. They are the rooting and sucking reflexes. There is here a hierarchical principle. William A. Mason describes it:

> The coordination of sucking and swallowing reflexes during feeding may be disrupted unless the infant monkey has its hands and feet firmly engaged. Grasping activities are intensified as nursing begins even when the infant is securely supported. The observation that young monkeys, chimpanzees, and children alternately open and close their hands or engage in various forms of finger play suggests an association between sucking and grasping may persist in a modified form at later stages of development.[2]

There are other reflexes with which the child is born that reveal its arboreality. There is the "preferred posture" of the infant, "positive supporting reactions," and a number of others that reveal an arboreal adaptation. In addition, there are embryonic manifestations of the fact, such as those relating to the development of the arms and legs. Further, there is the tendency of infants to intertwine the soles of their feet, some- It is this inherited arboreal foot posture which leads small children begin to walk, it is upon the outer sides of their feet that they place their weight, exactly as do nonhuman primates. It is this inherited arboreal foot-posture which leads small children to make holes in the outer sides of the soles of their shoes, and it explains why the heels of shoes always wear out first on the outer edge.

The newborn infant, then, is an arboreal infant and must be understood as such. The newborn possesses no reflexes or other

2. "The Social Development of Monkeys and Apes," in *Primate Behavior*, edited by Irven DeVore (New York: Holt, Rinehart and Winston, 1965) p. 519.

capabilities that reflect any adaptation to terrestrial living. All that the infant has going for it are those features and innate capabilities adaptive to the arboreal world. The newborn is not in any way a terrestrial creature. (For example, terrestrial young are genetically endowed from birth to move about on the ground, even if only to the extent of nuzzling up to the mother for nourishment and warmth, something comparable to the clinging-capability of the arboreal primate young.)

However, my point goes beyond such a broad declaration. It is only when we understand the arboreality of the newborn infant that we can understand the consequences of treating it in ways contradictory to that nature. What is at stake is not mere discomfort or even abuse. Survival itself is at issue.

In summary, the newborn infant possesses innate capabilities once absolutely essential to survival in arborea, but which are not needed for survival in terrestria, and it possesses no innate capabilities relating to existence in terrestria. Therefore, whatever the human infant does to survive in the terrestrial mode is the result of training by its mother (or other terrestrial adult).

From the perspective of the newborn infant, survival depends totally on its existing in an arboreal environment. From the perspective of the human species, every arboreal infant must be converted into a terrestrial adult. This is a central human predicament. Failure to provide the infant with an adequate arboreal environment will doom it; failure to terrestrialize the infant will doom the species.

This situation produces inevitable conflict, a struggle between genetic composition and cultural accumulation. The instinct of the infant is to preserve a species profile conforming to that of the arboreal environment. Hence, its various unconditioned reflexes so necessary to an arboreal species profile. The cultural needs of the adult are to create sufficient mortar so as to preserve species contact with the profile projected by the terrestrial environment. Since the arboreal profile and the terrestrial profile are incompatible, there erupts the inevitable conflict between infant and adult. Notwithstanding the wishful thinking of many, the infant is not a miniature adult, and neither is the adult an enlarged infant. They are, for all practical purposes, members of separate and distinct species, one arboreal, the other terrestrial.

The incompatibility of the infant and the adult is so enormous that save for one factor, the mother, there would be no possible resolution of the conflict. She is the mediator of difference, not so much by intent as by design. It is the function of the mother to present an arboreal profile to the newborn; it is her further function, when the child is slightly older, to bring it down out of the trees. First, the mother must provide an arboreal environment so that the arboreal infant may survive; then she must terrestrialize her child so that the species can survive.

It is when the mother seeks to terrestrialize her child that an inevitable conflict between parent and infant begins. It arises because the infant seeks to preserve its arboreal nature, something predicated on its genes, while the parent seeks to convert the infant so that it might, once past the dependency stage, survive in the terrestrial mode.

The human infant repeats on an individual basis the precise steps traveled by man's ancestors in their journey from arborea to terrestria. Like the phylogenetic experience, the journey of the infant is not voluntary. Quite literally, a superior primate forces it out of the tree of its origin and into terrestria.

St. Paul was not entirely correct when he said, "When I was a child, I spoke as a child, I thought as a child. Now that I have become a man, I have put away the things of a child." The truth is that neither Paul nor anyone else has ever himself "put away the things of a child." Those things have always been put away by others. And for a very important reason.

If the human child, an arboreal primate in every respect, were allowed the things of a child—if it were to grow into what its biology dictated—the result would be an adult arboreal primate totally unable to produce mortar and thereby preserve its existence. The consequences would be catastrophic. It is when we appreciate this fact that we can understand the agony of parents when, from their perspective, their children seem contrary, willful, and wanton.

However, we must also appreciate the situation of the child who, while going through the terrestrialization process, is being torn asunder by the demands of its biology (genes) and the demands of his parents that it come down out of the tree. When the mother hears the cry of her child, she is not listening to the petulant cry of a contrary child; she is listening to the cry of an arboreal creature being murdered.

Because the newborn infant is arboreal, it must have an arboreal environment in which to live. That is, every infant requires a mother-tree, for it is the mother-tree that provides all arboreal infants with both physical support and sustenance. Of course, among nonhuman primates, once past the dependency stage, the growing infant slowly transfers itself from the mother-tree to the actual trees of the forest.

Such being the case, how does the human mother create a mother-tree in which her newborn child may live? The human mother cannot fully duplicate the arboreal situation: The human infant cannot cling to her. But there are substitutes for clinging that can provide adequate body contact with the mother. Mothers in almost all societies, except certain advanced industrial ones, hold and support their babies in a variety of ways. Either someone—most often the mother—carries or holds the newborn almost all the time, or the child is held in some sort of sling or harness that the mother wears either on her front or her back. And at night, when the baby sleeps, it sleeps in the bed with the mother, thus preserving the close physical contact so necessary for the baby. At frequent intervals, the mother fondles, plays with, and otherwise makes direct physical contact with her baby. In addition, she nurses the baby whenever it shows hunger.

Is this sort of thing really necessary for the infant's well-being? Although he doesn't put it in terms of the Arboreal/ Terrestrial Conflict Thesis, James L. Halliday, in *Psychosocial Medicine*, answers the question this way:

[During the first few months following birth] there is a need for continuance of close body contact with the mother to satisfy the requirements of the kinesthetic and muscle senses. This requires that the baby be held firmly, nursed at intervals, rocked, stroked, talked to, and reassured. . . .

Infants deprived of their accustomed maternal body contact may develop a profound depression with lack of appetite, wasting, and even marasmus leading to death.[3]

Similarly, Albrecht Peiper, author of an exhaustive study of infants entitled *Cerebral Function in Infancy and Childhood*, remarks, "So well has nature equipped the infant for staying on his mother's body—for example, with the grasp reflexes and the rooting reflex—that civilization has yet been unsuccessful to the same degree in adapting him to his new abode, his own bed, which quite recently was forced on him against his will." [4]

From these two observations may be constructed the basic principle of the mother as mother-tree. First, there is the infant's need for stimulation, especially that of the skin, the body's largest sense organ. It contains the receptors for touch, pain, heat, and cold. Most important, stimulation of these receptors initiates reflexes that are important in adaptation to the environment. Also, skin stimulation appreciably affects the infant's respiratory, circulatory, digestive, eliminative, and nervous systems: ". . . Since the [human] infant from the beginning has the task of clinging to his mother's body, or finding the nipple, and of sucking, he needs first of all the senses of skin and taste, i.e., the lowest [evolutionary] senses which transmit the message of the most immediate environ-

3. New York: W. W. Norton, 1948, p. 244.
4. New York: Consultant's Bureau, 1963, p. 604.

ment to him because they are stimulated only by direct contact . . ." [5]

It is clear that an *active* participation by the mother is essential to the infant's survival. She cannot be passive. It is because the infant is born so helpless that it must be met by an arboreal environment (the mother) which will actively stimulate those reflexes so vital for survival and growth.

And then there is the matter of support. Whereas all mammal offspring need the sort of stimulation Halliday and Peiper emphasize, there is something unique about the need of the arboreal infant for support.

If the infant is supported by its mother from the beginning, and sleeps beside her from the beginning, it is relaxed, comfortable, and feels secure. Remove this close physical contact, and the infant quickly begins to fret and becomes conspicuously disturbed. There is in all arboreal primate infants a powerful need to be reassured at all times of the immediate presence of the mother. The very young infant clings to its mother continuously. Even as the infant is maturing and beginning to wander from its mother, at the slightest threat or uncertainty it retreats to its mother's body. Why, we might ask, is there this constant need for reassurance that the mother is there? Because in arborea the mother's immediate presence is essential for survival. The mother's presence is necessary as a support for her infant, thereby saving it from falling to the ground far below.

The importance of the mother-tree cannot be overemphasized. It goes beyond hunger or a particular pain, something specific and tangible that can be explained. Even a newborn infant can declare itself on such counts by crying. But how can a baby cry over the absence of its prime tree? The tree that supported its kind for tens of millions of years? It can't.

The shadow of the tree can be seen, however, when the crying baby is picked up; quickly the crying subsides. It can be

---

5. Ibid., p. 596.

seen when a simple gesture such as placing a hand on the abdomen will cause a fussing baby to calm down almost instantly. The shadow can be seen in institutions where well-nourished babies literally die from a lack of being held and handled.

The greatest obstacle to adequate mothering of newborn infants is mortar. The error in much of modern thinking about infant care is the belief that science can stamp out ignorance and thus guarantee human progress. This may be when we consider the needs of adults—although it is debatable. Society, and most especially an advanced industrial society, needs all the culture—mortar—it can get to maintain itself and the species profile. But the newborn infant needs absolutely no mortar to complete its species profile. Only the mind of the individual can manufacture mortar, and the newborn, for the first year, has no cerebral cortex function with which to create mortar or to relate to mortar in any way. In order to survive, it must have perpetual contact with the only environment in which it can exist: its mother. But—and here is an enormous proviso —only to the extent that the mother herself can become, vis-à-vis the infant, arboreal herself, can she provide her infant with a sustaining environment.

This is not to say that mothers must live in an arboreal environment, but that the mother must present an arboreal profile to her child. She cannot do this if she allows the mortar of her adult society to be part of the profile she projects to the infant. Separation, crib-sleeping, scheduled feeding, infrequent handling, allowing a baby "to cry itself out," and all the other paraphernalia of modern western infant care, do not comprise maternal care. They are forms of maternal *deprivation*, the sort of thing research with both human and nonhuman primate infants shows to be ruinous to the development and well-being of the infant. The mortared mother might very well feel great love for the child; this feeling, however, bears no viable fruit.

Mother love is the active participation by the mother in

meeting the needs of her child. It is not the mood or affectionate state of the mother, and should not be confused with a woman's love for motherhood and the narcissistic euphoria that resonates from such a woman. Mother love is the love for a child expressed in the activity of caring for the child's needs.

Infant care cannot be founded on science because science has no role to play where genes and environment are compatible. We can see the proof of this assertion in the child-rearing practices of primitive societies that possess almost no science, where infants are nurtured in the most natural way possible.

In *A Child's Mind*, Muriel Beadle reports on a test made on over three hundred Ugandan babies during their first year of life to see how their motor coordination compared with that of infants of the same age in western culture:

> The African babies came from lower class families where ancient tribal customs were still practiced. Babies remain with their mothers day and night. They are talked to, cuddled, and stroked; they are fed whenever they wish to eat; and they are watched for cues as to what they want to do—sit up, for instance—and are then helped to do it. The Uganda mother is wholly child-centered.
>
> . . . And the child she produces is noticeably superior to Western European or American children. At seven weeks, for example, he can sit up unaided and watch himself in a mirror; at seven months . . . he can walk to a box and look in it for toys. These accomplishments occur in our children at about 24 weeks and 15 months respectively.
>
> This superior co-ordination could be explained by earlier physiological maturation; on the whole, African people *do* mature earlier than Europeans. But that isn't the complete explanation, because the Uganda babies were also ahead of their Western-culture counterparts in adaptability to novel situations, social relationships, and language skills.

A few babies in the study came from the upper classes, which means their families were somewhat Westernized and therefore raised their children more as we do—less bodily contact with the mother, more emphasis on scheduled feedings, more attention to "training." *These particular African babies, Geber found, were much less precocious than the babies raised in the tribal environment.* [Italics added] [6]

It was only when male doctors and male "child specialists" began to prescribe for mothers and their infants in the latter part of the nineteenth century that new patterns of maternal care came into being. Instead of maternal care being the province of women who functioned on as instinctive a level as circumstances allowed—by projecting an arboreal profile—maternal care was taken over by terrestrialized men who sought —always with the best intentions—to transform the infant's environment from that of arborea to that of terrestria. The results were disastrous. Instead of seeing the infant for what it was, these men perceived it as a miniature adult, and they prescribed accordingly.

In 1852, England's Dr. Joel Shew wrote *Children: Their Hydropathic Management in Health and Disease*. Among the many authoritative utterances set forth was the following:

In no respect is a caution more necessary than in regard to nursing a child too frequently. If, as the common practice is, the stomach is too often replenished with food, the natural function of the organ will necessarily become perverted and enfeebled, and gripes, colic, flatulence, and crying will be the effect: nay, more, death itself is often the result. More children, a hundred fold, have been destroyed by overfeeding than by want of food. [7]

In addition, Dr. Shew was adamantly opposed to rocking infants in cradles, on the knee, or in any other way. Rocking a

---

6. New York: Doubleday, 1970, pp. 59–60.
7. New York: Fowler and Wells, 1852, p. 137.

baby to sleep was to rock it to either an early grave or insanity. "The reason why a child sleeps more readily when rocked is, that the motion of its head causes a degree of congestion in the brain; and the effect of this must, in the end, be to induce more or less debility of the part. . . . I myself knew one young lady well, who was rendered an idiot for life, as everyone believed, by her being swung a great deal in a basket, when a young child." [8]

Probably the most influential writer during the half century between 1894 and 1943 was Dr. L. Emmett Holt, Professor of Pediatrics at New York Polyclinic and Columbia University, who barged into the subject of infant care the way a bull might barge into a china shop. He addressed himself to every possible aspect of infant care, but in two areas he epitomized the ultimate in erroneous prescription. In the first, that of toilet training, he wrote as follows:

Q: At what age may an infant be [toilet] trained?
A: Normally by the second month if training is begun early.
Q: What is the best method of training?
A: A small chamber, about the size of a pint bowl, is placed between the nurse's [sic] knees, and upon this the infant is held, its back being against the nurse's chest and its body firmly supported. This should be done twice a day, after the morning and afternoon feedings, and always at the same hours. At first there may be necessary some local irritation, like that produced by tickling the anus or introducing just a piece of soap, as a suggestion of the purpose for which the baby is placed on the chamber; but in a surprisingly short time the position is all that is required. With most infants, after a few weeks the bowels will move as soon as the infant is placed on the chamber.[9]

8. Ibid., pp. 159–160.
9. New York: D. Appleton, 1907, p. 157.

This instruction appears in all fifteen editions of Holt's book, *The Care and Feeding of Children,* including the 1943 edition put out by his son. The only change in the 1943 edition is the instruction that the training might begin in the third or fourth month rather than the second.

In the matter of sleep, Dr. Holt prescribed as follows:

Q: Should a child sleep in the same bed with its mother or nurse?

A: Under no circumstances, if this can possibly be avoided. Very young infants have often been smothered by their mothers, by overlying during sleep.[10] If the infant sleeps with the mother, there is always the temptation to frequent nursing at night, which is injurious to both mother and child.

Q: How should a baby be put to sleep?

A: The room [a room separate from that of the mother, if at all possible] should be darkened and quiet, the child's hunger satisfied, and the child made generally comfortable and laid in its crib while awake.

Q: Is rocking necessary?

A: By no means. It is a habit easily acquired, but hard to break, and a very useless and sometimes injurious one.[11]

The Shews, the Holts, and their fellow-legionnaires inflicted incalculable harm on the children (and parents) of their eras. What is more, their theories and practices simply did not work. What they were about—even if they were not aware of it— was the terrestrialization of the infant. They were attempting to grab the newborn infant out of its arboreal tree, the mother, and hurl it to earth where, hopefully, it would stand on its own two feet—and work for its keep.

Their efforts were doomed. The newborn infant simply cannot be forcibly terrestrialized. You cannot do in ontogeny

---

10. Starting with the 1924 edition, he continues to forbid sleeping with the mother, but he deletes the passage about smothering.

11. Ibid., pp. 158–159.

what was not possible phylogenetically. Man's hominid ancestors were not *hurled* out of the trees and onto the ground where they stood on their own two feet. The terrestrialization of the species was a gradual process, and so it is with the individual infant.

Men have failed to terrestrialize infants, whereas from ages too remote for memory, mothers have succeeded. They have succeeded because, instead of ordering infants out of the tree, they have carefully carried them down—in their arms.

BREAKING THE
BOUGH

As HAS been seen earlier, man's terrestrialization was not an evolutionary process based upon genetic change, but was one based upon the creation of mortar. Hence, the base hominid brain has always remained the arboreal primate brain. Superimposed on this brain has been the terrestrial brain which serves, not to assist in creating a natural species profile, but to assist the organism in creating mortar so necessary to supplement the deficient natural species profile. Those functions of man's arboreal brain that cooperate to this end are encouraged. Those functions that interfere are inhibited. Thus, in the functioning of man's brain there exists the cortical inhibition of what have been called "nonadaptive reactions." Man's arboreal brain cannot be allowed to jeopardize his existence in the terrestrial mode. Since man's terrestrial experience began with the arboreal brain, and not a new one perfected for terrestrial existence, the brain he began with had to be the brain he ended up with—*as modified,* first by the inhibitory functions of the cortex, and second by the learning functions so necessary for the creation of mortar.

While, for example, the arboreal brain of man determines the need to urinate and defecate, the terrestrial brain inhibits spontaneous elimination and determines where and when elimination will take place. Man's sexual drive is a function of the arboreal brain; its control is a function of the terrestrial brain. Both inhibitory and regulatory systems are essential: In arborea there was no problem of soiling the nest, but in terrestria there is. In arborea, the species was sexually promiscuous; in terrestria, for reasons previously stated, this could not be allowed, and so man's arboreal sexual nature had to be inhibited and a regulatory system created that would conform man's sexual expression to his terrestrial needs.

The creative function of man's terrestrial brain concerns learning. This is essential to survival. If man were living in the environment to which he was genetically adapted, there would be no need for artificial extensions of the forelimbs; he could feed himself by natural means. But since man does not live in his natural environment, his genes are inadequate. Hence a substitute for genes is necessary. This substitute is learned activity which is passed on by individuals and not by genetic transmission.

The child, once he reaches the end of his first year, is ready to take on the burdens of terrestrial life, i.e., his neocortex is functioning; he is ready to be humanized. Fortunately, the child doesn't have to make genetic breakthroughs toward a terrestrial brain. He is born with it, even though during much of the first year it is not yet developed and functioning. But, there is the fact of potential. It is as if the child were a computer system that only needed programming. If the child is the computer, the mother is the programmer.

The mother, being the mother-tree of the newborn, is the foundation of the child's existence. On this base everything else is constructed, including the infant's humanization. If the mother has proved to be a firm, reliable mother-tree, the humanization process will take place with relative equanimity. If, on the other hand, the mother has been a wind-tossed arboreal perch that threatens to hurl the infant to the forest floor far below, humanization will be a painful process.

Because the mother not only exists as the supporting tree, but also as the feeding tree, in the child's mind, life and security come from the mother. All things come to the child by and through the mother. For good or ill, the conduit to terrestrial life is the mother. It is she who lifts her baby out of its bower and carries it down to earth. It is all summed up in the old nursery rhyme:

> Rock-a-bye baby, on the tree top,
> When the wind blows the cradle will rock,
> When the bough breaks the cradle will fall,
> Down will come baby, cradle and all.

Almost from the beginning, the mother prepares her child for the breaking of the bough. She goes up into the tree top where she gently rocks the cradle and softly hums tunes and plays little games that blend body and mind. Humanization begins almost imperceptibly.

The mother plays "finger-and-toe" games with her child. She hides her face behind her hands, cries out, and bares her face, to the delight of the child.

> This little pig went to market,
> This little pig stayed home,
> This little pig had roast beef,
> This little pig had none,
> And this little pig cried, wee, wee, wee!
> All the way home.

Thus, five little toes become five little pigs, and the baby gurgles.

> Pat-a-cake, pat-a-cake, baker's man,
> Bake me a cake as fast as you can;
> Pat it and prick it and mark it with B,
> Put it in the oven for baby and me.

Hands clap and faces wreathe into smiles as mother and baby play, just as they do with "Pease Porridge Hot." Sound, sight, touch; sound, sight, touch. The senses and the body blend to form a stairway down which the mother carries the infant from bower to earth. It is as if the anonymous rhymer suspected a profound truth when he wrote:

> Humpty Dumpty sat on a wall.
> Humpty Dumpty had a great fall.
> All the king's horses and all the king's men
> Couldn't put Humpty Dumpty together again.

In the same way, once the child begins his descent—once he has fallen out of the tree—there is no way to put him back together again the way he had once been.

There is genius behind the early nursery rhymes. The infant is drawn out of himself, gently, persuasively, by his mother who uses arboreal means to seduce her child out of his arboreal nest. The rhymes are like those of a free primate bounding from branch to branch in the tropical forest. Da-dum, da-dum, da-*dum*.

There is an amazing abundance of rhymes that involve animals. There is even Mother Goose. Who better to oversee a world of beasts and little children? After all, are not small children more like little beasts than grown people? Surely they feel more at home with cock-horses, hickety hens, and crooked cats than they do with fierce grownups who always talk of great and distant things rather than those small and close secrets understood by ponies, hens, and cats. The child's fascination with animals is as strong today, when most children see very few live animals, as it was when most families lived on farms. Children's attraction to animals is reminiscent of prehistoric man's absorption with animals, something seen in children's toys and in the many cave paintings of western Europe. There could well be a psychic connection.

But it is not the function of nursery rhymes to transform small children into terrestrial beings. Their function is to activate the mind. They seduce the infant into coming out of his natal shell, to use his mind and his senses, and to delight in the arboreality of everything to which he is exposed. This becomes more apparent when the child turns the pages of his first picture book.

These books are veritable jungles of color. The child, by his mother's side or on her lap, listens to the gamboling rhythms while his eyes dance among the succulent colors. This is no mere figure of speech. Primates have very acute stereoptical vision with strong color perception.

It is here, in the first books, that the child begins his great descent to the ground. Into his arboreal world of color and rhyme comes the first suggestion that there is more to this than mere play. Into his arboreal world are slipped some basic terrestrial values. There is, for example, a little lesson to be learned from the following:

> Little Boy Blue, come blow your horn,
> The sheep's in the meadow, the cow's in the corn.
> Where is the boy who looks after the sheep?
> He's under the haystack fast asleep.

The lesson is clear: Little boys shouldn't ignore responsibility when it is given them.

This rhyme teaches another lesson:

> Bye, baby bunting,
> Daddy's gone a-hunting,
> Gone to get a rabbit skin
> To wrap his baby bunting in.

Here the child begins to learn what sort of things a daddy does for his child—in particular, he learns about the hunt.

Numbers come to the child in a variety of ways:

> One, two,
> Buckle my shoe.
> Three, four,
> Knock on the door.
> Five, six,

> Pick up sticks.
> Seven, eight,
> Lay them straight.
> Nine, ten,
> A good fat hen.

The child learns about months, and their length, when he hears:

> Thirty days hath September,
> April, June, and November.
> All the rest have thirty-one
> Except February alone
> Which has twenty-eight days clear
> And twenty-nine in each leap year.

Also, through nursery rhymes the child begins to learn the differences between boys and girls:

> What are little boys made of?
> What are little boys made of?
> Frogs and snails
> And puppydog tails,
> That's what little boys are made of.
> What are little girls made of?
> What are little girls made of?
> Sugar and spice
> And all that's nice,
> That's what little girls are made of.

Then, of course, the child must be introduced to terrestrial fears:

> Little Miss Muffet
> Sat on a tuffet,
> Eating her curds and whey;
> There came a big spider,
> Who sat down beside her,
> And frightened Miss Muffet away.

There is even the matter of bedtime:

> Wee Willie Winkle runs through the town,
> Upstairs and downstairs in his nightgown
> Rapping at the window, crying through the lock,
> Are the children in their beds?
> For now it's eight o'clock.

And with the next rhyme, the child meets death—if only poetically:

> Solomon Grundy,
> Born on Monday,
> Christened on Tuesday,
> Married on Wednesday,
> Took ill on Thursday,
> Worse on Friday
> Died on Saturday,
> Buried on Sunday,
> That is the end
> Of Solomon Grundy.

Finally, we can begin to see the end of arboreal play with a rhyme like this one:

> There was an old woman who lived under a hill,
> If she's not gone, she lives there still.

Here we have the introduction of linear logic. Whereas life in arborea is flexuous, with primates able to move about in all directions and for any purpose, terrestrial life demands linearity. Once it was something as simple as the hunter getting sight of prey and then traversing as directly and quickly as possible the distance in as straight a line as possible. This could be accomplished either by the hunter or his surrogate, a spear, stone, or arrow. Today we know about linearity in such things as assembly lines, written language, and foot races.

It is essential that the child be transported from a flexuous world to one that is linear. This process begins with the coloring book.

In essence, the coloring book is a terrestrial environment in which the child is permitted to be arboreal. Within the lines provided—stark lines on a flat white background that give every appearance of a blueprint—the child may be flexuous. With his colored crayons the child can cavort as he wishes, provided he cavorts within the prescribed limits of the terrestrial ground plan: He may color as wildly as he wants, as long as he stays within the lines set down by terrestrial adults.

In one way or another—through the mother, through television, through a variety of ways—the child enters the world of stories. They are the easily digested kernels of terrestrial reality that slowly replace the soft diet of arboreal stuff and nonsense. Stories, however the disguise and whatever the form, are edifying. Not didactic, one hopes, but edifying, since children have an uncanny ability to distinguish between "today's sermon" and a good story.[1]

Ruth Tooze, author of the book *Storytelling,* has three basic rules for a good story: "First of all, the story will have a good plot with something of interest to resolve. In the second place, a good story not only meets you at some point of your experience but makes you want to go on from here to there, often equipping you for the going. It may take you on by widening your horizons or lengthening your point of view or deepening your understanding or lifting your spirit. In the third place, a good story with whose characters and action you so identify

---

1. In this analysis I do not include such things as play-games, the purpose of which is to help the child modify his conduct in such a way as to be a considerate citizen of society. These adjustive lessons are taught by the mother and companions. Nor am I including moral education that focuses attention on what is considered good or bad, as it in the main also concerns a child's social disposition. All primate mothers train their offspring in such matters, essential since all primates are social beings. These lessons are taught to all primate young. Our concern here is with the conversion of the arboreal infant into a terrestrial adult, a process unknown to other primates who face no such conversion problem.

will give you a sense of the relationship of this experience to total experience—this little piece of the universe and the universe." [2]

Resolution—the solution of a plotted problem—is the essential ingredient of a good story. Expressed a bit differently, life is a tale about problems that have to be solved. On such a muted note does the child first confront the problem of time-anxiety.

Resolution does not come quickly on the heels of the introduction of the problem. For example, "John, while playing in the forest, spied a most handsome pony in the middle of a clearing. Rising from a feast of berries, John walked over to the pony, petted it, took it home to a stable, and both lived happily ever after." This is no story, but rather an explanation of how young John got his pony. But if, in the telling, young John approaches the pony and the pony runs away, then we have the potential of a story, the story being concerned with John's efforts (simple or complicated) to possess the pony. If the pony runs away and John never looks for him, we have no story. If John searches for the pony and never finds him, here too we have no story, unless, of course, in the search John has other problems to resolve. But any such story resulting from the search would not have possession of the pony as its resolution.

Stories have as their primal element the search for something one doesn't have and which one wants. This search may involve an object or a state of being. The plot deals with obtaining, or the failure to obtain, the desired object or state of being. Essential to the plot is an obstructive element that makes arrival at the desired goal problematical. There is, then, the protagonist, the antagonist, and the objective. There is, even though not necessarily explicitly expressed, the passage of time. With these four essential elements we have a story. And this story, no matter what its manifest terms, is the basic story

---

2. Ibid., pp. 51–54.

of human existence. It is, in the final analysis, the story of time-anxiety.

It is interesting to note that nursery rhymes have no plot. As was said earlier, such rhymes are arboreal and hence lack the element of time-anxiety: the search for an object or state, the attainment of which is (at least technically) uncertain.

Put most simply, rhymes are *static* while stories are *active*. Thus, in the rhyme the child, as it were, can remain unmoved while in the story he must, in some way, be moved. Rhymes stay at Point A, while stories go from Point A to Point T. It is the movement from Point A to Point T that, combined with the obstacle (the antagonist), provides the dramatic element of the story. In a sense, movement *is* the story. And, of course, it is movement that distinguishes terrestrial existence from arboreal. It is the story of the arboreal child (Point A) moving to become the terrestrial adult (Point T). It is also the movement of man going from a state of rest (Point A) through an action essential to survival, to arrival at survival (Point T). In arborea there is no such movement, either of the infant or the adult. The infant doesn't go from being arboreal to terrestrial. He remains arboreal, even as an adult; hence, no movement. As for the adult, he doesn't face recurring crises that he must overcome if he is to survive.

This matter of survival in a hostile environment is so enormously important—it is the hinge of human existence—that every child must be taught, over and over and over again, his daily lesson.

Tooze's three rules of a good story start with the principle of plot resolution, which is actually the principle of survival. Wisely, her second rule concerns the appropriateness of the story to the particular circumstances and degree of development of the child. Her third rule concerns the relationship of the particular experience (the story) to total experience, or, as she expressed it, "this little piece of the universe and the universe."

Hand in hand, mother and child traverse the great and incalculable distance that separate the two worlds. It is she who can sing soft lullabies that waft her infant off to sleep, and it is she who must knock her child's shins on the sharp edge of terrestrial reality. And in the course of this journey—a story in itself—the child retraces the steps of human consciousness.

We have seen examples of this retracing in "finger-and-toe" games and in nursery rhymes, in which we were able to see the progression from the barest psycho-physiological beginnings of the newborn infant to the full experience of arboreality both in conjunction with the infant's psychophysical union with its mother and in its first efforts at leaving the mother and climbing into nursery trees. The essence of this stage is unity: unity with one's world, filled as it is with great color and flexuous movement, and with all sorts of beasts with whom the child feels an unfathomable affinity.

There then commences a small, scarcely perceptible break in this unity when the infant-child begins to slip into his mother's world, not under his own impetus, but under that of his mother. Heretofore it had been the mother who went up into the infant's bower; now, urged on by both mother and emerging consciousness, the infant-child picks up a crayon and steps inside terrestrial lines. He cannot return to arborea. For ever so long the infant-child lives in the extraordinary world of dawning reality in which events take place and changes occur, yet in which there seems to be no more efficient or necessary cause than magic itself.

In the beginning, in the ineffable moment of once-upon-a-time, as the child emerges from the shadows and into the light of fragmentary thought and perception, there is the beauty of magic. There is no cause and effect the way scientists mean that phrase, but there is being where once there was nonbeing, there is life where once there was only stillness, there is light where once there was darkness, there is Order where once there was Chaos. Out of this dim and primordial moment come all the magical stories of man.

How better to begin than with: "Once upon a time there

was a little chimney-sweep, and his name was Tom . . ."? Tom, the little chimney-sweep who cried "when he had to climb the dark flues, rubbing his poor knees and elbows raw; and when the soot got into his eyes, which it did every day in the week; and when his master beat him, which he did every day of the week . . . ," is the very Tom whom "the fairies washed . . . in the swift river, so thoroughly that not only his dirt, but his whole husk and shell were washed quite off him, and the pretty little real Tom was washed out of the inside of it, and swam away . . ." into the cool and tranquil world of the great trout, the dragonfly, the friendly lobster, and the countless fairies who saw that Tom was never harmed.

Man builds the great castles in which fairy kings have beautiful daughters, and old shoemakers have elves for helpers, and Puss-in-Boots strides about in great adventures. Out of Araby, a land of impenetrable mystery, comes Aladdin and his wonderful lamp, Ali Baba and the forty thieves, and Sinbad of the Seven Voyages. Where else but out of Araby could come the Enchanted Horse? Or the Magic Carpet? Or the great Bird of Paradise?

But then it must end. The child, like Mopsa the Fairy, must grow up. But worse, each mortal must face banishment forever from the magical kingdom, the way Jack had to. Mopsa, whom Jack had once carried in his pocket, taken care of, and loved, was now Queen Mopsa. Each child must do as Jack had to do that dreadful final day. "The bells had said he was to go home, and the fairy had told him how to go. Mopsa did not need him, she had so many people to take care of her now. . . . Oh, how sorrowful it all was! Had he really come up the fairy river, and seen those strange countries, and run away with Mopsa over those dangerous mountains, only to bring her to the very place she wished to fly from, and there to leave her, knowing that she wanted him no more, and that she was quite content?" Jack wished more than anything to remain in Mopsa's fairy land, but the moment came when Queen Mopsa, now so much older and wiser than Jack, returned his kiss, a tear falling on his cheek.

" 'Farewell!' she said, and she turned and went up the steps into the great hall; and while Jack gazed at her as she entered, and would have followed, but could not stir, the great doors closed together again, and he was left outside.

"Then he knew, without being told, that he should never enter them any more. He stood gazing at the castle; but it was still—no more fairy music sounded."

No more fairy music sounded . . . The death knell of childhood. It is the knell each child has heard as he has taken the final and irretrievable step into the world of conscious reality. A moment ago the child *knew*—he did not subsist on mere belief—that fairies and magic, elves and spells, witches and amulets were as real as the air he breathed; now he knows better. There is no Santa Claus, there is $E = MC^2$. And when that is known, fairy music can sound no more.

Neither fairy music nor the flaming wonder of childhood are stifled at once. Each dies a slow death. The first flicker comes when work replaces play and the child ceases to be an arboreal primate seeking to stretch into maturity, but instead becomes a protogroundling. It begins when adults deem it necessary that the child go to school.

The function of school is to train the child in culture: how to create mortar. It is in the matter of schooling that we can perceive man's great break with his anthropoid relatives. The chimpanzee, the gorilla, and the orangutan have no school. The young are trained primarily by the mother and secondarily by the members of the affinity group. Essentially, the training of the young centers around sociability: The infant must learn to live within the social confines of the affinity group. William A. Mason, commenting on infant training, writes:

> From [the mother] the infant learns to perceive the meaning of a gesture or a glance, discovers that food may not be taken with impunity . . . and finds that bites and slaps will be returned in kind.[3]

3. "The Social Development of Monkeys and Apes," in *Primate Behavior*, edited by Irven DeVore (New York: Holt, Rinehart and Winston, 1965) p. 531.

In other words, the infant learns how to behave within the group. He also learns, with species variations, what foods to eat and what ones to avoid; he also learns about sexual activity by observing. But, most significantly, the essentials of existence are the *donnés* of nature. Genetic composition determines the conduct. All that the infant needs to possess for survival is provided by its biology.

As we know, this is not so for man. Man must overcome his genetic deficiency vis-à-vis terrestrial living by means of mortar. It is this mortar that school is all about.

For untold millennia, "schooling" consisted of training boys for the hunt. They were handed over by their mothers to their fathers, who trained them to procure food. Girls, in contrast, had no real "schooling." They stayed with their mothers and learned about gathering and maternity.

The first schools that we know of were the *edubbas* of Sumer. These "tablet houses" had but one purpose: to produce the scribes necessary for the functioning of the economic and political processes of society. I have earlier referred to speech as the reproductive system of the mind, and to writing as the independent transmission system of culture. In this connection it is interesting to note that the first schools concerned themselves almost exclusively with perpetuation of the independent transmission system, so as to guarantee its future. Writing was, in this sense, the mortar of the mortar.

The post-hunt equivalents of the hunt are economic activities by which man provides the essentials of survival: food, clothing, and shelter. Modern schools seek to prepare children for economic activity. Until recently only boys went to school. Today, both girls and boys are trained in economic activity.

If anyone has any doubts as to the arboreal origins of man, he need only observe a typical school setting to become thoroughly convinced of the reality of man's arboreal past. The play areas of both nurseries and kindergartens are a mass of jungle gyms, teeter-totters, swings, slides, climbing ropes, tree houses, parallel bars, horizontal bars, and rings. There is even a horizontal

ladder that allows children to brachiate (swinging by the arms
from one hold to another) precisely as their ancestors did millions of years ago. Finally, there are trees. Place a child near
a tree and he will climb it.[4] Place a child in an arboreal setting
and his arboreal nature will take over and assert itself.

Survival demands that at a certain age the child climb down
out of the tree and begin his terrestrial training. Fortunately,
possibly because of deep residual memories of their own, adults
strip the child of his arboreality slowly. The greetings offered
the child by nursery and kindergarten are a blending of the
two worlds. In the foreground, as a reassurance, are the indicia
of arborea; in the background are the first hints of terrestria.
It is here in the child's first school that the fateful journey
begins. Largely it begins in the form of play—but play with a
purpose.

Dr. Marshall C. Jameson, a school principal, has outlined
the techniques and purposes of kindergarten: ". . . play is a
major *tool* [italics in original] which the teacher uses to promote and realize the goals of kindergarten." In his book *Helping Your Child Succeed in Elementary School*, Dr. Jameson
sets forth the goals of kindergarten.

(1) Learning to live with other children—learning the give
and take so necessary for school and life success. . . .
(2) Learning to listen, to follow increasingly difficult directions, to organize for work, to carry through on a
job, to pay attention, and even to sit still—all so very
necessary in the later program of learning to read.
(3) The creation of a wholesome attitude toward school.
(4) Establishing the foundations of good habits of work
and study.
(5) Increasing independence, self-control, and confidence
in one's self, which have been started in the home.[5]

4. It is a fascinating experience to watch a small child climb. His eyes
are on his hands; his feet function instinctively. You can see millions of
years roll back as instinct directs the feet unerringly to perches.
5. New York: G. P. Putnam's Sons, 1962, p. 20.

"To educate" is related to the Latin *ducere,* meaning to lead, guide, direct, head. During nearly the entire time man has existed on earth, something like 99 percent of his earthbound existence, the young males have been "led forth" by their fathers (or father-substitutes) to the hunt. They have, in other words, been educated to be hunters. This learning to become a hunter has not been restricted to the techniques of hunting. The techniques of almost anything are well within the competence of man's enormous brain. Education has always had as its base the establishment of a cultivated attitude toward the process of education and its goal. Even in something as remote from the ancient training for the hunt as the modern kindergarten we see the immemorial elements of conditioning the boy must go through before he can become what he must become.

He must, as Dr. Jameson tells us, learn to live with others. But this is not the sort of communal living that exists among arboreal primates. That sort of communal living is taught in the family situation. What Dr. Jameson is talking about is the ability to live with others in an enterprise that is on the one hand cooperative and on the other competitive.

Cooperation serves the purposes of the group, while competition serves the purposes of the individual. There is, inevitably, feedback from competition. The more competitive men are, the greater their survival value and hence a greater survival value for the group, not so much in terms of its internal effectiveness, but in relation to other groups.

Cooperation, Jameson's third goal, helps toward the establishment of wholesome attitudes toward school. What is meant by this is cooperation toward the whole process of education. As for his fourth goal, that of establishing good habits of work and study, Jameson recognizes that more than good intentions are necessary. One must get results.

Finally, there is the matter of "increasing independence, self-control, and confidence in one's self which have been started in the home." What this really means is independence from the maternal, and thereby arboreal, influence so characteristic of the home. In the beginning, the mother is the total environment of the child, projecting a completely arboreal profile to the newborn infant. As time passes, however, she must adjust her profile until finally she projects one that tends to direct the child (especially if it is a boy) toward terrestrial commitment. She lays the groundwork for the boy's ultimate masculinity, thus to prepare him for what lies ahead. She must urge her boy-child to develop those manly characteristics of stoicism, aggressiveness, and initiative that will be necessary if he is eventually to become a successful hunter. Boys are trained (shamed) not to cry when hurt, and in general not to show emotion. Because the girl-child doesn't have to overcome her essential nature and become a predator-hunter, she is raised—or has been until recent times—without these characteristics, and in default of them is typified as being passive.

Education, then, is a process that converts the arboreal, nonlethal, nonpredatory child into a terrestrial, lethal, predatory adult. Critical to the success of the process is the instilling of cooperative-competitive attitudes within the child. *Content* is secondary to *attitudes*. The child must be "psyched up" sufficiently to overcome his basic nonlethal nature and thus establish within him the ability to kill. Throughout the terrestrial history of man this process has been repeated generation after generation. On it has depended survival of the species.

Children, being the creatures they are, have never accepted the thought of an ordained existence. They are too wedded to the flexuous one to which they are born. This is not because they are perverse or are by nature unappreciative of parental interest in them. Children are simply arboreal primates. They *prefer* nothing, they *seek* nothing, they *oppose* nothing. Children, being by nature arboreal, have no teleological impulses. Children *are*. They are born into existence. They have no instinct to extend that existence beyond the limits dictated by the terms of their genetic composition. Just as the newborn chimpanzee will grow into the adult chimpanzee, so too the newborn child will grow into an arboreal adult.

But the human infant, because of factors discussed earlier, cannot grow into the fulfillment of its nature. It must have grafted on to it new buds that will extend the child in a new direction. This is the function of education: to lead the child into a new direction never intended by the child's original nature. The child, unlike other primates, cannot just *be*; he must have direction. Because directing the child beyond the scope of its nature violates that nature, the child, acting out of a survival imperative, seeks to reject the graft. Children have always rebelled against school.

Going back to the *edubba* of ancient Sumer, we find that discipline was a major problem. There was no sparing the rod. Kramer, in *The Sumerians*, tells of an essay written around 2,000 B.C., entitled "Schooldays," an anonymous recollection of an "old grad" that could have been written today. The day begins thus:

> When I arose early in the morning, I faced my mother and said to her: "Give me my lunch, I want to go to school!" My mother gave me two rolls, and I went to school. In school the fellow in charge of punctuality said: "Why are you late?" Afraid with a pounding heart, I entered before my teacher and made a respectful curtsy.

The day ends for the student when, home once more, he turns to the servants and says:

> I am thirsty, give me water to drink; I am hungry, give me bread to eat; wash my feet, set up [my] bed, I want to go to sleep. Wake me early in the morning, I must not be late lest my teacher cane me.[6]

In the same tenor is the Egyptian saying:

> Fortunate is a scribe that is skilled in his calling, a master of education. Persevere every day; thus shalt thou ob-

---

6. Chicago: University of Chicago Press, 1963, p. 38.

tain the mastery over it. . . . Spend no day in idleness, or thou wilt be beaten. The ear of a boy is on his back, and he harkeneth when he is beaten.[7]

In the Book of Proverbs there is a whole network of sayings relating to the proper instruction of boys of whom so much was demanded:

He who spares his rod hates his son, but he who loves him takes care to chastise him.

Chastise your son, for in this is hope; but do not desire his death.

Folly is close to the heart of a child, but the rod of discipline will drive it far from him.

Withhold not chastisement from a boy; if you beat him with the rod, he will not die. Beat him with the rod, and you will save him from the nether world.

The rod of correction gives wisdom, but a boy left to his whims disgraces his mother.[8]

Even medieval Christian education, an island of enlightenment amid a sea of European disrepair, was not to be respected by children. Adolphe E. Meyer records the difficulties:

Although Jesus had loved children, and had even manifested a rare tenderness for them, in this respect neither the [teaching] brothers nor sisters emulated him. Rather they accepted the popular principle of their time, namely, that children had no rights, with the result that not uncommonly a kind of instinctive antagonism reigned between the teacher and his learners. Unless spoken to they were to remain silent, and when addressing the abbot they were to make a knee. Never were they to fidget, or scratch themselves, or drape themselves against the wall, or seat themselves unbidden. Against such misdemeanors,

---

7. Leonard Cottrell, *Life under the Pharaohs* (New York: Holt, Rinehart and Winston, 1960), pp. 138–139.
8. 13:24; 19:18; 22:15; 23:13–14; 29:15.

and others equally unseemly, the teacher stood sentry, and
when, for all his care and admonition, they occurred none-
theless, he was quick to swing his ever-ready stick. "Learn
or depart," Winchester warned its newcomers, "a third
choice is to be flogged." [9]

The desideratum of modern education is the elimination of
the rod and the institution of reason in its place. Instead of
corporal punishment, moral and social suasion serve, at least in
theory, to convert the child.

John Dewey summed it up in his Pedagogic Creed when
he wrote: "I believe that school is primarily a social institution.
Education being a social process, the school is simply that
form of community life in which all those agencies are concentrated that will be most effective in bringing the child to
share in the inherited resources of the race, and to use his own
power for social ends." [10]

Almost a century after Dewey's exposition, Norman K.
Denzin wrote on the working out of Dewey's theory:

> At one level schools function . . . to Americanize the
> young. At the everyday level, however, abstract goals disap-
> pear, whether they be beliefs in democracy and equal op-
> portunity or myths concerning the value of education for
> upward mobility. In their place appears a massive norma-
> tive order that judges the child's development along such
> dimensions as poise, character, integrity, politeness, defer-
> ence, demeanor, emotional control, respect for authority
> and serious commitment to classroom protocol . . . [11]

It becomes painfully clear that while theories of education
change, the obdurateness of children remains constant. No

---

9. *An Educational History of the Western World* (New York: Mc-
Graw-Hill, 1965), p. 75.

10. *John Dewey on Education*, edited by Reginald D. Archambault
(New York: Modern Library, 1964), p. 430.

11. "Children and Their Caretakers," *Trans-Action*, now *Society*, Vol.
8, Nos. 9/10 (Whole No. 69) (July–August, 1971): 62–63.

matter what the final objective of a particular educational career may be, the child wants none of it. The child is happy as he is, being a child. He is born to it, his genes support his nature—in fact, they create his nature. It is man's terrestrial circumstance that produces the problem. The stress comes not from man's nature but from his circumstance. If man were able to exist in an environment for which his genetic composition had prepared him—as is the case with all other forms of life—there would be no need for schooling. There would be no need to superimpose artifice on a genetic structure. This artifice, this mortar, is essential to human survival. But no one likes it and no one accepts it, especially the young who are caught between their arboreal origins and their terrestrial destination.

OEDIPUS IN
THE VIENNA
WOODS

E VERY child, whether male or female, resists terrestrialization. Because the boy-child must inevitably become the
more terrestrialized—he must become a predator—his resistance is the greater. The focal point of this resistance is the
father. As a result, there is a quiet but heightened hostility
between boy and father. Most often this hostility is resolved
when the son accepts terrestrialization as his inevitable lot.

Sigmund Freud witnessed the hostility between the son and
the father and misread it. As a result, he constructed a most
remarkable myth that has endured through countless psycho-
analytical generations. It is the myth of the Oedipus complex.

Freud leaves no doubt as to the nature of the Oedipus complex, and he doesn't hesitate to assess its importance in human
development.

> There is no possible doubt that one of the most impor-
> tant sources of the sense of guilt which so often torments
> neurotic people is to be found in the Oedipus com-
> plex. . . .

Now what does direct observation of children, at the period of object-choice before the latency period, show us in regard to the Oedipus complex? Well, it is easy to see that the little man wants his mother all to himself, finds his father in the way, becomes restive when the latter takes upon himself to caress her, and shows his satisfaction when the father goes away or is absent. . . .

When the little boy shows the most open sexual curiosity about his mother, wants to sleep with her at night, insists on being in the room when she dresses, or even attempts physical acts of seduction . . . the erotic nature of this attachment to her is established without a doubt.[1]

In *The Interpretation of Dreams*, Freud places the Oedipus complex within the nucleus of all neuroses. The essence is sexual possession of the mother, the necessity of killing the intervening father, resultant guilt, and fear of castration by the father.

Bronislaw Malinowski was an early critic of Freud's principle of the universality of the Oedipus complex. As early as 1927 he saw something almost no one else did:

The complex exclusively known to the Freudian School, and assumed by them to be universal, I mean the Oedipus complex, corresponds essentially to our patrilineal Aryan family with the developed *patria potestas*, buttressed by Roman Law and Christian morals, and accentuated by the modern economic conditions of the well-to-do bourgeoisie. Yet this complex is assumed to exist in every savage or barbarous society. This certainly cannot be correct.[2]

Malinowski presents a most formidable refutation of Freud's Oedipal theme. He does so in the form of an analysis of the family situation among the Trobriand Islanders of northwest-

1. A *General Introduction to Psychoanalysis* (New York: Boni and Liveright, 1920), pp. 291–292.
2. *Sex and Repression in Savage Society* (New York: Harcourt Brace and Co., 1927), p. 20.

ern Melanesia. There the family system is matrilineal; kinship is calculated through the mother, not the father, as it is in the patrilineal systems of Europe and America. The boy or girl belongs to the mother's family, clan, and community. The boy succeeds to the dignities and social position of his mother's brother, not that of his own father. He also inherits his possessions from his mother's brother and not his father.

The mother's husband, the actual physical father of the child, is not regarded as the father. Children, in their belief, are inserted into the mother's womb as tiny spirits by the agency of the spirits of a deceased kinswoman of the mother. The mother's husband has the obligation to protect and cherish the children, to "receive them in his arms" when they are born, but they are not "his" in the sense of his having shared in their creation. According to Malinowski:

> The father is thus a beloved, benevolent friend, but not a recognized kinsman of the children. He is a stranger, having authority through his personal relations to the child, not through his sociological position in the lineage. Real kinship, that is, identity of substance, 'same body,' exists only through the mother. The authority over the children is vested in the mother's brother. Now this person, owing to the strict taboo which prevents all friendly relations between brothers and sisters, can never be intimate with the mother, or therefore with her household. . . . At his death his worldly goods pass to [the children's] keeping, and during his lifetime he has to hand over to them any special accomplishments he may possess—dances, songs, myths, magic, and crafts. *He also it is who supplies his sister and her household with food.* . . . To the father, therefore, the children look only for loving care and tender companionship. Their mother's brother represents the principle of discipline, authority, and executive power within the family. [Italics added][3]

------

3. Ibid., pp. 23–24.

Malinowski points out that the social and sexual forces at play in the patrilineal society are simply not present in the Trobriand family. That is, the father, especially the late-nineteenth-century father who was the stern, demanding, and judgmental father on whose beneficence, financial and otherwise, the family depended, and who possessed unlimited *potestas*, has no counterpart in Trobriand society.

As for sex, Malinowski writes: "First of all, . . . there is no condemnation of sex or sensuality as such, above all, no moral horror at the idea of infantile sexuality. The sensuous clinging of the child to his mother is allowed to take its natural course till it plays itself out and is diverted by other bodily interests." [4]

There never develops between son and father, or for that matter, between son and mother, those yearnings and conflicts so central to Freud's theory. However, there are repressive and formative forces among the Trobriands. There is the submission to matriarchal tribal laws and the prohibition of exogamy, which function in such a way as to produce their own complex. The former is brought about by the influences of the mother's brother, who in appealing to the boy's sense of honor, pride, and ambition, comes to resemble the father in western culture. "On the other hand," writes Malinowski, "both the efforts which he demands and the rivalry between successor and succeeded introduce the negative elements of jealousy and resentment. Thus an 'ambivalent' attitude is formed in which veneration assumes the acknowledged dominant place, while a repressed hatred manifests itself only indirectly." [5]

It is with the matter of exogamy that we discover the central taboo of the Trobriands: incest, not with the mother neces-

---

4. Ibid., p. 77. The "sensuous clinging" of the child is that of an arboreal infant clinging to its mother for survival purposes. When ready to leave the mother-tree for the actual trees, it slowly lets loose of the mother-tree.

5. Ibid., p. 79.

sarily, but with the sister. This taboo makes every accidental contact in sexual matters a crime, and thus makes the thought of the sister ever present, as well as constantly repressed.

Malinowski summarizes the two systems, that of western culture and that of the Trobriands, this way:

> . . . We see that in a patriarchal society, the infantile rivalries and the later social functions introduce into the attitude of the father and son, besides mutual attachment, also a certain amount of resentment and dislike. Between mother and son, on the other hand, the premature separation in infancy leaves a deep, unsatisfied craving which, later on, when sexual interests come in, is mixed up in memory with the new bodily longings, and assumes often an erotic character which comes up in dreams and other fantasies. In the Trobriands there is no friction between father and son, and all the infantile craving of the child for its mother is allowed gradually to spend itself in a natural spontaneous manner. The ambivalent attitude of veneration and dislike is felt between a man and his mother's brother, while the repressed sexual attitudes of incestuous temptation can be found only towards his sister.[6]

In brief, there is no substantive conflict between father and son. However, notwithstanding Malinowski's remarkable analysis, he passes over the central element in the family situation of the Trobriands that explains the absence of the Oedipal conflict. The uncle, not the father, is the one who provides the family's food, and it is the uncle who trains the boy to be a provider. In primordial terms, it is the uncle who is the hunter and it is the uncle who trains the boy to become a predator-hunter.

Margaret Mead, in *Coming of Age in Samoa*, describes in great detail the family structure—one significantly different from that of the Trobriands—and concludes that the family

6. Ibid., pp. 75–76.

system "seems to ensure the child against the development of the crippling attitudes which have been labeled Oedipus complexes, Electra complexes and so on."

In essence, what preserves the child is the absence of deeply channeled emotions involving the two parents, and the diffusion of parental authority. And, as with the Trobriands, there is no problem of guilt over infant sexuality.[7]

The Samoans do not suffer from the existence of a nuclear family situation. Thus, they don't participate in an isolated and deep emotion-bond involving husband and wife, as well as parents and children. Upon marriage, "The young couple live in the main household, simply receiving a bamboo pillow, a mosquito net and a pile of mats for their bed. . . . The wife works with all the other women of the household and waits upon all the men. *The husband shares the enterprises of the other men and boys*. . . . [Even] in the care of the young children and decisions as to their future, the uncles and aunts and grandparents participate as fully as the parents. It is only when a man is *matai* [the holder of a title, the head of a household] as well as a father, that he has control over his own children; and when this is so, the relationship is blurred in opposite fashion, for he has the same control over many other young people who are less closely related to him." [Italics added][8]

Mead, while discussing the coming of age in Samoa from the female's point of view, nevertheless, in the following passage reveals the central element in Samoan society that precludes the possibility of there being an Oedipus complex:

> Work consists of those necessary tasks which keep the social life going: planting and harvesting and preparation of food, fishing, house-building, mat-making, care of chil-

---

7. The sexual guilt mentioned by both Malinowski and Mead stems from the western practice of granting mortar a primacy over every other consideration. Sex must be so regulated as to subordinate it to the demands of mortar. Any sexual activity, whether of the young or the mature, that seeks to exist independent of mortar considerations is viewed as bad, thereby arousing guilt in the offender.

8. London: Penguin Books, 1954, p. 188.

dren . . . *these are the necessary activities of life, activities in which every member of the community, down to the smallest child, has a part.* . . . And there is always leisure . . . the result of a kindly climate, a small population, a well-integrated social system, and no social demands for spectacular expenditure. [Italics added][9]

It is because of diffusion of parental authority, the absence of guilt over infant sexuality, and the communal nature of work that there is no such thing as the Oedipus complex among Samoans.

As for Freud's contention that the Oedipus complex is universal, there is not a scintilla of proof. It is an assertion stemming from authority, not from evidence. Complexes, neuroses, fixations, and other manifestations of emotional disjointedness, arise from the impact of culture on the individual, and not from biology. Freud said No; that biological determinants produce elemental neuroses, such as that stemming from an unresolved Oedipus complex.

Clara Thompson, a psychoanalysist, has this to say about Freud's contention:

> . . . Basically [Freud] thought of the Oedipus complex as an inevitable biological stage of development. . . . Always he recognizes that culture plays a part, but he thinks of culture as the servant of biology. . . . In short, Freud assumed that the people he observed were typical specimens of universal human nature, and therefore the puritanical attitudes of Victorian society were believed to characterize human nature in general.[10]

In appraising Freud's Oedipus complex theory, it is interesting to note that his facts, the data on which he based his conclusion, were essentially correct. Freud saw a special and

9. Ibid., pp. 228–229.
10. *Psychoanalysis: Evolution and Development* (New York: Hermitage House, 1950), pp. 134–135.

close relationship between mother and son; he saw the hostility (balanced off against affection) between father and son. Where he misjudged his evidence was in seeing it in sexual terms. This error arose because Freud imagined nineteenth-century European man to be universal man, and in nineteenth-century European man, human sexuality lived a most corrosive life.

Added to the severe sexual inhibitions (accompanied by obsessive attention to sex) was the economic fanaticism of the latter part of the nineteenth century and the early part of the twentieth, in which man set off the productive explosion made possible by the long-smoldering Industrial Revolution. Men of this period were the great new hunters of the world. The hunt was everything, especially among the middle classes of Europe and America.

Freud's great error, that on which his Oedipal theory was based, was to assume the naturalness of man's economic circumstances as they existed at the time. What Freud failed to see, and what is becoming increasingly clear to modern man, is that the danger to man is exactly the reverse of what he imagined it to be. It was not sex that threatened man and corroded his most intimate relationships; it was civilization. To be more precise, it was man's terrestrial circumstance, in which survival demanded the conversion of each arboreal boy-child into a terrestrial predator, that threatened man and critically distorted the relationships within the family.

In the boy's early years he is the charge of his mother, whose job it is to fit the arboreal infant into the terrestrial mold. Because of the natural bond between a mammalian mother, especially a primate mother, and her child, this adjustment is relatively easy. The infant boy, for example, has almost no responsibilities other than those associated with the mother. He may help his mother clean up around the family residence (whether ancient cave or modern home), do a few errands, and even help as a gatherer of berries, fruits, nuts, and so on. Except for the fact that life is lived on earth, the existence of the boy is essentially arboreal—at least relatively.

When the father enters the picture, adjustment is set aside and conversion takes over. The boy, taken in hand by the father—or by the schoolteacher—is converted into a totally terrestrial creature. He is introduced for the first time to lethality (or its modern equivalent, confrontation-competition). He must learn to be a hunter.

This, then, involves two critical phenomena: Against his primordial (genetic) nature, he learns to be a predator; the father, also against his primordial (genetic) nature, has to assume the double role of a paternal figure and a pedagogue. Adding to the volatility of the situation, father and son confront each other in a lethal situation that is essential to survival. The son rebels not against his father but against this final assault on his arboreality. With his mother he experiences naturalness. She supports him, she feeds him, and she prepares him for what tens of millions of years of instinctual living lead him to expect: independence as an arboreal primate. Instead, as he arrives at the point where his expectations would expect to find independence, he is handed over to his father who, rather than escorting him to freedom, escorts him into a terrestrial prison where he must learn the deadly art of predation.[11]

The father is equally ensnared. It is not within his nature to be either paternal or a teacher, particularly a teacher of something against his own nature. To preserve the species, he must force his son to kill.

Freud saw the struggle between the son and his father, but he saw it in all the wrong hues. Warped by the obsessions of his time and place, he dreamed a terrifying dream born of Sophocles's mysterious genius. In the sensuous shadows of his

---

11. Kramer, in discussing the origin of certain concepts among the Sumerians, refers to the word *freedom*, which literally translated means "return to the mother." The literal meaning caused him great difficulty. He couldn't understand the relationship between freedom and returning to the mother. But when we realize that a return to the mother means freedom from the father and the lethal lessons to be taught by him, we can perceive the connection.

own fabrication, Freud saw a son lasciviously embracing his mother. What he could not see was a son clinging desperately to his mother and the arboreal life she represented. The voice of the father, calling to his son to be about a man's work, is the voice of Abraham calling to his beloved son Isaac—only there is no God to stay Abraham's hand, and the arboreal son is slain so that the terrestrial man might be born.

PART THREE

The Gallery

To sit for one's portrait is like being present
at one's own creation.

—ALEXANDER SMITH

   (*Dreamthorp: On Vagabonds*)

THE WARRIOR

THE HUMAN species, if it is to be understood, must be viewed in terms of its sequential development. First, there was the arboreal period which supplied the species with its arboreal premise. Second, there was the hunt era that was responsible for all of man's special terrestrial habituations. Third, there is the modern era, the post-hunt era, in which man exists in his production-consumption cocoon. As we have already observed, the arboreal premise endures to this day because of the secondary effect of mortar. In a somewhat similar fashion, though less firmly founded in genetic composition, the long hunt era retains a very strong hold over modern man who, even while out of the hunt era, acts in many instances as if he were still within it. Nowhere is this more clearly evident than in the matter of what has become known as "human aggression," something that was unleashed during the long and perilous hunt era, and that now seems virtually impossible to restrain. Human aggression, especially that represented by war, is man's most pressing problem. It must be understood and then controlled, or man faces extinction—possibly not today or even tomorrow, but someday soon. The threat is real and ever-present.

What, then, is human aggression? There is no settled meaning to the term. Some authorities say it is a learned and thereby cultural activity. Others say it is the outward form of an interior and instinctual force. Many place a very narrow meaning on aggression; others so broaden it as to include everything from outright war to an eyebrow raised in pique.

I believe that if we are to understand human aggression, we must first understand the term *aggression* as it is applied to nonhumans, for it was as an arboreal primate during the arboreal period that the species engaged in a form of aggression that was the foundation for that which was to come later. Once we have come to an understanding of that term, then perhaps we can see what became of it in the course of man's terrestrial experience.

The difficulty in discussing aggression—any aggression—arises over the connotations associated with the word. Even the dictionary adds to the difficulties. It defines aggression as "the action of a state in violating by force the rights of another state, particularly in territorial rights," and "an unprovoked offensive attack, invasion, or the like." [1] Because this sort of conduct is considered reprehensible by the majority of civilized peoples, the word "aggression" implies wrongdoing. This implication carries over to nonhumans as well. Therefore, in this discussion we must be very careful to avoid placing a subjective meaning on the word or else that which is actually a very natural form of conduct will be thought of as something slightly bad, which, of course, is not the case at all.

Konrad Lorenz supplies us with a refreshingly abrupt definition of aggression. He describes it as "the fighting instinct in beast and man which is directed *against* members of the same species." [2]

Louis Breger, on the other hand, says this of aggression:

Aggression is an instinctually bounded system involving the arousal of powerfully motivating emotions, most notably anger. [As with other systems] we should think of it as a total, integrated pattern which . . . may be broken

1. *The Random House Dictionary of the English Language, College Edition* (New York: Random House, 1968, 1969).
2. *On Aggression* (New York: Harcourt Brace Jovanovich, 1966), p. ix.

down into its action, physiological, and subjective com-
ponents. The actions of aggression are its most noticeable
aspect. Fighting, biting, clawing, hitting, loud sounds
such as shrieks and growls, threat gestures such as the
baring of teeth or positioning for attack, as well as subtler
actions such as widening the eyes or the erection of body
hair to create an appearance of greater size, are all promi-
nent. . . .[3]

If we accept the fact that aggression has something to do
with fighting (and all those actions subsumed thereunder),
what good is there in such conduct? What purpose does aggression serve?

Aggression is an adaptive mechanism. The forms and extents of aggression depend entirely on the adaptive needs of
a particular species. Those of the lion are vastly different from
those of the wildebeest. The same is true of the various species
of primates.

Charles H. Southwick writes of primate aggression this way:

[Aggression as an adaptive mechanism enables] primates
to meet a variety of environmental circumstances, to structure their social life in functional groups, and to survive
more satisfactorily in competitive communities. In addition, it may have favorable consequences in regulating
population size and a spatial distribution.[4]

On this point Washburn and David Hamburg observe that
it is important to consider both the individual actor and the
social system in which it is functioning, as evolution has produced a close correlation between the nature of the social system and the nature of the participants in the system. They
write: "Societies of gibbons, langurs, and macaques represent
different sociobiological adaptations, and . . . the form and

---

3. *From Instinct to Identity* (Englewood Cliffs, N.J.: Prentice-Hall,
1974), p. 42.
4. *Aggression among Non-Human Primates,* An Addison-Wesley
Module in Anthropology, Module 23, 1974, p. 3.

function of aggressive behavior are different in these groups." [5]

Such being the case, what do we discover when we examine arboreal primates and their various forms of aggression? Aggression, usually by adult males, is a form of assertive conduct, principally in the form of nonlethal display, occasionally reinforced by physical attack (even to the extent of occasionally inflicting harm—but very seldom death) employed to preserve a certain species's niche in the environment. Involved are: (1) defense against predators; (2) spacing and population regulation; (3) habitat utilization and range extension; (4) sexual selection; and (5) leadership selection.[6] In other words, aggression as here employed, means those assertive acts against others that, within the terms of the species/environment equation, will guarantee the three essentials of existence: protection from predators, sustenance, and sex. What forms assertion takes and the extent of that assertion depend on the species and the environmental circumstances in which it finds itself.

Aggression of this sort is possible against members of other species of animal, but this is rare, especially among primates who, rather than fighting nonprimates, especially predators, simply escape to the safety of the trees. Even within a species there is little interaction between members of different affinity groups except in the matter of boundary confrontations. Yet even that serves almost always to preserve territorial integrity without actual conflict.

Intragroup aggressions are the most numerous, occurring in most instances to preserve the social order and solidarity of the group. The purpose of this is to safeguard females and dependent offspring so that the group might survive.

Baboons and savanna-dwelling vervet monkeys live among lions, leopards, cheetahs, hyenas, jackals, wild dogs, and large raptorial birds. In such dangerous circumstances where preda-

---

5. "Aggressive Behavior in Old World Monkeys and Apes," in *Primates: Studies in Adaptation and Variability*, edited by Phyllis Jay (New York: Holt, Rinehart & Winston, 1968), p. 463.
6. From Southwick, *op. cit.*, pp. 23.

tion pressures are very great, they must maintain a high degree of vigilance, and be prepared to battle with powerful predators. To do this they must have a high degree of hierarchical order and discipline lest they be picked off one by one, thereby endangering the group's (as well as the species's) survival. On the other hand, the totally arboreal gibbon need only to engage in a ritual of morning yells to assert its presence in the world.

The purpose of these aggressions is not destructive, but designed to advance the interests of the species. *The intent is not to destroy or even harm another; it is to preserve the self,* and appropriate assertive actions are employed to this end. They are not destructive, they are conservative. They assist in the construction of a species profile that will match that of the environment.[7]

For these aggressions to be anything else, for them to seek out and destroy other members of the species, would make them counterproductive. Rather than adding to the species profile, such conduct would detract from it. The purpose of such aggression is clear if we imagine its absence. What if there were no hierarchy, or if there were a hierarchy, but no one worked to preserve it? What if adult males of a group were indifferent to the intrusions of members of another group? What if the strongest and ablest males didn't seek a sexual priority with females in estrus? What would happen to the group if the adult males failed to guard against approaching predators? Without these kinds of aggression, the species —any species—would quickly become extinct. With these aggressions a species achieves a viable balance in the species/ environment equation.

What, then, of adaptive aggressions when placed in the hands of man? In effect, they become *human aggressions* which have, regardless of their ultimate motive, the harming or de-

---

7. In this connection it must be remembered that other animals, including members of the affinity group, are part of the individual's environment.

struction of other members of the species as their purpose. By doing this they gravely jeopardize the species/environment equation, and thus survival itself.

The British psychoanalyst Anthony Storr has devoted an entire book to an attempt to discover the causes and nature of human aggression. In his *Human Aggression*, he reveals the visceral elements of his case for the presence of aggressively destructive tendencies in man. He writes:

> It is worth noting . . . that the words we use to describe intellectual effort are aggressive words. We *attack* problems, or *get our teeth into* them. We *master* a subject when we have *struggled with* and *overcome* its difficulties. We *sharpen* our wits, hoping our mind will develop *a keen edge,* in order that we may better *dissect* a problem into its component parts [italics in original].[7]

What Storr is describing, although he does not acknowledge it, is the circumstance in which human aggression began. He is describing the hunt, even if only indirectly. More particularly, he is describing the impact of the hunt on human thought and activity, for his "attack" on problems is a clear reflection of man's predatory conduct. In man's hands, aggression has become transformed from a conservative, adaptive activity into a form of predation, but not predation against prey; instead, predation against other men.

Human aggression, then is the very *opposite* of aggression in nature. The purpose of human aggression is destructive; it is designed to cause harm to others. It may be initiated out of a desire to preserve the self, but it involves harm—even death —to another. Nowhere else in the animal world is there such a policy.

The truly distinguishing feature of human aggression is its emphasis upon lethality. Even in those instances where the ultimate assertion is not employed, its presence is usually felt,

---

8. New York: Atheneum, 1968, unnumbered Introduction, p. 2 [sic].

for it is often only under the protective umbrella of lethality that subordinate aggressions can take place. No one dares act aggressively without the reinforcing prospect of lethality, for without it, the initial aggressor may be himself the recipient of lethality.

This is in sharp contrast to man's arboreal past, where in situations within the affinity group and between groups of the same species there was no lethality at all.[9] A system of display, threat, and ritual aggression preserved the internal order of the group; it assured the integrity of the group when confronted by intrusion.

That nonlethal primate of man's arboreal past entered the great labyrinth several million years ago, and emerged at the gates of Sumer some six thousand years ago as the creature *Homo sapiens,* hunter and warrior. Therefore, it must be concluded that somewhere between Point A and Point T a critical conversion took place, one that saw a nonlethal primate become both hunter and warrior. I put it this way because the hunt and war are inextricably linked: *War was invented to protect the hunt.*

Von Clausewitz has said that "war is . . . an act of force to compel our adversary to do our will. . . . Physical force is the means; to impose our will on the enemy is the object." In his most famous dictum, von Clausewitz wrote, "War is . . . a continuation of policy by other means . . ."

War during the hunt era was an act to compel an adversary to stay away from the hunt or it was an act to take the results of the hunt from another. It is when we come to the dictum that "war is a continuation of policy by other means" that we come to the basis of the proposition. The basic policy—the only policy—of early man was survival by the only means possible, the hunt. Thus, war was an activity engaged in only under extreme provocation.

---

9. Except in the possibly rare instances observed occasionally in modern primates today, in which sharp acts of aggression might accidently wound and even kill.

When did man invent war? There is no way of knowing. We do know that he apparently killed his own kind from a very early date. Leakey reports what he believes to have been the first murder, that of an Australopithecine child. If this is correct, then man killed his own almost from the beginning of the terrestrial period. This is reinforced by Dart's evidence of cannibalism among Australopithecines in South Africa. Joined with this fragmentary evidence is the question of the extinction of the Australopithecines. Did they enter a dead-end chamber in the labyrinth, or were they destroyed by a superior culture? The same might be asked of the much later Neanderthalers. We do know, however, that when we enter the historic period of man, we find war a fully developed institution. It is in Jericho and other communities actually older than Sumer that we learn of fortifications, towers, weapons, and other martial material of a highly sophisticated nature. When we come to Sumer we discover great epic poems detailing wars and extolling martial virtues.

The hunt is the key to war. There were three factors present in the hunt and each had to be reckoned with if man was to survive. Each of the three reflected a facet of lethality. First, man had to prepare himself, both with artificial extensions of the forelimbs and the necessary psychic state, to kill prey. Second, he had to prepare himself for a lethal counterattack by the prey or attacks by other predators. Third, he had to be ready to fend off the incursions of other humans who might seek to take his prey from him.

Becoming a hunter was a three-step process. A man had to be capable of going after prey and slaying it. He had to be ready at all times to fend off attacks by natural predators. And he had to protect his prey, either in hand or in prospect. It can be seen that the second consideration, that of danger from predators, put man on both sides of the issue. He was both hunter and hunted—and by natural predators far more powerful and capable than he, especially in the earlier period of terrestrial existence. Thus, man had to be capable of attack and counterattack in terms of prey and predator. This capability became transferable to the situation of interference by other humans so that when it came, the hunter/warrior was prepared, both in terms of weapons and psychic state, to launch both attacks and counterattacks on humans threatening the hunt.

With the end of the hunt era, there was an end to the danger from predators. But by this time hundreds of thousands of years of living in a defensive posture had so conditioned man for attack from predators that he continued to act as an armed displayer even when his conflicts involved other men: fellow arboreal primates. He responded to other men who interfered with his hunt—and here the hunt was economic activity—as if they were in fact predators threatening his source of food.

When in the post-hunt era we come upon war, we discover the continued need for the causal structure of the hunt, counter-hunt, and human interference. However, with man able to command his own food sources, there was no longer the occasion of attack and counterattack, once so necessary to produce the arousal state necessary to convert a nonlethal man into a killer. In order to achieve this essential conversion, it was necessary to do something very critical. Those seeking to wage war had to dehumanize the men they wished to destroy. By making them into something less than men—beasts— the ancient arousal system was brought into play, once again converting a nonlethal primate into a lethal warrior.

It was only when forced into the terrestrial mode against their will that man's hominid ancestors, contrary to their nature, took up, quite literally, the first pebble tool and began an aggressive career that saw them, as *artificial predators*, become aggressive to the point where they were not only able to kill regular prey, but also members of their own kind. However, this aggressive conduct was not the least bit pleasurable, as insisted upon by Storr, but an *in extremis* form of conduct absolutely essential if the species was to survive. In the first instance, it can quite literally be said, hominids took up weapons (known today, interestingly enough, as "arms"), which I describe as artificial extensions of the forelimbs, in order to do two things necessary for survival: protect themselves against natural predators far superior to them in natural terms, and provide themselves with sustenance. Because hominids were not natural predators, they lacked genetically based means to prevent intraspecies predation as well as restrained predation vis-à-vis extraspecies creatures. As a consequence, man the hunter/warrior has lacked a natural bias against killing his own kind and overkilling regular prey. The result has been war and excessive killing of prey to the point where, approximately ten thousand years ago, man in his greatest crisis of survival had to domesticate animals and grain in order to be certain of a constant source of food.

It is only when we view the entire sequence of arboreal primate > hominid > man that we see the slot in which to place "human aggression," a most unnatural activity, whether we are talking of hominids who were obliged to undertake it to survive in the prehistoric past, or of *Homo sapiens* who is seeking to end it in order to survive in the historic present.

If man is, as Storr says, an aggressive creature who takes pleasure in habitually destroying his own kind, then there is no hope whatever for man, for without fail, he will destroy himself. But what if he is not?

We may take as the first hint of the answer the fact that Storr himself, for all he says, does not find it possible to conclude that human aggression is an instinct. He confronts the issue in these words:

> Although we cannot give a straight forward and simple answer to the question "Is aggression an instinct?" what we can say is that, in man, as in other animals, there exists a physiological mechanism, which when stimulated, gives rise both to subjective feelings of anger and also to physical

changes which prepare the body for fighting. This mechanism is easily set off, and, like other emotional responses, it is stereotyped and, in this sense, "instinctive." [10]

It is in this quotation that we can observe the confusion over aggression. It is true, as Storr observes, that there is a physiological mechanism in both man and other animals that gives rise to aggression. The mechanism within man is precisely that which existed in arborea, because of the secondary effect of mortar. Man, prompted by the same stimuli as would evoke adaptive aggression in another primate, responds appropriately, but this response is transformed into an inappropriate response by the fact of the artificial extensions of the forelimbs: weapons. Take away those weapons, and man's aggressions would be those of any other arboreal primate in a comparable stimulus situation. It is the artificial extensions of the forelimbs (mortar) that convert an adaptive aggression into human aggression.

Something within man perceives the difficulty, for in manifesting human aggression, he strives almost always to practice human aggression only against those outside the affinity group. Most instances of serious human aggression do not occur within the affinity group. If they did, employing the means used in aggressions against other groups, the affinity group (family, clan, tribe, state) would be destroyed. This is in contrast to the situation in nature, where the great majority of adaptive aggressions take place within an affinity group. The sources of food for arboreal primates are immobile and contained within a fairly definitive territory. Therefore there is little interference by one group with another. Man, from the hominid on, had to pursue his food, and territories could not be maintained with any certainty. As a result, direct confrontation over prey was very probable a great deal of the time, thereby

10. *Ibid.*, p. 11. To call, as Storr does here, something "instinctive" (in quotes) because it is stereotyped behavior is very unscientific. Also, it is the equivalent of saying that conditioned responses are "instinctive," which, of course, is a contradiction in terms.

necessitating some system of protecting the hunt. Thus the greatest problems of survival were not within the group but between one affinity group and another. To exacerbate the problem, at the point of greatest confrontation, the representatives of the contending groups also were equipped with those artificial extensions of the forelimbs necessary for both the hunt and war. Add to that the heightened psychic state of the hunt, and you have human aggression. Once you have human aggression, you have all those subsidiary assertions—social, economic, and psychological violence—that flourish under the umbrella of the ultimate form of human aggression: the killing of another human.

However, it must be remembered that the hunt era was only an interregnum. It was not part of man's original arboreal existence; it is not part of man's contemporary existence. It was that fateful interim necessary for survival. It deformed man and it scarred him, but it did not change the essential nature of man. Despite the holdovers from the long hunt era, there is an overwhelming amount of evidence to prove the survival of man's original nature, not in some shrunken state, but in all of its pristine strength.

Violence and war are holdovers from the interregnum. They were emergency practices absolutely necessary to preserve the species at its time of greatest peril. Yet, despite their importance, they were as contrived as was the hunt they sought to protect. They were no more representative of the true nature of man than was the hunt itself. But they worked. Despite everything they preserved the mortar on which man relied for survival. Now that the hunt is over, man is once more able to assert his true nature, which is not lethal at all. Man is, in the final analysis, an arboreal primate.

There are many proofs of this, but one that I consider the most telling of all is the fact that man suffers intense emotional stress over war and violence. If they were natural, there would be no complaint. Does man complain about eating? About sex? No. He complains, however, when he cannot get adequate food, and he complains when he cannot engage in adequate sex. These are natural to man. War and violence are not. They have been expedients—and continue to be for those who respond to modern circumstances as if they still lived in the hunt era.

There can be little doubt that in the very beginning, hunters served as warriors. Indeed, depending on the scenario one wishes to conjure up, it is imaginable that with one thrust of a stone weapon the individual was acting as a hunter and with another thrust he was acting as a warrior fighting off those who would deprive him of the prey he just slew with his first thrust. In any event, what is significant is the fact that the same man using the same weapon at one time could serve as both hunter and as warrior. At the same time, the necessary heightened psychic state was present, intensified by the fact that in this man-to-man confrontation, each was responding to the other as if the other were a natural predator. Predator, yes, but not a natural predator of greatly superior lethal capabilities—rather an artificial predator caught in the crossfire of instinct and necessity. Between them in this confrontation was the source of survival. It was over this they fought—exactly as if two predators of different species were fighting, thereby ridding the confrontation of the rule against intraspecies predation. As a consequence, they fought to the death. In this way, then, hunting and warring were kindred and interrelated activities.

However, once the hunt was over, the life of the hunter was over. And when that happened, the individual lost two essentials: his weapons (as distinct from tools) and the heightened state necessary for both the hunt and war. In this condition, the individual—whether a herdsman, a farmer, or an artisan—was no longer capable of war. Discarding the weapons actually served to restore him to his prior condition where he was nonlethal, possessing only "grasping forelimbs." Lacking weapons and the need to use them, he lost the emotional state associated with lethal capabilities. What then of war? How could a nonlethal primate fight wars? Especially when he didn't have the two prerequisites: weapons and the emotional push?

Quite simply, he couldn't fight wars in that situation. But, since we know that wars have continued to this day, we must search out how, for a second time, a nonlethal primate could be converted into a lethal warrior. And here it must be noted that the original link between hunter and warrior is missing. Men who are not hunters are to be fashioned into warriors. Weapons must be provided, something that is not too difficult. What is just as necessary as weapons, however, and far more difficult, is the artificial inculcation of the heightened state absolutely necessary to becoming a warrior. Whereas once the hunt itself had produced the occasion, in the posthunt era something else would have to lift the would-be warrior to the emotional heights necessary for killing.

One of the first things we notice at Sumer is the presence of a military system. Undoubtedly this system had its roots in the depths of the labyrinth where the onetime practice of the hunter/warrior system gave way to specializations: Some men continued being hunters while others became warriors (and others became artists, tool-makers, etc.). Since everyone had to eat, the warrior, along with other nonhunter specialists, received some sort of compensation—proceeds of the hunt in the first instance.

Thus war became the warrior's hunt. He had, and continues to have, but one function: to wage war. For this he is supported, whether by direct proceeds of someone else's hunt or by some other compensation, such as money.

Now, it will be noted that other specialists, such as the artisan, the tool-maker, the priest, the scribe, and the farmer, also receive compensation of some sort or another, thereby making each specialty—each form of economic activity—a specialized form of the hunt. But what distinguishes the warrior specialty from all the others is that the warrior's function is to kill other human beings. For this he must have weapons and the necessary emotional state. The former is provided by the community; the latter is provided by the object of the warrior's hunt: the killing of other humans. Just as the earlier hunter had to rise to the needs of his work, so too must the warrior rise to his.

He does this in several ways. To begin with, there is the ancient association with the hunt, itself a lethal activity. He kills other men to protect the hunt, and he kills other men when they approach him like threatening predators. He responds to them as if they were natural predators. Because of these associations with a past that endured for hundreds of thousands of years, it has never been difficult to dredge up these past associations, even if only on the deepest unapprehended psychic level.

A second way the warrior rises to the needs of his work is through the practice of "military virtues." The Prussian militarist, Helmuth von Moltke, has probably best described these virtues in his historic dictum on war:

> Perpetual Peace is a dream—and not even a beautiful dream—and War is an integral part of God's ordering of the Universe. In War, man's noblest virtues come into play: courage and renunciation, fidelity to duty and a readiness for sacrifice that does not stop short of offering up Life itself.[11]

Courage and renunciation, fidelity to duty, and a readiness to sacrifice one's life—these are the military virtues. Yet when we examine them carefully, we find that they are also the "virtues" of the adult male primate protecting the affinity group. We can go further and say that they are "virtues" common to all creature life, from the primate mother caring for her offspring to the adult male protecting the affinity group. What distinguishes the military virtues is that they

---

11. Cited in Arnold Toynbee, *War and Civilization* (New York: Oxford University Press, 1950), p. 16.

have as their end-purpose lethality, which ordinary primate "virtues" don't. The rationale of military lethality is the protection of all the other hunts in society, from that of the artisan to that of the scribe. However, there is a critical lack of logic in that rationale.

Primates are fully capable of protecting the affinity group by nonlethal means. Therefore, the warrior who functions like the adult male of the primate affinity group should be able to protect his affinity group in the same way. After all, he is protecting his affinity group from members of the same species, other nonlethal primates (which is what man is, stripped of weapons). He is *not* protecting his affinity group from natural predators. It is here that the breakdown in logic occurs. It occurs as a result of the entanglement of the hunt and war, both ancient lethal activities.

It is this heritage that has fed the warrior in the post-hunt era. When he protects economic activity, he does so on ancient premises. Lethality and survival are mixed together in a foggy primordial memory that has as its postulate the principle that killing is the means of survival. Out of this postulate comes the conviction that to kill a member of a nonaffinity group in war is to kill a strange admixture of man and beast. That is why in all wars the enemy is stripped of his humanity and represented as some sort of beast. He must be made a beast in order to activate the ancient postulate that held killing to be the means of survival. By making the enemy a beast, he is thus made the requisite predator of the distant past, thereby justifying the right to kill him in self-defense. And it must be remembered that every warrior believes he is protecting his people even when he is boldly attacking others. He is protecting them by taking away the hunt of others and giving it to his own people (hence the practice of booty and reparations as a token of the underlying principles), or he is protecting them against the depredations of predators (who if they won would take everything away). Not only these psychic heritages are brought forth into the modern era; warriors, to maintain and protect their own hunt, which is a very real hunt, also arouse great terrestrial fears in the people, thereby inducing them to maintain the warrior class.

And yet, notwithstanding all this lethality, man has persisted in being nonlethal. Throughout all of recorded history he has resisted efforts to make him into a warrior. Whereas, in civilized society, there has always been an officer corps manning a military establishment and practicing the military virtues, as well as receiving the acclaim of the populace— after all, they protect the people and all their possessions— there has always been the difficult task of finding men to do the actual fighting, killing, and dying. It simply isn't in man to do these things. True, he may enjoy a good fight, but not the lethal kind. (When it is said that man may enjoy a good fight, what is meant is that he enjoys a bit of outlandish display. However, if the fight should become serious and bloody, all enjoyment flees—as do most of the participants.)

Men will fight when the proposition is real and immediate. They will fight when they are directly threatened. *In extremis*, they will often kill to preserve their own lives. They will also fight to protect their means of support when the threat is direct and immediate. Men will fight, when in desperate straits, for sustenance. If necessary, they will kill to obtain it.

However, when we talk of states or other large collections of people, we are talking of something entirely different. When the interests of the state are involved, even though they directly relate to the hunt, the individual doesn't feel the directness of the proposition. It then becomes the function of the state to induce him to participate. This is done either by cajolery, or in the alternative, by conscription.

Cajolery consists of elaborate promises of prestige, sexual pleasures and booty (to the victor belong the spoils!), camaraderie, etc., all of which appeals to his arboreal nature. Conscription consists of forcing the reluctant citizen into uniform. Once in the military, the realities assert themselves and the new soldier, whether volunteer or conscript, is reshaped into something entirely new. He is made into a killer of other men. Through rigid discipline, training, propaganda, and every other device at the command of those in charge, a nonlethal primate is converted into a warrior.

Samuel A. Stouffer and others prepared a mammoth sociological textbook on the American soldier of World War II. It considered what the army appeared to be like in the eyes of new conscripts. They reported:

> The Army was a new world for most civilian soldiers. Of its many contrasts with civilian institutions, there may be cited:
> 1. Its authoritarian organization demanding rigid obedience.
> 2. Its highly stratified social system, in which hierarchies of deference were formally and minutely established by official regulation, subject to penalties for infraction, on and off duty.
> 3. Its emphasis on traditional ways of doing things and its discouragement of initiative.[12]

Now, there is a purpose to this authoritarianism, stratification, and traditionalism. It is to lock the individual soldier—whether of Sumer or of the United States—into a situation where, in order to survive, he must become a trained killer of other men. He is given weapons, thus making him lethal, and he is given the psychological training to arrive at the heightened state necessary to employ those weapons in a lethal way.

Yet, despite all the elaborate efforts to convert this nonlethal primate into a lethal warrior, with an obstinacy that must drive militarists to despair, he refuses to convert.

General S. L. A. Marshall, in his field studies of the rate of fire among about four hundred infantry companies in the Central Pacific and European theaters of World War II, found that not more than 15 percent of the men interviewed had

---

12. *The American Soldier: Adjustment during Army Life*, vol. 1 (Princeton: Princeton University Press, 1949), p. 55.

actually fired a weapon at enemy positions or personnel during the course of entire engagements. Attempting to account for this, Marshall comments:

> The average firer will have less resistance to firing on a house or a tree than upon a human being. . . . [T]he average, normal man who is fitted into the uniform of an American ground soldier . . . is what his home, his religion, his schooling, and the moral code and ideals of his society have made him. The army cannot unmake him. . . . [Medical Corps psychiatrists in the European Theater] *found that fear of killing rather than fear of being killed, was the most common cause of battle failure in the individual* . . . [Italics added] [13]

Marshall goes on to observe that American society, at least until World War II, preached against war and aggression. While this may be seriously debated, it need not detract from the principal fact that the average (or should we say 85 percent?) soldier will more readily fire at nonhuman targets than at humans, for the reason assigned by Marshall. The Army cannot unmake a man: it cannot convert a nonlethal primate into a true lethal soldier.

Marshall acknowledges the problem, referring to such a soldier as a "conscientious objector, unknowing." But then he goes on to say that this condition "needs to be analyzed and understood if we are to prevail against it in the interests of battle efficiency." [14] That is, the nonlethal citizen must be converted into a lethal soldier. This is achieved, with at best only minimal results, by training and indoctrination. We can legitimately ask: What would happen to the Army if there were no such effort at conversion? Obviously there would be no soldiers. And if there were no soldiers—of combat quality— there would be no wars. There would be quarrels and disagreements among peoples, but there would be no wars. In such

13. *Men Against Fire* (New York: William Morrow, 1947), p. 78.
14. Ibid., p. 79.

event, we would witness man acting in accord with his arboreal nature. He would be, as he has always been, a great displayer, but without lethal artificial extensions of the forelimbs grafted on during the hunt era.

My purpose here is not to speak for or against war but to present evidence that the true nature of man is nonlethal. What should be sufficient to prove the point is that the matter is discussed at all. We do not inquire whether it is natural for man to eat or to engage in sex. We know that they are natural to man. We do, however, suffer over man's apparent warlike and lethal nature. We don't ponder the question of the lion's lethal nature, nor that of the tiger. We *know* they are lethal. It is when we raise the question of man's lethality that we confess a secret suspicion that he is not. The purpose of the present discussion has been to convert a suspicion into a certainty.

I must append a footnote to this discussion of war. Following war in the order of priorities subordinate to the ancient hunt is cannibalism, the means employed to obtain food when the hunt has failed.

There is abundant evidence of cannibalism from the earliest times. From *Australopithecus*, through Peking man, Neanderthal man, and Cro-Magnon man, to modern man, human flesh has been the emergency food of the species. Mesolithic and neolithic peoples, living between 10,000 and 2,000 B.C., perpetuated the ancient practice. Herodotus wrote of it in the fifth century B.C., as did a later Greek, Strabo, who just before the Christian era told of the practice among the Irish.

Norman Cohn, in *The Pursuit of the Millennium*, presents us with a most graphic picture of the practice as it occurred during the First Crusade. Although relatively modern, it could well serve as a model for the very earliest instances of the practice:

A large part—probably far the larger part—of the People's Crusade perished on its journey across Europe; but

enough survived to form in Syria and Palestine a corps
of vagabonds. . . . Barefoot, shaggy, clad in ragged sack-
cloth, covered in sores and filth, living on roots and grass
and also at times on the roasted corpses of their enemies,
they were such a ferocious band that any country they
passed through was utterly devastated. When they charged
into battle they gnashed their teeth as though they meant
to eat their enemies alive as well as dead.[15]

It is entirely possible that cannibalism came into being as
a result of warlike encounters between groups contending over
prey. If one of the groups failed completely in keeping any
prey as a result of the fray, it might have taken possession of
one or more of the other group's members to compensate for
the loss of prey. Being hungry, they would eat what they had
in hand. And when they did, they undoubtedly experienced
what many recent cannibals have experienced: that human
flesh is very tasty.[16] Here, also, might very well have begun
the practice of victorious armies taking prisoners of war and
either keeping them as living emergency food or putting them
to work as slaves.

From the very earliest times, slavery was a fully established
institution at Sumer, as was the taking of prisoners of war.
The earliest Sumerian written designation for "slave" was "man
of the mountains" or "woman of the mountains." On the basis
of philological evidence it is reasonable to conclude that the
earliest notion of "slave" was associated with the idea of "for-
eigner." It is logical to assume from this that some of the
earliest—if not the first—slaves were prisoners of war, rather
than members of impoverished families or debt-slaves.

---

15. New York: Harper & Row, 1957, p. 45.
16. Garry Hogg has written the definitive study in English of this
whole subject. In *Cannibalism and Human Sacrifice* (New York: Citadel
Press, 1966), he cites numerous authorities who describe the taste of
human flesh as being very much like sweet pork, and very tender. Fijians
call man "long pig," to distinguish him from "real pig." There are many
peoples who have greatly preferred "long pig" to any other meat.

It would seem from all this that slavery probably stemmed from cannibalism. Whether prisoners of war or whether acquired in some other circumstance, slaves were accumulated as a ready source of food, especially if there were more than could be eaten at the time of procurement. When man domesticated animals and grain there was no real need for emergency food in the form of other men. Therefore, men ceased being food and became the makers of food: they became slaves.

Evidence for this accumulation can be found in the very broad practice of only a few years ago when prisoners of war or victims of raiding parties were taken into slavery, where they performed services until wanted as food.

Hogg cites the artist and sculptor Herbert Ward who wrote A *Voice From the Congo*, in 1910:

> A visit to one of the slave-depots revealed a condition of savagery and suffering beyond all ordinary powers of description. It was not uncommon experience to witness upwards of a hundred captives, of both sexes and all ages, including infants in their mothers' arms, lying in groups. . . . The captives were exposed for sale with the sinister fate of being killed and eaten.
>
> Proportionately, a greater number of men than women fall victims to cannibalism, the reason being that women who are still young are esteemed as being of greater value by reason of their utility in growing and cooking food.[17]

The progression is there, I believe. The hunt > war > cannibalism > slavery. All revolve around food. In the beginning the slave (or prisoner of war) was food. Later he became the maker of food.

I have previously established the priorities subordinate to the hunt. Now I would like to show an historical instance of these priorities at work.

---

17. Hogg, op. cit., p. 108.

After World War I, Germany was in dire economic straits. Her hunt was in grave danger. It was so bad, it will be recalled, that in the twenties a wheelbarrow of paper money couldn't buy a loaf of bread.

Hitler came along and promised a New Order. He demanded *Lebensraum* and went to war to get it. Now, caught in the vortex of this primordial drive were the Jews, first of Germany and then of much of Europe. Before the war and during the early—and victorious—stages of the war, the Jews were persecuted and put into concentration camps, but for the most part they were not killed. It was only when the war began to turn against Germany that the systematic extermination of the Jews took place. In all, six million were destroyed. So intent were the Nazis in their determination to kill all the available Jews that they took them out of their various concentration camps (pens) and transported them to special extermination centers in—ironically yet appropriately—cattle cars. There they were not only gassed and otherwise killed, but their clothing was taken, jewelry confiscated, gold fillings extracted, bodies reduced to fat, and skin sometimes made into lampshades.

What is most extraordinary in this entire procedure is the fact that regular troop and military trains had to be shunted to rail sidings in order to allow the cattle trains priority. In other words, the war effort took second place to the efforts to get the Jews to extermination camps.

On the surface this simply doesn't make sense. It was not madness, however, that prompted the Nazis to shunt military trains; it was the ancient priorities.

The war was fought to protect the German hunt. When the war began to turn against the Germans, it had the secondary effect of seriously diminishing whatever hunt remained to the Germans. With the almost total collapse of the hunt, substitutes of all sorts were resorted to: ersatz food, synthetic oil, and a host of others. With the hunt failing, the substitute for the hunt had to be called into play. When the Nazis slaughtered the Jews and took their possessions—jewelry, gold inlays, bodies for soap, and skin for lampshades—they were practicing the greatest act of cannibalism in history. With the substitute hunt now under way, the war became secondary. The war would now have to protect cannibalism; it could not, as a subordinate activity, interfere with the substitute hunt. That is why the military trains were shunted to sidings, and that is why six million helpless Jews were led to slaughter: The Jews of Europe were the modern prey of a primordial hunt.

THE OBJECT

I T I S said in Genesis that the Lord God cast Adam into a deep sleep and, while he slept, took one of his ribs and fashioned it into woman. Whether this woman was Eve or whether it was Lilith depends on the particular legend. If we follow the Eve tradition, we encounter the serpent in the Garden and the great consequences that flow from that meeting. If we follow the Lilith tradition, we see her leave Adam in a pluperfect rage because he insisted that she assume the supine position during sexual intercourse.

From Eve we get all of humanity's problems; from Lilith we get the first protest movement. But Eve became subject to man and has, despite everything, become part of western tradition. Lilith, on the other hand, suffered a different fate: she went off somewhere to become a scarifying harridan, later to be invoked to frighten naughty children. What is significant is that both Eve and Lilith were the creations of male mythmakers.

Somewhat more recently, Eva Figes has sought to balance the scales by offering her opinion of Lilith. In *Patriarchal Attitudes*, she examines the situation faced by Lilith and then comments somewhat acidly, "If Lilith wants to be difficult about the recumbent posture she can always fly off in a rage and starve to death." [1]

---

1. New York: Stein and Day, 1970, p. 30.

Precisely. No one has better stated the condition of woman. Either woman submits to man or she loses whatever status, privileges, and immunities she might receive from him.

What offended Lilith, and what offends Figes, is female subordination. There is something so very symbolic about the female's subordinate position during intercourse. She is on the bottom, literally and figuratively. There is a whole conglomerate of factors that have placed woman in a subordinate position. Foremost is her economic dependence on the man. Because of the exigencies of the hunt, the female lost her capacity to satisfy her own sustenance needs. As a consequence she had to look to the male for whatever she was to receive. As a result of this prime dependence on the male, the female lost the freedom she had once known in arborea, and became, against her will, subject to the male. She lost her autonomy in all things, including sexual matters.

In arborea the female had to be in estrus before she would allow males to copulate; in terrestria she became the object of the male's sexual drives, irrespective of her own actual sexual receptivity. As for children, they, too, became the property of the male. While the mother might manage her small children, she did so within the framework provided by the male. In addition to all this, in many societies throughout history, should the female fail to provide the male with offspring, the remedies lay with the male, who could set the female aside and take a second wife in the hope that she would provide him with children—preferably sons.

Terrestrial existence has imposed on the species a division of labor along sexual lines. The male, in essence, takes command of the present. He is the hunter/wage-earner and provides for present needs. The female's prime function concerns the future. It is her responsibility to perpetuate the species or, as Helene Deutsch has expressed it, perform "her service to the species." [2] In actuality, the woman is permitted no more

---

2. *The Psychology of Women* (New York: Grune and Stratton, 1945) vol. II, p. 77.

than to produce the child and feed it during the early period. The mind of the child is provided for by the male.

Despite everything, it might seem that a mutuality should exist between the sexes: The male provides for present species needs, while the female provides for future needs of the species. The male satisfies the sustenance needs of the female; the female satisfies the sexual needs of the male. What is wrong with this arrangement is the fact that the male can exist with unsatisfied sexual needs, while the female cannot exist with unsatisfied sustenance needs. And it is this that provides the handle to the cudgel man holds over the head of woman.

It is in this respect that woman has become a sex object. She has almost no other identity. She has really no important function other than as a sexual being. The Sumerians understood this. In their earliest pictographs they reveal their concept of the nature of man and that of woman:

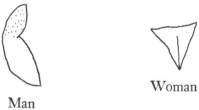

Man   Woman

The emphasis in the pictograph of man is upon the upper half of the body, especially the head. As for that of woman, there is only one feature: the pudendum.

There is another, and critical, aspect to the relationship between the sexes. As a result of the long hunt era, and the standards set by it for modern economic activity, the male has had to be extremely terrestrial. For the most part it has been the male who has created mortar. Being denied a significant role in mortar-production, and being relegated to such tasks as gathering and the rearing of children, the female has retained a greater degree of arboreality. Thus, there threatens a further problem between the sexes because of a species split.

The male is more terrestrial while the female tends to be more arboreal. Males have traditionally been obliged to be "down to earth," while females have been known to be more "flighty." Males tend to masculine things—such as war, politics, making money, and serious discussion—while females tend to female things—babies, household matters, spending money, and gossip.

Judith M. Bardwick and Elizabeth Douvan, in *Woman in Sexist Society*, express the proposition this way:

What are big boys made of? What are big boys made of?

Independence, aggression, competitiveness, leadership, task orientation, outward orientation, assertiveness, innovation, self-discipline, stoicism, activity, objectivity, analytic-mindedness, courage, unsentimentality, rationality, confidence, and emotional control.

What are big girls made of? What are big girls made of?

Dependence, passivity, fragility, low pain tolerance, non-aggression, non-competitiveness, inner orientation, interpersonal orientation, empathy, sensitivity, nurturance, subjectivity, intuitiveness, yieldingness, receptivity, inability to risk, emotional liability, supportiveness.[3]

The problem arises because male and female, to be able to survive in the terrestrial mode, have had to create an intimate relationship more or less on a one-to-one basis, something not necessary in arborea. It can be said, with great legitimacy, that the species living in terrestria is living in the midst of a great emergency requiring emergency tactics in order to salvage a desperate situation.

I have said earlier that in nature the female is the protagonist, whereas with the human species the male has assumed that role. This has arisen because of the demands of the hunt and the function of adult male primates in taking command in emergencies so as to be able to save the affinity group

---

3. "Ambivalence: The Socialization of Women," p. 147.

from danger, generally by leading it to safety. In the operations
of the human species, not only has the male had to become
the hunter in order that the species might survive, he has also
been seeking to lead the species back to arborea where, home
at last, it can be liberated from the unnatural demands of
terrestrial living. While this latter is actually a psychic matter, its expression takes the form of an effort to create neo-
arborea in terrestria. Yet even so, the dynamics of an emergency exist, during which the male has assumed, as he would
in arborea, the leadership necessary to escape from danger.

These two factors have produced a relational difficulty between the sexes. They have placed the female in her dependent and subordinate condition. And they have made of the
male a protagonist, something unknown in other primates.

In his dominant position, from which he has become the
law-maker concerning every aspect and detail of terrestrial existence, the male has established certain definitions. One of the
most bizarre has been the definition of woman.

Sigmund Freud has probably best exemplified male perspectives on the female. He considered them defective males. By
so proclaiming them, he fell into the error everyone falls into
when they establish modern man as the starting point and
standard of all human considerations. Freud had it backwards:
The man, if anything, is a defective female, in that he is
farther removed from his original arboreal condition than is
the female.

Once we understand this faulty perspective of Freud—and
all those who think as he did—we can understand his subsidiary opinions about women, a dread he projected onto all
men:

The man is afraid of being weakened by the woman, infected with her femininity and of then showing himself
incapable. The effect which coitus has of discharging tensions and causing flaccidity may be the prototype of what
the man fears; and the realization of the influence which

the woman gains over him through sexual intercourse, the consideration she thereby forces from him, may justify the extension of this fear.[4]

What Freud was fearful of, though probably it was an unconscious fear, was that women would distract men from their work. A woman, being relatively arboreal, might well so distract a man that he would cease producing mortar. It is entirely true that coitus discharges tensions, not only directly sexual tensions, but others as well, especially those that come from the problems surrounding the production of mortar. No other creature has them, only man. Most interesting is Freud's use of the term *flaccidity*, as if somehow he were equating post-coital flaccidity with general function flaccidity. What would happen, one could ask, if men were flaccid in their attitude toward mortar-production? The consequence would be disastrous. Woman, then, is the eternal temptress. Did she not tempt Adam to eat of the forbidden fruit? Look at the consequence of a momentary weakness of man when tempted by woman![5]

What is so paradoxical about this attitude is that it flies in the face of necessity. The species would be doomed were it not for sex. The procreative function of the female is natural. It is in no way "business" the way the making of mortar is. And this is the point. Woman acting as woman in sexual matters is acting naturally and according to her genes. Man, on the other hand, when he is "about his business" making mortar is not acting in accord with his nature. He is acting contrary to it. As a result, when he does act in accord with his nature, he is, even if only momentarily, turning his back on mortar. And when he does that, he jeopardizes survival.

---

4. "The Taboo of Virginity," in *Selected Works* (London: Hogarth Press, 1953–1966), pp. 198–199.

5. It has been suggested that the serpent who tempted Eve was actually a symbol of man's instinctual nature. If that is so, then Eve's temptation to Adam would represent an instinctual force at work, which, of course, is what I am suggesting here.

Because men *must* assert themselves in a most unnatural way to produce mortar, they must also exercise control over their sexual instincts. In fact, this need is so imperative that during the course of terrestrialization, control of sexual activity was shifted to the cerebral cortex so that it could be placed under conscious control. And the need for this control stems from the existence of terrestrial priorities that must be observed if man is to survive. First comes the hunt; second, war; third, cannibalism (slavery); fourth, training for the hunt. It is only when all factors relating specifically to the hunt are provided for that man can proceed to the fifth: sex. Since, in the rest of animal life, sex is an instinctual matter, the presence of a receptive female will cause the male to respond to her sexual signals by appropriate action. In the human species this cannot be allowed; the presence of female sexual signals at any moment could seriously interfere with mortar production. To forestall such a possibility, human sexual activity was placed under the control of the cerebral cortex.

This situation—the intertwining of sustenance and sex—has no counterpart in all of nature. In nature they are separate and distinct activities. With man they are tightly intertwined, with the male doing the intertwining.

In this regard we must observe the simultaneous operations of two previously separate and distinct functions as they slowly but inevitably come together, locking themselves into an unbreakable embrace. First is the familiar hunt. Since this artificial invention of man required almost all the conscious efforts of those responsible for its production, man had consciously to order the priorities of human existence. We have already seen these priorities. At the same time, and quite independent of masculine concern with mortar, was the female estrus cycle, a biological cycle that bore no relation to the artifice of mortar. Females, in this system, became sexually receptive on their own biological terms, which might or might not coincide with the sexual availability of the male. This is extremely important because unless the male sought to copulate with the female during the appropriate phase of the estrus cycle, the female would not accept him. The reproductive system of the species would be in jeopardy.

Something had to give. Obviously, the hunt could not fall back to allow the estrus system to function on its own terms. Sustenance comes before sex. So the estrus system had to give way to something that could subordinate itself to the needs of the male and his hunt and yet still provide for the reproductive needs of the species. The solution was the shift from the estrus cycle to the menstrual cycle—in terms of sexual receptivity.

The consequences of this shift have been enormous. Aside from the almost pure philosophical point that nature had to defer to artifice in an essential of existence, there is the matter of the sexual inviolability of the female giving way to violability.

In the estrus system it was the cyclical condition of the female that determined the time of copulation, the sole purpose of the system being to assure maximum prospects of impregnation. The key to the system was the sexual receptivity of the female; she allowed copulation only during the period when conception could take place. When she was ready, she sent out sexual signals such as swelling and coloration of the genital area, odor, and even sexual solicitation.

But once the shift set in, an entirely different situation was created—a situation that allowed a split between sexual activities and reproductive activities. With the new system, the female, *from the male point of view*, becomes sexually available 90 percent of the time, in contrast to only about 10 percent of the time under the estrus system. However, *from the female point of view*, she is reproductively receptive in precisely the limited way she had been while in the estrus system. As a consequence of the shift from one system to another, sexual activity began to be divorced from reproductive activity. Sexual activity came under the control of the male, while reproductive activity remained the province of the female. But from the male point of view, in the new system his sexual needs were provided for, and therefore the system was satisfactory. This, then, left the female in a situation where she had to violate her own sexual nature, which had always been related directly to reproduction. She was obliged to receive the male sexually when he wished it if she wished to survive, for it was the male who provided her with sustenance.

Every effort has been made to assure women that their subordinate position—socially and sexually—is perfectly natural. This assurance, it need hardly be added, has been given them by men, aided and abetted by a few functionary women who, obedient to the bell of sustenance, have echoed male assurances. A perusal of the literature—indeed, the actual experience of living—makes it clear that woman has but one function, and that is sexual. From Sumer to America, woman has been nothing but a pudendum. No. Worse, for when we peer at the pudendum long enough we begin to realize the full extent of female deficiency: She lacks a penis.

Nothing in all the analyses of humanity better reveals the sexual bias of men than the matter of the penis: With it you are everything; without it you are nothing. Indeed, so dogmatic is this belief that one is tempted to think of the penis as less a sexual organ than as a shillelagh with which to keep women in their place.

Nowhere is this thinking better exemplified than in Freud's "On the Sexual Theories of Children." It is a grim and terrifying view of a child's introduction to sex. There is, as Freud expressed it, the boy's "horror" upon discovering that a woman lacks a penis; a small girl's envy and shame upon discovering the boy's penis and her own lack of one; the child's struggle to grasp the mystery of reproduction, and especially the violence that children are said to impute to parental intercourse. "Whatever detail it may be that comes under their observation, [or fantasy]," Freud insisted, "in all cases they arrive at

. . . what we may call the *sadistic conception of coitus*, seeing in it something that the stronger person inflicts on the weaker one by force." [6]

In order to appreciate the problem of perspective, we must confront a most extraordinary statement by Sylvia Brody, a psychoanalyst who followed in Freud's footsteps. Indeed, she dogged them.

In the act of giving birth there is an efflorescence of masochistic and narcissistic gratifications (both often heightened by the high values placed upon natural child-birth). It is regarded as normal that for some time after delivery the ego boundary between the mother and her infant, who is partner to her gratification, is tenuous. [Helene] Deutsch . . . has described the simultaneous identity of mother and infant, the perception of the moving fetus as a moving penis, the unity of ego libido (narcissistic) and object of libido, the climactic expulsion of the incorporated object, and the reunion both achieved in lactation. From the beginning of the child's life, the mother's psychic freedom to invest the child with object libido partly depends upon her unconscious fantasy of him. If she perceives the child as a penis lost all over again, then the child will bear the brunt of her hostile envy in some more or less direct form. If she perceives the child as a penis regained, hers at last, its narcissistic value may be so great that she will have little object libido available for it. The situation will be different if she has accepted her femininity and feels her female sexuality as a positive biological and social attribute, because then her remaining dependence upon the child to restore her (the mother's) masculine narcissism will be less disturbing. [7]

---

6. *The Sexual Enlightenment of Children* (New York: Collier Books, 1963), p. 35.

7. *Patterns of Mothering* (New York: International Universities Press, 1956), p. 384.

Yet Freud and Brody are really the spiritual descendants of another writer who viewed the entire matter of sex and reproduction with unfeigned horror, notwithstanding the fact (or maybe because of the fact) of his own youthful rampant sexuality. I am referring to St. Augustine (A.D. 354–430), the Christian champion of Platonic thought and the arbiter of Christian morals for many centuries. In *The City of God* (XIV, 26) he offered his own thoughts on how infant generation might have taken place before the Fall:

> In such happy circumstances and general well-being [as existed in Paradise] we should be far from suspecting that offspring could not have been begotten without the disease of lust, but those parts, like all the rest, would be set in motion at the command of the will; and without the seductive stimulus of passion, with calmness of mind and with no corruption of the integrity of the body, the husband would lie upon the bosom of his wife. Nor ought we not to believe this because it cannot be proved by experiment. But rather, since no wild heat of passion would arouse those parts of the body, but a spontaneous power, according to the need, would be present.

Between Augustine, Freud, and Brody we have a triad of thought concerning human sexuality. Augustine wanted none of it. However, he accepted the generation of children, but only that they might eventually become citizens of the City of God. To him, the erect penis was anathema. Freud showed how everything sexual, when perceived by the child, was essentially traumatic, and that intercourse was a sadistic act. Brody then takes the matter on, viewing human sexuality from the reproductive perspective. Unfortunately, she can't see the child for the penis. Whether it is Penis Lost or Penis Found makes no difference, since the mother and child will suffer whichever way it goes.

In their thinking the basic standard is founded on the penis. If you possess one, you meet the standard; if you lack one, you are deficient. Naturally, everyone wants to meet the standard, and so those deprived of a penis envy those who have one. To get one, one might even have to visit Brody's fantasy world to find it.

Lisa Hobbs gives us a new look at this whole matter in *Love and Liberation* when she writes:

> Obviously, Freud was as incapable of understanding woman as a Florida cracker is incapable of understanding the black man. The harvest of his mentality is in his writing and nowhere is there a true accounting of the female spirit. There is not a whisper of female intellectuality, spirit, courage, insight, strength, unless it travels along the domestic route of Freud's approval. Like a gynecologist, he sat on a stool for fifty years before an imaginary stirruped woman, his eyes and mind fixated on her vagina. When he got up after fifty years he knew as much about real woman as the day he sat down. One wonders about his female patients whose cases he so meticulously recorded, those poor, wealthy, neurotic middle-class women suffocated by the domesticated roles that were strangling their psychic lives. One wonders why so many of them showed signs of hysteria. Could it not have been more the result of the treatment than the disease? [8]

There is a refreshing quality to Hobbs's invective. It is as if finally someone were audacious enough to suggest that "Freud has no clothes on." Also, her comparison of Freud to a Florida cracker is illustrative of the essential problem: The oppressor, to justify his oppression, must dehumanize the oppressed. Just as for centuries white people have characterized the black as intellectually deficient and sexually deficient (in the sense of being sexually irresponsible), so thinkers like Freud have dehumanized women. If anything could be said to dominate white thinking about black men, it is penis-envy, a con-

---

8. New York: McGraw-Hill, 1970, p. 56.

sequence of the myth of the black man's penis being bigger than the white man's. According to Freud, women envy men their penises.

Hobbs confronts the matter of "penis envy" formidably when she writes:

> The reality of Freud's existence *as a man* would surely lie in the authenticity of his relationship with women. Yet there is no evidence that he ever experienced this reality or realized its meaning or importance, or even suspected its existence. Not for a moment . . . does Freud appear to suspect himself or what his image of a desirable male-female relationship reveals about his own relationship with half the world. . . . His theory of "penis envy," springing from a basic faith in the superiority of the male, is basic to the whole psychiatric system to this day. The facts appear to me somewhat differently. Both sexes are drawn to possess one another's attributes, she to possess his penis, he to possess her vagina and breasts. This is not an expression of "envy" but rather proof of the basic dynamic of nature—the drawing together of the opposite and complementary sexes.[9]

There is, as Hobbs suggests, more than a penis between a male and female. Rather than Freud and his followers playing the game of "Penis, penis, who's got the penis?" as if the matter were one of theft and counter-theft, efforts should be made to see the *totality* of the bisexual nature of mammalian life. For example, and a baleful one at that, what if *both* males and females had lovely, sturdy, swinging penises? [10]

Freud's basic flaw was to mistake the penis for the whole man and to conclude that the absence of one made the woman somehow deficient. What Freud needed was to escape from

---

9. Ibid., p. 57.
10. Indeed, it is often observed that the clitoris is a small penis. In this event, any deficiencies would have to be based on size, thus basing envy on what the measuring tape says.

nineteen centuries of Christian culture, a cumulative process that reached its apotheosis in nineteenth-century genteel (if not necessarily gentile) Vienna, where female hysteria was as much a social disease as is twentieth-century body odor. If he could have risen above his times, Freud might have seen beyond the strictures of contemporary mores and might have seen into the authentic sexual nature of men and women, which is that stated by Hobbs: The sexes complement each other. Unfortunately Freud, so deeply immersed in contemporary neurosis, assumed that what appeared normal (that is, what seemed to work) was indeed actually normal. What never seems to have occurred to him was the neurosis of all of society insofar as it related to sex and the relationships between men and women. This, then, is one of his greatest deficiencies: His therapy had the purpose of reforming the individual so that he might better adjust to his society.

Freud not only established the masculine as the standard of human normality; he went further and established the late-nineteenth-century male as the standard of maleness. The nineteenth-century paterfamilias must stand as the most terrestrialized of all male figures. He was the end-product of countless centuries' struggle by the species to achieve a base on which to build neo-arborea. While it was the Industrial Revolution that allowed man to draw up the specifications for his project, it was the century encompassing the second half of the nineteenth and the first half of the twentieth that allowed man to engage in the Production Revolution. Under the banner of this revolution, man rallied all his forces. He dedicated his own best efforts in the cause of this revolution, and in addition, he dedicated woman's best efforts at bearing and nurturing infants. Because women were too arboreal for what man had in mind, the control of bearing and nurturing were taken over by men. Men became doctors in attendance at birth and they became pediatricians, prescribing for children.

Men also became the prescribers for women and their emotional ills. The first practitioner was Freud, and the medicine he offered was swallowed by both men and women. That what he offered was at best a placebo escaped everyone's notice for a very long time.

What made it work for so long was the fact that it helped finish off the terrestrialization process. Freudian thought, as exemplified by Freud and neo-Freudians, sought to conform everything so that it would better assist in the production of mortar. Freud, of course, didn't think in these terms. He thought in terms of civilization. He saw instinct, especially that manifested by human sexuality, as the great menace. And so, he wrote the following:

> . . . it is indeed one of the most important social tasks of education to restrain, confine, and subject to an individual control (itself identical with the demands of society) the sexual instinct when it breaks forth in the form of the reproductive function. In its own interests, accordingly, society would postpone the child's full development until it has attained a certain stage of intellectual maturity, since educability practically ceases with the full onset of the sexual instinct. Without this the instinct would break all bounds and the laboriously erected structure of civilization would be swept away.[11]

From his central viewpoint deep in the current of ongoing society, Freud saw the menace backward. He saw sexuality as threatening society. Yet in the following sentences, Freud sees the problem of society but nevertheless fails to see that it is society that should change, not man's sexual nature:

> Nor is the task of restraining it [man's sexual instinct] ever an easy one. . . . At bottom Society's motive is economic; since it has not the means enough to support life for its members without work on their part, it must see to it that the number of those members is restricted and

---

11. *A General Introduction to Psychoanalysis* (New York: Boni and Liveright, 1963), p. 273. This passage was originally written in 1920.

their energies directed away from sexual activities onto
their work—the eternal primordial struggle for existence,
therefore, persisting to the present day [1920].[12]

Freud was observing the priorities: first the hunt and its
subordinate activities, then sex. That is why he and his followers viewed woman as they did. She did not contribute to
the hunt. If anything, she threatened the hunt by her arboreal
and thus instinctual ways. Since, because of circumstances beyond her control, she was restricted to sexual matters, it was
her sexuality that men in their hunting mood viewed as the
great menace, as did Augustine centuries earlier.

There was, in this type of thinking, a very serious flaw:
Without human sexuality there could be no continuity of
the species. What complicated the matter was the divorce of
sexual activity, with its emphasis on pleasure, from reproductive activity, with its emphasis on the production of offspring.
Freud approached the problem this way:

> . . . it is a characteristic common to all . . . perver-
> sions that in them reproduction as an aim is put aside.
> This is actually the criterion by which we judge whether
> a sexual activity is perverse—if it departs from reproduc-
> tion in its aims and pursues the attainment of gratification
> independently. . . . The gulf and turning point in the de-
> velopment of the sexual life lies at the point of its sub-
> ordination to the purposes of reproduction. Everything
> that occurs before this conversion takes place, and every-
> thing which refuses to conform to it and serves the pursuit
> of gratification alone, is called by the unhonored title of
> "perversion" and as such is despised.[13]

And there we have it: Sex is to be put to the service of the
hunt. Sexual activity for its own sake, once it became split
from its strictly utilitarian function, that of reproduction, must

---

12. Ibid., p. 273.
13. Ibid., p. 277.

be held as a perversion lest it interfere with the hunt. What can be said of sex in what should now be called the Freudian Century that endured during the century of the Production Revolution, can be said of all human pleasures: They must be subordinated to the great hunt.

In the terrestrial mode of existence there has been little room or time for play. Just as one never sees the scalers of great mountains larking about lest they all fall and perish, so too the climb out of man's terrestrial prison has been too serious a venture to be sidetracked—or even untracked—by diversionary play or pleasure. It is a curiosity of human history that those at the very bottom who must work the very hardest have the most brutal and unrelieved lives, while those at the top—those who demonstrate their temporal success by the very fact of being at the top—have room in their lives for great leisure and almost unrelieved pleasure. In this connection, the work of Kinsey and others shows that the very poor of society have the most restrictive and reproduction-oriented sexual lives of society, while the more successful and educated emphasize the pleasure aspect of sex, in the course of which those practices termed "perversions" by Freud and traditional moralists are widely employed—and enjoyed.

While this might at first seem to be an anomaly, in fact it isn't, for the reason that those on the bottom of the economic heap—and they are the broad base of a pyramid—are seeking by dint of very hard work to arrive at the top, where neo-arborea is to be found. And once it has been found, there is no real need for hard work or productivity, including reproductive productivity. It is at this point that sexual pleasure can be enjoyed, and is, for its own sake.

But all that is to advance the discussion beyond the limits set by Freud and others who could not glimpse neo-arborea because they were in the midst of the great nineteenth-century hunt. Their standards, being imposed by the demands of the hunt, established the primacy of the masculine and the subordination of the feminine.

What, then, is it like to be in the feminine, and hence inferior, state demanded by men? Vivian Gornick tells us in blistering terms:

The terror of felt sexuality is the terror of our lives; the very essence of our existence. It pervades the culture, manifesting itself not only in the bodies of religious codes but in every aspect of moral law, every nuance of custom, every trace of human exchange, soaking through social intercourse: it is there in restaurants, on busses, in ships, on country roads, and on city streets; in university appointments and government decisions and pleasure trips and the popular arts. Everywhere—like some pernicious covering—can be felt the influence of that fear of the sexual self that has destroyed our childhoods, scarred our adolescences, forced us into loveless marriages, made of us dangerously repressed and corrupt people, and sometimes driven us mad. And deeply interwoven in the fabric of the cultural cloak is the image of woman: woman the temptress; woman the slut; woman the heartless bitch—luring men eternally toward spiritual death, making them come up against what they most fear and hate in themselves, pulling them down into the pit of themselves. . . . Woman herself is not locked in this profound struggle with the self; she is only the catalyst for man's struggle with himself. It is never too certain that woman has any self at all. What *is* certain is that onto woman is projected all that is worst in man's own view of himself, all that is primitive, immature, and degrading. In woman man has a kind of reverse reflection of himself: all of his sloth and weakness is there in full vibrance, and only a shadow of those higher emotions that will flame into full life in himself alone.[14]

14. "Woman as Outsider," in *Woman in Sexist Society*, edited by Vivian Gornick and Barbara K. Moran (New York: Basic Books, 1971), p. 78.

Gornick does a superb job in establishing the very basis of feminine existence: the terror of felt sexuality. When we read on, we quickly discern the cause of this terror: the rules of terrestrial existence by which the function of woman is established. Gornick also reveals the terror felt by the male. She observes that the man projects on the woman "all that is worst in man's own view of himself, all that is primitive, immature . . ." What she is saying, even if only indirectly, is that man fears his own arboreality ("all his sloth and weakness") in face of his terrestrial obligations.

What is probably most important in what Gornick says is her assertion that "It is never too certain that woman has any self at all . . ."

Woman possesses a quiddity, there can be no doubt about that, just as there can be no doubt about the quiddity of man. Each possesses an essential nature. It is when we come to the reflective matter of the self-image that we run head-on into the problem. And this most especially concerns the self-image of woman. In fact, this is so much of a problem that it might be better to say that woman does not have an image of self, but rather has adopted as her own the "self" prepared for her by man.

Dependency does not restrict itself to matters of sustenance. Just as the central element of mortar determines the nature and extent of all supportive and subsidiary mortar elements, so too the dependency of woman on man determines all the subsidiary elements of the relationship. This is inevitable. The purpose of mortar is to preserve a species profile in contact with that of the environment. The principal need for this contact is to assure sustenance. Around this core element everything collects on the principle that mortar attracts mortar. As far as woman is concerned the same principles hold true. She must present a "species" profile to man in order to maintain contact with the profile he, her "environment," projects. Failure to do this means extinction. And just as the profile of the terrestrial environment demands a great variety of accommodations by the species, so too the profile projected by man demands a great variety of accommodations by woman. Thus, if the men of a society demand that women wear veils and be totally segregated, they obey; if men demand submissive women with small appetites, they obey. To disobey is to lose contact with the profile of their "environment."

The matter can be put this way: The environment sets the terms of species existence; man sets the terms of woman's existence. Now, as we know, for the species to adapt to the terrestrial mode of existence it had to compensate for its genetic deficiencies by way of mortar. It did this by means of brain function. The same is true of woman. She has had to superimpose on her biological nature a network of mortar in order to survive in her "environment." She has done this by her brain or, as is often said, by her wits.

Just as the terrestrial environment has not been able to change the essential nature of the species because of its use of mortar, so too, man has not been able to change the essential nature of woman. She is, by virtue of her biology, the perpetuator of the species. Nothing can change that. What man has sought to do, however, is establish the terms of her functioning in this capacity. These terms are at sharp variance with those established by her true nature.

So there is a stress between the terms of woman's true nature and the terms of woman's existence as established by man. This, as might be expected, produces stress within woman. Her biological nature drives her in one direction; man seeks to drive her in another. Nowhere is this more clearly manifested than in the matter of sexual activity, and nowhere else is the problem of self-image or self-identity better revealed.

Rape is the ultimate death wish. It is the death wish operating at a level of self-sealing internalization. Men must come up against the external to give life to their expressive longing for violence, but women, in the grip of that same longing, come up against themselves. The woman's dream of rape is that of being pierced, torn, violated, challenged for her very existence by man. . . .

Implicit in the dream of rape is woman's true sense of herself, her true subconscious understanding of the actual position of value which she occupies in the life of the culture, her dread, long-felt conviction that she was not real to men. Her fantasies of rape are a culmination of the fact that she has always *been* raped. She is, preeminently, an object of lust; a creature upon whom the darker desires are realized; a source of release, of tension gathered and tension exploded; a creature with whom the agony of passion and the morbid fear of sexuality are associated.[15]

Woman's fear of rape stems from man's effort to distort her sexual nature. She cannot control the terms of her own sexuality; she must, as in all things, accept the terms laid down by man. We can begin to see the degree of violent stress experienced by woman in this situation when we compare it with that of any other female mammal who is sought for sexual assault by a male. Though such an eventuality is rare in nature, in those instances when it has been observed what the observer sees is a violent retaliation by the female. Under no circumstances will she allow a sexual assault by the male when she is not sexually receptive. She will turn and fight off the male with all the strength at her command.[16]

If woman, for any reason, rebels against the system in which she finds herself, she is labeled a neurotic, and she is treated accordingly. That is, she must submit to rape or pay the penalty.

The premise on which all traditional therapy for woman has been based has been her lack of sexual originality: She is a deficient male. She has been castrated and spends her life guilty of penis envy. If and when she reaches a point of maturity

---

15. Gornick, op. cit., pp. 76–77.
16. Sexual assaults among primates are not to be confused with acts of submission, which sometimes include "sexual mounting." These acts can include males as well as females.

where she gives up penis envy and accepts her own sexuality, she becomes normal and healthy.

Maria Torok, a psychoanalyst, in *Female Sexuality*, published as recently as 1970, opens her discussion of castration and penis envy by asking several questions. "Why is the feeling of castration and its corollary, penis envy, the universal lot of womanhood? Why do women so often renounce creative activity, their means of making the world? Why do they agree to shut themselves up in 'woman's quarters,' to 'be quiet in church,' in short, to prefer a dependent state?" [17]

What is important about Torok's analysis is her accommodation to subservience. She starts a most remarkable journey into obfuscation by throwing away the penis in, mind you, an essay on penis envy. She does so in these words:

> . . . [T]he penis itself—considered as a thing, an objective, biological, or even sociological reality—must be left aside in this essay on penis envy. For the penis itself is not involved in penis envy. . . . This part-object turns out to be an *ad hoc* invention to camouflage a desire. . . .
>
> However disguised, however hidden, the desire underlying penis envy cannot fail to show through. . . . *Penis envy will disappear by itself the day the patient no longer has that painful feeling of deficiency which caused it.* [Italics added] [18]

Essentially, a woman will drop all vestiges of penis envy when she has achieved mature female sexuality. According to

---

17. "The Significance of Penis Envy in Women," edited by Janine Chasseguet-Smirgel (Ann Arbor: University of Michigan Press, 1970), p. 167. (These questions clearly reveal Torok's failure to appreciate the true situation of woman. That she is a woman herself is beside the point. She is what in the idiom of the human rights movement would be called a "house maid," just as certain blacks are called "house niggers." Whether "maid" or "nigger," each is conforming to the rule of species profiles' conforming to the environment that provides sustenance. Undoubtedly, in Torok's case, the sustenance she depended on was "professional sustenance," something that could only be obtained by conforming to the profile projected by Freudians and neo-Freudians.)

18. Ibid., pp. 137–138.

Torok, penis envy obstructs orgastic completion, being an effort to repress genital fulfillment. However, we must remember that the penis is irrelevant. At best it is a screen behind which a woman's real desire lurks:

> Many women have the fanciful idea that the male sex organ possesses supreme qualities: infinite power for good or evil, a guarantee of its possessor's security, absolute freedom, immunity against anxiety or guilt, and a promise of pleasure, love and fulfillment of all his wishes. *Penis envy is always envy of an idealized penis.* [Italics in original] [19]

Yet, even the idealized penis is a screen. Behind that screen are anal-pregenital conflicts, as well as a specific, total or partial, inhibition of masturbation, or orgasm, and their concomitant fantasy activities. Torok then takes her next step in this curious psychic adventure:

> Penis envy appears now to be a disguised claim—not for the organ and the attribute of the other sex—but for *one's own desires for maturation and development by means of the encounter with oneself in conjunction with orgastic experiences and sexual identification.* [Italics in original] [20]

The point Torok is striving for is female maturity because its attainment will overcome penis envy. Maturity as a woman, it must be pointed out, means to fulfill woman's role of being passive, receptive, masochistic, and narcissistic. Torok clearly acknowledges woman's dependence on man. She explains it in terms of a mastery and rivalry blockage of the exit from the anal stage in a way that requires her to make herself into an appendage of the mother and later into the "phallus" of her husband who, in Torok's frame of reference, is the heir to the anal mother-image. In all of this, and leading to blockage, is female guilt!

This most extraordinary psychoanalytic legerdemain that

---

19. Ibid., p. 139.
20. Ibid., p. 142.

places woman in the sexual role and position of subservience in such a way as to assure her that both are normal and healthy, is genius born of desperation. What would happen, for example, if Torok, Freud, et al. had said that penis envy was just that, penis envy; and that woman's repudiation of this envy was neurotic, as was her acceptance of dependence? The fabric of society would be rent—as it is being today by such writers as Alix Shulman who, in *Woman in Sexist Society*, writes:

> . . . [O]ne wonders what might have been defined as the major male and female sex organs, the standard sexual position, the psychic "tasks of development" as Freud called them, and in fact, masculinity and femininity themselves, if women instead of men had composed not only the medical profession, but the dominant caste in society as well.[21]

In opposition to Torok et al., I would suggest that penis envy is one of woman's healthiest complaints. In virtually every society woman is subservient and dependent.[22] From her earliest moments the small girl and small boy are developed differently in terms of their self-concept and in terms of what is expected of them. The boy is to be aggressive, decisive, forceful, stoical; the girl is to be passive, receptive, submissive, emotional. Inevitably, every girl who becomes a woman has that moment of insight when she discovers herself, not so much in terms of her own identity, but in terms of her status in male-dominated society. She discovers herself *functionally*, and in so doing finds herself in an escape-proof prison. There is but one way out of this prison and the key that unlocks the gate is the male penis. That is, as a woman she is a prisoner; but with the male key in her possession she can unlock the gate and be free. She does not want the penis to be part of her; this would deny her own sex-

---

21. "Organs and Orgasms," op. cit., p. 204.
22. Exceptions are the Arapesh and Tchambuli societies in New Guinea. See Margaret Mead, *Sex and Temperament in Three Primitive Societies*, for details.

ual identity. She wants the *power* identified with the symbolic penis.[23] It is only when women have power that they can exist on independent and equal terms with men. Women don't want to deny their biology, for to do so would be to deny their own existence; what women want is to be free of male domination; women want unobstructed access to the meeting of their sustenance (and other) needs without being dependent on men for the meeting of these needs; also, women want their sexuality to serve *their* needs; women want to be the measure of their existence. Women want to be women, not "deficient males."

Nowhere in psychoanalytic literature is woman's subservience to the male principle better demonstrated than in the analysis of the sex act. Helene Deutsch, once described as more Freudian than Freud, takes on the task of examining the psychology of the sex act with ruthless loyalty to the male principle:

> The feminine woman, who is characterized by her struggle for a harmonious accord between the narcissistic forces of self-love and the masochistic forces of dangerous and painful giving, celebrates her greatest triumphs in her sexual functioning. In the sexual act her partner's elemental desire gratifies her self-love and helps her to accept masochistic pleasure without damaging her ego, while the psychologic promise of a child creates a satisfying future prospect for both tendencies.[24]

This is a devastating summary of human sexual relations. In Deutsch's terms, a "feminine" woman is passive, receptive, masochistic, and narcissistic. That is, she is Torok's female who has to struggle for an accord between her needs of self-love and

---

23. Simone de Beauvoir, in *The Second Sex*, expresses it this way: ". . . the childish desire (of the woman) for the penis is important in the life of the adult woman only if she feels her femininity as a mutilation; and then it is as a symbol of all the privileges of manhood that she wishes to appropriate the male organ."
24. *The Psychology of Women* (New York: Grune and Stratton, 1945), 2: 105.

"masochistic forces of dangerous and painful giving." Significant in this is the absence of any inquiry as to why "giving"
in the sexual act must be both dangerous and painful. What is
present, however, is the tacit admission that sexual intercourse
for the woman entails suffering. What is truly remarkable in
her thinking is the notion that suffering can be pleasurable.

According to Deutsch, sexual intercourse for both men and
women serves two related objectives: individual sexual satisfaction and reproduction. In the man, the reproductive function is joined to the sexual satisfaction he derives from the act.
In the woman, whatever pleasure she experiences is a prize
added, more or less like a bonus, to "her service to the species,"
i.e., reproduction. This difference between the experience of the
man and that of the woman according to Deutsch, results from
two circumstances:

> 1. In man, somatic satisfaction through the pleasurable
> discharge of the germ plasm and disposition of this plasm
> in a safe and fostering body are integral parts of a *single*
> act. The service to the species takes place at the same time
> as the sexual satisfaction and can subsequently be com-
> pletely disregarded by him.
>
> In woman, the goal of her germ plasm, that is to say, her
> service to the species, is realized only much later, after a
> certain fixed interval of time. . . .
>
> 2. Man can entrust the whole function to a *single* organ,
> while woman suffers from an overendowment, so to speak,
> which leads to complications . . .[25]

It is in these "complications" that we find the core of woman's difficulties. According to both Freud and Deutsch (as well
as their followers) there is a great struggle within the woman as
to which shall be her sex organ: the clitoris or the vagina. The
immature, neurotic woman clings to the clitoris, claiming it for
her sex organ. The mature woman sees to it that the clitoris

---

25. Ibid., pp. 77–78.

"resigns," transferring its pleasure sensations to the vagina. And it is here, in this remarkable myth of the struggle between the clitoris and the vagina, that we see the context in which female sexuality is forced to exist. It is the struggle between female sexual pleasure and male sexual pleasure. Intimately involved is the reproductive function of coitus (as distinguished from sexual pleasure).

From the man's point of view, the clitoris contributes nothing either to his sexual pleasure or to his urge for reproduction. Indeed, many men probably have never discovered the actual site of the clitoris. Of those who have, most probably ignore it, being too intent on their own pleasure, which directly involves the vagina, for it is the vagina that receives and embraces the penis and affords the occasion of stimulation so essential to male orgasm and ejaculation, thus advertently or inadvertently leading to the possibility of reproduction.

From the woman's point of view, it is the clitoris that provides pleasure, while the vagina provides babies. Between the man and the woman, therefore, we have a monumental cross-purpose. In terms of pleasure alone, the male doesn't need the clitoris, and the female doesn't need the penis.[26] In terms of reproduction, neither needs the clitoris and both need the penis and vagina. This, then, produces inevitable pleasure for the man, problematic pleasure for the woman, and for her, greater prospects for pregnancy. These are biological facts.

What complicates the situation are the social facts, and this is where Freud and Deutsch, as well as others, play such a pivotal role. By the myth, long since demolished, that the mature "feminine" woman transfers clitoral pleasure to the vagina, the woman's pleasure is thus lodged where it will do the *man* the most good. By outlawing clitoral pleasure, under the

---

26. That the penis stimulates the clitoral area is incidental to what the male does during coitus. In masturbation, which often is the only means for many women to achieve orgasm, the penis is totally absent. In both hetero- and homosexual relationships, of course, cunnilingus may also produce orgasm. The point is clear that clitoral pleasure is not dependent on the penis.

claim that it is an infantile form of sexuality at best, and by enthroning the vagina as the seat of female sexual pleasure, man forces woman to experience the sexual act on his terms. Whatever pleasure the woman derives from sexual intercourse is merely incidental to male pleasure.

It would seem—though the evidence is scant—that the development of the female orgasm came about in order to offset the problem of rape.

In the beginning, during the arboreal period, primate sexuality concerned itself exclusively with reproduction. Geoffrey Bourne observes that among the great apes there is little evidence that the female experiences any kind of orgasm. He relates the development of the female orgasm to erect posture. Desmond Morris, in *The Naked Ape*, suggests that nature supplied the human female with an orgasm in order to induce her into remaining in a horizontal position, relaxed and sleepy, after coitus in order to prevent the semen from oozing out of the vagina, which in an erect posture would fall because of gravity.

I would suggest a different reason, although both Bourne's and Morris's explanations may be contributory. The problem, as I see it, was rape. As I have already said, in nature a female not sexually receptive will refuse the male. As we have seen from the earlier discussion here, the estrus system gave way to the menstrual, and for the reasons set forth. However, the female's sexual receptivity remained unchanged. She could only conceive at certain times, regardless of what sexual activities might be engaged in at other times. However, there still remained the problem—and it was a genetic one—of the female refusing the male except during a limited phase of the cycle. Yet we know that women engage in sexual activities during nonconceptual phases of the menstrual cycle, and that they experience orgasm, and further, that when enjoying the pleasure aspect of sex, they manifest none of the rejection actions of the original primate.

Something, obviously, gave way. I believe the rejection principle gave way to the growing pleasure of sex as the orgasm began to make its appearance. I don't wish to play on words, but
since the female was absolutely dependent on the male, she
had to accept his sexual advances; thus we can see that she had
to make the best of it, and the only way she could do this was
to "lie back and enjoy it." Just as there was a shift, because of
selective pressures, from the estrus to the menstrual system, so
too, and at the same time, there were selective pressures away
from the rejection mechanism and toward the orgasm so as to
transform a rape into a sexually acceptable situation.

What bolsters this argument is the tenuous nature of the
orgasm. Man, whose orgasm and ejaculation are essential to
reproduction, can perform sexually with almost any woman
whether he cares for her or not. Woman, on the other hand,
seems to have an orgasm during interpersonal sex only when
the emotional climate is conducive to it. It is, of course, significant that in stressful situations the woman cannot reach an
orgasm, while in many instances, when alone and masturbating,
she can. It follows from this that the rejection mechanism is
functioning when the woman experiences no sexual pleasure
with a man and suffers from the all-too-common problem of
frigidity.

We can see the obverse of this principle in those situations
where, for whatever reason, a woman doesn't want sexual relations with a man. If she accepts him, no matter how reluctantly,
in most instances she will not have an orgasm, and what is
more, she will, even in the most subtle ways, let him know
about her reluctance. This, in turn, will affect the man so that
he will tend less and less to "impose" on the woman and instead wait for more certain signs that she is sexually receptive.

In less intimate relationships, we see the rejection principle
at work. An example—and they are legion—is the social situation where, for whatever reason, the male's sexual attraction to
the female is not returned in kind—again for whatever reason.
Any attempt on the man's part to become sexually intimate will

be rejected and almost always with social or emotional violence
If the man should persist, it is entirely possible that rape will
ensue, during which, despite her vigorous protests, the woman
will be "pierced, torn, violated, challenged for her very existence by man," as Gornick would put it.

However—and here we come the nub of the matter—should
the man succeed in *seducing* the woman, overcoming her rejection mechanism so that she will accept him sexually, sexual
intimacy may well result, at the culmination of which both man
and woman may have orgasms without either having the slightest thought of reproduction.

Among primates, and for that matter among mammalian life
in general, there is a direct relationship between the sexuality
of the female and that of the male. When the female is in
estrus, the male is sexually active; when the female is not, the
male is sexually inactive. In this system, the male in effect takes
his cue from the female. When the female is sexually receptive,
the male is sexually assertive; when she is not, the male is sexually dormant. There is a triggering mechanism present. The
female, who is the initiator, signals her sexual receptivity. This
signal triggers the sexual mechanism in the male and he takes
appropriate sexual action. This is not a seasonal matter among
primates the way it is among many mammal species. Everything
is tied to the matter of female receptivity, and as has been
pointed out earlier, female receptivity is signaled to the male
by what are generally termed "sexual signals," a combination
of one or more of the following: genital swelling, genital coloration, odor, and sexual solicitation which often takes the form of
"presenting."

When the species converted to the menstrual system, sexual
receptivity divided up into two forms of receptivity, that pertaining directly to sexual receptivity and that pertaining to
reproductive receptivity. From the male's point of view, there
has been no real way to ascertain reproductive receptivity, while
there has developed a whole network of "sexual signals" to ap-

prise the male of female sexual receptivity. These sexual signals, when transmitted to the male, trigger his sexual mechanism and he seeks to take appropriate sexual actions.

Such a system is virtually indistinguishable from that which existed when man's ancestors were arboreal primates—at least from the male's point of view. It is from the female's point of view that we perceive a significant difference, for when she signals, it could be that she is signaling that she is reproductively receptive or that she is sexually receptive, the two receptivities not being inevitably combined, though they may be.

This, then, brings us to a consideration of female sexual signals. As a preliminary matter, it must be observed that in humans, as among other primates, the signals must come from the female. There is no way for the male to send sex signals that will trigger a sexual mechanism in the female. A man might send signals by a variety of means and receive encouragement from the woman, but this is not the same as a signal triggering a mechanism. It is far more probable that the signals of the male (ineffective) are crossing those of the woman (effective).

Among humans, sexual signals are not as restrictive either in form or in purpose as they are with other primates. They cover a whole range of possibilities, from the purely biological to the social. The reason for this is that human sexuality has ranged extensively from the strict sexuality of arboreal primates. As the estrus system gave way to the menstrual, and as sexual activity drifted away from the purely reproductive process, sexual signals also began to drift from the strict limits established during the arboreal period. What complicated the entire development was the growing relationship between a designated female and a designated male which had, as its basis, female dependency. To secure her position vis-à-vis sustenance, the female had increasingly to insinuate herself with her designated male. To accomplish this necessary end, she developed a whole galaxy of sexual signals so as to bind the male more tightly to her sexually so that she could enhance her own survival prospects. And it is here, in this really desperate vortex, that female "beauty" came into the picture. The result of this has been to substitute the term "attractiveness" for that of "receptivity."

In the very simplest terms, the more attractive the woman, the greater her survival value. Attractiveness became a bargaining device for sustenance. Therefore, anything that served to make the female more attractive served as sexual signals to the male which, in turn, served her own needs of sustenance.

Attractiveness, as everyone knows, is extremely variable according to culture, and it covers a great variety of elements. First, logically, is physical attractiveness, that which is most often called "beauty." The girl-child may be pretty; only a woman can possess beauty. The child's body cannot emit sexual signals; a woman's can. When a girl crosses into puberty and begins to develop breasts and rounded hips, she becomes a woman as far as the man is concerned, and silently, her body speaking for her, she emits sexual signals which say, at the very least, that she is sexually alive. This fact alone is enough to trigger the sexual mechanism in the male.

In this matter of the body, particularly of the female breasts, I must take issue with Desmond Morris, who in *The Naked Ape* concluded that women's breasts were sexual signals. Under his theory, among male arboreal primates who copulate by means of a rear-entry into the female, the swollen genitals of the female serve as a sexual signal indicating receptivity, which of course is very true. His theory goes on to say that when man changed over to the woman-supine-subordinate, man-prone-superior system, the breasts evolved to their human size in order to act as sexual signals, more or less as a substitute for the old genital signaling system. The problem with this theory is that the breasts bear no relation whatever to sexual matters beyond that of being erogenous zones that sexually stimulate the female and not the male. But then, so do the ears, the mouth, the anus, and for some people, almost any part of the body.

There is a second problem with Morris's theory. In any number of cultures female breasts don't even serve as erogenous zones; they serve solely to feed babies.

Third, Morris confuses cause with effect. Contemporary female breasts are the result of a long process that began with ordinary primate breasts and ended with human breasts. The breasts at the onset of this process in no way could serve as sexual signals. A better way to put the matter is to say that some other principle was at work that adventitiously resulted in breasts that at the conclusion served as sexual signals, but to no greater extent than developing hips, pubic hair, and so on, all of which serve to indicate that the female has reached the reproductive stage of development. Breasts in and of themselves do not serve, nor have they ever served, as specific sexual signals: distinguishing a moment when the female is receptive to male sexual activity from a moment when she is not. In other words, breasts don't vary in any way so as to send appropriate sexual signals to the male.

Finally, and most important, a woman's breasts exist without any regard to her sexual receptivity. Breasts are a part of the anatomy, regardless of sexual cycles. They are a presence, not a sexual signal.

Why, then, human breasts as distinct from ordinary primate breasts? The answer lies with the needs of the suckling infant. When the female arboreal primate gives birth, the infant needs the mother's thick coat to cling to. Also, it will be recalled, most primate mothers do not assist the newborn in finding the nipples; the infant must climb the ventral surface to reach them. However, once it has found the nipples, the infant clings tightly to the mother's hair, fastens its mouth on the nipple, and sucks. Only infrequently will the mother assist the infant in nursing by holding it, and this only when she is not otherwise occupied.

When man's hominid ancestors were forced into the terrestrial mode of existence, as we have also seen, there was no longer a need to cling to the mother. Slowly the coat of hair disappeared. This resulted in a new and difficult situation for both infant and mother. There was no hair for the infant to cling to as it suckled. Therefore, the mother had to hold it as it nursed, and she had to hold the infant high up against her chest so that the infant could reach the nipple. Now, if the

nipple were a bit lower, it would be much easier on the mother.
Under this pressure, the nipple was slowly lowered to a position where, cradled in the mother's arm, the infant could reach
it. Stretching to present the nipple to the infant was the
breast.[27]

However, breasts may be a type of sexual signal, depending
on the culture and what the woman does to "present" them to
males. This, of course, has to do with the entire matter of female attractiveness—which is, for humans, almost entirely a
cultural matter once the female's body has matured to the reproductive age. What is germane to the present discussion is
not the great variety of signals that woman can send out. What
is critical is their great number.

In arborea, and within the confines of the affinity group,
there is at most an intermittent sending of signals. If we can
assume an average group of around forty primates, that would
mean that possibly half would be subadult. Of the twenty
adults, half would be male. That would leave ten adult females.
Of those ten, some would be pregnant, others would be nurturing infants, and some might be on the trailing end of their
procreative careers. That would mean that only a few adult
females would be in estrus at any one time and thereby sending
out sexual signals. And, finally, sex being what it is—a brief,
unemotional activity—there is not much involvement.[28]

In startling contrast to this is the human situation where,
instead of living in small groups, men live in large groups where
there are many adult females giving a full range of signals. And
what must be remembered in this is the fact that whatever the
interior state of the woman may be, it is only her outward state
that is perceived by the male—at least at some distance. Furthermore, in contrast to the arboreal primate situation, women

---

27. Elaine Morgan, in *The Descent of Woman*, comes more or less to
the same conclusion about breasts, although the setting for the development of woman's special breasts is on the shores of the ocean.

28. There is the amusing picture in one of Jane Goodall's books showing a male chimpanzee eating a banana while copulating. Or should I
say the male was copulating while eating? It is difficult to tell.

are sexually receptive 90 percent of the time. The result of all this is that the male is constantly and forever receiving sexual signals that trigger his own sexual mechanism, thus thrusting him into a responsive situation.

Needless to say, the male cannot appropriately respond to the signals. To do so, even though it would be in keeping with his nature, would produce social chaos, thereby seriously jeopardizing mortar. The solution is social inhibition. As human sexuality slowly began to superimpose itself on the base of primate sexuality, it was accompanied by inhibiting processes so as to protect the mortar so necessary for survival. As has been suggested earlier, this inhibiting process was produced by the developing brain. Because of the problems caused by sexual signals as they developed in the terrestrialization process, sexual activity had to come under the authority of the developing cerebral cortex. In the same way, and for the same reasons, the female came under the authority of the male. It was a situation forced on the species by the terrestrialization process.

We can see the reverse of the authoritarian principle, both of human sexuality and of the male over the female, when we enter the post-hunt era and begin to approach neo-arborea. Under these conditions, which will be discussed at length in "Omega," the male ceases to be a significant "environment" of the female, as well as a less critical conduit to the satisfaction of her needs. Thus, there being less of a contingency relationship, especially between sustenance and sex, the female can approach sexual matters more on her terms than on those of the male. She begins to be a sexual subject rather than a sexual object.

In addition there is occurring today a diminution of utilitarianism with the concomitant relaxation of terrestrial inhibitions placed on human sexuality. In this state, we begin to see the female move out from under the authority of the male and begin to express her sexuality on her own terms, not those handed to her by the male.

This is also true of the female's reproductive activity: In recent years we have seen increased instances of women having babies without the consent or the postparturition support of the father. *She* has the baby, not they. It is her baby, not his. Also, increasingly, the female who becomes pregnant terminates the pregnancy on her own initiative and without the consent or approval of the male involved. What is more, in very recent years it has become possible for a woman to become pregnant without the physical presence of the male, by means of artificial insemination. We are even now on the threshold of an age in which the woman's body is not necessary; "test tube" babies are on the horizon.

THE CHEAT

I DOUBT very much whether there has ever lived a man or woman who has unhesitatingly and wholeheartedly embraced human existence. Everyone, from time immemorial, has sought in one way or another to ameliorate the terms of terrestrial living. Either an attempt has been made to alter the terms of existence so as to make them more tolerable, or an attempt has been made to alter the perception of immutable reality. In either event, it is clear that man has sought, one way or another, to make his life into something it is not: acceptable. He has done so for but one reason: to survive in circumstances for which nature has not prepared him.

Man has attempted through myriad ways to circumvent the demands of terrestrial existence in order to arrive at an existence whose terms are more in keeping with his nature. In "The Cradle" we saw how each infant begins life as an arboreal creature living (hopefully) in the mother-tree. We have also seen how, through the efforts of the mother (or surrogate), every infant is taken from its natural environment and, willy-nilly, deposited into the terrestrial mode of existence. There, through the good offices of mortar, that remarkable artifice for which man's brain was created, man struggles for survival as best he can.

Survival, yes; acceptance, no. This is the great peculiarity of man. Whereas all other forms of animal life—if our presumptions are at all correct—conform to and accept the terms of their natural existence, man struggles against accepting the terrestrial terms of his existence, even though they mean survival. Behind the ramparts of mortar there lurks a creature who seeks to overthrow tyrannical terrestrial demands and replace them with the more congenial terms of arborea. This, upon reflection, only makes sense. Millions of generations of genetic development are not to be denied. They create, if anything, a form of genetic imperative.

Terrestrial man is a creature in exile: He seeks to return home. This notion is not a fanciful nor a symbolic ambition, but is founded on man's genes. However, man does not seek consciously to return to arborea. His mind is not stuffed with nostalgia. It can't be, for the simple reason that man's conscious mind is not arboreal; it is the creation of terrestrial existence. What actually drives man toward arborea is his body. It seeks a state of existence for which its genetic composition prepared it. It seeks to shrug off the oppressive mantle of terrestrial demands, a mantle that weighs down every natural expression of the body, so that it can rid itself of stress almost beyond its ability to support.

But man is confined to the terrestrial mode, presumably forever. Therefore, there is no possibility of a return to arborea. What, then, of the body? Must it always support the oppressive mantle of terrestrial demands? In a sense, yes. But in a second sense, the body has never really accepted the mantle, and has slipped it off time after time after time, whenever the chance has presented itself. It does so in a thousand different ways. It has always been so; it will always be so as long as the species exists in the terrestrial mode.

The basic premise of survival is mortar. Everyone, male and female, whether directly or indirectly, must participate in its production. That is why males have traditionally been hunters and why females have been the producers of hunters. Of course, in more modern times both males and females have actively produced mortar, leaving much of child-rearing to surrogate mothers. Further, in the modern era, the hunt has been replaced by economic activity.

The purpose of economic activity is to provide for the sustenance needs of the body. In brief, man works "by the sweat of his brow" for his daily bread. Or, put differently, work is the means by which man feeds himself. The end is sustenance, the means is work. If such be the case, and the end is sustenance, what would happen if in a given instance someone circumvented the means and went directly to the end? What I am proposing is this: that one might seek to eat without working. What then? Well, to begin with, we would have a very natural activity. It is *work* that is unnatural. No other mammal works to eat; why should a grounded arboreal primate have to? We know the answer: in order to eat. But—and here is the point—it is not natural to have to engage in indirect transactions; it is natural to go directly from need to satisfaction. This latter forms the premise of the body's existence. It has been necessary, as part of terrestrial living, to enact an unnatural system whereby work—an indirect transaction—becomes an integral factor of existence.

This is superbly exemplified by the 1936 Constitution of the Union of Soviet Socialist Republics, in which Article 12 stipulates, "In the U.S.S.R. the principle of socialism is realized: 'From each according to his ability, to each according to his work.'" [1] The article also stipulates an even more demanding proposition: "He who does not work, neither shall he eat." Yet such an edict is no harsher than that placed by God on Adam after expulsion from the Garden of Eden.

Still, despite the ordinances of God and man, the descendants of Adam have sought—and found—ways to avoid the burdensome regimen of labor. They have done so by applying terrestrial wit to the needs of the arboreal body. They have done so by a system of evasions, some of which are deemed "legal"

---

1. There is a significant difference between this provision and the dictum of Marx which said, "From each according to his abilities, to each according to his needs."

and some of which are "illegal." Only man is burdened with such categories of choice. All the rest of nature is bound by the terms of the species/environment equation. For man there is no such natural equation; relying as he must on mortar, he is obliged to formulate his own rules regarding that mortar and men's relationship to it. It is because man has the potential of choice with regard to mortar that rules have had to be forged. Because modern man has existed within the confines of such rules from time immemorial, he has failed to appreciate the period before, when there were no man-made rules, but only the law of nature. And yet, it is the very *fact* of these rules that proves the existence of alternatives. There is no need to legislate in matters where choice doesn't exist. It is because man appreciates the fact that he possesses alternative modes of behavior that he enacts laws in order to eliminate those alternatives that would interfere with the production of mortar. However, laws alone are not enough. Alone, they are nothing more than moral precepts. Laws require sanctions so as to increase the likelihood that they will be obeyed, thereby safeguarding mortar. It is because man understands the enormous temptation to ignore such things as moral precepts while in pursuit of sustenance and sex that sanctions are so necessary. In brief, the laws of man seek to curtail arboreal tendencies and to promote terrestrial interests.

The basic and essential code of man is contained in the Ten Commandments (or their equivalents in other systems of religion or philosophy). The first four commandments are, in a manner of speaking, enabling clauses. They establish the identity and primacy of the lawmaker. The fifth, which proscribes killing, is a reservation clause, denying the people the right to kill one another. Implicit, however, is the reservation of such power to the lawmaker. In this way, sanctions are reserved. The operative clauses, Commandments 6 through 10, are those that seek to proscribe certain forms of conduct. (It must be noted in this connection that all the operative clauses are in the negative form, there being no affirmative acts required of man.)

Adultery is clearly arboreal, reflecting as it does man's essential promiscuity in sexual matters. The admonition against stealing relates directly to mortar. Were it not for this rule, man, in obeying an instinct that deals in direct transactions, would take and use anything he needs. This is especially true of food. Thus we see that the two essentials of existence—sustenance and sex —are regulated.

What is said of adultery and stealing is also true of coveting another's wife or goods. This sort of thing is known as "nipping something in the bud," an acknowledgment that it is the mind that sets the body in motion. The commandment against bearing false witness is designed to prevent parole violations of the laws regulating sustenance and sex. This is a subtle and ingenious clause. It binds everyone to the law. For example, if a neighbor broke the law—say, regarding adultery—you could not say otherwise if you knew. In this manner, the neighbor is proven out. If, on the other hand, he did not commit adultery —if he behaved in the approved terrestrial manner—you could not accuse him of acting in an arboreal manner. So, no matter what the course of conduct, its arboreality or terrestriality will be exposed.

But despite all the laws built upon the fundamental ones set forth in the Ten Commandments, man continues to evade what might be called the "work laws" of terrestrial society. Neither, for that matter, does he obey the "sex laws" of society. In both instances, whenever conditions are favorable, he will insist on acting like an arboreal primate. And even when they aren't favorable, he will attempt to act in his natural capacity —and all too often get caught and pay the price. It is here that we encounter crime and punishment.

Property crimes best display man's refusal to accept terrestrialization; instead, they show man at his arboreal best.

Thievery of one sort or another—whether it be robbery, theft, embezzlement, larceny, fraud, tax evasion, or any other form of appropriation—is the taking of property belonging to someone else. Without the need to be metaphysical, we can safely assume that the thief takes something of value: that the property has value because of its limited supply and the investment of labor, however represented, by its owner. The purpose of property, whether owned individually or collectively, is to provide the means of sustenance. Therefore, when the thief takes another's property, he is attempting to get something for nothing. Put differently, he is attempting to eat without sweating.

No one really objects to thievery because everyone recognizes the thief in himself. Who, besides a few fanatics, would prefer to work hard when the fruits of labor could be had for the taking? No other creature works, yet all eat—or they become extinct. Of course, that is man's problem in the terrestrial mode: He cannot, in the main. *take* food. He must work for it, as has been pointed out earlier. But only terrestrial man works; arboreal man steals with exactly the same naturalness as shown by a chimpanzee in stealing anything that happens to catch his eye. The only difference is that in its natural habitat, the chimpanzee doesn't have to steal in order to feed itself. Man does, unless he works.

And yet, notwithstanding the patent realities of terrestrial existence, thievery is coextensive with terrestrial existence, and it is as ancient as man.

When we read the ancient Law of Hammurabi we see how sternly thievery was once treated (theft of temple property was punishable by death), as if by stern measures the thief in man could be driven out of him so as to preserve the honest toiler intact.

The primacy of thievery in crime can be seen in the crime figures of a modern society such as the United States. Walter Bromberg, M.D., in *Crime and the Mind*, lists crimes in the order of their frequency, based on arrests by police. First are misdemeanors, offenses such as disorderly conduct, vagrancy, and alcoholism, that are not specified as felonies. Then, listed in order of frequency, are:

2. Larceny (theft)
3. Assault, simple

4. Burglary
5. Gambling (promoting, permitting, or engaging in)
6. Auto theft
7. Assault, aggravated (felonious)
8. Sex offenses (including statutory rape)
9. Concealed weapons
10. Robbery
11. Forgery (and counterfeiting)
12. Narcotic drugs (sale, possession, and use)
13. Prostitution and commercialized vice
14. Rape, forcible
15. Murder and nonnegligent manslaughter [2]

As can be seen, four of the five most frequent crimes are arboreal: they relate to the illegal acquisition of property or they relate to gambling. Of the fourteen, nine can be broadly classified as arboreal. They are 2, 4, 5, 6, 8, 10, 11, 12, and 13.

To give some sort of sense of relativity in crime, in 1968, according to the FBI, there were 3,442,000 larcenies, 1,828,000 burglaries, 777,000 auto thefts, and 261,000 robberies in the United States. In contrast, there were only several thousand homicides.

Even these figures can't begin to reveal the pervasiveness of thievery in society. Tax frauds, shoplifting, industrial theft, corrupt contract practices—both public and private—false sickness claims by employees, and a thousand petty actions by virtually every citizen, young and old, rich and poor, public and private, testify to man's natural inclination to take what he wants or needs, regardless of what the rules of society say to the contrary.

It goes without saying that where there is an inclination, no matter how contrary to the rules, there will always be a source of supply—hence organized crime in the United States. Whether it is called the Mafia, Cosa Nostra, the Organization, or the Syndicate, or whether it is some City Hall "expediter" or a lawyer "with connections," there is always a ready supply of opportunities for everyone—if he wishes—to indulge his arbo-

---

2. New York: Macmillan, 1965, p. 78.

real inclinations to obtain something for nothing, or if not for nothing, then at a discount.

Crime and gambling are opposite sides of a common coin. Each seeks to get something for nothing. At least that is the ideal. In reality, both gambler and criminal may expend enormous amounts of energy and time—and even money—to arrive at the goal. But it is the goal that is important, not the incidental means.

From Aruba off the Venezuelan coast to Katmandu in Nepal, from Swaziland to Japan, and from Argentina to South Korea, gambling is an indispensable part of life. Gambling knows no race, religion, or creed. Neither does it respect age or social status.

Gambling, it appears, goes at least as far back as prehistoric times; crude dice have been discovered at a number of living sites. In ancient Egypt, losers were sent to quarries to work off their debt. Gambling predates China's four-thousand-year-old written history. In India, wagering on chariot races goes back to 2,500 B.C. Even the philosophical Greeks took up dice, and it is from them the goddess of gambling, Tyche, derives. The Romans, imitative in so many things, took Tyche from the Greeks and changed her name to Fortuna. She has been wandering the earth ever since.

In her wanderings, she has entered hovels as well as palaces, private homes as well as casinos, and church social halls as well as back alleys. She has precipitated, as her votaries believe, wagers between the gods in which Zeus was the heavens, Poseidon the sea, and Hades the underworld; she has played hob with countries, as when England and France went to war after Henry I lost heavily at dice to Louis. She has nudged historical migrations as when money, partly raised by lottery in England, financed the early Virginia colonies, and she even dallied with George Washington as he bet on cockfights. Quite properly, Fortuna could be called the spiritual mother of mankind, for it is she who seeks to nourish her children so that they need never grow up to become slaves to the human condition.

Almost everyone gambles. This is true whether we are talking of games of chance, the stock market, wagers on sporting events, bets on elections, gambling on a new clothes style, or flipping coins to see who gets the extra piece of cake. All, to varying degrees, are attempts to get something for nothing.

Gambling and working are antithetical concepts. As a result, they are at odds. Like its cousin, drink, gambling is the enemy of the working man—or so it is generally believed. Actually, gambling itself is big business. In fact, John Scarne, considered to be one of the world's leading authorities on gambling, says that gambling is the biggest business in America, the profits of which exceed the combined gross profits of U.S. Steel, General Electric, General Motors, Ford Motors, and Metropolitan Life. It is, he states in *Scarne's Complete Guide to Gambling*,[3] greater than the total combined gross profits of America's hundred largest industries.

The overall "handle"—the total amount wagered—is between $500 and $600 *billion* a year. With the gross national product about $1 trillion a year, that means that 50–60 percent of all the nation's wealth passes through the gambling conglomerate.

This size industry, of course must have its customers. Walter Wagner writes in *To Gamble or Not to Gamble*:

There are more than 90 million Americans who gamble. According to a New York Stock Exchange study, at the beginning of 1971 a record 31.9 million individuals owned the shares of all of America's public corporations. Thus there are [three times] more "stockholders" in the nations' number-one industry than in all other American industry combined. . . . Wayne Pearson of the Nevada Gaming Commission . . . [says] with bull's-eye accuracy: "Statistically, gambling is the normal thing. It's the nongambler who is abnormal in American society."[4]

---

3. New York: Simon and Schuster, 1961.
4. New York: World, 1972, p. 21.

There is nothing wrong with seeking to "pluck fruit from the tree." It is the most natural thing in the world to appease hunger by the nearest and most available means. All creatures other than man do precisely that. But man, as we know, must produce his bread "by the sweat of his brow": He must work. If *no one* worked and if everyone sought to pluck fruit, mortar would disappear, as would the human species. It is for this reason that society opposes both gambling and crime. Neither, in and of itself, produces mortar. Both are ways of eating without sweating: They are both, in brief, arboreal actions that cannot be tolerated in the terrestrial circumstance.

Gambling would not be tolerated were it not for the fact that by a remarkable stroke of serendipity, gambling is big business. But, it is a case of serendipity producing a petard, for with gambling such a profitable business for those who engage in it as a business, the arboreality of gambling is lost, because from the gambler's point of view there is so little fruit for him to pluck.

Gambling, whether legal or illegal, is business, the modern equivalent of the hunt, and hence is tolerated. Of course, society would prefer that there be no gambling, but on the theory that half a loaf (or half a hunt) is better than none, it winks at the vice and taxes it when it can. The danger, so the argument goes, is that too many people will devote their time to gambling and thus jeopardize mortar.

This argument—and it is as old as society—has been disproved by the work of the sociologist Nechama Tec, who made a study of gambling on soccer matches in Sweden. Her conclusions, published in *Gambling in Sweden*, show that gambling not only doesn't rend the garment of society, but that it actually serves as a useful safety valve to prevent the very sort of thing society fears.

Among the conclusions was this: That the propensity to gamble is greater among "those of the lower occupational class." The obverse of this was true: The more advantageous the social position, the less the likelihood of gambling.

Tec summarizes the findings of her study this way:

> . . . [G]ambling, while it does not lead to the disastrous consequences often assumed, does provide bettors with the hope for social advancement. The fact that segments of the population who are least capable of fulfilling their mobility aspirations *through conventional avenues* are most likely to gamble has important implications for the well-being of the bettors and, through these, society. By keeping alive hope for social betterment, gambling alleviates some of the frustrations derived from the obstacles which segments of the population encounter in seeking to fulfill their mobility aspirations. [Italics added] [5]

Thus, the safety value aspect of gambling. As Tec expresses it, "Instead of turning against the original source of their deprivations and unfulfilled aspirations, bettors are relieved through gambling of some of the frustrations and, hence, are less likely to attack the existing class structure."

Essentially, the steady gambler—such as the individual who regularly bets on Swedish soccer matches—is also a steady worker who "invests" a small portion of his income in the hope of making a lot of money. Most realize they won't strike it rich because of the odds. But still there is the dream, the realization of which would mean the end of working for a living and the beginning of an enjoyable life. It is the dream, implemented by action taken, that makes life worthwhile.

There is very little difference between the small gambler's investment in soccer matches and the majority of the more than 31 million who invest in the stock market. While some knowledge is presumed or is supplied by a qualified broker, the investor in the stock market is after precisely the same goal as the gambler and uses the same technique at getting rich: He bets (invests) on a stock or a group of stocks in the hopes they will go up in price. There is even a phrase for this type of in-

---

5. Totowa, N.J.: The Bedminster Press, 1964, p. 113.

vestor: "He plays the stock market." Another man might "play the horses."

Sociologists, psychoanalysts, and reformers have labored mightily to discover the nature of the gambler, thus to better understand him, thus to cure him, and thus to make him a more substantial citizen, someone who contributes to mortar.

A psychoanalyst cited by Wagner commented on Freud's analysis of Fyodor Dostoevsky's compulsive gambling: "Freud's classic study on Dostoevsky and parricide marks a high point in our literature on the psychology of gambling. The oedipal implications, irresistible character, need for self punishment derived from a deep-seated sense of guilt, and similar aspects have been elucidated in Freud's paper which also emphasizes the close relation between gambling and masturbation." [6]

Out of this morass of analytic nonsense there is, even if only inadvertently, one feature worth noting, that of the "oedipal implications." If we reject Freud's theory of the Oedipus complex and accept the one I have given earlier, we can readily see the implications, namely, that the gambler doesn't want to join the hunt.

What is interesting is the effort of nongamblers, especially those opposed to what is generally considered one of man's worst vices, to impute to gamblers a will to lose. While this may be true for a psychotic, which I am not sure can be proved, there is no basis for so appraising the ordinary or regular gambler. He wants to win. He does not want to lose. Wagner interviewed hundreds of gamblers in depth. His conclusion:

> A handful tentatively accepted the possibility of the will to lose, but the majority declared they all had a desire to break the house, from the fifty-cent numbers bettor to the high roller. Some gamblers fully realize that their chances of winning are all but non-existent, but they hope against

---

6. Op. cit., p. 217. Wagner cites another doctor, a psychiatrist, who says, "Gambling offers satisfaction possibilities for latent and unconscious homosexual, anal-sadistic, oral-receptive drives, and gratifications of unconscious needs for punishment."[!]

hope that they will win nevertheless. It is the desire to win, not to lose, that motivates gamblers.[7]

There are a few specialists who have made some modest successes in curing compulsive gamblers. Their technique is very simple: They induce the patient to forego gambling by reorienting his goals. "My approach," explained one Las Vegas psychiatrist to Wagner, "is to get a person in touch with his own feelings. I have a gambler ask himself: What are you doing to yourself financially, socially, psychologically? If he begins to feel despair, dismay, and agony because of what gambling is doing to him, this is an important breakthrough. He is then in a position to redirect his life . . ." The redirection of the person's life is toward "long term goals." [8] In other words, the cure for gambling is the terrestrialization of an otherwise arboreal individual.

Gamblers Anonymous, founded only as recently as 1957, provides what is probably the best profile of the compulsive gambler (who is actually an exaggerated arboreal type). They list three principal reasons for compulsive gambling:

1. *Inability and unwillingness to accept reality.* Hence, the escape into the dream world of gambling.

2. *Emotional insecurity.*

3. *Immaturity.* A desire to have all the good things in life without any great effort on his own part. Many G. A. members accept the fact that they are unwilling to grow up and unconsciously they seek to avoid mature responsibility.

The reality that gamblers—to varying degrees—are unable and unwilling to accept is the reality of terrestrial existence with its unnatural demands that each individual devote his life to preserving and perpetuating the mortar on which survival depends. The emotional insecurity they feel stems from the

7. Ibid., pp. 218–219.
8. Ibid., p. 225.

inability to exist in either the arboreal or terrestrial worlds. And the immaturity they feel is that of the infant seeking to cling to its mother who provides both the tree in which the infant lives and the food that nourishes it. In other words, the gambler—and that is most of mankind—is an arboreal primate seeking to remain what he is, an arboreal primate. His difficulty arises over the fact that he doesn't live in arborea; he lives in terrestria.

Not every terrestrial primate needs to gamble or steal in order to avoid work and still satisfy sustenance needs. A few—the very fortunate ones—inherit money which does the work, thus sparing the beneficiary from having personally to work. There are also those who, by good fortune and even a bit of hard work, have accumulated capital, which releases them from a direct participation in work itself. Instead of producing mortar, they oversee mortar-making mortar. In this relatively rare condition, there is a by-product of significance. By living off the income of capital, they need face no time-lag between the appearance of a need (or even "want," for that matter) and its satisfaction. It is the nearest man can get to an arboreal state. He doesn't work to produce mortar, his needs are taken care of as they appear, and he exists in the constant now. Also, he lacks a utilitarian relationship with anyone and, depending on his temperament, he can enjoy sex promiscuously. It is no wonder that such an individual is called a "playboy."

We can see now that there are a number of ways man seeks to alter the terms of his existence so as to make them more compatible with his arboreal nature. Essentially, it is a process by which he meets his needs without resort to mortar production. Of course, he avails himself of the fruits of mortar; otherwise he could not live in the terrestrial mode. As a consequence, he imposes an additional burden on those who actually produce mortar. If he "steals" the results of others' production, he is considered a criminal. If he "inherits" or "invests" on the basis of another's production, he is a worthy citizen.

But what of those who comprise the great mass of producers

who are neither criminal nor worthy, but who throughout their lives must labor to produce mortar? They have no way of altering the terms of their existence. Yet even they rebel against the oppressive demands of terrestrial living. Since they can't alter reality, they seek to alter their perception of it.

Eugene Marais, the South African naturalist who died in 1936, spent considerable time studying both man and baboon. In his posthumously published book *The Soul of the Ape* (for which we must be grateful to Robert Ardrey), he describes several phenomena pertinent to the present discussion. At one point he comments:

> The habitual use of poisons for the purpose of inducing euphoria—a feeling of mental well-being and happiness —is a universal remedy for the pain of consciousness. . . .
> I do not know of any human race, savage or cultured, which has not developed, or acquired from other races, the habit of using some poison, generally of vegetable origin, for the purpose of creating euphoria . . . On the other hand, I do not know of any species of animal under natural conditions that has discovered or acquired a knowledge of this kind and so formed a definite new habit.[8]

I would agree with Marais, save for his statement about the pain of consciousness *per se* causing pain. Rather I believe it is the content of human consciousness that causes pain. Of course it is possible to argue that man's heightened consciousness derives from his terrestrial predicament and thus, as per Marais, consciousness *per se* produces pain. To avoid a circular argument, I would emphasize the *content* aspect, rather than the fact of consciousness itself.

What is most interesting in what Marais has to say is the *fact* of the pain. Why should consciousness, whether *per se* or

---

8. New York, Atheneum, 1969, pp. 117–118. The manuscript was actually written (though never completed) in 1922.

per content, produce pain? Can it be that all existence is painful and that conscious awareness that one is alive raises the pain
to the conscious level? If this is proven to be true, then it would
seem that evolution—and hence, new life—should have ground
to a halt almost as it began. Either a form of stasis exists or we
are inevitably forced to agree with Freud's concept of the death
wish. It would seem, when all the evidence is marshaled, that
existence *per se* is not the cause of pain, but that certain aspects
of existence are capable of producing pain—and in fact do produce the pain to which Marais refers.

It is mortar that produces anxiety and hence pain. Man in
the terrestrial mode cannot experience stasis. He cannot rely
on his nature for survival; he must depend exclusively on artifice. As we know, this artifice must be made by him, thus obliging him to construct a constantly expanding system in which to
produce this artifice. It is, indeed, like the situation in *Alice in
Wonderland* in which one had to run in order to stand still.

Uncertainty concerning the fundamentals of human existence
produces the pain of anxiety. Man seeks in myriad ways to escape from this pain. Following the lead of Marais, we can observe that throughout known history and among all peoples
various poisons have been employed to deal with this pain,
either by diminishing it while allowing the individual to continue to function, or by terminating it in such a way as to cease
functioning altogether.

Marais describes a phenomenon—possibly for the first time
anywhere—that can best be described as "twilight melancholia." Significantly, it affects both man and, Marais discovered,
the baboons he observed for a number of years. "Normal mental pain in man," he writes, "generally speaking, is tidal in nature. With sunrise or during the early morning it is at its lowest
ebb, to reach its highest flow in the evening about the time of
the setting sun."

Marais, along with many others, observed that as evening
came, the people in their villages fell into a depression, or what
I prefer to call twilight melancholia. They became so disposed,

it must be pointed out, only when there was neither beer nor other intoxicant to drink. He writes:

> An air of quietness and dejection falls upon the village just about sunset. The men and women go listlessly and mournfully about such tasks as still remain to be done. The older people gather in sheltered corners or about the fireplaces, quite silent. Conversation ceases. No song is heard and no sound of musical instruments. It seems very much like the dejection of utter physical weariness. The little children are by no means exempt. All laughter ceases, the games come to an end and there is a general tendency to creep closer to the mothers and elders. . . . As the night falls, the scene changes. The fires are newly made. Conversation and laughter are heard once more. Songs and the sound of laughter are heard once more. Songs and the sound of music arise . . .[9]

What is most fascinating is that this same twilight melancholia was observed among the baboons Marais was studying. Before sunset, life in the troop was quite normal, with the younger members playing, the older ones "chattering," and so on. Then:

> With the setting sun and the first deepening of the shadows a singular transformation came over the entire scene. Silence fell upon them gradually. . . . The little ones crept cuddlingly into the protective arms of their mothers. . . . The older ones assumed attitudes of profound dejection. . . . And then from all sides would come the sound of mourning. . . . One need only compare them with a native village under the same conditions to realise beyond any shadow of doubt that you have here a representation of the same inherent pain of consciousness at the height of its diurnal rhythm. In the case of the baboons the condition also disappears with the settling

---

9. Ibid., pp. 134–135.

darkness. When the troop finally moved onto the krans or to the entrance of the sleeping cave, the games were re-sumed . . .[10]

Various explanations were offered, from the supernatural to the philosophical. The one most acceptable—if one can inter-pret Marais correctly—was the Boer explanation that the com-ing of night suggested the approach of death: "the utter futility of human life; the distressing certainty of the end of all things; and the helplessness and paltriness of man." Of all this, so the explanation went, the setting sun was the recurring symbol.

It would seem that what lay at the basis of the acute depres-sion was not the *certainty of the end* of all things, but the *un-certainty of the continuance* of all things. Once the uncertainty was over, life returned to normal. Also, during those times when intoxicants were available, the feeling of depression due to un-certainty was absent because awareness of the uncertainties of life were absent. It is the awareness of uncertainty that produces depression.

How then can we explain the behavior of the baboons? What uncertainties were there to cause a depression? We cannot, of course, know for sure. But it is significant that these baboons lived in an environment where they had no access to trees, but retired at night either to the rocks of the gorge-stream or to what Marais described as the sleeping cave. Thus they were vulnerable to predators, as they would not be if they were able to retire to the safety of trees. This could easily have produced a state of tension as they anticipated the night. This possibility is supported by the fact that Marais's experiments in induced intoxication of baboons in captivity showed that males were much more susceptible than were females. In this regard, it must be remembered that the males have the responsibility of protecting the troop.

It is a truism of human existence that where social regula-tions permit and when intoxicants are available, man dispels twilight melancholia by drinking or otherwise ingesting poison.

---

10. Ibid., pp. 138–139.

In western society, twilight melancholia is dispelled by the cocktail hour.

Ogden Nash, perspicacious in his wit, once wrote:

> There is something about a Martini,
> A tingle remarkably pleasant;
> A yellow, mellow Martini;
> I wish that I had one at present.
> There is something about a Martini,
> Ere the dining and dancing begin,
> And to tell you the truth,
> It is not the vermouth—
> I think that perhaps it's the gin.[11]

Nash, I believe, expressed the essence of drinking in his last two lines: "It is not the vermouth—/I think that perhaps it's the gin." While a few connoisseurs might attach shades of pleasure to various vintages, the bulk of men throughout the world drink for but one reason: to rid themselves, no matter how temporarily, of the pain of terrestrial existence.

There has always been an assumption in human existence that drinking intoxicating beverages of one sort or another will be permitted as long as it does not appreciably interfere with one's work. This assumption serves as a universal admission that man needs this succor in order to function. Drinking serves as a most essential safety valve, but no other species in nature knowingly consumes poison. Man's situation is such that only poison can alleviate his terrestrial suffering.

Dr. William B. Terhune, psychiatrist-founder of Silver Hill Foundation, devotes an entire book to the subject of sensible drinking, *The Safe Way to Drink: How to Prevent Alcohol Problems Before They Start*.[12] He explains his thesis in the

---

11. "A Drink with Something in It," in *The Face Is Familiar* (Garden City, New York: Garden City Publishing 1941), p. 267. Of course, there is Nash's shorter and more pungent observation: "Candy Is dandy/But liquor Is quicker." This from "Reflections on Ice Breaking," in *Verses from 1929 On* (Boston: Little, Brown, 1959) p. 37.

12. New York: William Morrow, 1968.

opening of his Introduction: "This book is based first on the premise that most of us are going to drink; second that it is unnecessary for the majority of drinkers to become victims of alcohol; and third, that through desire, decision and discipline, most people can escape alcohol dependency and habituation."

A few pages later, Terhune writes, "Man has enjoyed alcohol's pleasant effects for a long time . . . and it is possible to enjoy the effects of alcohol and escape its dangers."

Alcohol first anesthetizes the higher level of the central nervous system, especially the cerebral cortex where perception, memory, and judgment take place. This releases instinctive and emotional tendencies, with the result, to quote Terhune, "that people become purely emotional and overreact to events in a primitive, animalistic manner. Alcohol is the quickest possible descent from civilization to barbarism." [13]

I would suggest that what really happens is that alcohol serves to lift the drinker from civilization to arborea. I do not believe it is a mere coincidence that when one drinks, one "gets high." It is abundantly clear that when one is "high," terrestrial inhibitions evaporate and one becomes visibly arboreal. If we take the words used by Terhune to describe what happens when one drinks—becoming *emotional, primitive,* and *animalistic*—we can begin to see the drinker's ascent to arborea.

Arboreal primates, especially chimpanzees, are spontaneous in their expression of feeling; nothing is held back. Terrestrial man, however, has had to train himself to restrain emotional expression, a legacy from the hunting period when hunters had to be quiet while on the track of game and when silence was necessary to protect the affinity group from predators. This restraint is not natural, and when men feel restraint lifted, as they do when drinking, they are much freer to express whatever emotion they feel.

As for being primitive and animalistic, this is revealed by a lack of concern over terrestrial matters such as those structured

---

13. Ibid., pp. 26–27.

relationships existing between spouses and among social acquaintances; social actions that are built on certain conventions and amenities; and forms of responsibility such as those relating to money, time, and place.

Most significantly, alcohol suspends terrestrial restraints on sex, thus allowing both men and women to act arboreally: practice the sexual promiscuity so typical of arboreal primates. Nowhere is this shown more clearly than in the cocktail lounge or bar where men and women meet over a few drinks and then, depending on the mood and the moment, begin to act erotically.

Expressing the process in a negative way, as does Terhune when he writes, "A little alcohol usually produces a mild euphoria, somewhat dulls care, worry, guilt, failure, responsibility, and decreases the need for effort," we can still see the drinker leaving a terrestrial scene and entering the trees. The very states that are dulled by alcohol are those that one never sees in arboreal primates but only in terrestrial man.

There is a physiological explanation for the appearance of arboreal tendencies. The terrestrial brain, the portion of the cerebral cortex that evolved during man's terrestrialization process, is the first part of the brain affected by alcohol. It is anesthetized, leaving the "old" brain in which the limbic system is the highest brain complex, to run things. This brain knows nothing of terrestrial responsibilities and restraints. All it knows is the arboreal world. So, when it takes over, it allows the drinker to be himself: arboreal.[14]

In the lexicon of pharmacology, alcohol is considered a depressant ("downer"). The phenomenon I have just been discussing indicates an elevating process. Is there a contradiction? No. This is because moderate drinking inhibits the inhibitory function of the cerebral cortex, thus allowing for an elevated feeling. The problem the drinker faces, whether he gets an elevated feeling, or whether he goes beyond that to the de-

---

14. In the event that too much is drunk, this portion of the brain is closed down and unconsciousness or even death can occur.

pressed state, is that eventually he must return to the terrestrial world with its structured relationships, conventions, and responsibilities. That is, according to Terhune, the drinker must return to care, worry, guilt, failure, and effort.

Terhune reports, "In the course of a lifetime, one out of eight adults now living in the United States will become either alcoholic or seriously handicapped by alcohol-dependency." [15] The pain of terrestrial existence is simply too much for them, and they seek oblivion. These drinkers have long since passed the arboreal phase of drinking. They may have begun that way, but the climb down has proved too overwhelming and in the end going up is not worth the coming down, so they shut the whole system down.

Terhune, I think, best reveals the dichotomy between the needs of society and the needs of the alcoholic who withdraws from that society when he writes:

> The drinking man, i.e., the alcoholic is a defeated man. He has quit trying. Frequently, the very fact of his alcoholism is an admission that he has given up. Continued dependent drinking is an indication of failure. . . . We cannot drown our sorrows, nor our anger, frustration, failure and defeat, however hard we may try. Those who depend on alcohol as a way of life fly the white flag of surrender. They have become second-class citizens and, until they admit this to themselves, they are a mess.[16]

Terhune is terrestrial man expressing terrestrial man's horror and outrage at the escape of others from terrestrial bondage. Although we might argue that a psychiatrist should display a better understanding of alcoholism and possibly phrase the matter more temperately, nevertheless Terhune's words are those of a man bound to the terrestrial mode and its necessary ethic: utilitarianism. For example, what would happen if every-

---

15. Ibid., p. 11. Elsewhere (p. 50) he estimates that there are nine million confirmed alcoholics in this country.
16. Ibid., p. 44.

one ran up the white flag of surrender, to use Terhune's phrase? The species would become extinct very quickly as it is each man's utilitarianism that contributes toward the mortar so necessary to preserve the species profile. And if one out of eight Americans becomes an alcoholic, that means that much more work for the remainder.

Statistics on drinking are revealing. Of the male population in America, 75 percent are drinkers, as against 56 percent of the women. What is significant is that three times as many men as women are regular drinkers. What is more, for every female alcoholic there are seven or eight male alcoholics.

There is no objection to the easing of the pain of terrestrial living as long as it doesn't interfere with work. When it threatens to do so, then the full weight of society is brought to bear against the offending action. A classic example of this is the change in attitude exhibited in only the last few years toward cigarette smoking.

Unlike alcohol which seems to have been consumed as early as prehistoric times, tobacco is of recent origin. It was only in the middle of the sixteenth century that what Richard Blum calls the tobacco "epidemic" spread around the world like wildfire. What may have begun as early as the third century among the Arizona Indians was contained within the western hemisphere until 1555, when the first Europeans observed its use in Brazil. Then, within an historical moment, it was everywhere. In 1604, King James of England decried its use because so much money was "going up in smoke." Since he couldn't curtail tobacco's use, he taxed it heavily—something governments have been doing ever since. In 1638, the emperor of China ordered decapitation for users, but this order was unenforceable because of continuing and expanding use of the drug.

Blum, in *Society and Drugs*, suggests the basis for tobacco's rush to popularity:

The adoption of tobacco by a tremendous variety of non-literate societies and literate cultures with immense differ-

ences among them tends to rule out cultural and social
features as facilitators or determinants of tobacco-use innovation. Similarly, in almost all instances, the failure of
prohibitions adopted on the grounds of taste, health, religion, or criminal penalty to prevent adoption *emphasizes
the frailty of social controls when a society is faced with
an attractive substance, even if that substance serves no primary physiological need* . . . [Italics added] [17]

What then makes tobacco an "attractive substance?"[18] The
principal drug in tobacco is nicotine, which is toxic and addic-
tive, both psychologically and physiologically. Nicotine has
arousing properties. Contrary to popular belief, nicotine has no
sedative properties, but is actually a stimulant of the autonomic
and central nervous systems. Smoking serves to increase the
secretion of adrenalin, itself a stimulant. Adrenalin is a stress
hormone that aids in the organism's system of defense. Nicotine constricts the blood vessels, and the pulse and heart rate
increase because the heart must work harder to pump blood.

The overall effect of cigarette smoking is temporarily to assist the smoker to endure stress. We see this function in many
stress situations where the habituated smoker automatically
reaches for a cigarette at the beginning of the situation and
smokes heavily until the stress crisis is passed. It can be seen
that smoking has the opposite function of drinking. Whereas
drinking serves to reduce terrestrial involvement, smoking serves
to enhance terrestrial capabilities—if only in the short run.

What distinguishes smoking is its tendency toward counter-
productiveness. Cigarette smoking in any amount above the
base necessary to establish addiction is physically harmful. For
many years an ineffectual controversy fluttered about the issue,
but when solid evidence showed the full range of the harm
smoking can do, the United States government sought to warn

17. San Francisco: Jossey-Bass, 1969, 1: 94–95.
18. I assume by "no primary physiological need" Blum means no affirmative or nutritive need—otherwise his observation would fly in the
face of the facts.

people away from the danger. The cost of smoking was simply too great in illness, thereby diminishing productivity. Yet— and here is where Blum is so right—smoking goes right on. Even after cigarette commercials on radio and television were banned and packages were imprinted with warnings, smoking did not merely continue, it increased—thus the appeal of an "attractive substance."

If drinking serves to dispel twilight melancholia, smoking serves to dispel morning vapors. If drinking allows a temporary retreat from the pain of terrestrial living, smoking girds man for the demands of terrestrial struggle. The stress against which man drugs himself lasts from morning till night. Not even at night when he seeks relief from his daily ordeal by drinking can he put down his stress poison. As a result, he engages in contradictory practices of smoking and drinking. The result, in most instances, is a severe hangover the next morning. And for millions this goes on day after day, year after year, for the simple reason that the stress of terrestrial living never ends.

There are, quite literally, poisons for every occasion. Essentially, however, they do one of two things: Either they help one to function more effectively in the terrestrial mode, or they help one to escape the pain of terrestrial existence.

Psychotropic drugs—those whose main effects are on the nervous system—can be classified into six main groups:

1. *Sedative/hypnotics,* which lower mental alertness and bodily activity and induce sleep in elevated dosages. Examples are alcohol and barbiturates.

2. *Stimulants,* which decrease fatigue and increase mental and physical activity. Examples are caffeine and amphetamines.

3. *Major tranquilizers,* which calm anxiety and excitement. An example is meprobamate.

5. *Antidepressants,* which stimulate and raise the mood in mild or moderate depression. Examples are imipramine and phenelzine.

6. *Hallucinogens,* which cause profound distortions of mood,

perception, and thought processes. Examples are LSD and mescaline.[19]

It can readily be seen that these drugs have a yo-yo effect. Thus, they are variously known as uppers and downers. Their purpose is to help the individual rise up to the demands of terrestrial living or to sink down into indifference and oblivion. Whether one uses uppers or downers, however, is irrelevant. The point is that men and women—even young children—need the assistance of drugs that transform their conscious awareness of existence. The drugs serve a profound human need. No other creature needs to alter its perception of its circumstance. And lest one conclude that extensive drug use is peculiar to advanced industrial societies, it must be pointed out that Blum's research among 92 hunting and gathering societies showed that 57 used tobacco, 52 used alcohol, 40 used hallucinogens, and 15 used other stimulants of various kinds.

I believe, when it is all said and done, that the critical factor in the human equation is contained in the concept of *seeking.* Creatures other than man do not seek in the way man seeks. What they do, they do on the basis of their genetic nature. What man seeks is all that which cannot be obtained by his genes in the terrestrial mode. What man seeks, whether it is self-reflection or social satisfaction, or whatever, is beyond his genes and thus is in the realm of mortar. And when man must function on the basis of mortar, he enters the state of time-anxiety. He seeks to overcome this state one of two ways: by eliminating anxiety or by eliminating time. He can do the former by decreasing his terrestrial awareness through the effects of downers; he can do the latter through the effects of uppers. In either event, he alters his awareness of the world in which he lives because without so altering his awareness, he finds the world unendurable.

There is, finally, a last resort to the human condition: suicide.

---

19. From Gordon Claridge, *Drugs and Human Behavior* (New York: Praeger, 1970), p. 20.

When nothing else works, when mind-manipulation no longer provides relief, and when the pain becomes overwhelming, man destroys himself. Aside from the lemming, who marches en masse into the sea every seven years as a form of population control, man is the only creature to practice suicide. Man is the only creature attempting to exist in an environment for which he is not made. Suicides must sense this, for in a stroke, they leave it.

THE PRISONER

W H E N Jung was studying under Freud, and during the period of rising differences between the two men, Jung had this dream:

I was in "my house," apparently on the first floor, in a cozy, pleasant sitting room furnished in the manner of the 18th century. I was astonished that I had never seen this room before, and began to wonder what the ground floor was like. I went downstairs and found the place was rather dark, with panelled walls and heavy furniture dating from the 16th century or even earlier. My surprise and curiosity increased. I wanted to see more of the whole structure of this house. So I went down to the cellar, where I found a door opening onto a flight of stone steps that led to a large vaulted room. The floor consisted of large slabs of stone and the walls seemed very ancient. I examined the mortar and found it was mixed with splinters of brick. Obviously the walls were of Roman origin. I became increasingly excited. In one corner, I saw an iron ring on a stone slab. I pulled up the slab and saw yet another narrow flight of steps leading to a kind of cave, which seemed to be a prehistoric tomb containing two skulls, some bones and broken shards of pottery. Then I woke up.[1]

---

1. Carl Gustav Jung et al., *Man and His Symbols* (New York: Doubleday, 1964), p. 56.

Jung's interpretation of the dream centered on his difficulties with Freud. He felt it to be something of a liberating dream in that it symbolized his deep-seated resistance to Freud and that rather than having to function within terms established by Freud, henceforth he would be able to structure his own system of thought.

While this may be true, there is an aspect of his dream that symbolizes something far more fundamental, both in Jung and in all who have approached the subject of man's psyche.

Quite clearly, regardless of the specific frame of reference, the dream was an exploration of the past. And for our purposes, whether this past could be construed as being Jung's or that of mankind is irrelevant. What is important is that this was the way Jung perceived it. The exploration was twofold: into the past and into the depths. From a cozy, first-floor, eighteenth-century sitting-room, he descended into the past through a series of levels, each of which was earlier in time, darker, and deeper in the earth. In the end, he came to a "kind of cave," which seemed to be a prehistoric tomb, and in which he found two skulls, some bones, and broken shards of pottery. There, terminating the dream, Jung woke up.

There are two significant features to the dream as a whole. First, in going backward in time, Jung eventually travels to the bowels of the earth. Secondly, once back as far as he can go, he feels himself in a tomb, as if that is the *end* rather than the beginning. Or to put it slightly differently, in his explorations of the past, which go as far back as caves, Jung reaches a dead end. And at this dead end, there are traces of humanity, albeit dead: two skulls, some bones, and broken shards of pottery.

Jung's dream carried him as far back as possible in the history of the species. Jung knew about the late archeological discoveries in which skulls and jawbones of prehistoric men were discovered in and near European cave sites. Also, he knew of Darwin's work on the origin of the human species. The dream, so it seems to me, is one of those dead-end situations in which explorers of the past and of the psyche seem constantly to find themselves. The anthropological theory implicit in the dream seems to be this: When we go back in time we end up in a cave (or a reasonable facsimile thereof) where we find the bones of early man. Having gone back as far as we can go and finding ourselves thus placed in the symbolic cave, there is only one way left for us to go, and that is forward out of the cave and back to the present time (though it is fascinating to observe that Jung's dream had him living cozily in the eighteenth century, and not the early twentieth—before Darwin and modern anthropology).

I touch upon this point at the beginning in order to lay a proper foundation for all that follows in this chapter. Jung and Freud, and all the other explorers into the depths of man have proceeded on the assumption that man was (and is) a terrestrial being. All their theories of human psychology stem from this assumption. While it is true that they may willingly acknowledge, for whatever reason, the fact that man's ancestors may have originated in the trees, they construct their theories on the assumption that while man's *ancestors* may have originated in the trees, *man* lives on the ground.[2] There is in this dichotomy of thought the further assumption that when man's ancestors left the trees they took no psychic baggage with them.

They all, without exception, start the clock on man only after he is fully terrestrialized. In Jung's case, the clock begins in a cave. Freud, on the other hand, begins man's psychic profile with a "primal horde" living in the terrestrial mode where, unlike the situation in arborea, there exist the institutions of fatherhood and filialness and jealousy between father and son. What is even more outstanding in Freud's whole system of thought is his "masculine psychology," in which the male is the standard of normality, while the female is a deficient male, something that could only arise out of an evaluation of the species in the terrestrial mode.

---

2. This is precisely the problem of the anthropologist and the paleontologist, as was discussed earlier.

The essential problem in attempting to work with the data and theories provided by Freud and Jung, just to mention the two most significant explorers of the human psyche, is that of perspective. They, and almost everyone after, have proceeded on the basis of a modern's perspective of man's past—a past, significantly, that began in the terrestrial mode of existence. This approach inevitably establishes the basis of man's nature and thus of his normality (and abnormality) as being that of modern man. Previous man, especially prehistoric man, is thus perceived as a lesser man, rather than man being a lesser arboreal primate. It is this perspective that makes it conceptually impossible that man ever possessed an arboreal period that in any way could play a role in man's psychic history.

Other explorers of man's psychic nature, unable for one reason or another to perceive the relevance of the arboreal period, have sought to establish an ancient base on which to construct a theory. Their base is extrapolated from the most ancient of myths, epics and legends from around the world that are only, at the most, several thousands of years old. They are, in fact, only as old as written language. Thus, they seek by indirection to perceive that which they believe cannot be seen directly. It is for this reason that Jung sought, through his collective unconscious with its archetypes, or primordial images, to construct a psychic history as well as a psychic beginning for man.

Whether going backward in time or whether going forward from a far-too-recent point in man's history, the various explorers of man's psyche have all constructed both theories and models on the presence within man of unconscious and conscious minds that are in perpetual conflict. Implicit—and absolutely unavoidable—in this sort of a construct is a creature whose entire existence from primordial time to the present has been rent by this conflict. The result of this inescapable conclusion is that conflict between the conscious and unconscious is an inherent characteristic of man's psyche, that all men, of all time, have had this conflict within them. What, then, if there were a period when there was no conscious mind? Clearly, there could be no conflict. *This* possibility has never occurred to any of the theorists. The problem posed by these theories is similar to that concerning man and tools: man, ergo tools. Here the proposition states: man, ergo two minds in conflict. This conclusion is inevitable if one looks backward across the human landscape. Everywhere one turns—even as far back as Sumer— there is man suffering from two minds. However, if we go forward—as we have frequently done in this work—we discover an entirely different landscape.

In the foreground, on the branch of a tree, as it were, we discover an arboreal primate who can only be described as of one mind. It acts in conformity with its nature as that nature has been determined by the species/environment equation. It has a brain; in fact, the most advanced brain produced by evolution. It has had to be in order to guide the primate to successful existence in the demanding arboreal environment. This brain, however, did not begin *de novo* in arborea. It was the culmination of millions of years of brain development that began with the simple Chordate. As environment became more and more complex, a more and more complex brain was required so that the organism could properly relate to the environment. The critical thing to observe in brain progression is the absence of conflict between the older and newer parts of the brain. They work harmoniously in a combined effort to increase the survival possibilities of the various species. There is only one exception to this process, and that is man. And the reason for this is that man's history has not been one in which the species has sought to perfect its relationship to its environment, but has been a history of attempting to adapt to a second and hostile environment for which natural evolution had not adapted the species. Whereas other forms of life evolved improved brains to cope better with their natural environment, man had to grow a new brain in order to cope with a new one. It is from this historical perspective that we must view the relationship between man's conscious and unconscious minds—and the conflict between them.

There is inevitable conflict within even integrated brain systems. But this is not the sort of conflict experienced by man. In all advanced brains other than man's, it is the purpose of the cerebral cortex to resolve conflicts that arise from conflicting information (stimuli) provided by the senses, both internal and external. If a male primate, for example, sees both a sexually receptive female and a predator, or if it feels hunger and sees a predator, it must make a decision on how to resolve the conflicts. This is the function of the cerebral cortex. But there is within the species/environment equation a full range of possible solutions. A phyletic memory system, built up over millions of years of evolution, provides a repertoire of responses no matter what the combination of conflicting stimuli might be. It was in order to increase phyletic memory and thus to be able more adequately to resolve conflicts produced by contending stimuli from an increasingly complex environment that the cerebral cortex came into existence in the first place and then evolved in complexity, reaching its ultimate perfection in the arboreal primate.

It is the phyletic memory that provides solutions to conflicts provided by stimuli from within and without the organism. All stimuli can be fed into the system, integrated, evaluated, and then sent to the "memory bank" of the phyletic memory, where past responses have been recorded. The brain selects the appropriate response to whatever combination of stimuli are presented and these are transmitted to the appropriate motor systems, and action takes place.

Phyletic memory is the genetic buildup of successful responses to stimuli. For this to be possible the species profile must conform to that of the environment. In such case, the phyletic memory of the individual will serve its needs in that environment. There is no conflict between parts of the brain that cannot be resolved by phyletic memory.

Man's arboreal ancestors had such an integrated brain system with its phyletic memory. However, when they were obliged to leave the trees and establish a terrestrial existence, they entered an environment in which arboreal responses would be totally inappropriate and would inevitably lead the species to extinction. Therefore, a whole new set of responses that would relate the organism to the terrestrial environment were required. In this circumstance, the old phyletic memory was useless. Worse, it was counterproductive.

Because hominids did not evolve naturally into terrestrial creatures, there was no opportunity for natural evolution slowly to evolve a new brain that could integrate the old memory system with the new. The problem of hominids—and hence the initiating cause for the creation of a revolutionary new brain system—was raised by the fact of mortar with its secondary effect of preserving the original arboreal genes. Such being the case, the original arboreal brain remained intact and sought at all times to function as if it were still regulating an organism living in arborea.

This arboreal brain continues to function in man today and is the instigating force that perpetuates all of modern man's arboreal tendencies, such as those of sustenance and sex. It is, in fact, the brain that manifests itself as the unconscious mind of man. And it is this unconscious mind that seeks to meet the needs of the body. In summary, then, it can be said that *the unconscious mind is the mind of the arboreal body of man*. The source of this mind is the arboreal brain, an end-product of natural evolution. As a consequence, this brain, with its unconscious manifestations, is immutable; it cannot be changed. It is essential to understand that this unconscious mind is the mind of the body; it regulates and coordinates all bodily functions and needs, from sleep and sex, to sustenance and elimination. Finally, this mind functions on the basis of phyletic memory: It responds to stimuli, both internal and external, on the basis of what its phyletic memory tells it. This phyletic memory is related directly to the arboreal environment.

This mind quite obviously could not be allowed to function in the terrestrial mode. And yet, being the mind of the body, it could not be extinguished, for to do so would have extinguished life itself. Regardless of where a creature lives, it must be able to eat, to sleep, and to eliminate, and for the sake of the species, it has to have sexual activity. Since the arboreal mind could not be put away, it had to be superimposed upon in such a way as to accommodate the body to the demands of the terrestrial environment. Such things as sustenance, sex, sleep, and elimination would have to come under the supervisory control of a mind that had as its premise the establishment of a proper species/environment equation. The body would be allowed to function, but its arboreal tendencies would be subjected to the inhibitory regulations of the terrestrial mind.

To do all this required something absolutely unique. It could not be a mind guided by a second phyletic memory. If such an anomaly occurred there would be two rigid and immutable memory systems seeking to pull the body in totally opposite directions. The result would be utter immobility and death for the species. This, then, meant that a genetic memory system could not be used. What was needed was a supple, variable mind that could reconcile the needs of the body with the demands of the environment in such a way as to preserve contact between the species profile and that of the environment.

We have met this mind before. It is the mind that produced man's mortar. And because of the demands of mortar, it is also the mind that produced speech. I am referring to the conscious mind.

This mind is the manifestation of that portion of the brain that was created during the terrestrial period. Most specifically it has been the special development of the human cerebral cortex, and especially the frontal lobes, that has produced the conscious mind.

That such a mind could be produced at all is one of the great innovations of all living matter. That it came into being at all was made possible by the plasticity of the primate brain. Without this original plasticity the earliest hominids could not have survived in the terrestrial mode. Selective pressures created added plasticity so that the mind needed to guide man ever further away from arboreal origins could keep pace. As it kept pace, and as the needs of mortar grew ever greater, the transmission of this mind's content from one individual to another grew increasingly essential. At a certain critical moment, man developed speech, thus guaranteeing the reproduction and transmission of the conscious mind. Just as genes transmit the unconscious mind from generation to generation, language transmits the conscious mind from generation to generation. In this way the arboreal and terrestrial minds have been passed on over the hundreds and thousands of human generations.

In summary, the unconscious mind, man's arboreal mind with its phyletic memory, is the fundamental mind of man. Superimposed on it is the supple, culturally acquired conscious mind, the terrestrial mind, that seeks to regulate or suppress, as appropriate, the arboreal mind so as to guarantee survival of the species in the terrestrial mode.

Since the arboreal mind is fixed and the terrestrial mind is variable, this means that the content of the conscious mind can vary from individual to individual and from social group to social group. It is, then, the content of the conscious mind that determines the nature of, and the extent of, any conflict that exists between the two minds.

Contrary to the thinking of most scholars, it is not the unconscious mind that plagues man. It is the conscious mind that, notwithstanding its semblance of rationality, is the basis of all human irrationality, from eccentricity through neurosis to psychosis.

It is because of the problems created by consciousness that I have emphasized at several earlier moments the essential fact of human existence: The further man gets from his arboreal origins, *and hence further from the sovereignty of his arboreal mind,* the greater the stress caused by the Arboreal/Terrestrial Conflict.

Pivotal in all this is the fact that the greater the scope of the conscious mind in its attempt to solve terrestrial problems, the greater the suppression of the arboreal mind. And it must always be remembered that it is the arboreal, unconscious, mind on which man's existence depends. The conscious mind may regulate and suppress, but the one thing it cannot do is originate anything. Without the unconscious mind as a foundation, the conscious mind would have nothing on which to affix its regulatory functions. More: It would have no basis for existence. And neither would man.

Built upon consciousness is self-consciousness, although more thorough reflection on the point would indicate that consciousness *per se* is self-consciousness, no matter how limited it might be. There is, for example, the self-consciousness of Goodall's chimpanzees as they prepare, in advance, their little sticks for fishing for termites. This activity, in reality, is an instance of a triangular relationship that involves an awareness by the chimpanzee of self, of termites, and the connecting link, the stick. The importance of this triangular situation lies in the fact that it involves an indirect transaction, something that man, from the very earliest terrestrial moment on, has had to employ if he would eat. In the arboreal period, however, there was no need of an indirect transaction, and hence no need for the conceptual triangle. On the other hand, once terrestrialization commenced, consciousness of growing proportions was essential in order that, through the operations of the conscious mind, increasing mortar might be produced.

The unconscious mind seeks constantly to meet the needs of the body. So does the conscious mind, but in a more indirect and derivative way. Unfortunately, they function on the basis of different "clocks." The "clock" of the unconscious mind is that founded on the rhythms of the arboreal primate body living in an arboreal environment. That of the conscious mind is based upon the rhythms of life in the terrestrial mode, not, it should be pointed out, on the rhythms of the body.

In arborea, there existed for man's hominid ancestors a simple system of "time." Hunger was satisfied by a continuous

process of eating—as much as eight hours a day.[3] While sleeping and other activities interrupted the eating process, there
was still never any bodily stress stemming from an unmet need.
The rhythms of eating and nourishment were predicated on the
balance between the organism and the environment. As for sex,
the female was sexually active when her body was prepared for
conception. From the male point of view, he copulated upon
receipt of sexual signals from the female. In other words, stimuli, whether internal or external, resulted in immediate response. The actions were direct: hunger sensations > eating;
sexual signals > copulation. It could be said, regardless of any
awareness or lack of awareness of time, that the species in the
arboreal mode existed in the constant *now*. That is, there was
no appreciable delay between the appearance of a need and its
satisfaction. Further, the satisfaction was a direct satisfaction,
the result of a direct transaction.

In terrestria there is a different sort of time, thus producing
a "clock" of its own. Notwithstanding the actual body needs,
the satisfaction of these needs must fit into the time schedule
of the terrestrial clock. For example, the satisfaction of sustenance needs is achieved indirectly and only after uncertainty,
if at all. The body might need sustenance now, but circumstances, such as a poor hunt, may postpone satisfaction for an
extensive period. This produces stress on the body as well as
time-anxiety. As a consequence of this problem, all other needs
of the body—sex, sleep, elimination—must reset their clock so
as to subordinate themselves to the dominating sustenance
problem.

The body exists in the constant *now*. Its needs are genetically determined and are immutable. The satisfaction of those
needs has become, during the process of terrestrialization, increasingly indirect and postponed. Adding to the problem has
been the uncertainty of satisfaction because of the uncertainty

---

3. This is calculated on the basis of modern observations of chimpanzees in their natural habitat.

of mortar, on which man depends for survival. If the mind of the body exists in the constant now, then the conscious mind exists in the inconstant future. Man's problem is that he possesses an arboreal body attempting to survive under the direction of a terrestrial mind.

The stress resulting from body and conscious mind existing, literally, in different worlds is incalculable—and inescapable. In effect, the human organism as a total entity seeks to live in two worlds and in two time zones. The body claims one world and one time zone for its own; the conscious mind, another world and another time zone. The unconscious mind—the mind of the body and thereby the mind of immediacy—is being regulated and suppressed by the mind of mortar, the mind of uncertainty, and the mind of futurity. The consequence is a conflict of enormous magnitude and a conflict without ultimate resolution.

There is no escape from the terrestrial prison and therefore there is no escape from this conflict, which, as we know, is manifested in two ways, by time-anxiety and by body stress. For man to avoid psychic extinction or a complete shutdown of the body, he must achieve a balance between the demands of the body and the demands of terrestrial living. Thus far in his existence he has failed. In fact, instead of achieving a balance, he has extended the problem to the point of critical danger to survival. The worst offenders in this regard have been the psychotherapists who have aggravated the very problem they have set out to solve. Rather than establish a balance within their patients, they have increased the already critical imbalance that drove their patients to seek help in the first place.

Regardless of the guise of the individual's problem, it inevitably turns out to be one of identity. This is not an abstract identity, but that of the individual in his social context. It arises as a result of consciousness—of self and of the surrounding milieu. It is here that we must confront the uniquely human problem of the psychic profile. *For the individual to survive in*

the terrestrial mode, it is essential that his psychic profile con-
form to the psychic profile projected by the society in which
he lives.

In the beginning, and for most of man's terrestrial existence,
man's essential task was to present a species profile—largely
through the instrumentality of mortar—that would conform to
the profile projected by the natural environment. However, as
was pointed out in the last section of "The Labyrinth," once
man incorporated nature into his cultural cocoon by domesticating animals and grains, this need was drastically reduced and,
in fact, as man continually encroached on those aspects of nature outside his cocoon, the time came when, for all practical
purposes, the environment had no substantive profile to project
to man. In this condition, all the necessary elements for human
survival were under the control of man. At this point, man's
break with nature was complete.

When this occurred, the exterior lines, as it were, gave way
in importance to the interior lines of the human community.
This took place because individuals became more dependent
on each other than on the environment. When this happened,
and it happened with the beginnings of civilization, it became
essential for the individual to maintain a personal profile in
contact with that of the group. For the individual to lose contact with the group profile meant extinction. This came about
as a result of the intermediacy of the group between the individual and necessary protection, sustenance, and sex. Thus it
can be seen that individual indirect transactions so necessary
for sustenance became doubly indirect and, being doubly indirect, heightened both time-anxiety and body stress to that
degree.

However, this matter of a personal profile is not a tangible
reflection of the mortar necessary to maintain a species profile
in contact with that of the environment. Physical sustenance
is not the issue; rather the issue revolves around the social relationship between the individual and society, as it is society as a

whole that proves to be the conduit to the satisfaction of body needs. As a result, and to guarantee its own survival that it might continue to act as the necessary conduit to the satisfaction of body needs, society projects a profile with which the individual must maintain contact if he is to meet and satisfy his body needs.

This profile projected by the individual I call a psychic profile, because it is the mental processes of the individual that make it possible to maintain contact with the profile of society, and not a physical one.

Note the priorities: The body's needs are served by the mind. It is not the other way around, as so many think. It is not, and never has been, a case of the body serving the mind (or of the body being the corruptible vessel of the soul). The function of man's mental processes in their entirety is to serve the needs of the body. That means—and this is critical to any meaningful understanding of human psychology—that an unhealthy or debilitated psychic life will seriously interfere with physical health.[4] It is not the reverse. The body does not determine mental health; mental health determines physical health.[5]

The question arises as to why man throughout history has placed such a priority upon the mind, creating the strong impression that everything, including the body, serves its needs. It is like the problem of the key appearing more important than the lock which, in turn, seems more important than the door which seems more important than the room to which it leads which, again, seems more important than the contents of the room, which, when we look at the entire matter, is why the key was forged in the first instance: to get at the contents of the

---

4. As will be discussed later, even "mental" or "emotional" illness is at root a physical condition.

5. This is a problem distinct from genetically based physical problems for which there is no solution. There is nothing one can do about a malformed heart, for example. Such a condition, as experience shows, can have an effect upon mental health to the extent that the physical condition can produce subsidiary mental, or emotional, problems.

room. The same sort of sequence can be shown to exist in terms of the confusion of mind and body, especially with man. The mind is necessary to lead the body through a maze of social doors, leading ultimately to the meeting of the needs of the body. It is not the reverse: The room does not exist any more for the key than the body exists for the mind. Yet, if a play on words may be permitted, the mind is the key to meeting the needs of the body. Especially is this evident in the case of man's relatively recent cocoon, where to go from body need to satisfaction involves so many indirect transactions that a key is needed to unlock all the intervening social doors. The key is man's mind, and as the key must fit the terms of the lock, so too must man's mind conform to the terms of society; hence the need for the individual to project a psychic profile.

He would prefer, if possible, to project a species profile to the environment and thereby engage in a direct transaction. Or perhaps it would be better to say that the *body* would prefer to so engage itself with the environment. But, as we know, man cannot do this. Also, as we know, man's conscious mind serves as an intermediary between the needs of the body and the demands of the terrestrial environment. However, the conscious mind is not an impartial intermediary. It contains a strong terrestrial bias, since its function is to conform the body to the demands of terrestrial living. At the same time the body and its unconscious mind have what can only be described as an eternally arboreal bias. Hence, conflict.

While it has been the declared purpose of psychotherapists to reduce and even—theoretically—eliminate this conflict, they have failed lamentably because they have proceeded in the wrong direction. In essence, they have sought to end the conflict by rendering the unconscious harmless. Beginning with Freud, who called the unconscious a seething caldron, psychotherapists have attempted to subject this caldron to reason, but with disastrous results.

The fact is that the unconscious mind has reason of its own.

It is a reason that guided the destiny of millions of generations of arboreal primates. If it is a seething caldron, it is so because of the incarceration of its reason in the prison of conscious reason, a thoroughly terrestrial reason. The conflict that exists between the two minds of man is like that of prisoner and jailer. The prisoner wants his freedom; the jailer wants to confine his prisoner. The crisis presented to each is enormous. The prisoner is being stifled to death by what from his perspective is madness without a shred of reason to justify it. The prisoner is guiltless, natural, and vital. He wishes merely to live as he once lived before imprisonment. The jailer, from his perspective, has good reason to confine his unruly, unrepentant, and subversive prisoner who, if let loose, would go on a rampage that would, quite literally, destroy civilization.

However, if we still pursue the analogy, the jailer must allow some activity on the part of the prisoner. He cannot be allowed to waste away, for if that happened, in a manner of speaking the jailer would be out of a job and, lacking a means of support, would himself perish.

As is true of all creatures in captivity, the prisoner here is severely restricted in what he can do, and what he can do is determined by his jailer. If in a particular case the jailer is unduly oppressive and extremely restrictive in what he allows the prisoner to do—always, it seems, with the emphasis on what the prisoner cannot do—there will ensue a serious collapse of the prisoner. If, on the other hand, the jailer is lax, allowing the prisoner virtually free rein, there is a great risk of an attempted escape.

If the conscious mind, with its terrestrial bias, overly restricts or suppresses the unconscious mind with its arboreal bias, the entire system breaks down and mental illness is the result. Yet, even as we apprehend the term *mental illness*, we must immediately be aware that what really stops functioning properly is man's brain. It fails to function as a brain (in the same manner that a nonfunctioning or improperly functioning liver or pancreas fails to function as a liver or pancreas, with the appropriate accompanying consequences). Mental illness, in other words, is at base a physical condition.

What, on the other hand, if the jailer is lax and allows the prisoner to have his way? Then, instead of mental illness, we have "social illness." When the arboreal nature of man is allowed to express itself independently of the inhibitory control of the conscious mind, society breaks down. This breakdown is manifested in such antiterrestrial activities as sexual promiscuity, violation of laws relating to property, refusal to engage in the hunt, and every other activity strictly arboreal.

Whether the jailer is harsh or lax, the resulting conduct is considered deviant. Deviance of either sort, if sufficiently extended, can well result in individual and species extinction. Under a harsh jailer the organism simply ceases to function, its vital processes stifled. Under a lax master, the terrestrialization of man, absolutely essential for survival in the terrestrial mode, is set aside, thus destroying the mortar on which survival depends.

Balance is essential. There must be a *modus vivendi* between the two minds if man is to survive. While it may be that the unconscious mind would prefer an arboreal niche in which to be itself, untrammeled by the harsh demands of the terrestrial mind, it simply cannot be allowed its preference. Similarly, the conscious mind cannot exist on its own. To do so would be to destroy its basis of existence as well as whatever *raison d'être* it has.

It is clear that a reconciliation is necessary. Man—subjective man—has sought to effect one. As the conscious mind began to make its appearance in the experience of the species and as the individual began to distinguish itself from the totality of the species, there began to appear what modern psychologists call the ego. It is the ego which perceives the triangle mentioned a bit earlier. Without the triangle of self, object, and intermediary, there would be no need of consciousness and hence no need for an ego. It is the function of the ego to reconcile the needs of the body with the demands of the environment by means of the intermediary.

This is precisely where the difficulties of psychotherapy begin: in the matter of the nature and function of the ego. Every effort is made to press the psychic profile of the individual as firmly as possible against the psychic profile of the group, so as to increase survival possibilities of the individual. To this end, psychoanalysts have endowed the ego with a strong terrestrial bias, with the result that an already critical imbalance becomes that much more critical.

Freud, in *An Outline of Psychoanalysis*, confirms the notion that the principal function of the ego is self-preservation. He observes that the ego must learn to cope with the external world in a variety of ways. Then he writes:

> As regards *internal* events in relation to the id, [the ego] performs [its] task by gaining control over the demands of the instincts, by deciding whether they shall be allowed to obtain satisfaction, by postponing that satisfaction . . . or by suppressing their excitations completely. [Italics in original] [6]

This is entirely as it should be; the ego is functioning as an intermediary, and thereby acting as an agent of reconciliation. The difficulty arises, however, when we encounter Freud's superego. Beginning with the child we see the superego as being:

> . . . not merely the personalities of the parents themselves but also racial, national, and family traditions handed on through them as well as the demands of the immediate social milieu which they represent. In the same way, an individual's superego in the course of his development takes over contributions from later successors and

6. New York: W. W. Norton, 1949, p. 15.

substitutes of his parents, such as teachers, admired figures in public life, or high social ideals.[7]

The only difference between the superego of the child and that of the adult is the degree of subjectivity. In the child the superego very directly represents parental values; in the adult, it is more objective and has as its basis more or less the ethical standards of society. The terrestrial bias in such a system is clear. The result is effort by the individual, whether on his own or through the therapeutic efforts of another, to conform to the ideal created by the superego which means conformance to terrestrial society. Thus the ego strives toward terrestrial values.

One of the signs of maturity, according to Freud and those who follow him, is that of gratification-postponement. It is, if possible, more than a sign of maturity: It is a mark of virtue, and indisputable evidence of a cure. It is, paradoxically, one of those measuring rods that no one questions. And yet gratification-postponement is the very thing guaranteed to produce time-anxiety and body stress. Notwithstanding, the individual is taught from infancy to *seek* it, not merely to accept it as one of life's inevitable conditions, much as one accepts gravity. Yet, if one were to add weight so as to be able to experience a greater awareness of gravity, he would be thought quite irrational. But not so with regard to increasing ability to accept greater and greater gratification-postponement. That way lies maturity—within the framework of this system of thought.

Jung is more elusive. Unlike the dogmatic Freud, who creates a theory and fills it with almost tangible figures such as the id, ego, and superego, Jung proceeds almost mystically to construct the psyche of man with the aid of gray figures such as the persona and the shadow. Caught between, as it were, is the ego. And being caught between, the ego is pulled in opposite directions. It is when Jung talks of the ego in military terms that we can begin to see what he means:

---

7. *Ibid.*, p. 17.

The individual ego could be conceived as the commander of a small army in the struggle with his environment—a war not infrequently on two fronts, before him the struggle for existence, in the rear the struggle against his own rebellious instinctual nature.[8]

What Jung presents us with is the image of a war on two fronts. On one is a struggle *for* existence in the terrestrial environment; on the other is a struggle *against* arboreal instinct. It is in this war that the persona, the face which one presents to the world (the psychic profile), seeks to make contact with the elements of survival. Yet, there is the rear-guard action necessary to keep the shadow (arboreality) under control so as not to interfere with survival efforts. What is significant to the present discussion is not the outcome of the war, but rather the fact that a war is under way and that the main front relates to the social environment.

In opposition to Freud and Jung, and their followers, are those who seek to "cure" emotional problems by staying almost completely away from the person and instead focusing their attention, as well as that of the patient, on externals such as conditioning. Behaviorism, including its subsidiary schools, sees the individual only in relation to his social environment. B. F. Skinner, in seeking to set the "self" on some unreachable shelf, writes, ". . . a self is simply a device for representing a *functionally unified system of responses.*" (Italics in original)[9] In these systems of therapeutic thought, there is no "ego" within the person; whatever "ego" there is is that of the observer who replaces "bad habits" with "good habits" by way of conditioning that will alter behavior in a way so as to relate the individual to his social environment.

Lost amid the efforts to strengthen the bond between the individual's psychic profile and the psychic profile of the group is the foundation of human existence: the body. When the

8. *The Structure and Dynamics of the Psyche* (New York: Pantheon, 1960), p. 360.
9. *Science and Human Behavior* (New York: The Free Press, 1953) p. 285.

criterion of normality and of mental health is conformity to the demands of terrestrial living, the essential problem of man is not solved; it is made worse. This again raises the question of the content of the conscious mind. Just as it can contain so much that is of a terrestrial bias, thus exacerbating the problem, so too it can contain elements with an arboreal bias so as to begin to establish greater balance, thereby reducing both time-anxiety and body stress. While this might seem to be something of a contradiction in that the body with its unconscious mind has no content in the sense that the conscious mind does, any contradiction is more apparent than real. The purpose of introducing elements of arboreal bias into the conscious mind cannot in any way affect the unconscious mind directly. However, such content can permit the individual to place limits on the terrestrial bias by counteracting it with arboreal bias. The purpose of such an indirect solution is to reduce the drive toward increased terrestrialization and hopefully reverse the process so that the individual's drives and activities can slow down to the point where body stress can be lessened, thereby improving overall health and even longevity prospects. As it is, the species is being driven to an early grave.

It should be noted that just above I only mention a reduction of body stress and nothing about time-anxiety. This omission is intentional. One of the reasons much of psychotherapy seems to work is that it satisfies the conscious mind. The patient, under the subtle prodding of the therapist, comes to a vision of normality and well-being. Indeed, it can be said with frightening legitimacy that the transmitted values of the therapist become the new superego of the patient. In this condition, once the patient's self-image matches that of the therapist's projected image, the patient believes himself well. Of course, what has happened is that the psychic profile of the patient has adjusted itself to that of the therapist. What is not accounted for, and what goes on silently suffering, is the patient's body, which requires that its needs be met now and not in some uncertain future.

*   *   *

Man, of necessity, is future-oriented. The story of his progress from pebble tool to automated assembly-line is the story of his developing cerebral cortex, most particularly the frontal lobes, for it was the development of the frontal lobes that made it possible for man to project himself into the future, thereby to guarantee his survival in the terrestrial mode.

There is, of course, no way to observe directly the development of man's most unique attributes. When and how these things began and then developed are lost in the ancient labyrinth. Fortunately, there is another way to observe the process, and that is in reverse. We can observe what happens with the loss of those remarkable lobes, and when we do we see the essential arboreal primate before it was imprisoned in the terrestrial mode; we see a creature living exclusively in the present, without any concern for the future. We see someone without body stress and time-anxiety.

Over the centuries tentative probings—and endless theorizing—had confirmed most scholars in the belief that the frontal lobes were the seat of intelligence and the locus in which all that made man man were stored. It took the most extraordinary experience of one Phineas Gage in 1848 to set everything aside. Gage, foreman of a road construction gang in England, was the victim of an unusual accident. A charge of dynamite exploded prematurely and drove an iron tamping rod, nearly four feet long and one and one-fourth inches thick, through his brain. The rod entered high on his left cheek and emerged through the top of his head. Gage was as good as dead.

For about an hour Gage lay on the ground, stunned. Then, to everyone's astonishment, he was able to walk away to see a doctor. On the way he talked with composure about the great hole in his head. He survived for twelve years after the accident, dying in San Francisco under circumstances that required an autopsy. It was then discovered that both the left and right frontal lobes of his brain had been heavily damaged.

That Gage did not die at the moment the heavy bar tore through his head was surprise enough. What sent the medical profession scurrying to its theories was the transformation of

Gage after the accident. The fact that most disturbed them was the *absence* of spectacular change. Gage continued to be competent, he suffered no loss of memory, and he was entirely capable of working as a foreman.

What changes took place were not those contemporary theory could have foreseen. It was his personality, not his in-intellectual equipment, that had been transformed. Before the accident he had been considerate and well-integrated. After the accident he was fitful, and, as one commentator later wrote, ". . . irreverent, indulging frequently in gross profanity and manifesting little consideration for others. He had become obstinate, yet capricious and vacillating. With these new traits he could no longer be trusted to supervise others. In fact, he showed little inclination toward work of any kind, but instead chose to travel around, making a living by exhibiting himself and his tamping iron . . ." [10]

It was only when psychosurgery came along that a systematic study could be made of man minus his frontal lobes. In this procedure segments of the frontal lobes are either removed or are surgically isolated from the rest of the brain. Mary Frances Robinson, in *Psychosurgery and the Self*, has described the net effect of such procedures: "Psychosurgery changes the structure of the self through reducing the capacity for the feeling of *self continuity*." (Italics added) [11]

Walter Freeman and James W. Watts, two experienced American psychosurgeons, have written of the futurity principle:

> With the intact brain the individual is able to foresee, to forecast the results of certain activities that he is to initiate in the future, and he can visualize what effect these actions will have upon himself and upon his environment. . . .

10. Dean E. Woolridge, *The Machinery of the Brain* (New York: McGraw-Hill, 1963), p. 147.

11. Mary Frances Robinson and Walter Freeman (New York: Grune & Stratton, 1954), p. 15.

. . . Insight demands that the individual shall erect in his mind an image of himself in relation to the outside world, and he can do this only if he projects himself into the future and sees himself as he should appear.[12]

According to their research, frontal lobe disease or elimination results in inertia, lack of ambition, a reduction in consecutive thinking, loss of what we know as self-consciousness, indifference to the opinions of others, and satisfaction with inferior performance of tasks. Secondary effects of the condition are euphoria, evasion, bluffing, talkativeness, aggressive behavior, teasing, inattention, poor judgment, and what the authors label "indecent acts." Writing of the effects of prefrontal lobotomy they say:

What is accomplished by the operation is a separation of the ability of the individual to project himself into the future and the feeling tone that accompanies this. We speak of smashing the fantasy life. It is the inner sensations, ideas, recollections, ambitions and disappointments, the regrets for the past and the fears for the future, that are particularly affected this way.[13]

There is, then, in the normal individual, a continuity of self. It begins in the past, through memory; it continues in the present by means of present awareness; and it extends into the future via projected imagination. By this method of self-continuity man is capable of creating mortar and thereby surviving. Because he has had to create mortar on an ever-increasing basis, man has had to project himself on an ever-increasing basis into the future, thus requiring extended continuity of self. This can be seen, by way of example, in the matter of fatherhood and filialness. When, in the course of terrestrialization, the hunt became more demanding and hence more consuming of the lives of the adult males, there developed a growing need for more

---

12. *Psychosurgery in The Treatment of Mental Disorders and Intractable Pain*, 2d ed. (Springfield, Ill.: Charles C. Thomas, 1950), pp. 530–531.
13. Ibid., p. 531.

continuity of self. Since the adult males could not extend themselves beyond themselves, any greater extended continuity had to be achieved through the younger males. For this to happen, the older males had to extend their own continuity through specific younger males so that the hunt could be perpetuated. (Of course, the ultimate extension of the continuity of self can be seen in the notion of perpetual life after death.)

Since survival in the terrestrial mode demands continuity of self, or as we might otherwise express it, continuity of the ego, what happens when there is a discontinuity as a result of disease or surgery?

The psychiatrist S. Spafford Acherly has given us an answer in a remarkable case he was able to observe for a period of thirty years. It concerned one J. P. who was born almost totally devoid of frontal lobes. J. P. was born in 1912; he began to walk and talk at one year. Throughout infancy and early preschool childhood his general intelligence and development were reported as being unimpaired. However, there were two features that stood out: He wandered a great deal, notwithstanding severe beatings by way of punishment, and he possessed what Acherly describes as Chesterfieldian manners.[14] What is significant about his wanderings, which began at two and a half and continued for the rest of his life, was the fact that he never expressed fear, even though as a very small child he would be found miles away from his home.

J. P. had trouble from the very beginning of his school years. Acherly writes of a rather humorous and revealing incident: "The first grade teacher had just finished writing a letter to the parents complimenting them on having such a polite, well-mannered child who was such a good influence in the class, when she looked up and found him exposing himself to children and masturbating openly." [15]

Acherly summarizes this period of J. P.'s life:

14. The details of the case are presented in "A Case of Paranatal Bilateral Frontal Lobe Defect Observed for Thirty Years," *Symposium on the Frontal Granular Cortex and Behavior*, edited by J. M. Warren and K. Ahert (New York: McGraw-Hill, 1964).
15. Ibid., p. 194.

Reading skill was always good; mathematics always poor. He passed the first three grades but was forced to repeat the fourth and fifth. He got by in school largely because of his reading, spelling, and language ability, but was disobedient, truant, and a poor helper at home, could never seem to finish household chores he was expected to do unless closely supervised. No friends of either sex. Heartily disliked by the boys at school and in the neighborhood . . . never was known to escape into daydreaming or moviegoing; always a "goer" rather than a "sitter" or a "doer." Never learned how to get along with his peers. *He has been a stranger in this world without knowing it.* [Italics added] [16]

Because of repeated incidents over a period of years, such as masturbation, truancy, stealing (mostly from home), thrusting himself into the center of attention with no self-consciousness, excessive boastfulness, and extreme unpopularity with other students, J. P. was transferred from school to school. Finally, after stealing a teacher's car, he was sent to reform school.

Acherly summarizes J. P. as an adolescent:

His adolescent years appeared no different from his pre-adolescent years—no close friendships with either boys or girls, in fact, no friendships at all of either sex. He took a girl to the hotel for dinner one night and when she was in the powder room he took her purse and ended up in Alabama. Always the same polite little boy; little adolescent rebellion against authority even though father disciplined the boy severely. We were surprised at the curious lack of the usual dependency-independency struggles; no direct or indirect evidences of lovemaking or increased goal-directed sexual activities. No sentimentalizing the mother or other women; no great enthusiasms or periods of dejection or discouragement. Seldom, if ever, cried even when severely punished.[17]

---

16. Ibid., p. 194.
17. Ibid., p. 194.

J. P.'s health as a young man was excellent. He was alert-looking, responsive, talkative, of sturdy build and had never suffered from serious illness. As a personality he was always distinguished for his stereotyped, forthright, but excessive politeness and courtly manners without being ingratiating. He sought to be useful and important. He was indignant when others didn't measure up.

It wasn't until he was nineteen that his true condition was suspected, and it wasn't until late 1933, when J. P. was almost twenty-one, that he was operated on to explore the area of the frontal lobes. It was then that their almost total absence was discovered. After a brief stay in the hospital, J. P. was released and almost immediately pawned his mother's rings, took his uncle's car, and drove to Chicago. He came home drunk and for the first and only time threatened his father. He was sent to the state hospital, but soon escaped and went to Colorado. Returned, he was again put in the state hospital—in the closed ward—where he was generally unhappy but was able to do useful work when closely supervised. That is, until he walked off several months later.

Once free of the hospital, the pattern of behavior was essentially the same as in previous years. He was never able to hold down a job for more than a few weeks, primarily because of erratic performance. At various times he was a salesman, factory worker, night watchman, orderly, gas-station attendant, errand boy, bus-driver, and truck-driver.

In 1948, when J. P. was thirty-six years old, Acherly and an associate made an evaluation. They asked themselves this question: How long could J. P. continue to hold up in the face of daily defeat, rejection, and frustration with the loss of flexibility associated with advancing age? The reply they gave to the question came fifteen years later when they concluded that nothing had changed. J. P. was J. P., only older. Acherly writes: "Compared with the average human being with an intact brain, his defenselessness, vulnerability, and helplessness are nothing short of tragic. Fortunately, his organic brain condition has so blunted his sensibilities or so raised the threshold of response that he appears unaware of his total life situation."

Acherly summarized his impressions through 1948:

> . . . What seemed to command our attention and sympathy was his "aloneness"—detachment not from the immediate physical environment of things and people, but from anything beyond that—anything that gave meaning to life, love, friendship, comradeship. *He is indeed a veritable stranger in this world with no other world to flee to for comfort.* . . . [Italics added]
>
> In short, we saw here a case of arrested development that showed itself most strikingly for all practical purposes in the social sphere. Simple social feeling and goodwill are there, but he is limited in his ability to amplify, elaborate, nurse, and implement this social feeling. . . . His total drive system seems weak and ineffectual—sexual, aggressive, or mastery and self-preservative functions—all seem as reduced in their essence as are his abstract intellectual functions. All seem simple, rudimentary, undeveloped, and arrested.[18]

Acherly concludes his survey of J. P.'s life by writing: "Our patient is now about fifty years of age. He has not changed essentially in the last 30 years in health, looks, or behavior. He is the same refreshingly simple, uncomplicated, straightforward, outrageously boastful or indignant little boy." [19]

What is interesting in all of Acherly's restatement of J. P.'s history is not so much what J. P. lacked, but what, according to Acherly, humans living in modern society possess. In contrasting J. P. to normal people, Acherly wrote of J. P.'s helplessness, vulnerability, and defenselessness, in contrast "with the average human being who can rationalize his position in terms of repression, conversion, substitution, sublimation, masochistic self-pity, or aggressive offense." In so cataloguing the capacities

18. Ibid., p. 204.
19. Ibid., p. 205.

of the normal human, Acherly has succinctly described the functions of the frontal lobes.

J. P. quite obviously could not survive in terrestrial society without the assistance of others. No one could without adequately functioning frontal lobes. Without them, the individual lacks all continuity of self and hence cannot project himself into the future. As a result of this deficiency, he cannot produce mortar. On the other hand, with a fully operative cerebral cortex, the individual possesses reflective and projective capabilities by means of which he can prepare for the future.

What, we must now ask, if there are things of the past remembered that when projected into the future make the *anticipation* of the future a painful experience? When we have that condition we have anxiety; and when that anxiety reaches a critical level the individual shuts himself off from the future by way of neurosis or psychosis as effectively as if born without frontal lobes or as if a surgeon had performed psychosurgery. The fact of the matter is that psychosurgery is performed for precisely the reason that anxiety has proven absolutely unbearable and has so incapacitated the individual to function that the only way to be able to endure the present is to interrupt, by surgical means, the continuity of self, thereby cutting him off from the future.

Since the future cannot be excised, it is effectively removed from contemplation by surgically removing the past. This is done by separating the frontal lobes from the thalamus, the gateway to the lobes, which acts as a central collection agency for the various sensory data collected by the rest of the brain. In other words, painful data and conscious awareness of them are kept apart. By this separation, though the painful data continue to exist, the individual loses the ability to grasp their significance.

Just as there is a continuity of self in the normal individual, there is also a continuity of meaning. Whereas the small child lives in discrete, isolated segments of time, the older child (generally six and older) and the adult possess an integrating system whereby all the past discrete elements of personal history are integrated and synthesized into a comprehensive system, producing for the individual a generalized perception of the self in relation to the rest of the world. If this is a relatively pleasant perception, the individual is considered normal because of his ability to function on the basis of that perception. If the perception is painful and if as a result the individual by a variety of means seeks to shut off that painful perception, he is considered neurotic or psychotic, depending on the degree of shutdown. This synthesis of past experience is the function of the frontal lobes, and by isolating them from the rest of the brain —whether by surgery or shutdown—the individual is spared the pain of contemplating the future. As a result, he exists in the constant now.

It is for this reason that frontal lobotomy patients live in the concrete present and even though experiencing everything and anything from intractable pain to psychotic symptoms, never fret over them or worry about the future. Pain, even pain that was unbearable before surgery, becomes bearable because there is no way of projecting the pain into the endless future. There is, in effect, no memory of past pain and no anxiety about future pain. Psychotic symptoms may exist, but as they too are separated from the past and future they can be lived with, pretty much as many people adjust complacently to minor idiosyncrasies. The *significance* of pain and symptoms is absent because the individual exists in the concrete now.

However, the fact that the conscious mind does not apprehend the past or experience anxiety over the future does not mean that the individual isn't suffering. He is, only he isn't consciously aware of it. His body is suffering—silently. This is seen in high blood pressure, sweating, bodily tension, and a whole variety of possible manifestations. Indeed, as I just observed, post-lobotomy patients often continue to experience physical pain and psychotic symptoms—which is the only way that the body can marshal its defenses against threats to its existence.

What is outstanding in all of this is the fact that the body continues to suffer the consequences of existence in the terrestrial mode regardless of the state of consciousness of suffering. Because of ever-expanding mortar requirements, constantly expanding consciousness of a markedly terrestrial bias is required. As a consequence of this, greater and greater restraints are placed on the body. The now of the body is stretched to the breaking point by futurity demands. The body, in protest and to protect its very existence, constantly responds. Shutdowns occur with increasing frequency; neuroses and psychoses grow in number and in intensity as the body struggles for survival. And what do therapists do? They completely ignore the body except to prescribe palliatives such as tranquilizers and sleeping pills as a method of anesthetizing the body so that its complaints can't be heard. While they are attempting to silence the complaining body (even to the extent of psychosurgery), they are focusing their professional attention on the mind in an effort to conform it more closely to the terrestrial demands of society. Not only do they ignore the silent cries of the body, they prescribe for the mind in such as way as to squeeze the body almost to death. Could anything be more deleterious? Could anything more speedily bring the species to the brink of extinction?

The entire subject of psychotherapy has come upon hard times, as if something very deep in man were protesting against this onslaught against survival. Once Freud was the messiah of a sane new world. Then flaws in his thinking began to be discerned. His great theory of man broke up into a dozen or more microtheories. Then, in something redolent of the break within Christianity, Freud and Freudianism were declared anathema and the conflict within man was set aside as a fiction in order to make room for the conflict between the individual and society. Whatever was wrong with man was the result of bad habits. Recondition man and these habits will disappear, leaving a healthy social being in its place. And yet, despite macro- and microtheories, despite conditioning and reconditioning, hospital admissions grow while more and more individuals apply faddish poultices to their fevered minds. There is even a new hypothesis, obviously the result of the cornering of reason, that says, "I'm Okay, You're Okay," as if all man had to do was to convince himself, as per Norman Vincent Peale, that positive thinking will overcome reality.

I have intimated earlier what I believe to be the source of the problem: The conscious mind. The mind is the key, but it is not the content of the matter. Unfortunately, almost everyone thinks key and content are the same. One way or another, so the general belief is, you can alter the mind and thereby solve man's existential problems. This would be true if all man possessed were a variable conscious mind. It is possible to so alter that mind as to produce every conceivable type of creature, from a Caligula to a Francis of Assisi and from an Einstein to a Jack Ruby.

But man is not merely a variable conscious mind; the rock on which everything subsists is the body with its genetically based, immutable, unconscious mind that no amount of tampering with can change. The unavoidable *fact* of human existence is man's arboreal body. Any effort to adjust man to terrestrial living must take that fact into consideration. To ignore man's arboreal body is to ignore the basic—and unalterable—nature of man. To know of this premise of life and then to proceed as if it were unimportant is to proceed through deadly folly, for if it is ignored much longer there will be no premise from which to proceed in any direction, for the body of man will have ceased to exist because its now-ness will have been so stretched into a state of futurity that it will simply, and quietly, break into pieces. It is doing so increasingly every day.

It is not necessary to remain fixed upon the plight of those who must have recourse to the analyst's couch, the encounter group's circle, the hospital's bed, or the psychosurgeon's knife, to see the universal problem of terrestrialized man. The problem can be seen in everyday existence as lived by everyday people. A woman is overweight, so she goes to one of her doctors, who prescribes amphetamines (her other doctors care, *seriatim*, for her skin, her feet, her teeth, her eyes, her bones, her stomach, etc. Almost no one is available to take care of *her*.). A child is having problems in school and is sent to the school psychologist, who prescribes tranquilizers or, in an extreme case, divorce for the parents. A man is having difficulties in his job, and the company psychologist gives him a battery of vocational tests, plus an open-ended prescription for sleeping pills, so that the man can at least get a full eight hours' sleep at night.

There really is no need to extend the point. The odds are that the reader is on a regimen of drugs, illegal or legal, marijuana or alcohol, and following a routine of anxiety ranging from vocation to sex. So the reader *knows* the problem in all its subtle and intimate ramifications.

What has been needed for a very long time has been something to put an end to drug regimens and routines of pervasive anxiety. Man—one is tempted to say indomitable man—has faced, in his long and turbulent terrestrial career, a series of crises, and he has overcome them, a subject I have discussed elsewhere. They concerned, in order: sustenance, climate control, a reproduction system for the conscious mind, and finally, in the penultimate crisis, a means of freeing the species from the vagaries of nature by incorporating nature into man's cocoon. The solutions, as we know, were tools, fire, speech, and domestication of animals and grain.

What is remarkable about both crises and solutions is that they all directly and specifically concerned the survival of the body. Man's extraordinary terrestrial mind was created for just one purpose: To assist the body to survive. It would seem, then, that the crisis represented by the great cave paintings of western Europe, once overcome, would have ushered man into, if not the ultimate millennium, then at least a terrestrial millennium in which an acceptable solution to a basically insoluble problem had been found. Man, under these circumstances, could at least survive. An arboreal primate, by virtue of a unique brain, could survive in the terrestrial mode by means of mortar. Mortar was, and is, the key to survival.

But the brain has proved to be the stumbling block. Instead of remaining the key in a sequence leading to ultimate content —the brain leading to the satisfaction of body needs—the key has become the point of existence itself. Man measures himself by his mind, not by his body. And he does so because in every critical evaluation of his situation he proceeds in reverse. He operates on the great false premise that man is the measure of all things. He argues—and evaluates—from a conclusion, not from an original premise. If we untangle the logical sequence and then set it straight, we discover that the *conclusion* is man, and that the premise is an arboreal primate seeking to exist in the terrestrial environment. The key to this impossibility is man's mind, which has the ability to fashion the mortar absolutely essential to the survival of his arboreal body in the terrestrial mode. Mortar, then, exists for the body. This being the case, the mind exists to make mortar so that the arboreal body, caught in the terrestrial prison, might survive. The mind has no other purpose than that. It is the servant of the body. Or, put a bit differently, the mind is the servant of survival—it is not the object of survival. And yet, it is this key, this mesmerizing key, that grants man his favored position among all creatures. The mind is the very thing that separates man from beast. It is the thing that makes man—man. Nothing frightens him more than the loss of this unique attribute. Nothing humiliates him more than to have his reason suspect. But still, the mind is only the servant of the body. And being such, it must be put to the service of the body. Nowhere is this more urgently needed than in the matter of psychotherapy which, for the most part has completely ignored the body. In so doing, it has jeopardized man to the point of extinction.

And it is this jeopardy that is now confronting man with his ultimate crisis. He has, in his construction of mortar, reached the point where the construct has become more important than its purpose. Means have become ends. Thus ignored, the real ends have entered a state of extreme jeopardy. This, in turn, places the species in jeopardy. This is man's current crisis.

THE DREAMER

O F A L L man's inventions, the most remarkable has been religion. It, more than anything else, has given purpose to man's life. Indeed, without it man would be forever mired in terrestrial living—just like any other beast. If such were the case, there would be no purpose to life. The consequence of this would be catastrophic, for life without purpose would not be worth living, and once found not worth living would be quickly extinguished.

If we return to man's arboreal ancestors we find them living without religion. When we come upon Sumer we discover a fully evolved system of religion. Therefore, we must conclude that between Point A and Point T, religion was invented. The question is: Why?

Previously we have explored the various crises that arose during the terrestrialization process. They concerned sustenance, control of the environment, and communication, all of which related directly to mortar. Tools, fire, speech, and such inventions as paternity, filialness, the family, and so on were essential to survival in the terrestrial mode. In essence, they made it possible for an arboreal primate to exist in terrestria.

What, then, of religion? Where does it fit into the terrestrialization process? In a sense, religion serves as a mediator between the arboreal aspirations of man and his terrestrial circumstances. It makes terrestrial life bearable by promising a return to arborea. Viewed this way, religion can be conceived of as a part of psychic mortar. However, in a larger sense, religion is the guidance system of the species in its efforts at returning to arborea. It is this that gives purpose to life, one great purpose of life for the species being to return to arborea where it belongs.

As I have said elsewhere, this desire to return to arborea is not a conscious desire for the reason that the conscious mind is a terrestrial mind. What drives man to seek a return to arborea is his arboreal body which today, because of the secondary effect of mortar, is genetically the same as it was while the species lived in arborea. Man's conscious mind has translated this bodily assertion into dynamic symbolic processes it calls religion. Religion serves as a promise by the conscious mind to the body that it will be liberated from its terrestrial prison and allowed to return to its natural habitat, arborea. But the great stumbling block, the thing that makes the promise a lie, is the fact that the conscious mind knows through its reasoning processes that the body can never return to arborea. It is because of this that religion rests, not on reason, but on faith,[1] not on what one can legitimately anticipate, but on what one hopes for. Only when faith and hope can leap the barrier of reason can one become religious and believe that someday he will return to arborea—even if he has to wait until a second lifetime, or a thousand earthly lives have passed—to make the journey home.

For thousands of years man has sought to explain his origins. Until modern anthropology began to rummage around in the great labyrinth of time, man had to be content with myths, those curious figments Mircea Eliade describes as *"truth par excellence."* Myths are myths because the conscious mind cannot penetrate far enough back in time to explain events that took place before its own existence. But there are shadowy memories that inform myths; whether we call them phyletic

---

1. Faith is a state of mind derived from a commingling of reason and aspiration. The reasoning here is provided by the conscious mind; aspiration from the unconscious mind.

memory, race memory, or as per Jung, the collective unconscious, they are there.[2] We see these shadows in the great
cosmogonic myths, and we see them in the great religious
myths of every period and place.

The most commonly recurring element in all mythologies is
that of a paradisiacal past. Virtually all peoples of every period
and place have a myth of a time—a very early time lost in primordial mists—when men lived in a sublime paradise. They
enjoyed immortality, spontaneity, freedom, and, as Eliade tells
us, "the possibility of ascending into Heaven and *easily meeting*
with the gods; friendship with the animals and knowledge of
their language." [Italics in original] [3]

In this time, or as Eliade informs us, *in illo tempore*, Heaven
and Earth were very close to each other, or Heaven was easily
accessible, either by climbing a tree or a tropical creeper or ladder, or by scaling a mountain. In effect, these myths reveal primordial man enjoying a beatitude, a spontaneity and freedom,
which he lost as a consequence of a *fall*, something that occurred after a mythical event that caused a rupture between
Heaven and Earth. In other words, man's fall came after the
rupture between Heaven and Earth. "*In illo tempore*," Eliade
writes, ". . . the gods came down to earth and mingled with
men; and men, for their part, could go up to Heaven . . ."

When, a few centuries ago, the Noble Savage was discovered
in the course of voyages of discovery, he was envied by Europeans for his freedom and his way of life deep in the bosom of
nature. Here truly was the Golden Age rediscovered. However,
these noble savages revealed an awareness of having lost their
own version of a primordial paradise. The myths varied from
culture to culture, but they had certain shared features: man

---

2. It is entirely probable that man's arboreal ancestors possessed a
rudimentary consciousness comparable to modern chimpanzees, which
make tools for termite-fishing. This could be a sufficient base on which
to build the structure of man's future consciousness.

3. *Myths, Dreams, and Mysteries* (New York: Harper & Row, 1960),
p. 60.

was immortal, he was able to meet God face to face, he was happy, and did not have to work for his food.

In *Images and Symbols*, Eliade sets forth the principle of "The Centre," that is, a place sacred above all other places. He writes: "The most widely distributed variant of the symbolism of the centre is the Cosmic Tree, situated in the middle of the Universe . . . Vedic India, ancient China, and the Germanic mythology, as well as the 'primitive' religions, all held different versions of this Cosmic Tree whose roots plunged down into Hell, and whose branches reached Heaven." [4]

And then, of course, there are the trees in the Garden of Eden—but we will get to that in a moment.

I think it is abundantly clear that behind the mythical façade there exists the reality of arborea. Before Time, in the Beginning, man's arboreal ancestors experienced precisely what myths tell us: spontaneity, freedom, and immortality.[5] There was no need to work in order to eat and they easily were able to meet and mingle with other primates, and, in a sense, understand the language of other animals. This existence, an existence that was the very center of everything, took place in the trees. Then there occurred that "mythical event," that rupture between Heaven and Earth that resulted in the *fall*. That is, the species was denied access to the trees. Paradise was lost—or rather, arborea was lost.

The second most universal "mythical-memory" among men is that of nostalgia. Man seeks to return to that primordial paradise. Whether one follows the primitive shaman or the Christian priest there is a path to be followed: It leads to that primordial paradise. "At the *commencement* as at the *end* of the religious history of humanity, we find again the same nostalgia for Paradise. If we take account of the fact that this nostalgia for Paradise was similarly discernible in the general religious conduct of men in the archaic societies, we are justified in supposing that the mythical remembrance of a non-historical hap-

4. New York: Sheed & Ward, 1961, p. 44.
5. Immortality in the sense that there was no awareness of death.

piness has haunted humanity from the moment when man first became aware of his situation in the Cosmos." [6]

What is striking about Eliade's observation is his use of the phrase "the mythical remembrance of a nonhistorical happiness." He is to myths what the traditional paleontologist is to arborea. As outstanding as Eliade is as a scholar of myths, he cannot, for whatever reason, translate mythical elements into their actual—even if prehistorical—counterparts. What is most curious about myth-collectors, including many besides Eliade, is that they consider myths as myths, or fanciful stories of fancied origins, without ever considering the possibility that these states actually existed and that these occurrences actually happened. It is *not* a mythical remembrance that produces profound nostalgia. It is *actual* remembrance of *actual* states and events that produces this nostalgia. After all, what is nostalgia but a longing for things of the past? If there were no actual past, how could there be nostalgia? Nostalgia is real, just as the arboreal past was real. It is this nostalgia that prompts the religious impulse in man, an impulse that is universal.

There is, of course, a problem. No matter how powerful the tug of nostalgia may be—and it is exceedingly powerful—there is always an impediment to any return to the paradisaical past. This impediment is a necessary factor in all religious systems, for if there were no impediment there would be the real possibility of a direct and immediate return. Man knows that he cannot go back; he has always known this. It is this very knowledge that prompted him to invent religion in the first place. And yet, he must believe in the *possibility* of a return. That is, he must dream dreams of the past and then project them into the future where he might achieve the desired state.

Man is like any exile who, even while in the deepest possible foreign dungeon, remembers his homeland and dreams of the day when he will be free to return there. This is so even when he knows he will never get free. But it is the one thing that

---

6. Eliade, *Myths, Dreams, and Mysteries*, p. 71.

sustains life. It is the only thing that gives life a purpose. The loss of this dream will plunge the prisoner into the deepest despair.

Yet this dream has an impediment of its own, reflecting the impediment to a return. The matter involved is manifested by the gods.

Every religious system has its immortal god or gods who are, in one way or another, the creators of the universe, the earth, and man. They possess, to varying degrees, remarkable powers over man. In addition, many mingle with humans on earth, though it is extremely rare that a mere human can ascend to the celestial abode of the gods—and return safely. In some systems the gods are very remote and awesome in their power; in others, they are quite near and quite human in their frailties.

There is in virtually all religious systems a strange ambivalence of feeling, something that is a mixture of love and fear, of attraction and repulsion, in connection with the gods. There is a profound desire for a reconciliation with the gods, yet an almost equally strong desire to escape them.

Finally, there is the matter of man's *fall*, an element present in just about every system. If not a fall, then something that separates man from the gods. In any event, there is a divorce for which men feel a greater or lesser sense of guilt.

Religious systems establish a relationship between fallen man and a celestial god or gods. Once that relationship is established, religious thought branches out into a multitude of themes. But regardless of the variations, the basic dynamics are there, consisting of an effort on the part of fallen man to affect a return to that state of being in which he once lived in harmony with a celestial god or gods. In this way, and only in this way, can man achieve the serenity he so desperately seeks. In every system, however, there is a critical impediment to achieving this end. In actuality, this impediment—regardless of its nature—cannot be surmounted, because man knows he cannot return to arborea. He is confined to his terrestrial prison and can only escape by way of fantasy or by way of death. And it is for this reason that death has become the pivot on which all religious thought turns. It is the one event in every man's life that liberates him from the confines of the terrestrial environment, permitting him to return to arborea by way of fantasy. Yet even in death there is a problem. To go to arborea is to confront the superior primate (primates) that drove man's arboreal ancestors out of arborea millions of years ago. Here we see the ultimate function of religion: *to assist man in finding a way to appease God so that God will allow man back into arborea.* In the idiom of my thesis, it would be expressed this way: The function of religion is to assist the inferior primate in finding a way to appease the superior primate so that it might get back into arborea. However, I think it best to use the terms *man* and *god* here because the problem is man's, not that of the original primate.

If religion is man's most remarkable invention, then surely the concept of life after death is the most extraordinary feature of that invention. And yet, despite everything, it is the heart of religion. It is, in another sense, the one thing that makes terrestrial living bearable. Lord Tennyson once proclaimed, "If there is no immortality, I shall hurl myself into the sea." Bismark remarked, "Without the hope of an afterlife this life is not even worth the effort of getting dressed in the morning." It was Paul who wrote that if Christ is not risen, then all is in vain.

The purpose of an afterlife is not to extend man's present terrestrial existence into the farthest reaches of the future. It is to give man an opportunity to escape his terrestrial prison that he might ascend to arborea. Since his reason tells him that he cannot, *in this life,* escape his prison, his imagination creates a second life in which he can accomplish his goal.

Unfortunately, it is not that easy a proposition, even in an afterlife. There is the matter of the body. And here man's genius fully reveals itself. It is man's body that confines man to the terrestrial mode, it is the body that is the prison. Freed of it, he would be able to ascend to arborea. In all the more sophisticated religions, it is the body that is the cause of man's fallen state. It must be chastised in this life; it must be shed in the second life if man is to achieve arborea. Yet, *something* of man must ascend to arborea. This something man calls his "soul." What, then, is the soul? It is the protagonist of man's imaginary afterlife. Just as man's fantasy worlds are incorporeal, so of necessity are its inhabitants. We can see this principle in literature, where Agamemnon and Holden Caulfield are as real to certain readers as Julius Caesar and Louis Pasteur are to students of history. It is because the soul and its world, the afterlife, are of such vital concern to man that they possess a "reality" almost impossible to resist. No one will shed his blood for Agamemnon, for Agamemnon is not vital. But millions have shed their blood for the protagonist in their fantasized future life. This, it must be pointed out, is not a form of madness, but is a condition of the mind brought about by the incarcerated condition of man's arboreal body. When the body of man, *in reality*, has most of the terrestrial restrictions lifted from it, this fantasy future life disappears, something that will be discussed later. The point I want to make here is that as long as serious terrestrial restrictions affect the body, the mind will fashion a fantasy world in which man escapes to arborea. It is the only way man can endure terrestrial existence. He may live in terrestria, but he dreams of home.

The difficulty in living within most religious systems stems from the remoteness of the gods. The distance between them and lowly man is actually an unspannable chasm. On one side recline the impersonal and indifferent gods; on the other is struggling man, who almost abandons hope of returning home. All that he can aspire to is a shedding of the body so that he can be rid of suffering. As for the soul, all it can hope for is oblivion.

Death for the Sumerians was scarcely a release at all. Life for man was but to serve the needs of the gods. When service was finished, man died, whereupon he descended into a twilight

and equivocal world not too unlike the one from which he
came. This is not dissimilar from the beliefs of the modern
Australian aborigine whose past, present, and future lives are
part of a single continuum in which the various periods are
barely identifiable, one from the other.

It was because the gods were so remote that, in the period of
the Third Dynasty of Ur, a new practice came into being. It
was to prepare the foundations of Judaism and eventually Christianity. It all began with a change in burial rites. Until about
2000 B.C., the dead had been buried in regular cemeteries. With
the commencement of the Larsa Dynasty there came the rule
that the dead were to be buried in or under the houses of the
living.

Sir Leonard Woolley, along with Kramer, one of the world's
great Sumerologists, has described the arrangement:

> At the rear of the house, i.e., as far as possible from the
> part into which strangers would be admitted, there was a
> long narrow court roofed for half its length; under the
> pavement of the open half was the brick-built family vault
> (it might contain a dozen bodies) and the roofed half was
> a chapel dedicated to the worship of the family god.[7]

At the same time that there was a change in the site of burial,
there developed a change in the rite. Until this time, personal
items of a varied nature had been buried in the tomb with the
body. Henceforth in Ur the door to the burial vault would be
closed and a clay water jug and a platter placed *outside* the
vault. Nothing was placed inside the vault. The reasoning was
this: The dead man continued to live in his home. He was,
even in death, still a member of the family; he required no special tomb furniture or fittings because everything in the house
was considered to be at his disposal.

All this occurred at the time of a significant shift in religious
practices. The center of the new practice was the domestic

---

7. Leonard Woolley and Jacquetta Hawkes, *Prehistory and the Beginnings of Civilization* (New York: Harper & Row, 1963), p. 713.

chapel, a place more intimate and personal than the great formal temples with their rigid ceremonials. The complaint, as I have said, lay with remoteness. The gods—and there was a pantheon of them—were simply too remote and unapproachable. This was reflected in the great temples and their priesthoods. To overcome this deficiency, from an early time on the individual would place himself under some lesser member of the pantheon, one who ranked as his "personal deity," and safeguarded his interests and interceded for him with the major gods.[8] However, this personal deity was not chosen at random. Woolley writes on this point:

> Just as the great god was immanent in the city state, so the family, which was the ultimate social unit, more real and more vivid than the state itself . . . was the manifestation of a deity; that deity, whose high priest was the head of the house, had no distinctive name and needed none, because he *was* the family and could not be distinguished from it. [Italics in original] [9]

It was to this personal deity that members of the family prayed in their domestic chapels. Because there were so many of these special deities and because each family had its own deity, there was no need to fashion names for them. They were nameless. They *were*, as Woolley has observed, the family.

The importance of this rather obscure and transient practice lies in the fact that Abraham was born in Ur during the period when this practice was most in vogue. According to Hebrew tradition, the proper home of the family was Harran, but a branch of the family had established itself at Ur. There Abraham was born. Harran and Ur were the capitals of the two earthly realms of which Nannar, the Moon God, was the king, and anyone living in either city acknowledged the supreme au-

---

8. A Christian counterpart to this would be prayer to a saint or the Blessed Virgin, though, of course, they were not gods. The hope would be that the intercession of the saint would aid the cause of the petitioner.

9. Op. cit., Wooley and Hawkes, p. 713.

thority of the Moon God. This included Abraham's family, whose religious roots, despite some possible Semitic relics that might have endured to the time, were Sumerian.

The household of Terah, Abraham's father, followed the religious practices of Ur, "when every house possessed its domestic chapel beneath whose pavement lay the graves of the family's forebears and when family worship filled the void left in man's religious consciousness by the growing elusiveness of temple ritual and by Nannar's failure to protect his kingdom against foreign enemies." [10] We see this in the case of Jacob who, when he made a covenant with his cousin Laban, invoked the sanction of just this family god, "The God of Abraham and the God of Nabor, the God of their father."

There is, of course, the great invocation of "The God of Abraham, of Isaac and Jacob," that establishes for all time the God of Judaism. This ineffable God, this God without a name, this God without an image, was not a remote and abstract god such as those that surrounded the Jews in their long and turbulent history. This God was the personal deity of the family of Abraham that was originally prayed to in Ur. When Jacob and Laban entered their covenant, however, this onetime family god with whom there had been a sense of intimacy and who had served as an intermediary with the great and remote gods, had evolved into an unnamed, and unnameable, divine being which personified the family—and later the tribe—throughout all its generations and which was for its members the operative force in all family and tribe affairs.[11] The story of this evolution is contained in the story of Abraham's removal from Ur and his wanderings in the land of Canaan.

Abraham's removal of himself and his family from Ur to Harran was not religiously significant because the cult of the

---

10. Ibid., p. 742.
11. The later Moses identified the old and nameless god with Yahweh, whose worship had been widespread for a long time among the western Semites. This identification of the family god of the patriarchal clan gained stature through Moses and without change of character became the God of Israel.

family god existed there as it had at Ur. It was only when he migrated into relatively barbarian Palestine that the first step was taken which led to the isolation of the Jews as a "peculiar people," and which ultimately led to Christianity, history's most powerful guidance system to arborea.

Abraham's migrations placed certain restrictions on his practice of religion. Nannar the Moon God could not cross the frontier and enter the land of Canaan. To do so would infringe on the territorial rights of the established gods of Canaan. Also, Nannar required a large temple in which to be housed, as well as a retinue of attendants to perform their temple service. A pastoral people lacked a residence for a temple and its staff. As a result, Nannar had to be left behind in Sumer.

A novel condition existed in Canaan as far as Abraham was concerned. Being a pastoral people, the family of Abraham, along with their servants and flocks, had to remain in the countryside and not, as a rule, enter the Canaanite villages and towns where the gods of Canaan, in the tradition of the times, were ensconced in their temples and where tradition required obeisance by those sojourning in the region. Yet, the religious needs of Abraham and his people demanded some form of expression. The solution lay in the practices relating to their family god. Because in a sense, the god *was* the family and was thereby immanent *in* the family, wherever the family went, there went the family's god, unencumbered by temples and attendants, and unimpeded by frontiers. The head of the family (there were no priests necessary in this system, thus Judaism is a religion without a priest caste) conducted the worship of the family god—"the God of Abraham, of Isaac and Jacob"—in the traditional manner, sacrificing to him, not in any temple, but upon a makeshift altar set up wherever they camped.[12]

In this way, then, the world's most unique religious system, that relating to a personal god, was established. The conse-

---

12. It was not until the time of Solomon, between eight hundred and one thousand years after Abraham, that the first temple was built in Jerusalem.

quences for man have been enormous, for it has been this personal god who has repaired the rupture between heaven and earth, thus making it possible for man to return to arborea.

But the return home was not to be through Judaism, for Judaism was the faith of the tribes of Israel and this faith concerned itself with a future messianic age in this world. It is in Isaiah (61:5–6) that we read:

> And strangers shall stand and shall feed your flocks; and the sons of strangers shall be your husbandmen, and the dressers of your vines. But you shall be called the priests of the Lord. To you it shall be said: Ye ministers of our God, you shall eat the riches of the Gentiles, and you shall pride yourselves in their glory.

It was, however, the gentiles who prevailed, and they presented the Israelites with bitter portions, the final one coming A.D. 70 when Roman legions destroyed Jerusalem.

It is only when we understand the real relationships between any god and man that we can fully grasp the Judeo-Christian concepts of God and man. Neither concept, it must be pointed out, is readily ascertainable on the basis of what religion tells us.

It is said that man is made "in the image and likeness of God." It is also said, by those who reject religion, that "God is made in the image and likeness of man." In reality, the relationship between the two figures is that between one primate and another as they originally existed many millions of years ago in arborea. This relationship was an immediate and contiguous one, very unlike that projected in every system of ancient myths except one, that of the Israelites.

If we follow the Biblical lines of development in the relationship between the two figures, we come across a primordial garden in Eden. "The Lord God," Genesis tells us, "made to grow out of the ground all kinds of trees pleasant to the sight and good for food." Among the many trees pleasant of sight and good for food were the tree of life (cf. Eliade's Cosmic Tree) and the tree of the knowledge of good and evil. Man—here meant as male and female—lived in a natural condition, immortal and without need to work in order to eat. Clearly, the author of Genesis is describing arborea. Arborea—paradise—is lost because of an act of disobedience, an act, interestingly enough, related to a tree. An angry God expels Adam and Eve from arborea. As a consequence, they lose their immortality, their naturalness, and they become obliged to suffer: Eve, in child-bearing; Adam, in working for food. Most critical of all, they can never return to arborea, for God placed "the Cherubim, and the flaming sword, which turned every way, to guard the way to the tree of life." This expulsion is the *fall* for which later Christian writers would blame the fallen condition of man. The fall—what an apt, yet inadvertent term!—was occasioned by an act of disobedience by man's first parents, which henceforth would be known as original sin, an affliction that would have to be borne by all subsequent humans: All children born of woman would be born into the terrestrial mode of existence, and not the arboreal. Original sin is the birthmark of humanity. It is that which forever separates man and God, man and arborea. All this is the result of the fall: the exile of the species from arborea. Were it not for the fall (described as a fall from grace), man and God would continue to be united and man would continue to be immortal, sustained by the tree of life. In short, were it not for the fall, man would still be in arborea.

What must be observed in this process is the power of God. It would not be sufficient for the Biblical God to be angry with Adam and Eve, no matter how legitimate (or illegitimate, for that matter) his anger might be. What is necessary is that God possess the power to expel them from the garden. It reflects the power of the original superior primate to force man's arboreal ancestors from arborea.

One of the most unusual aspects to this story of man's fall is his great sense of guilt. The loss of paradise—union with God —is the result of some moral defect in man. While theologians attribute man's fall to some spiritual flaw that leads to a transgression of one of God's ordinances, thereby inducing a deep sense of guilt, it would seem that an anthropological explanation for the fall would be more appropriate.

A deficiency of some sort—we have no way of knowing its precise nature—made man's arboreal ancestors inferior to certain other primates.[13] Because of this deficiency, superior primates were able to exclude them from arborea during the prolonged aridation in Africa. This physical deficiency man translates into a spiritual deficiency for which he feels guilt.

What is unique about the Judeo-Christian sense of guilt is its enormity. No other religious system so heavily accentuates guilt. But then, no other system has a personal god who, in human terms, is the father whom the son has disobeyed. Or, rather, there is the father who drove the son from the family home. Since the father is a good father, a just father, he would not drive the son out unless the son had done something to deserve it. Therefore, as this principle of projection provides, the son is guilty of some transgression.

In reality there is no basis for man's sense of guilt. Yet this guilt, especially as experienced in the Judeo-Christian system, has had a very important part to play in the development of doctrine. It has provided a powerful incentive to seek a reconciliation with God and thereby a return to arborea. Reinforcing this incentive is the doctrine of punishment. Because man transgressed God's ordinance, he not only has been denied beatitude, he has warranted punishment—and for an eternity coextensive with that to be enjoyed in paradise. Punishment consists of eternal damnation and consignment to hell which, in digest, is an extension of terrestrial existence both in degree of suffering and in duration. This life, then, is the testing ground for the future. The goal is arborea; hell is perpetuated terrestrial existence.

Reconciliation requires a purification of the self. No sinner may enter the presence of God. Upon translation, this means

---

13. See pp. 46–50 *supra* for a discussion of the competition between African monkeys of the Miocene and contemporary apes.

that man the primate must cure the defects that made him inferior to the expelling primate. Only in this way can he return to arborea.

In all this can be seen the love/fear, attraction/repulsion factors in man's relation with God, something alluded to earlier. If we observe Judaism for a moment, we see that man's fear of God was so overwhelming as to preclude all chance of a return to arborea. That is why in Judaic thought there is no substantial body of doctrine relating to a heavenly paradise after death. What there is is tentative and equivocal, an argument occurring over whether the promised messiah would bring the existing world order to an end and inaugurate a timeless sphere in which the righteous would lead a purely spiritual existence freed from the trammels of the flesh, or whether the messianic period would be only a transitory stage between this world and the next. In any event, opinion was divided. This open question was settled for all time when Christianity formulated its position.

In Christianity, the jealous, unapproachable, and vengeful God of Judaism is replaced with a just, forgiving, and merciful God with whom a reconciliation is possible, thus assuring the faithful that salvation itself is possible. This has been the great Christian message.

Christianity, above all other religions, is one of salvation. Whereas Judaism really seeks to avoid confronting the question, and Buddhism and Hinduism seek blessed evaporation into nothingness, Christianity offers salvation. It promises arborea to the faithful.[14] Indeed, Christianity has no other purpose. It is because of this that Christianity has been so important in the history of man—not because it could in fact produce salvation in the form of life after death, but because it provided the framework in which it was possible to achieve neo-arborea on earth. And this remarkable feat has never been possible in any other religious system.

---

14. Islam also offers salvation, but many of Islam's features are those of Christianity, as modified by later thinking.

I am not suggesting that other religions don't have salvation as their purpose; they do, because the very purpose of religion is to serve as a guidance system back to arborea. Where others fail, and where Christianity succeeds, is in the matter of a guide. The basis of Buddhism and of Hinduism is salvation: release from terrestrial suffering. But these religious systems lack an immediacy between means and ends. Means and ends are widely separated. At base, the individual is on his own when he attempts to span the great distance between this world of suffering and later release.

It was the Christ figure who proclaimed, "I am the way." And indeed he was. He was, in effect, the one who would lead the faithful to the Father in Heaven.

The great distinguishing feature of both Judaism and Christianity is the sense of family. God was the family deity of ancient Ur. In Judaism this God was part of the family; he was in reality *the* great patriarch. And being such, he was feared and unapproachable. Any effort to come close to this patriarch was done in great fear—and alone. Witness Moses when he came to Horeb, the mountain of God:

> There an angel of the Lord appeared to him in fire flaming out of a bush. . . . When the Lord saw him coming over to look at the bush more closely, God called out to him from the bush, "Moses! Moses!" He answered, "Here I am." God said, "Come no nearer! Remove the sandals from your feet, for the place where you stand is holy ground. I am the God of your father," he continued, "the God of Abraham, the God of Isaac, the God of Jacob." Moses hid his face, for he was afraid to look at God.[15]

If Moses must hide his eyes, what then of lesser men? As a consequence of the awfulness of God, Jews have been concerned with the future messiah who will lead them into the kingdom of this world.

---

15. Exodus 3:2–6.

But then there came that most unusual figure of history. Indeed, so unusual was he that some question whether he really ever existed. I am, of course, referring to Jesus Christ. For our purposes it makes no difference whether he was a real historical figure, though it seems most likely that he was. What is important is, not that he lived, but that men have for several thousand years acted on the assumption that he did. What is more, they have acted on the basis of certain assertions made by and about him.

Christianity, unlike any other religion, derives its essential dynamism from the facts of the life of its founder. The central fact is the death and resurrection of Jesus. Now, this principle of death and resurrection was not unique to him. As early as Sumer there is the great Gilgamesh, there is the Egyptian Osiris, as well as many others. It is no wonder: Man, from the very beginning, has sought to return to arborea. Knowing he could not do so directly in this life, he has imagined the return as occurring in a second life. But for this to happen, death would have to occur. Only after death could the resurrection take place.

Who of the last several thousand years looks to the resurrection of Gilgamesh or of Osiris as a promise of his own resurrection? No one. There is no bond between the living and Gilgamesh or Osiris. There was none in their times, there is none today.

But with Jesus there is a bond. It is a bond created because Jesus was both "true God and true man." But, in a sense, so were Gilgamesh and the others. With Jesus, however, both he and the believer shared a common father. This was the great distinction between Christianity and all other religious systems. As man, Jesus could teach his disciples to pray, "Our Father who art in Heaven . . . ," and as God, he could proclaim, "Before Abraham was, I am." He was, then, the Son of the Father as well as the son of the father. And being such he was both God and brother to man.

What made it work—and that which has given Christianity

its enormous force—was that Jesus "overcame" death. He died on the cross (tree), was buried, and on the third day was raised. Later he ascended into Heaven where he sits at the right hand of the Father.

This is, on its face, a most remarkable story. To the faithful it is remarkable in its promise; to the skeptic it is remarkable in its violation of reality. It cannot be dismissed as fanciful mythology; neither can it be accepted literally. What, then, is it all about?

To answer the question we must place the Christ story in the context of man's historical circumstance. For hundreds of thousands of years—from the time of *Homo erectus* onward—man had wandered the earth in pursuit of survival. Slowly, his migrations shrank and eventually he began to lead a settled existence. Civilization dawned—as did speculation. Why speculation? What was it in man that prompted him to inquire about his nature, his origins, and his destiny? As rising consciousness began to probe the frontiers of awareness, man began increasingly to extend the scope of his speculations. Then came that moment in human history when man's mind became flooded with a new consciousness, one that made certain vital connections between his nature, his origins, and his destiny. This moment was the sixth century B.C. In this century all the major religions except Hinduism started almost simultaneously. Prince Gautama, the Buddha (c. 566–486 B.C.) in India; Confucius (551–479 B.C.) in China; Zoroaster (c. 598–540 B.C.) in Persia; and Deutero-Isaiah (second Isaiah) about 550 B.C.[16]

Man was seeking to reach back into the past and also toward the future to explain his earthly condition, his beginnings and his ends. He made vital connections, but they weren't the ultimate connections that would provide the ultimate answers. During the period when Jesus lived more connections were being made; horizons were becoming extended. Yet, it wasn't until three centuries after the death of Jesus that the final connec-

---

16. Judaism had no single founder, but the sixth-century work done by Deutero-Isaiah in Babylon was critical in establishing the Judaic religion.

tion was established. It happened at the Council of Nicaea A.D. 325, and it was made in the form of a statement on the personality of Jesus: "Our Lord Jesus Christ, Son of God, the only begotten of the Father, being of the substance of the Father, God of God, Light of Light, very God of very God, begotten not made, consubstantial with the Father . . ."

Jesus was of the same substance as the Father and had existed with the Father from the very beginning. This is a tremendously important insight into the nature of man. It evidences an awareness, however dim, of man's origins. This becomes clear when we substitute the word *primate* for *Father*. When we do, we see that man is of the same substance as the primate. In this way, and for the first time, the nature of man is glimpsed—not fully seen, but at least glimpsed. In those days anything more was beyond conscious awareness. That is why Jesus had to be both "true God and true man," that is, true primate and true man. Only when the divine aspect shucked the human aspect could it ascend to heaven, thereby confirming the belief that in death heaven could be attained. That which was of man's nature was condemned to terrestrial living; that which was of primate/god's nature could ascend to arboreal living.

It wasn't until the nineteenth century, when Darwin announced his evolutionary theory, that the symbolism of Christianity was set aside so that new consciousness could express in explicit terms what only symbolic terms could express before. In actual fact, there is no substantive difference between Darwin's theory and the Nicene Creed. They both express the nature of man and his origins.

There remains but one more speculation, that concerning man's destiny.

When we confront the question of man's destiny, we confront the hard kernel of existential reality. There are, in actuality, two possibilities: Man lives and then dies; or man lives, dies, and then enters a second state, or life, depending on the particular religious system. In the Christian faith, there is life after death which lasts for eternity, either in heaven or in hell.

It is significant that life after death is a concept that exists only in some sort of religious system of thought and is based upon faith rather than reason. Indeed, were reason alone to be applied to the matter, not only the concept of life after death but religion itself would crumble. What is truly extraordinary is that for countless centuries, faith has been able to move the mountain of reason and carry man through this life and into the next.

What should attract our attention is not only the faith of believers, but the force behind that faith. What, we should ask, prompts such faith that men and women will sacrifice everything, including their lives, in its behalf? In a way, the question is unanswerable. To the faithful it is so abundantly clear as to require none; to the disbeliever, no answer could possibly satisfy.

Of course, we know that to the believer, eternal life is everything; that after this probationary existence, if the believer dies in a state of grace, he will enjoy eternity with God. But there is more to it than dry certitude. Let us listen to John as he writes of his Apocalyptic vision: "And I saw the holy city, New Jerusalem, coming down out of heaven from God . . . and I heard a loud voice from the throne saying, 'Behold the dwelling of God with men, and he will dwell with them. And they will be his people, and God himself will be with them as their God. And God will wipe away every tear from their eyes. And death shall be no more; neither shall there be mourning, nor crying, nor pain anymore, for the former things have passed away.'" [17]

It is in the final phrase—"for the former things have passed away"—that we can glimpse a prime ingredient of heaven. Previously we have seen that heaven has been affirmatively conceived of as a state of being in which the individual enjoys immortality, naturalness, and general well being. Here we can perceive the *negative* aspect of heaven in that those in the

17. Apocalypse 21:2–4.

heavenly state will not mourn, not cry, not suffer pain, for these "former things [will] have passed away."

What John is saying is that the afflictions of terrestrial living will be done away with. *This* is the enormous attraction of heaven. It is really impossible for anyone to grasp the notion of immortality or naturalness. heaven as an affirmative concept is virtually incomprehensible. Even Paul was without words in describing it: "I know a man in Christ [Paul himself] who fourteen years ago—whether in the body I do not know, or out of the body I do not know, God knows—such a one was caught up to the third heaven . . . and heard secret words that man may not repeat . . ." [18] But what every human born into the terrestrial world knows is suffering, both of the mind and of the body. The great attraction of heaven is the release from time-anxiety and body stress. This is why there is in religion a great circular movement that begins with a paradisaical past, goes through earthly suffering, and then returns to paradise in a future life. By this great movement the individual restores his original condition, and by doing this escapes the pain of earthly existence.

In the idiom of my thesis, the circular movement begins in arborea, dips down into existence in the terrestrial mode, and then ascends once again to arborea. By doing this, the species goes from its natural state to terrestria for which it is not genetically equipped and as a consequence of which it experiences time-anxiety and body stress. Then, to be rid of time-anxiety and body stress, it seeks to regain arborea.

For thousands of years man was subjected to the extremes of time-anxiety and body stress in the terrestrial mode of existence. During these thousands of years he sought relief. None was available. The masses of people knew nothing but birth, suffering, and death. Increasingly, the body came under the inhibitory control of the conscious mind. In defense of the organism the mind constructed a most unusual type of psychic mortar whose function was to reduce body stress so that the

18. 2 Corinthians 12:2–4.

organism could continue to function in the terrestrial mode. This psychic mortar was religion, and its greatest expression was Christianity whose assuring message was peace, the heart of which was contained in the Sermon on the Mount when Jesus said to the multitude:

> Therefore I say to you, do not be anxious for your life, what you shall eat; nor yet for your body, what you shall put on. Is not the life a greater thing than the food and the body than the clothing? Look at the birds of the air: they do not sow, or reap, or gather into barns; yet your heavenly Father feeds them. Are not you of much more value than they? But which of you by being anxious about it can add to his stature a single cubit?
>
> And as for clothing, why are you anxious? Consider how the lilies of the field grow; they neither toil nor spin, yet I say to you that not even Solomon in all his glory was arrayed like one of these. But if God so clothes the grass of the field which flourishes today but tomorrow is thrown into the oven, how much more, O you of little faith?
>
> Therefore, do not be anxious, saying "What shall we eat?" or "What shall we drink?" or "What are we to put on?" (for after all these things the Gentiles seek); for your Father knows that you need all these things. But seek first the kingdom of God and his justice, and all these things shall be given you besides.

Four times Jesus urged the people not to be anxious about the problems of existence; his admonition: "But seek first the kingdom of God and his justice, and all these things shall be given to you besides."

And Paul in his epistle to the Philippians concludes by saying, "Rejoice in the Lord always; again I say, rejoice. . . . The Lord is near. Have no anxiety, but in every prayer and supplication with thanksgiving let your petitions be made known to God. And may the peace of God which surpasses all understanding guard your hearts and your minds in Christ Jesus." [19]

19. Philippians 4:4–7. In comparable words, he concludes 2 Corinthians, Ephesians, 1 Thessalonians, 2 Thessalonians, and Hebrews.

The summary statement of Christianity is contained in the Sermon on the Mount, for it establishes the conditions of suffering man and it promises those who so suffer the reward of heaven: the poor in spirit, the meek, those who mourn, those who hunger and thirst for justice, the merciful, the clean of heart, the peace-makers, and those who suffer persecution for justice's sake and for Jesus's sake.

It is significant that not everyone will go to heaven. Certain conditions must be met, as everyone in the Christian West knows. There is an assumption that such should be the case, that a sense of justice demands conditions for entry into heaven. But why should this be? The species certainly did not choose to enter terrestrial existence; it was forced into it, much against its will (against its genetic nature). The same is true of the individual; he does not choose to enter into existence; it is forced upon him under circumstances for which nature has not prepared him. Whereas the species was sent into exile, the individual is born in exile. Yet in either case terrestrial existence has not been chosen.

What is true of Christianity is true of all other religions; though in others the concepts of guilt, reward, and punishment are more muted, they are present. Why couldn't it be that *everyone* born of woman would be promised this return to arborea? Surely such a doctrine would not interfere with terrestrial living for in every religion we see that man is, in effect, ruled by two sets of laws: the laws of God and the laws of man. In no way would violation of the laws of God interfere with those of man. In fact, were the laws of God to be abrogated, there would be greater devotion to the laws of man, since in many ways the laws of God contravene, both in the letter and in the spirit, those of man. Another way of expressing it would be to say that the laws of arborea do not interfere with the laws of terrestria. Since an unconditional opportunity to return to arborea in a second life would not interfere with terrestrial existence in this life, why has man found it necessary to create conditions for such a return?

Actually, *man* has not created those conditions; primates

have. Elsewhere I have discussed the matter of the usual pattern in nature in which the female is the protagonist while the male is a peripheral figure. Among primates, the exception to this rule is found in those emergency situations when the affinity group is being menaced by predators. In such cases, the adult males assume the protagonist leadership role, to lead the group to safety. This is a particular problem when the group is on the ground. The adult males must take command and see to it that everyone escapes to the trees. For this reason there is a need for social solidarity and physical proximity, and it has been the need for mobility in this circumstance that has provided one of the reasons why dependent infants must be able to cling, unaided, to their mothers. Anyone, young or old, female or male, who violates the rule, who leaves the group, who straggles, or who fails to heed the warning cries and activities of the adult males will be ready prey for any approaching predator. Whoever fails to make it to the trees is in grave danger of being devoured by a predator. It could be said that those who make it to the trees are saved, while those who remain below are lost forever.[20]

Of all the Christian parables, probably the most moving is the one of the lost sheep: "If a man have a hundred sheep, and one of them stray, will he not leave the ninety-nine in the mountains and go in search of the one that has strayed? And if he happens to find it, amen I say to you, he rejoices over it more than over the ninety-nine that did not go astray." There is also the parable of the woman who loses one of ten drachmas and then searches carefully for the one that is lost. Upon find-

---

20. In Matthew (18:5), as well as in Mark (9:41) and Luke (17:2), Jesus speaks in very strong terms of those who cause children to sin (". . . it were better for him to have a great millstone hung around his neck, and to be drowned in the depths of the sea.") This undoubtedly arises from the fact that the arboreal primate infant, which clings to its mother and perforce must go wherever she goes, may well be led to "sin," and thus to death, by the mother wandering from the affinity group while on the ground. The strength of Jesus's admonition arises from the dependence of the infant on the mother, and where she goes or fails to go determines the fate of the clinging infant.

ing it she says to her friends and neighbors, "Rejoice with me, for I have found the drachma that I had lost." Finally, there is the Prodigal Son who, upon repentence and return to the father, is robed and sandaled, with a ring placed on his finger. Then the fatted calf is prepared. Whereupon his joyous father exclaims, "Let us eat and make merry; because this my son was dead, and has come to life again; he was lost, and is found."

Indeed, the great point of Jesus's earthly mission was to save not the just, but the sinner. He outraged the Pharisees and the scribes because he associated with sinners—publicans and harlots. He was in every respect the good shepherd who was seeking to save his sheep by leading them to heaven. The symbolism is overwhelming in its profound psychological impact. It even extends to the concept of the Mystical Body of Christ, by which all followers of Christ are, in effect, part of Christ: part of the affinity group that Christ is to lead to arborea.

This explains the great urging by Paul that none be lost. He created in this connection the great Christian dichotomy, that between the Spirit and the Flesh. In his famous Epistle to the Galatians he writes:

> Now the works of the flesh are manifest, which are immorality, uncleanness, licentiousness, idolatry, witchcrafts, enmities, contentions, jealousies, anger, quarrels, factions, parties, envies, murders, drunkenness, carousings, and such like. And concerning these I warn you, as I have warned you, that they who do such things will not attain the kingdom of God.

What Paul is inveighing against are those things that will destroy the solidarity so necessary for salvation. They are those works that will lead one astray. Instead, he pleads for what he calls, most ironically, yet appropriately, the *fruit* of the Spirit, which are: "charity, peace, patience, kindness, goodness, faith, modesty, continency . . ."

The early period of Christianity was one of watchfulness;

Christ would soon appear calling the faithful to heaven. Woe
to them who were not ready! For had he not warned them?

Watch therefore, for you do not know at what hour your
Lord is to come. But of this be assured, that if the house-
holder had known at what hour the thief was coming, he
would certainly have watched, and not have let his house
be broken into. Therefore you also must be ready, because
at an hour that you do not expect, the Son of Man will
come. . . .

If a wicked servant says to himself, "My master delays
his coming," and begins to beat his fellow-servant, and to
eat and drink with drunkards, the master of that servant
will come on a day he does not expect, and in an hour he
does not know, and will cut him asunder and make him
share the lot of the hypocrites. There will be the weeping
and gnashing of teeth.[21]

Paul warns the Thessalonians that the Lord "is to come like
a thief in the night," and admonishes them to be wakeful and
sober. This is one of the major themes of Christianity and why
everyone should remain "children of light," that is, in a state
of grace. For what would happen if Christ called and someone
were beyond his hearing? What, we must ask, of those who
have strayed?

Going back to the primate situation, if the adult males took
command in the emergency situation and warned loudly, but
one of the affinity group had wandered too far away or for some
reason didn't hear the warning, it would in all likelihood be
killed and eaten by a predator. This raises the interesting question of why a single primate would wander from the group.
There are really only two reasons: one, in search of food; two,
in response to sexual signals. Translating this principle to the
human situation (where man's essential genes, it must be remembered, are identical to those of the original primate), we
can see how "the flesh" can be the cause of damnation. Paul,

---

21. Matthew 24:42–50.

particularly, was concerned with the problem and wrote, "And they who belong in Christ have crucified their flesh with its passions and desires."

Speaking in anthropological terms, there can be little doubt that primates first began coming to the ground in search of food on the ground, or to be able to travel to isolated trees to get food there. In any event, it can be said that "the flesh" brought them to the ground. It was this form of preadaptation that made it possible for man's arboreal ancestors to survive once forced out of the trees. Had it not been for this pre-adaptation, in all likelihood man's arboreal ancestors would have become extinct while still living in the trees. While security and repose were only possible in arborea, the needs of the body require frequent descent to terrestria. In Christian terms, this has been translated to mean that man is a "slave" to the flesh, that for some reason, he has a natural tendency— even a preference—for things of the flesh. It can thus be seen that for both primate and man, "the flesh" can deprive them of the tree of life. (Paul, speaking of the wicked: "Their end is ruin, their god is their belly . . . they mind the things of earth." [22]) And that is why it is so hard for him to be awake and watchful and why it is so easy for him to go astray.

What, then, if someone should fall asleep and not hear the call? He would, quite simply, perish. If a primate, it would be devoured by some predator; if a man, he would be consumed by the fires of Hell.

One of the great arguments among early Christian thinkers concerned the duration of hell (there was no argument among them as to the existence of hell; others since have argued that point). Origen said the suffering of hell would cease when sinners have fully undergone a punishment proportionate to their crimes. St. John Chrysostom, Cyril of Alexandria, and Augustine said No; condemnation was perpetual. There would seem to be no way of knowing for certain—some

22. Philippians 3:19.

primates left below might well escape a potential predator; on the other hand, they might not.

The concept of hell is one of man's oldest beliefs. Until the time of Christianity it was a concept not in very sharp focus; it existed, but without the full clarity given to it by Christianity. One modern author described the requirements of hell this way:

> Hell had to be as terrifying as imagination could make it. But imagination was limited by the vistas of the mind. In other words, when men fantasized devils, they had grotesque but recognizable forms; they had bodies like men, or wolves, or serpents, and their expressions were frightful, but each face, mutilated, altered, exaggerated, *was a face* . . . [Italics in original] [23]

I'm not so sure that Paine's theory is correct. While it is true that Hell is populated with all sorts of grotesque and terrifying creatures, I don't agree that man's imagination conjured them up. Rather, I believe it was memory that dragged them up out of man's early and terrifying past.

The terrestrialization process involved a number of concurrent phenomena. Among them were a change in the body from that of an arboreal primate to man, a constant struggle with other animals, many of which were larger and more powerful and, most important, rising consciousness. Devils and demons are, in every culture, a strange and unsettling mixture of man and beast or a mixture of recognizable beast and exaggerated beast. I can think of nothing that would have struck the primate's rising consciousness as more hellish than to be caught in the confines of terrestria. Long before man came to dominate the animal world, he was in a most precarious state: half-predator, half-prey. At any moment he might be consumed—by a predatory beast, or even by one of his own kind. Thus, there

---

23. Lauran Paine, *The Hierarchy of Hell* (New York: Hippocrene Books, 1972), p. 11.

could be considerable confusion as to what form of beast was doing what to whom.

Hell, even in its more sophisticated forms, seems to be an exaggerated surrealistic expression of the most terrifying aspects of terrestrial existence. The pains of the damned are really the pains and stresses of an arboreal primate seeking to exist in the terrestrial mode, raised to the ultimate degree. The purpose of terrestrialized man is to return to arborea. What, then, if he should fail? For eternity—forever—he will be obliged to remain in terrestria, where he will experience all the pains and stresses of terrestrial living—forever and to an almost unimaginable degree. This hell is not pure fantasy; it is a remembrance of things past that were very real and very terrifying.

At the same time that man was seeking life everlasting in heaven, he was also seeking an earthly millennium. The search was first made within the Jewish tradition, and when Christianity made its appearance the practice continued unabated. The only real difference between the two lay in the Jewish promise of a future Messiah and the Christian promise of a return of the already existing Messiah. In either case, the object was the same: Heaven on earth.

Promises of the millennium, sometimes called chiliasm, quickly came under the close scrutiny of the Church, and in the third century Origen sought to present the kingdom of heaven as something not related to time and place, but only to the souls of the faithful. That is, paradise would be achieved only after death, not in this life and on this earth. After Constantine (274–337), when the Church became supreme in the Mediterranean world, ecclesiastical disapproval of chiliasm became emphatic, for the Church had a mission: to lead souls to heaven. It could not stand by and see men seeking paradise on earth.

Notwithstanding this, in the fourth century, the eloquent Lactantius, following a tradition begun by John in his Apocalypse, sought converts to Christianity by promising a millen-

nium laced with bloody vengeance on the unrighteous. When
victory came, the millennium would begin. He describes the
scene thus:

> When peace has been brought about and every evil sup-
> pressed, that righteous and victorious King [Christ] will
> carry out a great judgment on the earth of the living and
> the dead, and will hand over all heathen peoples to servi-
> tude under the righteous who are alive, and will raise the
> [righteous] dead to eternal life and will himself reign with
> them on earth, and will found the Holy City, and this king-
> dom of the righteous shall last for a thousand years.
> Throughout that time the stars shall be brighter, and the
> brightness of the sun shall be increased, and the moon shall
> not wane. Then the rain of blessing shall descend from
> God morning and evening, and the earth shall bear all
> fruits without man's labour. Honey in abundance shall drip
> from the rocks, fountains of milk and wine shall burst
> forth. The beasts of the forests shall put away their wild-
> ness and become tame . . . no longer shall any animal
> live by bloodshed. For God shall supply all with abundant
> and guiltless food.[24]

The terms of Lactantius's vision are unmistakable: He is describing a terrestrial arborea in which lethality and human labor
are done away with; quite literally he is describing a land of
milk and honey. What is significant about this vision, and all
the visions of chiliasm through the centuries, is that man will
enjoy paradise on earth. He will not have to wait until a second
life. Of course, the vision is of the future, but that is secondary
to the primacy of the fact that living men, men of flesh and
blood, might someday enjoy the fruits, if I may put it that way,
of arborea while living in the terrestrial mode. What, we might
ask, would the Christian Church do if in fact such promises as
those made by Lactantius were actually forthcoming? We need

---

24. Cited in Norman Cohn, *The Pursuit of the Millennium* (N.J.:
Essential Books, 1957), p. 12.

not dwell on the specifics of his vision, but on the principles lying beneath the surface of the symbols in our search for the answer.

Here we come to the matter of what man has sought—and continues to seek—as the consummate life. What is it that has always prompted the search for heaven in a second life, or paradise in this one? And, for that matter, what is it that the Buddhist seeks? Or, anyone, in the final analysis?

There can be no denying that in various ways man seeks to rid himself of the sufferings brought into his life by the conditions of terrestrial living. We have seen how the religious impulse seeks to attain as directly as possible a reconstitution of arboreal life even if it is necessary to postpone its realization until a second, fantasy, life. In chiliasm we see something less demanding. Milk and honey, yes; but note that the element of immortality is gone. Man is now asking for a life without those elements that make terrestrial existence so unnatural and hence so painful. He is asking that he not have to work to satisfy his sustenance needs, and he asks for the end of lethality.

The underlying purpose of Buddhism, enunciated by Gautama himself, has been to find a way to end human suffering. Salvation, in Buddhism, means the ultimate liberation from the necessity of suffering. Nirvana has been described as being "permanent, stable, imperishable, immovable, ageless, deathless, unborn, and unbecome . . . it is power, bliss and happiness, the secure refuge, the shelter, and the place of unassailable safety; . . . it is the real Truth and the supreme Reality; . . . it is the Good, the supreme goal and the one and only consummation of our life, the eternal, hidden, and incomprehensible Peace." [25]

Peace, whether in the idiom of eastern or western thought, is the absence of suffering, or harmony between man and the world he lives in. When we pierce all the symbols of religious and chiliastic expressions, we come to the heart of the matter,

---

25. Edward Conze, *Buddhism: Its Essence and Development* (New York: Harper & Row, 1959), p. 40.

which is the desire by man to live at peace with his world, to be in harmony with his environment. That is why, on the one hand, he seeks to ascend to arborea, and on the other, why he seeks to bring arborea down to terrestria. By doing one or the other (it makes no difference which), man eliminates his need for mortar. He can engage in direct transactions to satisfy his sustenance needs, and by being able directly to satisfy this need, he no longer suffers from either time-anxiety or body stress. When this state of existence pertains, the contingent and subordinate condition of sex is done away with, and we thereby have an end to sexual utilitarianism. And when this occurs, man will exist totally in a natural state. Finally, since there would be no more mortar, there could be no more lethality. In brief, man can exist in harmony with his environment because the profile of the environment is met by a species profile that is entirely a genetically created profile.

For thousands of years man has had to suffer through this world to arrive at the next in order to realize this harmony. Short of that he has had to rely on visions of a future earthly paradise. But in either event, harmony has had to be postponed; it could not be realized in the life of the dreamer—that is, until the genius of man began to transform the world into a new paradise, not in fantasy, but in fact.

THE HUNTER

I F M A N had never existed, had there never been that climatic catastrophe that drove an innocuous and inferior primate from the world of the trees, it is most likely that evolution would have proceeded along lines earlier established by its thrust in time. There would have existed an arboreal world occupied by a wide variety of primates, other mammals such as the squirrel and the sloth, and a great host of birds, insects, and occasional trepassers such as snakes and predaceous mammals. As for the terrestrial world, it would have enlarged on the pattern established many millions of years earlier, with its delicate balance between predator and prey, and between animal and plant life. We can catch glimpses of this possibility in the few lingering remnants of the past that have escaped the hand of man, places like the great animal preserves of Africa.

But man came to be, and as a result, he had to establish a place for himself. It must be noted that evolution did not provide for man and therefore did not set aside a place for him. Whatever place man would occupy, he would have to stake out on his own. And to do so, he would inevitably have to dispossess those already there. Yet even as man has sought a place for himself in terrestria, he has not been able to escape his origins. He has always maintained a link with his arboreal past. In the last chapter we saw a manifestation of this in his yearning for heaven, or in default of heaven, then the millennium.

Even when man seeks to address himself to the concrete problems of terrestrial living, he cannot let go of the past. We see this most clearly in his efforts at establishing civilization.

Being an arboreal primate, man functions on the basis of male dominance and hierarchy.[1] There is always—with the rarest of short-term exceptions—the leading male under whom there is a descending hierarchy that eventually reaches the masses of the people. For most of man's known history, the leading male has been a kinglike figure.

When we reach back into ancient time to discover the origins of kings, we reach into mists in which it is hard to distinguish between a king and a god, so mingled are they in myth. In any event, there is great confusion as to whether the king is descended from a god, whether he is in fact a god, or whether his authority comes from the gods. Out of this mist we derive the concept of the divine origin of kings as well as the Divine Right of Kings, something that has stamped human history indelibly until the most recent times.

In the earliest systems the gods, having assumed, bestowed, or permitted kingship, were acting with a design. What they required of men was their own ease and support. Their means for securing these was work by men and order among them. As the connecting link between the gods and the people, the king was, as a rule, priest as well as king. This proved to be a facet of the ruler as hard to distinguish from the king as was the king from a god.

So what we see in the ruler is someone who by reaching down into the world and its people was profane, and who by reaching up into the world of the gods was divine. The latter pretension gave the king enormous authority; the former extension gave him great power. In some systems, such as the Sumerian, the purpose of human existence was to serve the needs of the gods. When we come to the very much later and more sophisticated

---

1. This is so notwithstanding sporadic efforts in the past and a concentrated effort today by women to share in matters of dominance and hierarchy.

system of the Hebrews, the god intrudes conspicuously into the history of his people. But still, there is the curious and significant intermingling of men and gods. And in every instance known there is the awe-inspiring superiority of the god or gods and the almost crippling inferiority of man. I say "curious and significant" because the contrived nature of the gods is really a reflection of the true nature of the superior primates that drove man's primate ancestors out of arborea.

It is almost impossible to ignore the parallel between primates and gods, as each has played such a critical role in man's history. The primate figure is the one that drove man's arboreal ancestors out of arborea and saw to it that they never returned; the god figure drove man's human ancestors out of heaven (paradise) and saw to it that neither they nor their descendants ever returned. Although we can't reconstruct the actual relationship between the original primates, we can detect the elements of a genuine hierarchy in the god-man situation. There were, of course, the gods and there were the masses of men. Linking them, somewhat as an envoy from and to the world of each, was the king figure. While man, he was the link with divinity. Or was he a divine link with humanity? That was the beguiling question.

This is not an exercise in abstract theory, but one of the truly determinative facts in human history, for when we come to the threshold of the modern era, we come to Paul, who set the pattern for all future historical development when he proclaimed: "Let everyone be subject to the higher authorities, for there exists no authority except from God, and those who exist have been appointed by God. Therefore he who resists the authority resists the ordinance of God; and they that resist bring on themselves condemnation. For rulers are a terror not to good work but to the evil. Dost thou wish, then, not to fear the authority? Do what is good and thou wilt have praise from it. For it is God's minister to thee for good. But if thou dost what is evil, fear, for not without reason does it carry the sword. For it is God's minister, an avenger to execute wrath on him who does evil. Wherefore you must needs be subject, not only because of the wrath, but also for conscience' sake. For this is also why you pay tribute, for they are the ministers of God, serving unto this very end. Render to all men whatever is their due; tribute to whom tribute is due; taxes to whom taxes are due; fear to whom fear is due; honor to whom honor is due." [2]

This famous principle enunciated by Paul became the fundamental law of western civilization for over a thousand years. It established the legitimacy and authority of the state as being handed down from God. Not only that, but it granted to the state those sanctions necessary to reinforce its authority and the means by which the state could guarantee its own continuity. The state was, in reality, an earthly extension of God's kingdom. The consequences of this were incalculable, for the individual's response to the authority of the state was calculated as a response to God's authority. Thus, there was no escape from God, his authority, and his power of life and death. Whatever one did as a citizen of the state directly affected his eternal destiny. Or, in the idiom of my thesis, what the citizen did vis-à-vis the state had a direct bearing on his prospects of achieving arborea.

Of course, when Paul laid down this rule, there was no immediate prospect of its coming into play, since Rome had its own state system. But from the time of Constantine on, when the Church began to assume conspicuous social and political proportions, a onetime theory began to be an operative principle of civil life in Europe and eventually in all of western civilization.

For over a thousand years, European man lived in two hierarchical systems, that of the state and that of the Church. However, since the authority of the king was derived from God, European man actually lived in a single hierarchical system that had two phases to it—the temporal and the spiritual—or, put differently, the terrestrial and the arboreal.

---

2. Romans 13:1–7.

Modern scholarship has been harsh on the European civilization that prevailed between the fall of the Roman Empire and the beginning of the Renaissance. Indeed, it is usually called the "Dark Ages." The complaint lies with the viselike grip of Feudalism on the body and the equally viselike hold of the Church on the soul of man. It is true that Europe was in a vise—and that it stagnated terribly. But not for the obvious reasons. Among most historians, scholasticism, with its heavy emphasis on authority, is blamed for the lack of intellectual development. If one wanted to know something about the stars, for example, one went either to the Scriptures or to the bishop. One did not take up a telescope (even had one existed) and peer at the heavens.

Everything temporal was determined by one's birth, as established by the rules of feudalism, and everything else was determined by one's death, as established by the law of the Church. Experimentation, exploration, independent thinking, the searching out of alternatives to the rules of existence simply didn't occur. Nor were they really wanted.

This condition was the result of the kingly/priestly system under which society operated during the centuries when Europe and Christendom were coextensive. The system was quite simple. Under it, everyone knew precisely where he stood, both in this life and in the next. Under feudalism, the individual, regardless of station, was part of a system of reciprocal duties, as well as the beneficiary of protection from those of higher station. Even among the class of nobles this held true, right up to the ultimate protection offered by the pope. Within the Church, to which everyone was born, there was a system of sacraments that properly utilized assured eternal salvation.

What this arrangement provided, of course, was security, and in both worlds. What characterizes such a system is its exclusive emphasis on the past. There are no extensions into the future; there are only reliances on what has come before, in that distant past represented by God, or rather, by what lies behind the figure of God, the arboreal period.

Under such a system, what could be gained by turning one's back on those who led one to ultimate fulfillment? It would be the same as going the wrong way on a one-way street. The preoccupation of European man was with eternity. Under this system of thought, as propounded by the Church, eternity could be gained only through the kingly/priestly gateway. Because of this, they turned their backs on worldly matters and in a manner of speaking, while keeping their gaze upward and backwards, they reluctantly backed into each new century. Quite rightly it could be said that they were in the world, but not of the world.

What made it all work, and it must be remembered that it worked for well over a thousand years, was the central position of the Church which, as it has itself expressed it, held the keys to the kingdom of heaven. No man could go to the Father, except through the Son, and no one could get to the Son except through the Church of Rome. It was an immutable assertion, the contravention of which would condemn the transgressor to eternal damnation. Further, should he fall into the hands of the state or the Church, not only was eternal hell awaiting him; so were the minions of the state, who—more or less to prepare the soul for its own suffering in due course—subjected the body to torture and death.

There was no alternative. Man was bound to the chain linking him to heaven my way of the European State and its one true Church. Under this system there was no room for personality or individuality. It mattered not a whit whether the king was a knave or the priest a whoremonger, so long as each possessed his office legitimately: the king by way of blood, the priest by way of the laying on of hands. It was the office that conferred authority and thereby power, not the merits of the individual. Europe functioned under this unalterable principle for more than ten monotonous centuries. Change was an unwelcome threat.

And yet, change did occur. It occurred partly as a result of what might be best called the terrestrialization of the Church and partly as the result of the incursion of eastern ideas. Both were necessary. Eastern ideas alone could not have successfully assailed the intellectual ramparts of Europe. What was needed was something behind the battlements that would sow discontent so as to deliver the keys out of the hands of the Roman Church. Only this way could a true alternative be possible.

Catholic Europe was all of a piece—or it was nothing. Either all roads led to Rome and thereby to heaven, or they led every which way and thereby to perdition. Jesus had once said that he was the way, but by the fifteenth century many others were saying, even if quietly, that the Church had lost its way—worse, that the Church of Rome was an impediment to salvation, that it had cast away the ancient truth and was mired in superstition and temporal distractions. This last was an historical inversion of a very ancient circumstance. In the beginning, confusion had arisen as to what of the ruler was earthly and what heavenly. By one means or another, the king was elevated to the hemline of divinity. Thus, the direction to be taken by those under the king was through the king and up toward the divine. When the leaders of the Church assumed temporal power and became princes of the Church, there occurred the lowering of the priest to the rank of mere mortal, thereby sundering the link between earthly man and heaven. Yet an alternative began to arise. If it had not, there is an overwhelming likelihood that European man, despite the failures of the Catholic Church, would have continued to seek heaven through the instrumentality of the Church. Why? Because he wanted heaven and if, to gain it, he had to go through the portals of the Church—or the sewers of terrestrial living for that matter —he would do so.

Between them, the Renaissance and the Reformation provided European man with new alternatives. In effect, they changed the landscape from that of something vertical and narrow to something horizontal and broad.[3] A number of critical factors exerted pressure to so transform the landscape of Euro-

---

3. In architecture this is reflected in the change from the vertical and narrow Gothic to the horizontal and broad neoclassic and the ornamental —even flamboyant—Baroque.

pean thought. Trade with the East infused new ideas, especially
those of ancient Greece. Increased trade produced a rising middle class that was neither princely nor beggarly. It became an
important wedge between the ruler and the masses. In time, it
would grow and engulf them both. In time, it would hold the
purse strings of civilization—and morality. Indeed, it would
be this middle class that would inaugurate the neo-arboreal
era of human history.

The principal event, of course, was the Protestant Revolution. From the earliest days of Paul there had always been those
who picked at the seamless garment of Christianity. In most
instances they picked off at most bits of lint, but in time, as
the centuries passed, the pile of lint grew until it acquired
enough substance to form a second garment, that of Protestantism.

The central problem concerned man's relation to God. Under
the Catholic system, a man was separated from God by a religious hierarchy, just as he was separated from his king by his
feudal superiors. Access to God could be achieved only through
the intercessions of the clergy as they administered the sacraments. Under the Protestant system, the clerical hierarchy was
done away with and each man had direct access to God. The
authority of the Church was replaced with the authority of the
conscience as molded and guided by the Bible, God's great instrument made available to the mass of humanity by the invention of the printing press. The doctrine of the universal priest-
hood, of the right and duty of the believer to a personal
responsibility, replaced, for much of Europe, the doctrine of
the primacy of the Church. (The Church, of course, had the
Bible, but rather than allowing the laity to read it, the Church
read it, as interpreted by the Church, to the laity.)

This new doctrine inevitably affected the relationship between the state and religion. Under the old system, the state
was subordinate to the Church; in Protestant Europe, the
Church was under the state. Under Catholicism, the Church
could guarantee citizens of the state access to heaven; with Prot-

estantism, the state could assure the Church access to potential believers. Here we can begin to see the trend away from the narrow and vertical, and toward the broad and horizontal. The state no longer served the Church; if anything the Church served the state. What, then, of access to God? That was between the individual and God. Neither Church nor state was a necessary conduit. For the first time in a thousand years there occurs a separation of Church and state vis-à-vis heaven. Man now had two personalities, one temporal, one spiritual. In this new-found condition, he could live fully in this world while preparing for the next. He lived under the state; he was a citizen first, then a believer. Finally, living in the world, the Protestant believed that if one was to serve God in one's personal life, it would not be unnatural to see one's work as part of one's service to God: One could dedicate one's temporal life to God. In time, it would become possible to equate temporal success with morality, rather on the principle that as ye sow, so shall ye reap, or in translation, as you sow the seeds of material success in this world, so shall you reap the reward of eternal life in the next.

The Reformation, as can be seen, turned man around. Instead of looking backward, he now looked around him; instead of taking everything on ecclesiastical authority, he began to question, to experiment, and to explore this world, in the course of which he discovered the New World—and the New Order of things.

Sir Thomas More, in the early sixteenth century, wrote his *Utopia*, probably the most famous of all fantastic flights to perfection. However, he was neither the first nor the last utopian. Plato's *Republic* and Plutarch's *Life of Lycurgus* came much before, and Campanello's *The City of the Sun*, Bacon's *New Atlantis*, and many others followed in the next four centuries.

Unlike earlier notions of the millennium which had Christ coming down to earth in order to institute his thousand-year reign, the utopians had man as their protagonist as he sought to perfect life on earth by his own efforts. Essentially, all utopias have sought man's happiness. As to the means, there have been two principal theories. In one, the happiness of man was to be achieved through material well-being, by man sinking his individuality into the group, and through the perfection of the state. The other, while demanding a measure of material well-being, considered that happiness was the result of the free expression of man's personality, unencumbered by an arbitrary moral code or by the interests of the state. In brief, happiness could be achieved by mass man or by individual man. What cuts through the differences of the two schools is the fact that it was *man* who could achieve happiness; he need not have it thrust upon him by a benevolent god in a future world or even in this one.

There is another important feature to these uptopias: They all saw man as achieving happiness on this earth, in this life, by virtue of his own labor. It is in these utopias that we begin to see the first faint outlines of man's plans for creating neoarborea. But to be able to create neo-arborea, man would have to sever all ties with the past; he would have to let loose of the kingly/priestly strings; in short, he would have to begin all over again, much as Noah had had to after the Flood. Instead of surviving a flood, however, those who would make a new beginning would have to cross a vast ocean to a New World where they would forge neo-arborea out of a primordial wilderness. In effect, what the Puritan Pilgrims came upon in America was a second Garden of Eden, where all that man would need for heaven on earth was provided, not by a jealous and demanding God, but by a munificent Nature that made but one demand: hard work.

This, of course, was eminently compatible with the morality of the original New Englanders and even that of those who planted civilization in the southern colonies, for the extremely personal God they transported across the ocean to the New Canaan was the God of Salvation through hard work, even if not the God of good works. While this may seem paradoxical, it isn't. The God of the New World was the God of the New Dispensation who, while decrying the display of worldly goods, praised the storing of this world's goods in the treasure vaults of the next. The fruit of this world was to hang not on the limbs of a temporal tree, but rather on those of the tree of eternal life.

This was not so much the result of the forging of a new and pure theology by those who founded the American colonies as it was the pragmatic acceptance of reality. For the state had succeeded the Church—or any church, for that matter—as the primary source of power.

Paul in his time might properly have said that the power of the state came from God, but certainly Machiavelli could not have echoed such an ancient and anachronistic dictum, for by the fifteenth century a new world had come into being. It was a temporal world with its emphasis on tangibles rather than on spirits, on commerce with other men rather than with long-dead saints, and on the body rather than on the soul. It had come into being, not like a thief in the night, but like a man reaching an inevitable conclusion, a conclusion we must now examine.

The great purpose behind all the religious movements founded in the sixth century B.C., as extended by later developments such as those shown in Christianity and Islam, was to extricate man, an arboreal primate, from a hostile and alien terrestrial environment for which he was not genetically adapted. Religions arose as a means of salvaging an impossible situation. Man could not return to arborea; he could not accommodate himself to terrestria.

In his mind, man might imagine that he is, in fact, a terrestrial creature, or he might continue to believe he is an arboreal primate. It is not unlike the conundrum of the philosopher who poses the dilemma: "Am I a man dreaming I am a butterfly, or am I a butterfly dreaming I am a man?" This is not an idle question nor an abstract game. Man has always been torn between what he imagines to be his two natures, often expressed as the conflict between what he is and what he would be, between his higher and lower natures, between the spirit and the flesh, between—finally—good and evil. Always, no matter what the form of the conflict or the idiom of the ultimate dilemma, there is what man believes to be the conflict within himself between the higher and the lower. In every instance, the higher can be translated to mean the arboreal or the original nature of man, while the lower can be translated to mean the terrestrial or the fallen (or even corrupted) condition of man.

In every act of accommodation to terrestrial living, man at the same time has sought to safeguard his arboreality, and he has done so by one of two devices: either by altering the terms of external reality so that they might better resemble various aspects of arboreal existence, or by altering his perception of terrestrial reality. Earlier we saw how reality might be altered, and how perception might be altered by the use of drugs. Here I wish to concentrate on the second method of altering perception: through fantasy, especially by the fantasy of religion.

We can never know for certain what the origins of religion were. They are lost in the shadows of the labyrinth. But we can perceive what seems to me to be a remarkably clear relationship. The religious impulse appears to have manifested itself at approximately the time when the great cave paintings of western Europe began. This is so, give or take a few millennia, which on the scale of time contained in the labyrinth is quite negligible. This is precisely the time when we find evidence of ritual burials and small cult objects, such as the famous "Venuses." This is also the time just prior to that when man no longer looked directly to nature to provide him with food, but began to grow his own in the form of domesticated animals and grain.

In this regard, we might divide the long span of man's terrestrial existence into two periods. In the first—and longest— man subsisted on what nature had to provide. In this sense, man was dependent; also, he was without responsibility for the provision of sustenance. In the second period—that of the last ten to twelve thousand years—man has ceased being dependent on nature and instead has become responsible for the provision of his own sustenance. Thus, we can see that during the long period of the hunt, man was dependently irresponsible; he survived on what nature could provide. In the post-hunt era man has become, of necessity, independently responsible; to survive, he has had to provide his own sources of sustenance. And it is at this juncture that man begins his great invention of formal religion.

Until Zoroaster in the sixth century B.C., while there was what we call religion, there was no great sense of responsibility. There was no clear-cut concept of good and evil as moral principles, there was no substantial reward for good, nor was there abiding punishment for evil. Prior religious sentiments placed man more or less at the mercy of the gods. He was dependent on the gods—and helpless to affect his own fate. With Zoroaster we have the introduction of personal responsibility and the prospect of man's being able to do something about his own destiny.

The significance of this lies in the fact that for millennia man had labored mightily to provide sustenance for himself in this world without connecting what was done in this life with the next life. It would seem that in the sixth century B.C., man began to make the connection between the two worlds, with himself occupying the central and responsible role.

This concept of personal responsibility, though born in the sixth century B.C., remained nonfunctional for more than twenty centuries because of the inability of the individual to extricate himself from the grip of the state and the Church. In a very large sense, the state and the Church assumed much of the responsibility for the destiny of the individual in the form of either the religion of the state (whether profane or divine) or the religion of the Church. With the Reformation of the sixteenth century, came an entirely new situation. The state, now making no profession of divinity, ruled the bodies of men.

The churches, except for the Catholic, provided an ambience in which the private religion of the individual might exist. True, the various churches directed the form of religion, but they could not direct the content, especially the subjective content, of the individual's religion. Thus at last, we discover the individual assuming direct responsibility for his own destiny, which included a keen appreciation of the relationship between personal acts in this life and rewards and punishments in the next.

It might well be said that for the first time in man's long and tortured terrestrial sojourn he was able to practice religion in its pure form. That is, each man could determine for himself how he was going to create a guidance system to arborea. Man became, for the first time, a responsible creature, and the core of his responsibility concerned the provision of sustenance. That is, the individual ceased being irresponsibly dependent on the state or the Church, and became independently responsible for the provision of his own sustenance in this world and the next.

It was in this state of consciousness that European man began the settlement of the New World. With the independence of the colonies begins the final phase of human development, that in which the arboreal primate becomes transformed into the neo-arboreal primate. No longer does man seek to return, in this life or the next, to arborea. Instead, he seeks to construct neo-arborea on earth. The Paradise Lost of Europe became, in 1776, the Paradise Found of America.

The United States of America was the first country ever established by a thoroughly conscious act. Further, it was an act that intentionally severed all ties with the past: It formally cut the strings attached to the kingly/priestly principle. In its place it formulated the cultural/scientific principle that had for its major premise the newly discovered concept of material progress.

To a very large extent America was made possible by certain European accomplishments. Among the most important were the Industrial Revolution begun by the English and the concept of progress begun by the French (the latter producing the milieu in which the former could bear fruit).[4]

Significantly, Europe did not directly benefit from the social and intellectual roilings taking place within itself. It was to be the new people, the Americans, who would become the first and leading beneficiaries of an exclusively European phenomenon. But such a turn of events could be predicted. Europe, despite its scattering of terrestrially oriented thinkers, was founded on the kingly/priestly principle, under which the leadership and the power of the state derived their legitimacy from the link between earth and heaven. Even as America was growing more and more independent of heaven and even as France produced some of history's most worldly thinkers, its king still proceeded under the authority granted him by Divine Right. It would take a bloody revolution to deprive the king of both his Divine Right and his divine life. What was true of France was also true of the rest of Europe. Even today, when Europe has become so heavily influenced by the American cultural/scientific principle, it still possesses counteracting remnants of the kingly/priestly principle, with the result that Europe is being torn between two possible loyalties, one to the past and one to the future.

America is indeed the New World. It has no history in the European sense. It began as Europe might have begun had it commenced its career in the seventeenth century instead of in the mists that arose in the East as much as ten thousand years ago. Yet, it was the experience of Europe over the millennia, and especially during the Christian era, that led to the American experience. Had there been no New World, Europe would have turned its energies inward to accomplish its own revolution. It would, undoubtedly, have been a painful and pro-

---

4. It is not a coincidence that the Industrial Revolution and the Age of Reason (and that of the Enlightenment) concurred. With the birth of prospects for improving terrestrial existence came the rational philosophy to support it.

tracted process, but it would have occurred—and probably in the long run, more to the world's advantage than has been the result of the American adventure.

If anyone could be said to symbolize the irony and the agony of America, it would be Jonathan Edwards, New England's greatest preacher, not only of the eighteenth century, but of any century. Edwards contained within himself the greatest of all paradoxes, for within his soul was contained the dying embers of a flame lit eighteen centuries earlier, while within his loins was the great seed of the future. He was able to proclaim from the pulpit, "All children are by nature children of wrath, and are in danger of eternal damnation in Hell," and that children "are infinitely more hateful than vipers." Yet, in his marriage bed, he and his remarkable wife, Sarah, conspired to spawn eleven children, all of whom lived to maturity, a truly extraordinary accomplishment for a period that saw most children die before puberty. Yet it was not the mere fact of having eleven children that sets Edwards apart from other men, for that was a common occurrence, but that though he was a man of God, nevertheless six of his children were born on Sunday. While this means nothing today, in those days there was the assumption that a child born on a Sunday had been conceived on a Sunday. Thus, for a preacher's wife to have child after child born on a Sunday suggested—nay, proved—that one of Christendom's most renowned hellfire and brimstone preachers had not devoted the entire Sabbath to God, but had shared the holy day with his wife in carnal pleasure, thus jeopardizing not only the souls of himself and his wife, but those of the children as well. I don't pass on this bit of irrefutable gossip in any sense of reproach or even amusement, but in order to display the paradoxes within Edwards and, indeed, within the society in which Edwards lived.

There was nothing this poor struggling Christian feared more, or detested more, than sins of the flesh, and nothing revealed the sins of the flesh more than sex, the products of which were children. As a spiritual descendant of Augustine who held that the only Christian purpose that could justify and thereby compensate for sex was the hope that children might, in death, become citizens of the City of God, and the spiritual child of Calvin who feared that the City of God would not get children in death, but that hell would, Edwards hoped fearfully for the City of God, but dreaded—and expected—that most children, including his own, would end in hell.

In a famous sermon addressed to parents, Edwards said:

> The saints in glory will see [the suffering of those in Hell], and be far more sensible of it than now we can possibly be. They will be far more sensible how dreadful the wrath of God is, and will better understand how terrible the sufferings of the damned are; yet this will be no occasion of grief to them; but on the contrary, when they have this sight, it will excite them to joyful praise. . . .
>
> The suffering of those in Hell will be an occasion of their rejoicing, as the *glory of God* will appear in it. [Italics in original.] [5]

In what was probably one of Edwards's most famous hellfire and brimstone sermons, entitled "Sinners in the Hands of An Angry God," he had this to say to his congregation:

> The God that holds you over the pit of hell, much as one holds a spider, or some loathsome insect over the fire, abhors you, and is dreadfully provoked—his wrath toward you burns like fire; he looks upon you as worthy of nothing else, but to be cast onto the fire; he is of purer eyes than to bear to have you in his sight; you are ten thousand times more abominable in his eyes, than the most hateful venomous serpent is in ours. [6]

---

5. *The Works of Jonathan Edwards* (London: Ball, Arnold, and Co., 1840), 2:208–209.

6. Quoted in *Puritan Sage, Collected Writings* of *Jonathan Edwards*, edited by Virgilius Ferm (New York: Library Publishers, 1953), p. 372.

Surely Edwards, loved all his own children,[7] and therefore he must have worried over them as he recalled the words of the founder of his faith who, in his *Institutes of the Christian Religion,* wrote, "Let us hold this, then, as an undoubted truth, which no opposition can ever shake . . . that man's heart is so thoroughly infected by the poison of sin, that it cannot produce anything but what is corrupt . . ." What would Edwards have thought of his direct descendants who, by 1900, included among them the following: 13 college presidents, 65 professors, 30 judges, 80 public office holders—including 3 U.S. senators, 3 governors, 3 mayors of large cities, a vice president of the United States, and a controller of the U.S. Treasury—as well as 100 lawyers and the dean of an outstanding law school? What would he have thought of the members of his family who by that year had written 135 books? Or of those of his family who entered the ministry in droves and sent 100 missionaries overseas? Or of his direct descendants who by 1900 had become the heads of many large coal mines and directors of vast oil interests and silver mines? Finally, as one scholar who researched more than 1,400 descendants of the marriage of Jonathan and Sarah wrote, "There is scarcely any great American industry that has not had one of this family among its chief promoters. . . . The family has cost the country nothing in pauperism, in crime, in hospital or asylum service; on the contrary, it represents the highest usefulness." Whither these descendants of Edwards? heaven or hell? There is little doubt that Edwards himself would have deplored their worldliness out of an earnest fear that it would seriously jeopardize their salvation. They on the other hand, would have thought Edwards old-fashioned and narrow-minded. In a sense, both would have been right—from their special perspectives.

Edwards was one of the last of a breed. He lived in a vertical and narrow world that saw the only hope of man as lying in

7. He did very much, according to Elisabeth D. Dodds, whose biography, *Marriage to a Difficult Man,* is a chronicle of family life and paternal love.

escape to arborea. This world could not be redeemed; therefore, it must be shut away lest it interfere with man's escape.
His descendants, in contrast, lived in a horizontal and broad
world in which the prospects were enormous. They saw, as no
one before had seen, that the earth possessed great potential.
To their way of thinking the earth could be redeemed, could
be made into a terrestrial paradise. They were like Moses leading the Israelites out of Egyptian slavery and into the Promised
Land. And like Moses, they were never to see the Promised
Land. That would be for others.

The central difficulty of the American experience was that
it replaced one fantasy with another, and while doing so took
the rules of one and applied them to the other.

The original fantasy was Salvation that saw peace and harmony as being possible only in an afterlife in a reunion with
God—or, in the idiom of my thesis, a return to arborea after
death. Salvation was everything, nothing could be allowed to
stand in its way. All the rules of terrestrial living were formed
around this objective, and they were based on the principle
that the end justified the means. The body could be imprisoned, tortured, even destroyed in pursuit of this policy. Anything and everything that contributed to the enjoyment of
this life could be confiscated if deemed a threat to eternal life.

The second fantasy, that on which America was built, was
Success. In contrast to the Salvation fantasy, which was based
on the kingly/priestly principle, the Success fantasy was based
on the cultural/scientific principle. The former, as has been
pointed out, focuses attention on matters past and above. The
latter focuses attention on matters future and below. It is, in
every way, the terrestrial counterpart to a quest for arborea.
It is, in brief, a quest for neo-arborea. And its rules are precisely
the same as those that apply to the Salvation fantasy; indeed,
this is inevitable since both are seeking the same result, though
by going in opposite directions.

The end justifies the means. Anything and everything that
will advance the cause of Success is allowed; anything that

threatens to interfere is disallowed. That means, since Success lies in the future, that the present will be sacrificed as necessary to the future, just as, in Salvation, this life is sacrificed to the needs of the next. However, whereas Salvation may require the sacrifice of the body to save the soul, with Success it is the soul that may have to be sacrificed, since the body is as indispensable to Success as the soul is to Salvation.

It is in the matter of the body that we come across the connecting link between Salvation and Success. In both fantasies it is the body that bears the burden. In the case of Salvation the body is disciplined in order to still its natural tendencies since they tend to mire it down in the terrestrial world, thus jeopardizing the soul's return to arborea. With Success, the body is disciplined for the very same reason: to still its natural tendencies which are to exist in the *now*.

The American adventure to transform the elements of terrestrial living so that they might resemble those of arboreal living—has sacrificed everything to achieve this end. The adventure began in the eighteenth century, leapt forward in the nineteenth, and reached its goal in the twentieth—only it doesn't know it and keeps rushing into the future, discarding the present as if it were an impediment rather than accepting it as the only place life can exist.

There is a further element in the American experience, one that has no counterpart in the Salvation fantasy. It concerns the matter of responsibility. As was said earlier in this chapter, religion and responsibility are inextricably linked. Both, it will be recalled, arose when man had to assume responsibility for providing the source of his sustenance. This responsibility has been lacking in the American experience because of the remarkable state of the vast continent that lay before the onrushing settlers. The fecundity of the continent became legendary: All man had to do was "pluck the fruit from the trees." To those contemplating this cornucopia, it appeared as if it were inexhaustible. Therefore, there was no need to worry over replacing what was replaceable or conserving what was irreplaceable. This condition, of course, strongly paralleled the situation before man entered his cocoon. All American man had to do was take what was there. When that was gone, there would be more where that came from.

This belief had an enormous effect on the people, most of whom had come from deprived backgrounds where almost nothing was certain. It made possible the fantasy of Success. Opportunity was there; all anyone had to do was pluck it. This remarkable opinion was held by everyone, not merely those born to better families or those granted better educations.

Just as there were the spiritual virtues that secured one's entry into heaven, so too there were virtues associated with Success. One of the earliest proponents of such virtues was Cotton Mather, who proclaimed, "I tell you with diligence a man may do marvelous things. Young man, work hard while you are young; you'll reap the effects of it when you are old . . . Let your business engross the most of your time." [8] As a matter of fact, most influential promoters of Success were ministers of the gospel. The most famous were Horatio Alger, Jr., William Makepeace Thayer, and Russell H. Conwell —all ministers—who urged the youth of America to cultivate the character ethic, something that later would evolve into the Protestant Ethic. Success would surely come to any young lad who possessed the following character traits: industry, frugality, perseverance, initiative, sobriety, punctuality, courage, self-reliance, patience, and honesty.

In their sphere these virtues were the equivalent of the virtues of the Spirit pronounced by Paul in his Epistle to the Galatians: charity, joy, peace, patience, kindness, goodness, faith, modesty, and continency. The purpose of both sets of virtues was to lift the individual out of the present and move him in one of two directions, either to Salvation or to Success. The great menace to either Salvation or Success was an inert body that allowed itself to remain in the present. Or,

---

8. Cited in Richard M. Huber, *The American Idea of Success* (New York: McGraw-Hill, 1971), p. 12.

as Paul expressed it, the flesh with its lusts was the great menace to Salvation. Similarly, the flesh, with its tendencies toward indolence, endangered Success. That was why sex, alcohol, and rich fathers were so terrible: They tempted youth to indulge itself in affairs of the present, thereby ignoring the future, whether that future be Salvation or Success.

Success can only be understood if it is realized that it could never be achieved. It was something one strove for. As the Declaration of Independence put it, it was the object of "the pursuit of happiness." One pursued it; one did not attain it. Making money was not Success. It was what one did with money that counted. Success included social responsibility. It was John Wesley, the founder of Methodism, who wrote:

> Make all you can honestly;
> Save all you can prudently;
> Give all you can possibly.[9]

Using one's acquired wealth for social purposes, whether for public libraries, for sparing animals and children from cruelty, or whatever, was only logical. It kept successful men occupied with things outside themselves—at least in theory. Thus preoccupied, the individual would not concentrate on himself and his own pleasures. That is, he would not reside in the *now*. Instead, he would continue to be future-oriented.

What is noteworthy in this scheme of Success, from its basis in the character ethic to its conclusion in giving away "all you can possibly," is the means involved. It reveals a significant split within man. On the one hand there is the gospel of fraternity, while on the other is the gospel of fratricide. In the last century it has been possible for a man to go to church on Sunday and to the market place on Monday and never detect within himself a split between the Sunday Christian and the Monday hunter. It is as if they are two entirely separate people. And in a way they are.

---

9. *Ibid.*, p. 64.

Man cannot be both hunter and Christian. They are contradictory concepts. Either a man is going to seek peace and harmony in a second life, or he is going to seek it in this life. A man cannot go in two directions at the same time. Yet, paradoxically, both types derive from a common need, and both have been propelled by the same impulse. What completes the paradox is that the enabling influence of both emanated from a single figure, the Protestant clergyman. But then it must be remembered that the Protestant clergyman, from colonial beginnings until the twentieth century, was the pedagogue of society. He administered almost no sacraments. Instead, he taught, first about the means of Salvation, then about the means of Success. In doing so, he touched his audience in a most tender spot: their utter dissatisfaction with terrestrial living. Salvation or Success—it didn't really make much difference which—would deliver man from the pit of terrestrial existence. Whatever ultimate choice the individual made, he would become free of terrestrial restraints. He would never again have to slave at providing sustenance; he would be free of utilitarian relationship; and he would be free of time-anxiety and body stress. Whichever decision he made—Salvation or Success—he would be free—ultimately. It was the paths to these ultimate goals that separated Christian and hunter. The Christian, by and large, endured this life in order to attain the next. The hunter, however, had to conquer this life. He had to become terrestrial in order to attain what he was after: Success. To do this, to conquer in the terrestrial mode, he had to become quite literally a hunter. That is, he had to become something he was not: a lethal predator.

I have described elsewhere the problems of man, an arboreal primate, becoming a predator. There was the obvious problem of creating "artificial extensions of the forelimbs" that would convert a nonlethal primate into a hunter of prey. In the post-hunt era, these artificial extensions have been not weapons, but tools—tools in the largest possible meaning of the word. They could only be provided by education.

The ferocity of American ambition for education stemmed from the fact that there was almost no lag between the time when men were literally hunters and the time when they traded musket for writing slate. Indeed, for many on or near the frontier, the same individual often was both hunter and student.

Thus the clergyman could preach the goals of Salvation and Success, but he could not do much more than point the way. He could extol the virtues of industry, thrift, and so on, but he could not preach the one vital sermon so necessary for Success: bloody competition. Because man lacks the instincts of a predator and because he lacks the "tooth and claw" of the predator, he has been obliged to resort to every device in obtaining the prey he seeks. From the days of *Australopithecus* on he has been a scavenger, a trickster, a trapper, a stampeder, a plunderer, and a killer in order to obtain prey. Of necessity, he has had to continue being a scavenger, a trickster, a trapper, a stampeder, a plunderer and a killer in order to attain Success—in the world of business.

To understand this, we must realize the difference between survival and Success. In the very earliest period, when man had no more than stone tools, all he could aspire to was survival. To a large extent, man was at the mercy of the elements of terrestrial living. He struggled merely to preserve species contact with the environment. Anything beyond that was impossible, primarily because he lacked the tools. The same thing held true of the early cocoon period. All man could do was bring the natural elements, such as animals and grain, together so that they could perform their natural reproductive processes. For a very long time, man's control of these elements was marginal. Drought, disease, pestilence—almost anything could threaten the basis of human survival. This precarious existence endured until the Industrial Revolution. Then everything changed.

Essentially, the Industrial Revolution provided man with a new system of tools whereby he could adequately control the elements of terrestrial living. This was done in two ways. First, these new tools enabled him to control such living elements in nature as drought, disease, pestilence, and so on. By so doing, he was able to increase the yield of natural elements under his control, thereby solving his food problem. Second, the new system of tools allowed man for the first time to utilize the nonliving elements of nature in such a way as to transform the living conditions in the terrestrial mode so that eventually they came to resemble in a remarkable way the terms of arboreal existence.

The Production Revolution of the nineteenth century, using the tools begun by the Industrial Revolution, constructed the foundation on which twentieth-century neo-arborea is based. As a result, man is capable of controlling all the significant features of his existence. He can ignore the seasons, as well as day and night. He can escape from any weather that he finds uncomfortable and enter one he prefers. He can eat seasonal foods out of their season. And finally, he has established a system of production that can function largely on its own.

Man can do all these things, and yet there are actually few beneficiaries of this ability. The majority of the world's people live in the depths of terrestria, grubbing for sustenance, subject to disease, oppressed by tyrants, and suffering from perpetual despair. If man is ever to enjoy peace, he must eliminate the great chasm between the few who are able to live in neo-arborea and the many confined to their terrestrial prison.

As things are there should be no need for man to suffer from a lag between a body need and its satisfaction. Therefore, there should be no need for time-anxiety and body stress to exist. Man is fully capable of reproducing the conditions of arborea while existing in terrestria. And yet, we all know that modern man—especially when on the rim of neo-arborea—suffers as never before from both time-anxiety and body stress. Why?

Most of the uncertainties that plagued man from his earliest terrestrial moments on are gone. He has perfected a cyclical system in which he can control the creation of life and the termination of life. He can take the living and the nonliving elements of nature and combine them into a fantastic cocoon that in every way resembles the original arboreal habitat of the species. Why, then, does modern man feel such unbearable stress? Why such pervasive anxiety? Why does he struggle as if he were in some engulfing quagmire?

The answer, I believe, lies in the fact that man, while on the rim of neo-arborea, finds himself also on the threshold of neo-terrestria, a condition brought about by such a total immersion in terrestrial processes that produce neo-arborea so as to prevent man from extricating himself from terrestria. As a result, man is at a crossroads, torn apart by a conflict between ends and means.

Man cannot remain long at the crossroads; he must push on to a decision. Whichever decision he makes will set the course of the future. As to the duration of the future, that depends on which decision man makes.

PART IV

Janus

Lintel and threshold, greetings, and fare you
well. Today, for the last time, I step outside
my home and my country . . .
        —PLAUTUS, *The Merchant*

A PHOENIX
RISING OUT OF
MORTAR

MAN is not an abstraction; he is a living being, existing in time and place. He is never completely one thing or another; he is never totally arboreal or terrestrial. He is a mixture of the two. While his nature is arboreal, his terrestrial circumstances demand that he act in a terrestrial way. Yet, he is never totally terrestrial, because at all times his arboreal nature seeks ways to manifest itself. Given the merest crack in terrestrial mortar, man will act arboreally. When the crack becomes a broad avenue, man becomes almost totally arboreal.

In the past, very few humans ever lived lives that allowed them to act arboreally. The lot of the overwhelming majority was oppressive and extremely terrestrial. They lived only to work for the creation of subsistence mortar. So thin was the line between survival and extinction that they scarcely could afford the luxury of rest. A drought, a flood, a bad winter, a blight, an invasion, civil strife—almost anything could sweep whole populations into their graves. For these people mortar was dangerously thin and fragile. But above them (how apt a word!) were the few who were sustained by the many. They

were royalty, the class of men most closely related to the gods.
They were sustained by the masses, from whom they took
whatever they wanted. The masses were the tree that both fed
and supported members of royalty so that they might lead
arboreal lives—or at least relatively arboreal lives.

Within their domains, kings—and sometimes lesser nobility
—had virtually absolute power; it could be said that their every
wish was someone else's command. Because they were the
pivotal figures in the kingly/priestly principle, their persons
were frequently inviolable, thus sparing them from predators.
But whether inviolable or not—regicide was not unknown—
they were greatly above the ordinary mortal. The security and
the well-being, even the life, of the subject, was dependent on
the king, who was suspended, as it were, from heaven. The
king's power was from God; therefore he was not dependent
on the people. Upon his death, no new king was elevated from
below; there was descent of the crown through the bloodline
—or there was a struggle between members of the next echelon
of arboreal figures.

The king enjoyed whatever luxuries his kingdom possessed.
He had a retinue of servants so that his needs could be provided for with 'a minimum of delay. While he had a queen
for reasons of state, he had other women to satisfy his sexual
desires. Thus, in matters of body needs, from sustenance to
sex, the king led a relatively arboreal existence.

Nevertheless, he was obliged to perform useful functions,
thereby giving him utilitarian value. He had to rule, to maintain order in the kingdom and peaceful relations with other
states; he had to dispense justice, even if only of a sort. And
in emergencies he had to fight wars. In this way, then, he
was obliged to be lethal.

As long as the kingly/priestly principle obtained, the vast
multitudes were obliged to be almost totally terrestrial. Whatever arboreality they might experience had to be that of fantasy, principally in the form of religion. And it is no coincidence that the original appeal of all the great religions was to

the oppressed masses, the terrestrial masses, who could glimpse the prospect of arboreal living only in a future life, never in this one.

When the United States cut itself off from the kingly/priestly principle, it cut itself off from the past, where both tradition and privilege had had their origins. As a reaction to the past, there was instituted the cult of egalitarianism, which reduced everyone to the least common denominator.

Because the Americans distrusted kingly prerogatives—to say nothing of kingly abuses—they not only did not inaugurate their own kingly system, they forbade many kingly tyrannical practices. This they did by attaching the Bill of Rights to the Constitution. As a consequence, tyranny could not come at the American people from above. At the same time, however, this closing of the heavenly skylight also served to prevent anyone from climbing up through the opening so as to be able to lead anything resembling an arboreal life.

Since privilege from above was precluded, whatever privilege was to enter the American system would have to come up from below. This would require the creation of a broad and powerful middle class which could only come into existence as a result of the presence of excess mortar. Subsistence mortar, that which barely sustained the lowest group of workers, could never create the conditions necessary for an arboreal existence. What was needed was subsistence living—extremely terrestrial living—under conditions that would allow the accumulation of excess mortar.

America, isolated from the kingly/priestly principle that inhibited significant change in Europe during the critical century 1790–1890, and functioning on the cultural/scientific principle, was the ideal arena in which man could begin the construction of neo-arborea, where a remarkably large percentage of the population could eventually be released from the bondage of terrestrial extremes and begin to lead arboreal lives. The task was accomplished by very hard work and very little arboreality.

It is difficult at this point in our history fully to appreciate the enormousness of the explosion of mortar in America. During the nineteenth century the frontier raced westward at a rate of almost thirty miles a year. When the Civil War began, the industrialized North had to send to Europe for much of its early armaments as well as for its uniforms. Yet scarcely forty years later, America was the world's leading industrial power. During these forty years, almost thirteen million immigrants arrived in the country, providing the basis for subsistence mortar on which the rest of the population could build the industrial edifice that would produce excess mortar. Industry, frugality, perseverance, initiative, sobriety, punctuality, courage, self-reliance, patience, and honesty—the most terrestrial of virtues that man could devise—were the very virtues that created excess mortar. And yet, even as they created the conditions for arboreal living, they created a new person: the terrestrialist, someone who could never experience arboreal living.

Before the time of the terrestrialist, man had to survive on subsistence terrestrial fare while he dreamed of arborea, whether in abstract form or in religious form. Only those few born or raised above the masses, could experience arboreal living. Thus, for all practical purposes, there was literally nothing on earth that could produce the conditions necessary for arboreal living.

However, once it became possible for even the lowest-born to produce the conditions that would allow for arboreal existence, an entirely new situation pertained. Work, not birth, could produce the conditions that would allow for arboreality. Instead of privilege riding on the backs of the masses, the masses would ride on the back of productivity. Man would produce his own arborea. To do that, however, man would have to become a terrestrialist. He would have to work as never before, with singlemindedness and devotion and a total disregard for present ease and comfort, in order to create the necessary conditions. And yet, in becoming such a terrestrialist to accomplish such an objective, he produced within himself an insoluble dilemma. Man, so the dilemma went, must work to produce arboreal conditions; if he ceases to work so that he might enjoy the arborea he has created, the conditions will vanish and arborea will be lost and man will be right back where he once was: mired down in terrestria with no chance of escape.

The dilemma arises over the matter of production: Man must produce if he is to consume. Before his break with nature, he could consume what nature produced in direct transactions. When forced into the terrestrial mode, indirect transactions, involving artificial extensions of the forelimbs, were necessary if man was to consume what nature produced. When man entered his cocoon he had to become a producer. Thus, he began to be on both sides of the production-consumption process.

As a result of this situation, man produces to consume, so that he might be able to produce in order to consume, etc., etc., etc. It is an endless cycle. To be a producer, man must exist in a contingency-dependency status and possess utilitarian value. Further, he must inevitably experience time-anxiety and body stress. In addition, so as to preserve and perpetuate mortar, all subsidiary institutions and practices must remain rigidly in place. Hence, the perpetuation of the social-sexual subordination of women, the family, paternity, filialness, war, slavery, and education.

It can be seen from this that man, even when he has produced the conditions necessary for arboreal living, must continue to function as a terrestrialist who produces what man has always sought, but who can't consume what he has produced. That is, he can't stop acting in a terrestrial way in order to be able to enjoy what he has produced—arborea.

That is the dilemma. Is there any way to break through it? Another way of posing the question is that: Must man always be future-oriented to such an extent that he cannot live fully in the present? That really is the ultimate question. Ever since the beginning of the terrestrialization process, man has had to leave the constant now and organize existence around the inconstant future. In the beginning it was something as simple and brief as picking up a pebble with which later to kill an animal or prepare an already scavenged one for food. In the twentieth century, just the preparation for a role in the production process may take ten or twenty years during which some form of dependency on others exists and during which many body needs may be frustrated or postponed, especially those concerned with sex.

The ethic on which the American system of production was built was one of present denial for future benefit. In the earliest years, this future was actually that of a future life. But as productivity grew, the delay was shortened. In theory, at least, one could enjoy this life, but only after long years devoted to hard work and self-denial. (It will be recalled that Cotton Mather's admonition was addressed to the young man to work now so that he might "reap the effects" of it when old.) In time, this principle gave way to the one that broke up the long year of work into brief respites of a week or two of vacation; the work week was reduced to six and then five days, and the work day from sixteen hours to ten and then eight, and now frequently less.

This is a critical process that graphically illustrates man's efforts to live in the present as much as possible. In its original form, the individual had to provide for his own future, from that of the two-week vacation to that of final retirement. He produced, as it were, for his own consumption. But then the process became cooperative, largely due to the efforts of labor unions. And it is here we begin to glimpse the beginning of one of man's most ingenious techniques in creating arboreal conditions.

Before the beginning of cooperative efforts, if a worker became ill or had an accident, he and his family suffered as long as he was absent from work. And, should the worker die—on the job or off the job, it made no difference—the family lost everything: They lost their source of sustenance. Nothing but a worker's own ability to save provided the money for his old age. This was a precarious situation for the worker. An illness, an economic recession, the illness of a spouse or child—anything could threaten the security of the worker and his family. There was, in this system, a direct personal relationship between production and consumption. It was very simple: Work and you get paid; don't work and you don't get paid; what you do with your pay is your business. It was a system in which the great majority lived on subsistence mortar that could shatter at any moment—and often did.

It is with the beginning of trade unionism that we begin to see something totally new in the human productive process. There began to develop a slight separation between a worker's productivity and his compensation. The effect of this is incalculable. It means that for the first time there is a breakup in the production-consumption process. When a worker can be ill or have an accident or take a vacation and be paid for the time he is not working, we witness the historic phenomenon of man being able to consume without having produced. It means that no matter how slight the separation, human productivity is beginning to assume an aspect of nature's productivity: Something is produced at least to some degree without man's participation in the process.

What made it possible was the increased productivity of the nonhuman elements in the process. The artificial extension of man's grasping forelimbs—mortar—was producing, on an expanding basis, other mortar, thereby releasing man from part of the process. Mortar was at last producing mortar, not in the sense that man's brain (mortar) was producing mortar (the extensions). That had already been done in the past. It was a case of the extensions (mortar), independent of man's brain, producing production and consumer goods (mortar).

What this means, then, is that man had by the end of the nineteenth century reached the point where he could begin to turn over part of the production process to mortar so that he could begin to live in the present. He could live, even if only for a brief time, on what mortar alone could produce. It was as important a moment in the terrestrial life of man as Yuri Gagarin's first suborbital flight into space was to space travel. It showed that it could be done, that man now could create the conditions that would support arboreal living, just as Gagarin's flight showed that man could exist in a weightless condition which, in a sense, is exactly what mortar allows man to do: exist without being weighted down by terrestrial conditions.

Despite the obvious good that labor unions could do for the working man in the early years of struggle, there was powerful opposition to them, not only from the capitalist class but even from many of the workers. To understand this remarkable phenomenon, we must look to Europe, where a new philosophy was taking shape: socialism.

Everything Marx was after was contained in that famous aphorism: "From each according to his abilities, to each according to his needs." It must be noted that it is a disjunctive statement, unlike that of the 1936 Soviet Constitution, which said, "From each according to his abilities, to each according to his work." Marx is telling us that each must contribute what he can to the production process. But then he does not go on to say, as the Soviet Constitution does, that each receives exclusively on the basis of work performed, but rather that each receives on the basis of *need*. He separates the production cycle from the consumption cycle. It is not a matter of x hours of work for y units of pay and then go fend for yourself. He says work as you are able, but receive what you need. He destroys the ability of the owner of the means of production to control the consumption side of the total process, which is what industry throughout the world was doing at that time. The owners of the means of production sought to control both sides of the production-consumption process so as to perpetuate the dependency—and marginal—status of the workers. As long as there was no outside force seeking to influence the relationship between employer and worker, there existed in the relationship something similar to that of the earlier relationship between master and slave, in which the slave was contingent on the master while the master escaped any contingency relationship, with the net result that the master enjoyed a remarkably arboreal existence.

In the industrial situation, the employers were not the operators and managers of the factories, they were the shareholders of the corporations that made the production system possible. Their money (mortar) worked for them so that they might not have to work. And under the then current theory of capitalism, the rule was to pay the worker only enough to keep him producing without gain or loss of effectiveness. Therefore, he could only be paid in relation to his own productivity. Anything more, and the profits of the shareholders would be reduced, thereby endangering their own arboreality. As a consequence, they fought bitterly to prevent the unshackling of the worker from the production line. They thought, quite erroneously, that his emancipation would mean their own enslavement to terrestrial practices. And as I have said before, everyone given the slightest opportunity will seek to act in accordance with his arboreal nature. He will do anything to escape from the bondage imposed on him by terrestrial living.

That was why Marx and his socialism were so hated: They posed a threat to the arboreal lives of the owners of production. His cry, "Workers of the world unite, you have nothing to lose but your chains!" threatened to reenslave the capitalist. Take away his mortar, his investment capital, and he would have to reenter the production-consumption process and lead a terrestrial life. It was for fear of this that they strongly opposed all unionism and socialism.

What was wrong with capitalist thinking was its failure to identify its own arboreal aspirations with those of the workers. It was the classic posture for capital and labor to be in opposition. Capital's gain was labor's loss, and vice versa. While this might have been true when labor's contribution to production was excessively large because of the small role of machinery, once machines (mortar) began playing a larger and larger role, it became clear that both capital and labor would benefit together from production, because both could begin to rely more and more on mortar producing what needed to be produced for consumption.

There was another fundamental error in capitalist thinking. Workers were conceived of as producers, but not necessarily consumers, of the products they produced. Henry Ford saw something in 1914 that no one else did when he raised his workers' daily pay to five dollars and at the same time lowered the price of his cars (to the utter horror of his financial advisors). By doing this, Ford put his workers on both sides of the production-consumption process.

Until this time, consumption above that necessary for bare subsistence was reserved for the small capitalist class that used the production of others to create the foundation of their own arboreal existence. Not only did the man have mortar (capital) working for him; the woman of the family did also, in the form of servants who did the menial and manual labor within the home. However, once the worker was able to be on both sides of the production-consumption process, the arboreal class began to grow with extraordinary speed, and it wasn't very long before both capitalist and worker began to enjoy a mutual arboreality. In fact, it wasn't very long before the wages of labor reached a point where both the capitalist and his wife had to reduce labor's role, substituting for it more and more machinery in the factory and in the home. Servants, like the workers, had become consumers. Henceforth, machinery (mortar) would work for capitalist and worker alike. The result has been that with very few exceptions, the life of the worker today in the consumption cycle is indistinguishable from that of the capitalist. He has as many servants in the home as does the capitalist, he has at least one private automobile, he has access to the most expensive medical and dental care, and he is paid when hurt, ill, on vacation, and retired. It can rightly be said that in the modern era a worker's paradise has been achieved.

REVOLUTION...

THE TERMS of arboreal existence are present. What prevents so many from experiencing it, even as they utilize the accouterments of such an existence, is their preoccupation with terrestrial means. They function as if full personal participation were essential to the success of the process. They believe that the ethic of the arboreal period must be the same as that which produced it. These are the terrestrialists I mentioned earlier.

It is not merely a question of attitudes toward production and consumption, with present production taking precedence over present consumption; it is a matter of the entire fabric of terrestrial existence that includes everything from the hunt itself to war, slavery, and education, as well as such institutions as the family, filialness, paternity, and the social-sexual subservience of women. There is in America today a conflict between the arboreal and terrestrial aspects of man as they confront each other.

In 1954, the Supreme Court of the United States, in its famous decision, *Brown* v. *Board of Education*, in effect ruled that black citizens were *de jure Homo sapiens* and could no longer be restricted to second-class citizenship under the guise of "separate but equal" school facilities. Since then there have been a series of liberation movements that have had as their purpose the certification that certain other classes of people are, indeed, also *de jure* members of the species.

The long struggle of black people in this country, as well
as those of the brown, the red, and the yellow, is well known.
This is not an exclusively domestic affair in the United States,
but an international phenomenon that reveals a rising consciousness occurring on a very wide scale.

Only after this racial movement had begun, and in fact had
reached its peak, did the second significant movement commence, that of women. Women, too, were no longer going to
be treated as sex objects and second-class citizens.

Next in sequence came the Gay Liberation movement,
which demanded that homosexuals be treated as full members
of the species, and that oppression and exclusion stop.

The most recent movement, one that oddly enough lacks
a name, is that of prison inmates, who are rising up in protest
against subhuman conditions and treatment within prisons.
Like those before them, they are demanding that they be
treated as human beings.

The subordination of racial groups, women, homosexuals,
and prison inmates was a consequence of the rigid system that
was necessary to perfect the production process to the point
where it could begin to gain some autonomy through the increased use of mortar. At this point, the system's need for
absolute rigidity was gone. It was as if shackles had been taken
off everyone involved, allowing them to move about as they
wished. Being humans—arboreal primates—they have begun
to move about in arboreal ways.

In terms of the liberation movements I have mentioned,
those of the races occupies the first position, since they relate
directly to the production process. In this country, all minorities were previously consigned to lower-echelon work. They provided the cheap, massive understructure that supported the
production leaders. Unless they were firmly kept in their subordinate, but significantly contributory, position the structure
on which the white production-leaders stood would have col-
lapsed, wrecking everything. However, once the relation between the superior white worker and the production process

loosened, the once-rigid subordination of the minorities also loosened, allowing minorities to become more mobile.

Women's liberation was able to follow that of the races because once the rigid rules of the hunt were loosened, the various sexual rules could become more fluid. Terrestrial sexual relations were geared directly to the demands of the hunt, placing the woman in a dependent status. However, once production begins to become slightly independent of the male, the male becomes a less critical conduit between a woman and the meeting of her body needs. She now becomes less dependent on the male, allowing her to relate more directly to the source of those things that will meet her body needs. In addition, the conditional relationship between her dependent economic status and her sexuality is lessened, thereby giving her greater choice in her sexual life and in the matter of having as many or as few babies as she chooses. Since a human relation to production is no longer as important as it once was, there is less need for production workers. As a result, reproduction is freed from its demands and individual women can determine the size of their families without reference to the needs of society.

Once sexual relations became loosened between men and women, sexual relations between members of the same sex became loosened. Sex has lost some of its utilitarian role since production needs less sexual support. This being the case, homosexuals no longer appear to be a menace to the previous sexual utilitarianism society demanded.

In this regard, since utilitarianism has become diminished, sexual activity does not have to be restricted to coitus, since offspring are not the necessary object of sexual activity. Thus we see a loosening of the restrictions as to what acts may be performed in both hetero- and homosexual relationships. Further, because individualized sex no longer interferes with the production process, greater exposure to sexually stimulating situations can be permitted. We see this in the relaxation of literary, theatrical, and cinematic censorship, and in the ability of increasing numbers of people to discuss openly virtually every aspect of human sexuality, including most significantly the matter of the female orgasm. When a woman possessed an essentially utilitarian role in sexual matters, whether she had an orgasm or in any way experienced pleasure in sexual activity was completely beside the point. However, once she lost this utilitarian role, her needs were allowed to come forward and be an important aspect of her sexual activity.

The progression in the liberation movements was from that of the worker in the production process to that of contingent sexual roles within the system. We can now witness the third movement, which concerns the problem of the individual who refuses to conform to the rules of the system: the prison inmate. Under the old system, violations of the law were severely dealt with in order to preserve the rigid system, and a convicted felon was incarcerated as a way of punishment and as a means to prevent the infection of general society by those who refused to function according to the laws created to protect and promote the production process. Prison inmates, of all members of society, were of the lowest order. In this country, for example, a felon lost most of his civil rights, including the right to vote. Whether in prison or on parole or upon completion of sentence, he was a pariah for the rest of his life, lacking the status of *Homo sapiens* in every essential way, from his almost total inability to obtain decent work on the outside to his being denied the ability to participate in ordinary civil activities. He was, at best, a beast to be beaten and hounded all the days of his life.

But once the cleavage between personal participation and the production process began to grow, and as utilitarianism began to lose its central position in human relationships, new attitudes began to develop toward the law instituted to reinforce this utilitarianism. While most criminal laws remained unchanged, their interpretation by the courts, especially the Supreme Court of the United States, underwent significant change. For the first time in history, more and more attention

was being paid to the rights of the individual who was suspected of crime and who in fact was in prison for crime. He
became, at last, a *de jure* member of the species and as such
was entitled to the rights and immunities enjoyed by members
of the species.

There is another aspect to the matter of criminal law that
bears scrutiny. Under the old law, because of its harshness
and because of the public attitude toward crime, there was a
reciprocal attitude on the part of those breaking the law. It
was one largely of hopelessness and isolation. However, under
the new dispensation, attitudes on both sides of the law have
changed. As for the criminal, he feels less bound by the law
—which, it must be remembered, is the law of utilitarianism
—and prefers to function in accord with what we might call
the laws of arborea, under the terms of which there is no private property and one takes what one wants when one wants
it. As a result, crime is on the increase. This is so, not because
of any laxity in the enforcement of the law, but because of
the weakening of the premise on which the law rests.

Other liberation movements have been attempted, but because they lack a direct or dependency relationship to the
hunt, they have failed. Most conspicuous has been the efforts
of the university students. As students, they lack any direct relationship to the production process, and they lack a dependent sexual relationship; thus any relaxation of the production
process would not be reflected in the situation of the student.
On the other hand, because students have had a direct stake
in military conscription, they have played an important role
in the struggle against it, something to be discussed later.

One of the most neglected minorities has been the aged.
Though they have sought to establish "Senior Power," they
have failed because of the absence of any relationship to the
production process. They live in the post-production period of
their lives, and therefore any relaxation of the process would
find no echo in their situation.

There is in the various liberation movements a central dynamic that is significantly affecting the lives of everyone. This dynamic is the emerging *I*. Until this emergence, everyone had a utilitarian role to play; as a result, everyone had a utilitarian identity. A man, as the protagonist of society, had the most utilitarian identities. He was an employee or employer, a husband, a father, a member of a church and of a political party, and so on through an almost limitless list of possible identifications. A man who lacked the first three identities, to a very large extent, lacked any real identity. He failed to function as he must function in the production of mortar, and he failed his sexual responsibility to create future workers and to assist in preparing them, especially in their value systems, for later participation in the production of mortar.

A woman in this system also possessed utilitarian identities. She was, in her formative years, a virgin who could only surrender her virginity to her husband. Upon marriage, she was a wife, a mother, a member of a church and of a political party, and on through organizations that contributed something to the social good of the community. As with the man, if she lacked an identity as a wife and as a mother, it was as if she had no identity at all. She was not part of the rigid system and she failed in a most critical way to produce the future of the system. She had really only one function: that of producing babies and then terrestrializing them for the good of the society in which she lived.

What was true of adults was true also of children. Above a certain age, the age when play left off and work began, a child was a student. He had no other identity because he was mere potential, not actuality. It was virtually as impossible to conceive of a child divorced from his student identity as it would have been to conceive of the child growing into maturity without becoming, by that fact alone, a series of utilitarian identities. Indeed, it was to attain these later identities that the child was a student. And that was why education was so vital. It was the guarantor of the future.

This matter of utilitarian identities produced certain problems for those who did not fit into the scheme of things. What, for example, of the artist? He produced works of art—paintings, music, poetry, and so forth—but works of art are not part of physical mortar. At best they are part of psychic mortar, in that in a variety of ways they ameliorate the severe terms of terrestrial living. But this art has to be "paid for" by someone supporting the artist. Until most recently the artist was supported by patrons or he supported himself by other means. It is because the artist was so dependent on the largesse of his patron, and so low on the economic scale, that he was very low in the social order of things. This was especially true in Europe and America until the rapid expansion of the middle class produced many new "patrons" who, instead of supporting the artist *in toto*, supported him piecemeal by buying his output. This, then, placed the artist in the market place, where his output helped in the circulation of mortar (money) and in the creation of mortar, such as art galleries and agents.

In contrast to the nonproductive artist, there was the prostitute. She had a distinct utilitarian identity and a utilitarian value, yet in almost every legal jurisdiction she was outlawed. The question is: Why? She performed a useful and marketable service, or under the law of supply and demand she would have disappeared long ago. It cannot seriously be argued that she threatened the stability of the family. Human history gives no evidence whatsoever of this. Then why was she so bad that laws had to be enacted against her—laws, incidentally, that were never adequately enforced either against the woman or her male customers? The prostitute was a living example of man's arboreality. To grant her legitimacy would be to grant man's arboreal sexuality legitimacy, and that could not be allowed. The prostitute was an embarrassing link with the past.

One of the great misconceptions about prostitutes is that they do not enjoy sex. This is not true. In a *Playboy* interview, William Masters, the famous researcher into sexual matters, pointed out that second only to economic reasons, most prostitutes enter the profession and remain in it for the sex it offers. This only makes sense. Being an arboreal primate, the prostitute is sexually promiscuous. And so is the male of the species. It is because man is sexually promiscuous that monogamy is a burden for both males and females. Prostitutes relieve this burden for the male. The female, under the system, lacked independence and therefore could not easily practice sexual promiscuity. Instead, she had to be circumspect when opportunity appeared which, in most societies, was extremely rare. Infidelity by a wife was an act of insubordination and hence reprehensible. Infidelity by a husband was not an act of insubordination because of the male's dominant position, and hence was easily forgiven.

Another problem the prostitute posed was that of disconnecting sexual activity from its procreative function. If enough males discharged their sexual tensions with prostitutes, the terrestrial function of sex would be thwarted. This could not be allowed.

Finally, the prostitute violated the order of things. Women were intended to be wives and mothers. They were not to be independent and thereby free of the usual dependency role of the woman. If, for example, all women became prostitutes, there would be a complete breakdown of the system with the resultant loss of all prospect for the future where hopes of arborea were to be realized. Under the utilitarian identity rule, women had their place, and that was in the home.

However, once utilitarianism is ended, everything loosens up and people may act out their needs as they see fit, without regard to utilitarian values. This means the emergence of the individual as an individual, and not as part of something else. What makes this possible is the increasing independence of the production process from human participation. Mortar thus produces mortar, thereby allowing man to exist in neo-arborea, where his arboreal nature is free to express itself. Sustained by mortar, even if only partially, man can live part of life in the now. And when he does, he acts as he wishes, without re-

gard to utilitarian consequences. With our arrival in neo-
arborea, the emergency conditions of terrestrial living are over,
and when that happens, terrestrial rules are replaced by arboreal rules and man begins to function naturally: as an arboreal primate.

Consider the family, for example. In terrestria the family is
the basic unit of society. For reasons explained elsewhere, male
and female had to form a permanent union out of which children were produced so that in time the mature children could
provide support for the old and also perpetuate the species. All
this was necessary because of the demands of the original hunt
and those of subsequent economic activity. At stake, of course,
was the production of mortar. But once mortar begins producing itself, the need for man to make it is reduced. And
when this happens the demand for the terrestrial family arrangement is reduced.

One of the first conspicuous fissures in the solidarity of the
family has been the rising divorce rate that began its climb
only a relatively few years ago. The "sanctity" of marriage
gave way to the "sanctity" of the individual who had a right
to happiness or at least the right to change his mind. Another
way to express it is to say that the utilitarian value of the family gave way to the personal preferences of the people in it.
Increasingly over the last few decades, wives have become independent of husbands especially in legal and property rights.
They have ceased being restricted to a dependency status, and
can now relate directly to mortar.

The great fracture within the family has been that between
parents and children. While in the past there have been "generation gaps," which the maturity of children always seemed
to close, today there is something distinctly new. For the first
time in human history, sons and daughters are not following
the leads of their parents. They, far more than their parents,
sense the possibilities of arborea.

One of the outstanding symbols of the estrangement between parents and sons is the matter of hair. Although the

violence of parental reaction to the long hair of sons has now
died down somewhat [1] only a few years ago it was the cause
of the breakup of family relationships. Hair is extremely visible, and when sons begin to let this visible symbol speak for
them, it says something that both infuriates parents—especially
fathers—and frightens them. The long hair of sons is a signal
to parents that they are not going to join the hunt. Short hair
and clean-shaven faces are the grooming style of the modern
hunter. Sons have reacted to this by letting their hair grow
long and their faces develop beards. In another, earlier age,
such use of hair would have been compatible with the standards set by the then hunters. But in the modern era they are
a clear signal of rejection.

At the same time, clothes and lifestyles have changed. Again,
to set themselves off from their hunting fathers, sons wear
tacky and even cast-off clothes. However, it is in the matter
of lifestyles that there is the greatest cleavage between parents
and children. Essentially, children have started to lead arboreal
lives, withdrawing from competitive situations such as school
and careers. They have formed various types of small communities where efforts are made to share whatever anyone has.
Most of these efforts fail, not because of differences among the
participants, but because they are experimenting with something very primordial that has suffered from a long intervening
period in which intense competition was the perennial lifestyle.

Probably the most unnerving practice for parents, especially
mothers, is the sexual promiscuity of daughters. Since marriage is not the sacrosanct institution it once was, and since
daughters don't need to enter a dependency situation at a

---

1. Today, hair is less troublesome for two reasons. First, long hair,
beards, mustaches, and other visible lifestyle manifestations are increasingly common, and most of the population is becoming used to them.
Second, many features of the "hippie" lifestyle have been coopted by
society as a defensive measure and to take economic advantage of the
styles. Thus, there are the so-called "mod" styles that make for economic
profit. Hair, etc., once the symbol of the lifestyle of a portion of the
populace, has now become the hair style of the many, thus losing its
original quality and effect.

relatively young age, bringing with them their virginity as a wedding present to their husbands, the natural primate sexuality of the young is expressing itself.[2] They seek only temporary relationships that are not based on utilitarian values, but on the values of the particular individuals involved. In this arboreal climate young women have babies without the prior social necessity of marriage. The baby is the *mother's* baby; it is not that of the father. If and when the relationship that created the child ends, the mother takes her baby wherever she goes.

The new generation of maturing young people work at jobs. Most seek fields compatible with their lifestyles. Those who must take what they can find—and they are the vast majority —refuse to make careers out of their jobs. They work to "earn the bread" to live the lives they want. Mostly they obtain subsistence incomes, but this doesn't disturb them at all. They have learned that a lot of mortar isn't necessary to sustain life. Instead, what they have discovered is the ability to live as much as possible in the constant now. In this connection, they have discovered their bodies, and having found them, they have sought to relate to them—or, as it is sometimes put, they "get it all together."

The complaint is raised against the young people that they are the products of a permissive society. This is merely defensive pejoration. If the society is permissive—which I am not saying—it has been the terrestrial parents who have made it so. But this would be to concoct a contradiction in terms. Terrestrial parents—actually the greatest hunters in man's long history—produced the arboreal conditions that have allowed their children to begin to live an arboreal existence. The significant fact is that it is the children of the successful middle-class who comprise the bulk of the arboreal generation. Those previously confined to existing on subsistence mortar are now

---

2. It is significant that the natural sexual promiscuity of young boys and men has never been seriously interfered with, a situation creating what is known as the double standard. But then, boys don't have babies nor is their virginity a wedding present to their brides—male virginity has no market value.

climbing up to the middle class so that eventually they, or their children, might make the final leap into the trees.

Unfortunately, even tragically in many instances, most parents can't see the situation in its real colors. They see the only way to live as that of extreme terrestrialists. What they don't see is that the age of the extreme terrestrialist is past, that man has entered a stage where the terrestrialist can let up and begin to live in the now—even if only part of the time. What inhibits the terrestrialist from doing this is his preoccupation with the future. He is like the great hunter who has returned to his village laden down with game but who, even as he lays the game down, still feels its weight on his back.

One of the most remarkable aspects to this generational situation is revealed in the conflict between older and younger religious thinkers. It is being proclaimed today that God is dead. Religion, as never before, is suffering from drift and disinterest. Church membership is down, church attendance is down, church support is down. Within the Catholic Church, priests and nuns are leaving their vocations in record numbers. Celibacy is being challenged, the authority of the pope is being challenged, and the once tightly structured system of thought is unraveling. The individual, not the organized structure of the Church, is becoming the controlling factor in the religious lives of the people, especially the younger.

The reason for all this is not hard to find. The function of religion has been to serve as a guidance system to arborea. With man on the rim of neo-arborea, there is little need for guidance. God is dead, as it were, because he is not needed. The impulse in man that formulated the concept of God is no longer present in those beginning to experience the arboreal life. In arborea, there are no gods—just other primates—and that is why those retaining residual elements of the religious impulse are using church instrumentalities to perfect relations between people, not between man and a dissolving God.

Education is in crisis. A most elaborate system was once constructed to produce the terrestrialists who would build the foundations of neo-arborea. Now that great need doesn't exist. What does exist is a need to prepare technicians to manage the mortar-producing mortar—and on an ever-decreasing basis. What is not needed is an educational system that seeks to produce confrontation-competitors on the one hand and conformists on the other. Curricula are being rearranged to reflect changing conditions. There is less emphasis on the staples of education, the three R's, and more on interpersonal situations. Grades and competitive scoring, especially on the university level, are decreasing in importance. However, the problem of education that is producing the current crisis concerns its future. Instead of growing and producing the sort of student produced a generation ago, education must begin to see its changing place in society. There is less need for the educational processes, simply because there is less need for hunters in the developing arboreal era. In this connection, it must be remembered that education is not natural to man. It is something built up as a necessary ingredient of mortar. Therefore, once its need becomes decreasingly necessary, the natural inclination of man takes over, and he seeks ways to rid himself of this unnatural accretion.

The system has been organized so as automatically to feed small children into the educational processes and keep them there until they are minimally qualified to enter the production process. Teachers are rebelling because none of it has the urgent meaning it once had. In fact, to many it has no meaning at all.

There is, finally, one more critical area of conflict that is breaking up the family and at the same time threatening to break up society. This conflict concerns the place of lethality in the life of the species. By nature man is neither a predator nor a perpetrator of human aggression; terrestrial circumstances once obliged him to adopt these measures if he was to survive.[3] As living conditions slowly begin to acquire arboreal aspects,

3. This rather complex subject is dealt with extensively in "The Labyrinth."

man is beginning to revert to his original nonlethal self. As far
back as the last years of the nineteenth century, when there was
scarcely a hint of arborea in the air, efforts were begun by
various states to put an end to war. World War I, the logical
extension of terrestrial living's principles, resulted in efforts to
create some sort of system that might lessen the prospects of
war. The League of Nations failed badly; the United Nations
isn't really doing much better today. The reason is that states,
not people, are represented. States, by their very nature, are
terrestrial institutions that can only act and react on the basis
of terrestrial premises, and one of the major premises of terrestrial living—at least for man—is lethality.[4]

The Southeast Asian war was an excellent example of a state
seeking to function in terrestrial ways while a broad spectrum
of its people insisted on acting in an arboreal way. At no time
during all the years of that war was the American hunt in
danger, notwithstanding various efforts to convince the people
that it was. American credibility, America's obligations to
nations depending on it for leadership, and a host of other
arguments were advanced to try and persuade the American
people that something of great national concern was present
in the wretched little countries of North and South Vietnam.
Nothing worked, especially among most of the young.

Something visceral persuaded a great many people that war
was not the solution to the problems of war-ravaged Vietnam.
Foremost among them were the young. The confrontation was
total. On one side was all the power of the world's mightiest
terrestrial state, possessing the most devastating lethal capability in the history of man. Functioning on exclusively terrestrial assumptions, this side sought to impose its will on American youth. Opposed to the monstrous lethal force of the mili-

---

4. It is significant that the two peace conferences at The Hague (1899,
1907) were approached cynically and even with hostility by most of the
world's leading states, which went through the motions only because of
the strong public pressures within their various countries for an end to
armaments and war. This is an excellent example of the terrestriality of
the state being challenged by the arboreality of people.

tary establishment was a ragtag bunch of disorganized and nonviolent protesters, mounted on picket lines and camped in doorways. It was a classic confrontation between the terrestrialist and the arborealist. Neither side could understand the other. To the terrestrialist an aphorism like "Make love, not war" was either incomprehensible or obscenely treasonous. To the arborealist, the napalming of helpless women and children was the act of an obscene madman.

In this titanic struggle the young men were the heart of the opposition to war. Yet they were the most vulnerable, being subject to the draft. It was the poor and the oppressed who were sent to wage the war; their affluent brothers, those most arboreal, mobilized the youth against the war, employing every technique from draft-dodging to going to prison rather than fight the war.

This confrontation between terrestrialist and arborealist obliged fathers and sons to stare at each other across a breachless chasm. The father saw the conduct of the son as threatening the very foundations of survival; the son, in turn, saw the father threatening the foundations of existence. The issue over which terrestrial father and arboreal son divided concerned the role of lethality in man's life. The father saw the enemy as a predator and demanded counter-lethality. The son saw human beings on the other side of the fighting line. Expressions of solidarity with the people of the NLF and North Vietnam were acknowledgements of common identity as members of the species. Since intraspecies killing is inimical to the survival of the species, it simply couldn't be permitted. The father, on the other hand, saw these same people as threats to the safety of the United States ("If we don't fight them in Vietnam, we'll have to fight them in California"), endowing them with almost superhuman capabilities. The paranoia of the father was a classic restatement of the fears of the early terrestrial hominids menaced by actual predators.

The issue presented by the young—and by a sprinkling of older people—goes beyond the question of the ultimate form of lethality. It concerns the state of mind that can produce this escalated lethality. It has been terrestrial competition in all its dimensions that has produced the type of thinking that can result in lethal action. Social violence, economic violence, psychological violence have all been aspects of terrestrial lethality. The arborealist sees them as menacing as the final act, for they prepare the way for the final act. As a consequence, the arborealist seeks to do away with all forms of terrestrial violence, whether social, economic, psychological, or military.

This is not to suggest that arborealists are moral and that terrestrialists are immoral. The terrestrialist wants an end to lethality. It is the goal of everyone, but of course lethality can only be arrived at on certain terms that the terrestrialist sincerely believes are necessary. It is not a question of morality; it is a question of perspective. To the terrestrialist, lethality is a regrettable necessity. To the arborealist it is regrettable insanity. To the arborealist an end to all forms of violence is absolutely essential; to the terrestrialist, nonviolence guarantees the loss of everything held precious: life, freedom, and prosperity.

The debate continues. But the fact that should attract our attention is that the debate exists at all. Without the constantly increasing numbers of arborealists, whatever flickering debate that might have once arisen would have been stamped out long ago. Only when man exists in fully realized arboreal circumstances will he be able to divest himself of terrestrial lethality. The difficulty of the present moment is that man is only on the rim of neo-arborea. And that places him in a most dangerous position, for he could as easily topple out of neo-arborea as into it. The forces are that delicately balanced.

In this section I have attempted to set forth the two revolutionary forces at work in man today. They are the emergent *I* and the resurgence of nonlethality, two aspects of that original primate that has since become man. They comprise two essential parts of man's nature that have not changed in all the millions of years man has struggled to survive in the terrestrial mode. They have remained submerged all this time. But now arboreal circumstances are beginning to reappear, and with their appearance, these two prime arboreal qualities of man are beginning to make their appearance. And as they do, they stare directly at two counterrevolutionary forces that are their implacable foes.

...AND COUNTER-REVOLUTION

WHILE it is true that man is on the rim of neo-arborea, it is also true that he is on the threshold of neo-terrestria. Man has established a network of processes by which he lives so that he might attain Salvation or Success. In neither effort is the *now* taken into consideration other than to serve as an avenue leading somewhere else. The *now* has no end-value; it has only process-value. Yet these processes are threatening to become ends themselves, thereby projecting man into a dead-end situation from which there may well be no extrication. This is the result not so much of objective reality as of subjective disposition, which has produced a dedication to the processes that is almost impossible to overcome. It is very much like religious faith: one doesn't give it up easily, especially when it is the means of Salvation.

Man is becoming as wedded to the processes as he has always been to the goal. It is this that produces a great contradiction within him: that between terrestrial means and arboreal ends. The threat provoked by this contradiction is that man will continue to apply himself to the means in such an intense way that they will become the ends of his existence. In such an event man will enter neo-terrestria. If he does, the consequences will be ruinous, for when he arrives in neo-terrestria he will become entwined in two processes that will plunge him into extinction. One process, that of production-consumption, will use up all available mortar, thereby depriving man of a means of maintaining a species profile to match that of the environment. In the alternative, the second process, the military process, will transform lethality into neo-lethality, which will exterminate the species.

The essential difficulty in the production-consumption process centers around two propositions. First, whereas once production existed so that man might consume, today man consumes in order to perpetuate production. Second, whereas the process once functioned to serve man's needs, now man exists to serve the needs of the process. Both reversals are the result of means becoming ends, and they became ends when the process achieved an existence independent of man's control. Independence gave the process a type of "environmental profile" to which man has had to match a "species profile" and, as we know in the case of nature, nature's profile is the one that must be conformed to by the species. It is not the other way around. Similarly, whatever profile the production process presents, man must conform to it. What is extraordinary about this situation is that man created the process and now has lost control of it. He could reassert his control and return to the conditions that pertained before the reversals, but he doesn't, because he has no instinct for any aspect of the process. All he has is accumulated mortar that is beginning to crumble. What makes the reversal work is man's instinct to consume. It is the basis of survival.

The corporation is one of man's most remarkable inventions. Actually, there is no such thing as a corporation. That which is called a corporation lacks all tangible reality. Instead, there is an assumption, an understanding, among people that a mythical entity, called a corporation, shall exist to serve certain needs. The corporation exists to assist man in escaping personal responsibility for what he is about to do or what he is in the process of doing. To add to the grotesqueness of the situation, in America there is even the legal fiction that a corporation is a person, a straight-faced assertion made by the Supreme Court of the United States so that corporations might benefit from the Fourteenth Amendment clause relating to equal protection of the laws. This is essential if corporations are to travel from state to state, itself a novel concept, without arbitrary restraints being placed upon them. There is another distinguishing feature of a corporation. For all practical purposes it is immortal. It cannot die a natural death; it must be intentionally put away. But that is not the end. It can, even when put to death, be resurrected the next day. In addition to all this, probably the most unique talent of the corporation is its ability to make things, move things, sell things—in short, do everything man can do, and a lot more—all of which is quite something when it is realized that a corporation is a mythical entity, an assumption on the part of men.

But it serves man's purposes—or it is intended to. What causes the difficulties is the almost mystical effect the corporation has on those connected with it. The principal attitude demanded by the corporation of those who work for it is complete loyalty. Should anyone act in any way the corporation deems disloyal, he is discharged. The effect of this power is to divorce the corporation from human principles. The corporation can do things inimical to the interests and well-being of people, and nothing can be done about it. If an employee complains—say, of price-gouging, of doing ecological harm, or of withholding benefits from the public, such as potential new products and processes—he will be fired. If an outsider complains, he has no standing in the company and can in no way affect corporate policy. The board of directors and the senior officers can do such things, but they are directors and senior officers because of special loyalty and proven service to the corporation. What we have, and this is no exaggeration, is a system that allows to function in man's midst an extra-species entity that has no loyalty to the people, no responsibility to the people, and no liability to the people. This is true even though the corporation is a mythical entity created by man.

What we see when we examine the corporation more closely is man's faulty imitation of nature. With the corporation he tries to reproduce nature's capabilities, which are independent of man's control. Both nature and the corporation have no responsibility toward man; they owe no loyalty to man; both are not liable to man. Yet both produce the things man needs to consume, and in both, to extract what he needs to consume, man must cooperate with and work for both. Neither the corporation nor nature work for man. It is the other way around.

What, on the other hand, of the ownership of the corporation? If we are talking of large corporations, there is no meaningful ownership. Many people own very small portions and have no control. The corporation, through its executive officers, has all the effective control. As for the small corporation, its owners and executive officers are almost always the same people, and the reason the corporation exists is to exempt ownership from responsibility.[1] The owner can work for the corporation and in this capacity he is not responsible for what the corporation does. So, either way, the corporation proceeds, independent of ownership.

There is no way around the matter. The corporation is a most remarkable fictional cocoon inside man's cocoon. It is man's small imitation of nature. It is the heart of the production process.

It is the *process*, not production, that is important. The concern of those managing the production of goods and services is not with goods and services, but with the preservation of the corporate entity creating them. The needs of the public are

---

1. By far, limited liability is the most common reason that people incorporate small businesses.

not considered; they are exploited for the benefit of the production process. Modern history is replete with countless instances
in which inferior, defective, and dangerous products, as well as
fraudulent and defective services, have been sold to the public.
In addition, there is the growing problem of pollution stemming from the production process itself and from the goods it
sells to the public. Also, there is the problem of inflation, the
net effect of which is to create increasingly inferior goods and
services at increasingly higher prices. What is alarming to the
public is the fact that almost nothing can be done to correct
these conditions. As Calvin Coolidge once put it, "The business of America is business." The codicil could read, "And
the business of government is business." Despite appearances,
it is business that controls the government, both in the elective
process which is financed by business interests, and in the
legislative process which is dominated almost totally by business interests. As for the public, Commodore William Vander-
bilt spoke the mind of business when he said, "The public be
damned." Indeed, this principle has its legal form, which says,
Caveat emptor! "Let the buyer beware!"

It is when a member of the public, a consumer, seeks redress
in the judicial system that he discovers the truth about the
situation. Ignoring the usual David and Goliath confrontation
(where this David almost never wins) and going to the substance, the laws of the various jurisdictions in this country have
been designed to protect business from litigation by the public.[2]
The legal doctrines are endless: contributory negligence, assumption of the risk, warranty limitations, contracted
exemptions, and, of course, *Caveat emptor*, are but a few of
the many protective legal devices that have accrued over the

---

2. As recently as 1973, the U.S. Supreme Court put a new and enormous obstacle in the way of class action suits to redress certain wrongs
committed by industry by requiring each plaintiff to prove ten thousand
dollars' damages or more. Further, it wasn't until the late 1960s that
Congress enacted "truth in packaging" and "truth in lending" laws. Until then, it was perfectly legal for corporations to lie and deceive in both
areas, with the public helpless to do anything about it.

years. And even when the occasional consumer plaintiff recovers a judgment, and the defendant corporation pays (only after endless and costly appellate delays), the monies paid are added to the cost of doing business and eventually are passed on to the public.

It should be clear by now that the production process has been and continues to be completely out of human control. It is a law unto itself and the first principle of the law is that of survival.

The connecting link between production and consumption is the advertising industry, which has as its sole function the artificial stimulation of consumption (and the transmutation of irresponsible business leaders into responsible business leaders). They are the ones who package the production process and then sell it to the people as if it were sugar plums.

In the age of mass production and controlled competition, there is inevitable standardization. Taking such consumer products as beer, cigarettes, cosmetics, canned foods, and automobiles, there is no difference whatever between comparable brands. A beer is a beer, one cigarette (of a grade) is indistinguishable from another, cosmetics don't even need to be commented on, one brand of tomato sauce is like all brands of tomato sauce, and a Ford and a comparably priced Chevrolet are fraternal twins.

With advertising so profusely fraudulent, and the people increasingly cynical about the lies cast in their direction, how is it possible for advertising to work? It works because, more than anything else, it appeals to the arboreal nature of the people. This is especially so since the advent of color television, for the baubles on the screen look so very much like great succulent bunches of fruit hanging from the tree of plenty that one is almost ready to reach into the set and grab them.

Among the great yet typical practitioners of the arboreal art of seduction are the promoters of beauty aids. Use Product X, and you will become instantly sexy. It makes no difference whether the product is for women or men; the same principle is used. There are two factors present: the first is instant gratification; the second, sexual desirability, most often in terms of being sexually desirable to all members of the opposite sex. Hence, between the two factors, there is instant sexual promiscuity.

The essence of advertising appeals is the instant removal of terrestrial problems. One eats marvelous foods with absolutely no trouble or time consumed whatsoever in preparing them; one enjoys the luxury of a beautiful automobile while at the same time suffering no inconvenience such as cost, which appears in the advertisements as a throwaway item. Every automobile is better than all the others—and, miraculously, each is cheaper. With the automobile of the moment—it makes no difference about the brand—you are *someone*. You have arrived, whether among the gods or among the smart starters, depending on the market being appealed to. In every instance, you are better off than before. And should anyone suffer time-anxiety or body stress, there are instant cures for these terrestrial ills. Patently inadequate medicines are offered as the catch-all solutions to upset stomachs, headaches, constipation, clogged sinuses, and bad breath. Sustenance, sex, and a general sense of euphoria are the message, regardless of the medium. By *medium*, I mean here the packaged product or service. Marshall McLuhan spoke of the medium as being both the message and the massage. He was quite wrong on both counts. The medium is irrelevant. It is neither the message or the massage. The message and the massage are contained in the arboreal dreams awakened by the promise. That is what moves the consumer. This is true whether radio, television, billboards, newspapers, magazines, or skywriting is used as the formal medium.

All that, however, is only part of the process of inducement. What was missing for a long time and is now present is the extension of the process beyond the limits of realization.

World War II created a large reservoir of money for the American people that couldn't be spent during the war years.

With the end of the war and the restructuring of the economy, consumer goods once again became available, and on a scale never before known. Production leaped because consumption, reinforced by a large reservoir of cash, called for it. Household items, automobiles, processed foods, clothing, recreation products, and a thousand other consumer goods were produced to meet the consumption demand. This economic activity followed the classic lines of a free economy, and especially one founded on the Protestant Ethic of industry and frugality— or, in the realm of consumption, cash and carry. Credit was reserved for those who didn't actually need it, such as the wealthy and the successful business concern. The rest of society was educated to believe that credit was a near occasion of sin, in addition to being unavailable to them.

Essentially, this was a terrestrial economy, one in which there was a realistic relation between production and consumption. There was a balance on both sides of the equation. But this very balance placed a limit on the production-consumption process. By placing a limit on it, in effect a limitation was placed on the ability to produce neo-arborea. This was the result of a direct ratio between production and consumption. If this ratio were to be maintained, the trek to neo-arborea would be halted unbearably close to its attainment.

Credit became essential. Credit is to consumption what increased automation is to production. Each releases man at least to some extent from the total process, thereby allowing him to live in the now. Thus, just as mortar on the production side of the process frees man, so too mortar—credit—on the consumption side frees him, even if only temporarily. Most significantly, credit allows man to satisfy his needs (and wants) now, rather than postponing them. By doing this he reduces time-anxiety and body stress. Quite literally, he can have what he wants when he wants it without working for it. What sublime arborea! But, as everyone knows, there is a catch to it all.

By use of credit systems, man is given the illusion of arborea while being actually more securely locked into his terrestrial prison. By use of credit, one mortgages the future. And to whom is the future mortgaged? Directly to the production-consumption process.

The advertising industry has done a brilliant job in packaging the entire concept of consumer credit. They have converted stern neoclassic banks into indulgent mothers who will let Johnny play now as long as he does his chores later. What best symbolizes this system is the slogan of Bankamericard: "Think of it as money." Therein lies the bold deception. Properly speaking, you possess money after you have received it, whether by way of work, gift, or discovery. To think of a credit card as money is to pervert the meaning of language. But there is much more method than madness to this bizarre adventure in Alice in Arborealand.

The promoters of this practice, the great banks, know that between 60 percent and 75 percent of their credit customers will fail to pay their credit charges on time. The real profits of the $122-billion-a-year consumer-credit business comes from the interest on late payments, which run anywhere from 18 percent to 25 percent. Banks and the sellers of consumer goods and services rely on the public's arboreality to produce their profits.

There is in this enormous phantasmagoria a fatal flaw. It is not, as it might seem, a competition for arborea, in which the exploitation of the consumer by the producer provides for the latter's arborea at the expense of the former. It must be remembered that the same individual, from bank president to store clerk, is on both sides of the equation. What puts everyone in this double role is the terrestrial circumstance that man must produce mortar to survive, and the universal need of every creature to consume in order to satisfy sustenance needs. The problem presented by the modern production-consumption process is that of ends and means being reversed. By inducing the individual (on a very large scale) to want more than he needs, so that he mortgages his future to the process, you tie him to both production and consumption, thereby guaranteeing the perpetuation of the production process.

It is argued—and by the promoters of production—that it is consumer demand that is obliging production to increase its output. In fact, they have coined an opprobrious word to describe the situation: consumerism. This is a case of the worst sinner casting the first stone. The question of whether there is this consumerism can be resolved by asking one simple question: Who makes the decisions regarding the factors of production? The consumer is not consulted, except by polls and testings conducted by industry to analyze what the buyer will buy. The decisions affecting production are made exclusively by the producers. Russia, after its 1917 revolution, sought to create a system in which there would be the dictatorship of the proletariat, the purpose of which was to place the means of production in the hands of the workers. While this was a noble theory, in reality the means of production are in the hands of industrial and state leaders. The consumer's needs are ignored in Russia as they are in the United States. In very recent years, beginning efforts have been made to consider the consumer's needs. Various governmental agencies have been created for this purpose. And there have been people like Ralph Nader who have sought to attack the worst crimes of industry. But always the consumer opposition to what industry does comes after the fact, never before. That is why Detroit cars are recalled after their sale, and that is why the various governmental agencies have to proceed by way of putting a stop to flagrantly false advertising and by ordering companies to cease and desist from certain harmful practices.

In the normal cycle of production and consumption, the consumer, despite arboreal blandishments, faces terrestrial reality when he confronts both what he has purchased and what he will have to pay over a period of time, including interest. The most mischief is done to the consumer's arboreal aspirations. He is promised sugar plums and instead receives something consisting of artificial flavors, artificial colors, and artificial values.

Nevertheles, despite the crushing effect of reality, he continues
to succumb because he continues to be an arboreal primate.
He *wants* to believe that this scent or that breakfast food will
transport him to arborea, that this brokerage house or that
savings-and-loan will free him from having to produce mortar,
and that this tonic or that poultice will relieve him from the
pains of terrestrial living. And because he wants to believe, he
buys.

There is in this new production-consumption process a disastrous reversal of a second sort. In the past, Salvation or Success lay in the future; the present was the time of struggle and
travail. It served, despite its flaws, to give meaning to the future.
Today, however, this is reversed. Now, as the process has
evolved, the individual can realize his arboreal aspirations today, but it is his future that is blighted. He plays now and pays
later or, to put it differently, he experiences aspects of arborea
now and pays for this by facing terrestria tomorrow. In other
words, every time he goes up into the trees where sugar plums
live, he must come down to earth again where the bills must be
paid. In this way, countless times in the life of the individual,
he repeats the species experience of being expelled from arborea, and he bitterly resents it and protests against it. Unfortunately, once he enters the process there is nothing he can do
about it. He may receive a shoddy imitation of arborea, but he
must still pay the producer in hard coin. That means he must
continue to function on the production side knowing even as
he does so that the arborea of which he dreams, and which is
projected to him by false promises and equally false products,
is no longer attainable. He has seen arborea, or a reasonable
facsimile thereof, and it is not to be his. Everything belongs to
Bankamericard—at 18 percent. Because of this his frustrations
mount; they have mounted now to the point where an explosion is imminent.

It would seem that the solution should be for man to regain
control of the means of production, now lost because the means
are in the nonhuman hands of corporations. This would appear
doubly possible because men and women work for the corpora-

tions, as well as serving as consumers. The solution would seem to lie in a genuine form of consumerism that would work to achieve a balance between the two sides of the process, thereby creating an extra dividend, that of the individual reducing the conflict within himself between his productive and consumptive aspects, something that is currently forcing him to act alternately as predator and prey and to feel abused on both counts.

Even if this were to be achieved, however, there would remain another problem that is nowhere near as easily solved. It concerns the nature of mortar.

For a very long time man lived an existence divorced from nature, but it was an existence nevertheless compatible with nature. Though he domesticated animals and grains, this was a cooperative effort by which man, his animals, and his grain foodstuffs were part of the cycle of life. Everything born lived and died, and then returned to the earth, where its organic elements remingled with the earth from which new life came.

However, when we consider the artificial extensions of man's forelimbs that made it possible for him to live in the terrestrial mode, we see an entirely different situation. Once a pebble was fashioned into a pebble tool, it could never go back to being a mere pebble, and once ore was made into metal it could never go back to being mere ore. Further, once fuel needed to produce these extensions and then to feed them was used, it could not be recycled.

The principle at work is quite simple. Those forms of mortar that are directly related to the organic nature of man, such as natural food, are part of the cycle of nature and can be replaced. Those forms of mortar that form part of the artificial extensions of the forelimbs or are necessary to feed those extensions cannot be recycled and cannot be replaced.[3]

---

3. Except for wood, all the other extensions such as metals and plastics cannot be recycled and cannot be replaced. Also, except for wood-based fuels, the fuels necessary to feed the artificial extensions cannot be recycled or replaced. Each is a one-way item, thus excluding it from natural cycles.

The problem is conspicuously clear in modern times. The problem we are here concerned with is the relationship between human productivity and mortar productivity. It has been increasing mortar productivity that has allowed for decreasing human productivity, thereby releasing man from a rigid relationship to production. The consequence of this, as we have seen, is the reappearance of arboreal tendencies, the result of being on the rim of neo-arborea.

The dilemma should be evident. With a limited supply of artificial mortar, there is a limited amount of artificial arborea available to man. Because there are limited sources of metals and fuels, the time will come when man will be on the threshold of another monumental crisis, equal in size to those of the past. Had man's ancestors failed to make tools, that would have been the end of the species. Had they failed to domesticate fire, they would have perished, because they could not move into cold climates to follow their migrating food supplies. Had they failed to invent speech, they would not have had a method of reproducing the conscious mind, and mortar would have crumbled. And had they not developed the cocoon in which to produce their own sources of food, man would have perished from starvation.

The crisis man faces today is of comparable importance. He has locked himself into his cocoon so tightly that he is completely dependent on mortar for survival. Within this cocoon he has created a contingent neo-arborea, made possible by the heightened use of mortar. If man continues to use up mortar, especially that which cannot be recycled or replaced, it won't be long until there is no more mortar. When this happens, man will begin to lose touch with the walls of his cocoon. Indeed, the walls themselves, being made of mortar, will begin to crumble, thus exposing modern man to the precise hazard faced by his most ancient ancestors: that of preserving species contact with the environment. In this circumstance, how will man be able to compensate for his genetic deficiencies and project a species profile that will conform to the profile projected by the terrestrial environment? What could man utilize as mortar?

Quite obviously, man would have to revert to living under conditions that preceded the stage when metals, oil, gas, and coal were available. This would mean that mortar could no longer be constructed of modern metals and could not be fed by modern fuels. The consequence of this would be to deprive man of modern mortar's contribution to production, leaving man and other living elements as the sole agents of production. The result would be a return to the old terrestrial processes by which man survived for hundreds of thousands of years. This being so, there would be the total loss of neo-arborea. What is worse, there would be the loss of all hope of ever achieving it, for man would know that the elements needed were no longer available. At this point man would be helplessly and hopelessly mired down in terrestria, an alien utterly unable to escape and just as unable to adjust adequately to the conditions of terrestrial existence.

The present worldwide energy crisis is a harbinger of things to come. Recessions, depressions, national and personal hardships, the lowering of living standards, the need to make sacrifices, and the uncertainty of the future are nothing compared to what the situation will be in the future once mortar begins to give out. Today hoarding, black markets, and myriad forms of cheating are already beginning to appear, just as they always appear when there is an emergency such as war or a natural disaster. People, from businessmen to householders, are seeking to protect their positions. Essentially, they are seeking to preserve the basic elements of neo-arborea. To this end, they will lie, cheat, and steal. What, then, when they must witness more than the decline of neo-arborea, when they must witness the end of neo-arborea?

Man will never allow himself to be expelled once again from arborea. He will resist with every ounce of his strength. He will do so because should he lose arborea this time, there will never be a chance for another. And then man will lose the will to live. But when we consider all the factors of the present crisis, there is little prospect that man will ever even reach the point of losing the will to live, for before reaching that point, he will have destroyed himself with his painfully acquired neo-lethality.

THE FATE OF
THE PHOENIX

WITHIN modern man there is a delicate balance between revolutionary and counterrevolutionary forces. On one side are marshaled the emergent *I* and nonviolence; on the other are the production-consumption process and the military process, the source of neo-lethality. The revolutionary forces represent the arboreal nature of man; the counterrevolutionary forces, the terrestrial habituations of man. Significantly, it has been terrestrial habituations that have created the conditions making possible the reappearance of arboreal behavior, having by terrestrial means produced arboreal conditions, even if only to a limited extent. In other words, neo-arborea rests on terrestrial foundations. And it has been this fact that has led to neo-lethality, the consequence of a calamitous miscalculation of the situation.

The miscalculation concerns the efficacy of lethality. Before proceding, however, I must make it clear that I am not here discussing lethality only in its ultimate form, that of actual killing. I am incorporating into the term all the aggressive tendencies that man has acquired during the terrestrialization process. They include every kind of violence, from social, economic, psychological, and physical, to killing itself. In this regard, I conceive of lethality as being a disposition by which one feels free to impose his will on others by means of social, economic, psychological, and physical violence, reserving at all times the ultimate imposition: that of death. In other words, the subject is human aggression.

It is not merely that man possesses the weapons of universal destruction. Given certain circumstances, he may never actually use them. We should be more concerned with the state of mind that could produce such weapons. While some might speak of their use as the "unthinkable," their very existence is proof that the unthinkable has been very carefully thought out and put into readiness. However, even if they are never used, the threat of their use comprises a form of lethal violence, just as a parent's threat to beat a child is a form of lethal violence even though the child is not actually struck.

Psychological violence is a relatively new phenomenon. It has achieved its greatest impetus through the operation of the behaviorist school of psychology which seeks to condition and control man's external conduct by internal psychological means. Social and economic violence are comparatively old and are universally known and practiced. They serve as control mechanisms by which one group seeks to dominate another. Yet, as powerful as these are, they derive their power not from their own nature but from the nature of the sanction behind them: physical force that reaches its ultimate expression in lethality.

The miscalculation I am referring to concerns the actual efficacy of the ultimate sanction standing behind all lesser and indirect forms of violence. The miscalculation stems from a faulty premise relating to terrestrial existence. It is that man must be lethal in order to survive (here I am restricting the term *lethal* to intraspecies killing, not that by which man secures animal food). While once during the critical hunt era he had quite literally to kill in order to protect himself from natural predators, in the post-hunt era man, having destroyed or banished all natural predators to remote enclaves, has no such need. As a consequence, there is no need of lethality for protective purposes. Yet, as we know, man practices lethality. He does so on the erroneous assumption that the new hunt—economic activity, the central element of mortar—needs the same protective system that the old hunt had to have.[1]

It is entirely true that the conditions necessary for neo-arborea have been produced by terrestrial means, and that arboreal conditions are the result of modern mortar. But what is not true is that lethality is any longer a necessary part of mortar. The proof for this is found in the fact that tools, not weapons, have created the mortar necessary for the creation of neo-arborea, and in the further fact that lethality, rather than supporting and protecting the process, has proven to be an interference with it. In other words, lethality no longer functions to protect the hunt; instead it menaces the hunt. Yet, despite the realities, it persists, especially in its institutionalized form, the military process.

The heart of the problem is the military establishment. Wars come and go; there are periods of peace. Yet at all times and in all seasons there is the military establishment which has as its *raison d'être* the military process, which has but one function, to serve the needs of the state. But instead of serving the needs of the state the military establishment uses the state to further the interests of the military process so as to serve the ends of the military establishment, which is that of self-perpetuation. Whereas once wars were intended to protect the hunt, today wars are the pegs on which the military establishment hangs its cloak of legitimacy.

To do so, it awakens primordial fears that bear no relation to contemporary reality. Having awakened them, it forces others to do the killing and dying on its behalf. In contrast to the production process, which raises visions of sugar plums to induce participation, the military process arouses enormous terrestrial fears that go back to man's desperate years when he was close to being overwhelmed by terrestrial beasts.

---

1. See "The Warrior" for details on this point.

The enemy of the military establishment is nonviolence, perpetual peace is anathema, and universal disarmament is a recurring nightmare, for if these were to prevail the military process would fade away, taking with it all those who benefit from it.

The most dangerous member of society is the militarist. It is not only that his values run counter to the professed values of the ordinary citizen who simply doesn't want to serve in his process. That is bad enough. Far more inimical, however, is the fact that he is the only one in society with weapons. It is an axiom of history that he who controls the military controls the state. We need only refer to ancient Rome and modern Latin America to see this principle in operation. As for the United States, today it is struggling to keep the military under civilian control—and it is not being very successful.

Even in societies where there is no perceptible menace, there is a military establishment. Switzerland hasn't fought a war for centuries, yet it maintains a strong military establishment.

The militarist is the last of the great hunters. His prey is other men. He enjoys a special place in almost every society because he safeguards the society that honors him. As can be seen, there is a large circular argument here, punctuated by a critical inconsistency. He doesn't always safeguard the society he is pledged to safeguard. In fact, half the establishments which actually engage in war fail in this regard, since in war there is generally a winner and a loser. Yet, despite the outcome of individual wars, the militarist and his establishment go on. Classic examples of this proposition are the German General Staffs that suffered defeats in World Wars I and II; yet, upon termination of the embarrassing losses, they survived (despite the efforts of the Allies to destroy that of World War II) and carried on almost as if nothing had happened.

The remarkable thing is that there really is no need for a military establishment. Lethality is not needed to preserve order among nonlethal primates. Man today, having laid his weapons down at the end of the hunt era so that he might pick up the tools of production, is again a nonlethal primate. Only the militarist has weapons, and for this he is feared. The rest of mankind fears him exactly as man's ancient ancestors feared the deadly predator, and with a dreadful sense of hopelessness. What can a nonlethal primate do against the deadliest predator the world has ever seen? Absolutely nothing. That is precisely the state of affairs the militarist wants, as it guarantees the perpetuation of the military process on which he depends. He is the exact counterpart of the corporate officer who exploits the consumer in order to preserve the corporation which provides for his needs. This is true even though the modern course of the military process, as in the case of the production-consumption process, is set for disaster.

And yet, the militarist himself, like other men, is a non-lethal primate. He is no more a predator than was the original primate forced out of arborea. However, just as the species turned to predation in order to survive, so too men turn to the military process in order to support themselves. Those who are seduced by patriotic themes and assurances of God's blessing (thus assuring themselves of eternal arborea), enter the military as a career, not as a means of killing or being killed. They are no different from the corporate officer or anyone else who employs various devices to gain sustenance. It is because man lacks a direct relation to the source of sustenance that he must resort to indirect transactions. Among the indirect transactions available are those of the military and the corporate officer— or the writer of books. The militarist, for whatever reason,[2] enters the military process because it is a conduit leading to the satisfaction of his sustenance needs. Once he has connected with a conduit to sustenance, he will not quickly let go. To do so would threaten his survival. It is so with everyone. Once

---

2. There are special inducements relating to every profession. Family tradition; nationalistic propaganda, lack of alternatives, and other factors combine to induce someone to enter the military.

a connection is made with a conduit to sustenance, everyone is loath to let go.

As we have seen in the discussion of the production-consumption process, man always seeks to reduce his participation in indirect transactions. He seeks to replace himself with machines—mortar. The very same thing is true of the militarist. It is this urge for arboreal conditions that prompts him to perfect the military process so that mortar might effectively replace him.

Historically, the militarist has always sought arboreal existence. Once the bloody battle or war is over, the victor takes possession of the spoils. When not engaged in active fighting, the lot of the militarist has been almost always one of relative indolence—especially for the officer corps. They are, because of who they are, well provided for by the state. In fact, they do not contribute in any way to the creation of mortar. They merely stand by to protect national mortar in times of emergency. So, all in all, the life of the militarist has proved to be quite arboreal.

In his pursuit of arborea, even if it is along bloody paths, the militarist has constantly sought to improve the conditions of his profession. In this he has been remarkably like the private citizen who works at a job. As the Industrial and Production Revolutions perfected the production-consumption process, so did they serve to perfect the military process, until by the end of World War II the American military process had perfected the atom bomb which became, in time, the basis of the hydrogen bomb. With the hydrogen bomb we enter the age of neo-lethality, for with it we enter an age where wars can lead to no conclusion but death and destruction. Thus lethality, once the means to ends, now becomes an end in itself. It serves no useful purpose.

There are two major problems faced by the military process. In the contemporary scene, the process has lost a critical peg. It cannot wage a war to its logical conclusion: to the point where one state can unilaterally impose its will on another, as in von Clausewitz's famous dictum. It must fall short of such a conclusion and permit political resolutions. It can't even function as a threatening sword poised above any political negotiations, for to follow through with ultimate force would obliterate the problem as well as much of the earthly landscape. The Korean War, the Vietnam War, the Indochina War, and the constantly recurring wars of the Middle East are important examples of truncated wars in which traditional martial principles do not and cannot function, for if they did, they would jeopardize the military process itself, thereby denying those in the process of the mortar on which they depend for survival.

There is, unfortunately, an additional consequence flowing from the modern situation. If war cannot be fought to its conclusion, if there is no final object to a war, what purpose can be served by beginning it or, for that matter, continuing it once it has begun? If all war does is provide the pretext for negotiations toward a political settlement, why not bypass the expense of war and go directly to political settlement? This has been the precise object of the United Nations. It has been the goal of all internationalists and pacifists. It would seem that it should be the desire of everyone. But it isn't. Not everyone wants peace. War, especially truncated war, is simply too profitable for those within the military process. To understand this, we must look at the relationship between the military process and the production-consumption process, or between the military economy and the general economy.

Some students of economics, such as Seymour Melman, describe the military economy as parasitic in that it subsists on the general economy. I'm not so sure that it is as parasitic as it is competitive. It doesn't use the general economy as much as it appropriates to its own use those resources that would ordinarily be applied to the general economy. Or, in the idiom of my thesis, the military process competes directly with the production-consumption process. And when each year, as in the United States, the military process has an annual budget of some $80 billion, it is significant competition to even the strongest economic system. It is a budget that is greater than the national budgets of all but a handful of the largest states. In fact, because of its enormous economic system, the military process in a country like the United States is in effect a state within a state. The problem is, it is a predator state within a nonpredator state, and it is in the process of eating at the vitals of the host state by virtue of the fact that it requires increasing increments of input to preserve its mortar. As a consequence, it heightens its competitive position with the general economy, taking increasing increments from it, thereby threatening the arboreal aspirations of those subsisting on the general economy. As the demands of the military process increase, the general economy resists that much more, obliging the military to exert ever more pressure so that its demands might be met. We see this increasingly in the United States where the military process offers increasingly complex and costly weapons systems and the Congress protests over the extravagance, waste, and spiraling costs. This objection is met by naked threats that the United States is suffering this or that "gap" vis-à-vis the Russians.

There is a final problem faced by the military process. When wars do come along now, their prosecution is so costly in terms of weapons that the wars must be curtailed lest they bankrupt those fighting. Only the United States could have waged a war as costly as that fought in Southeast Asia. Somewhat over $100 billion were directly spent on this ill-fated adventure that ended up in a temporary cease-fire and American withdrawal.[3] The Yom Kippur War of 1973 between Israel and the Arab nations, though fought for only a number of weeks, left all sides in a critical condition with regard to their weaponry. Billions went up in smoke so that negotiations might begin.

The problem here is similar to that of the production-

---

3. Since World War II the United States has invested over a trillion dollars on its military process.

consumption process. More and more mortar is going into the military process—and there is only so much mortar available. What will the military process do when mortar starts to become critically scarce? What of the confrontation between the production-consumption process and the military process in the face of scarce mortar? Here is where we encounter the ultimate dilemma of man, that between his terrestrial fears and his arboreal aspirations.

In the final analysis, man is caught up in a conflict between his arboreal nature and the terrestrial processes that have made it possible for him to survive. It is a case of arboreal ends being dependent on terrestrial means. The great danger is that of converting means into ends, for if that is done, neo-arborea falls victim to neo-terrestria and man will be destroyed.

It is an inescapable truth that man is dependent on mortar. However, there is the question of how much mortar, and what kind of mortar, man requires. I do not believe, even for an instant, that man needs all the mortar declared necessary by the production-consumption process. Neither do I believe that man needs lethal mortar. Man has always overshot the mark in his efforts at being an artificial predator and an artificial producer. He overkilled during the hunt era; he overproduces today. He has failed on both counts because he has lacked an instinct for either. In the post-hunt era, man no longer needs lethality. We can begin to see a subtle awareness of this fact in the new function of war, which is to trigger political, i.e., nonviolent, solutions to conflicts. What we have, then, is a reintroduction of display—greatly exaggerated—the arboreal primate's system of social regulation.

The key to both problems, that of production and lethality, is a matter of the quantity and quality of mortar necessary in order to experience neo-arboreal living. There is no set amount. What is necessary is that there be enough to allow the individual to live in the now. Processes have no now; they are always future-oriented. But the body lives in the now. This has always been the great missing link with the past—and with the

future. Man, in his great concern with means and ends, has for
the most part lost track of that to which means should address themselves: the body. It is the body that experiences
body stress, and it is the mind that experiences this stress as
time-anxiety. When the body is unnecessarily burdened by
production-consumption processes, all prospects for its living
without crippling stress are totally lost, no matter how arboreal
the terms of existence may appear.

It has been man's great anxiety about achieving neo-arborea
that has proved the greatest obstacle to its attainment. It has
provoked him to employ such measures as lethality and its
conclusionary descendant, neo-lethality, and it has provoked
him to launch the modern production-consumption process.
What he has not done is to seize the moment in which to *be*.

The youth have glimpsed neo-arborea in a way the older
generation can never hope to glimpse it. Like an arboreal primate infant who has clung to its mother-tree as she has laboriously climbed back into the trees, young people have begun
to let go of the mother and to test the tree itself. It is not a
perfect tree, and even an arboreal primate must climb around
in its search for food and a place to sleep at night. The important thing is that it is there. Man has planted the tree; now
he can begin to live in it.

TOWARD MERE
EXISTENCE

THERE are no secret consolations contained in the Arboreal/Terrestrial Conflict Thesis. Virtually all other explanations of man, of his origins, and of his destiny, possess within them the seeds of hope for something more than existence. I have nothing to offer but mere existence.

Yet what I offer is actual, not illusory; now, not postponed. If we scan the countless exploratory efforts of man throughout his long and turbulent history, we discover that every conceivable attempt has been made to construct a hypothetical beatific existence, unfortunately always in the remote and contingent future. The fatal flaw within them all, something I am convinced man has sensed all along, is that they have so influenced man as to prevent him from ever experiencing existence itself.

There can be no denying the very real consolations of religion. It is the one thing that pierces death and overcomes its finality. Under the terms of my thesis, we live this life and die—completely. Nothing is left behind, nothing lives on. Religion, on the other hand, makes a very rich promise, even if the promise can never be fulfilled. It is that death is not final. Speaking from the perspective of a man who has reached the half-century mark and who must now begin to think of the eventual ending of my own existence, it would be a sublime supplement to my personal life to know that upon my death I would enter an eternal state in which I would live forever in the midst of my loved ones.[1]

Death, in the religious system of thought, is the great entrance way to something almost beyond human expectation. It is this expectancy that gives religion its universal appeal. Death, in the system of thought born of my Arboreal/Terrestrial Conflict Thesis, is the terminal point of human existence. The grave contains no hope. When I die, I become cut off from my family, my dearest friends, and even from myself.

What is so remarkable about much of humanity is that it clings to the hope of something eternal while completely ignoring everything contained within time. Family, friends, even the individual himself is ignored in the quest for the eternal, whether that be a spiritual eternal or a great temporal millennium. Or, when not ignored, family, friends, and the individual himself are roundly abused for the sake of obsessive thoughts that lie just beyond reach—even beyond comprehension in many cases.

For those not wrapped up in an obsession with eternity there is the sort of gossamer offered by men like Erich von Däniken, whose *Chariots of the Gods?* fills them with impatient hope of rescue. I join them in their fantasy. After all, what could be more marvelous than the prospect of having ineffable gods (members of the family?) from another galaxy come for us and take us to our inheritance several thousand light years from terrestrial suffering? This is the great expectation inherent in all such fairy tales. Behind the veil of fantasy

---

1. Religionists, of course, argue that no one can prove there is no such thing as eternal life after death. That is true, but since they make the assertion of life after death, the burden of proof is on them to prove their assertion. My present argument is that death terminates life, something that is self-evident. Therefore, I have carried my burden forward as far as it can be taken. Anyone wishing to argue for life after death must, of necessity, pick up the burden where I have put it down: with death.

lies the great truth of our existences: that none of this is real, that soon we will be transported to our true world where every great possibility, like giant sugar plums, shall be ours. Alas, there is no *deus ex machina*. There is for us earthlings only this earth with its cycle of birth, life, and death. There is nothing beyond this earth, at least for us. The earth is our cradle, our home, our burial ground. It is the compass of our existence. Since this is the case, perhaps the time has come for us to forego the outer reaches of space and fantasy so that we can begin to live within the compass of existence.

For several million years man has been engaged in the great search for a way home. It began at the foot of the original tree.[2] Driven from there into the great savanna of terrestrial existence, man has dedicated his life to something beyond mere existence. Impelled by body stress occasioned by the anomaly of an arboreal primate seeking to exist in the terrestrial world, man has sought to remedy that stress by overthrowing the tyranny of terrestrial existence that makes demands on the body it cannot meet unaided. In all this time man has sought to return home. He cannot. In default, he has struggled to construct arborea on earth. In doing so, he has committed the fault of all exiles. He has invested arboreal life with features it never had. Man has idealized arborea beyond all reasonable limits. We can see this in his concept of heaven and even in that of Eden.

Adam and Eve, it would seem, led an idyllic existence. There were no predators, food was plentiful, the weather was perfect, and there were no mosquitoes, no indigestion, no death, and no taxes.

Of course, arborea was nothing of the sort. There were invading predators, though not to the extent found in terrestria; food was not always plentiful—its decline forced man's an-

---

2. Which has its religious counterpart in the concept of the foot of the cross, where the Christian pilgrimage to salvation begins, and in the concept of the foot of the tree of wisdom, where the Buddhist religion begins its pilgrimage for enlightenment.

cestors out of the trees; the weather was not perfect—rain, drought, and storms occurred; undoubtedly there were torment- ing mosquitoes and other irritants (primates spend a great amount of time grooming each other); wild animals have al- ways suffered stomach and other physical disorders; and, of course, death has always been as common as birth. (True, arboreal primates do not pay taxes. They don't because there is no mortar that has to be paid for.)

Arborea never was paradise; it never will be. Look to the great apes in their natural habitats: They face all the existential problems faced by other creatures—including man. The only difference between their situation and that of man is that they are naturally equipped to cope with their environment, while man is not. While it is true that without mortar man could not exist, it is equally true that with mortar he can exist as fully in the terrestrial mode as can arboreal primates in arborea, *provided* that he seeks essentially the same existence as that lived by other primates. That existence is one in which, for the most part, man—like other creatures—lives in his body and not somewhere else, such as in a distant millennium or an infinitely remote eternity.

As it is, man occupies this existence as if it were the prelude to another. The victim of this disorientation is his body, which suffers from extreme stress. The amount of stress is directly proportional to the amount of disorientation. Therefore, the more future-oriented man is, the more body stress (as well as time-anxiety): the less future-oriented, the less stress.

Man cannot live without at least some mortar. Therefore, he cannot exist solely in the now. He must effect a balance be- tween the present needs of the body and those of the future. This need for balance is not unique with man. Other primates achieve it. The mother with dependent offspring often must delay her needs so that those of her infant may be met. The adult male must maintain vigilance in his protection of the affinity group. For both, many hours each day are consumed in gaining sustenance. They must all endure the prospect of predators; they must accept the storm as they accept the warm sun. Potential or actual conflict among the leading males is always present, even if quickly resolved by nonlethal displays. Primates clearly experience fear—and they complain about it—but they also know pleasure and excitement, and, too, they experience death—not just the fact of death, but something beyond. Confused mothers sometimes carry dead infants around with them for days. Members of an affinity group sense the trailing off of one of its members as it becomes enfeebled and begins its descent into death. If some of this seems almost human, it must be remembered that such primates are man, but man without mortar.

The second oldest search of man has been for meaning. Western civilization is drenched in the lore of ancient Greek philosophers who asked the unanswerable question about existence. The meaning they found existed only in the mind. Ever since, Western man has looked to the mind for meaning. In doing so, rather than finding meaning, he has found a thousand variations on the common theme of suffering.

Life consists of a continuum of nows. True, the mind might rise above the now and project into the future, but having done that it must always return to the now where the core of existence lies. I may plan for tomorrow, but tomorrow might never arrive. Even should tomorrow arrive it might not do so on my terms. In that event, I must adjust myself to the fact. This is so whether I live for another week or another half-century. Regardless of what I may want for tomorrow or a thousand tomorrows, the final decision rests with my body, which exists in the constant now.

The mind is the body's guide, not its master. Therefore, the mind must serve the needs of the body and not today hold the body captive for the sake of a future that exists as a hypothesis in my mind. Tomorrow, however, is a contingency with real potential for actuality and therefore cannot be ignored. To do so would be to invite extinction. But in providing for tomorrow, today should not be mortgaged for tomorrow to the extent that it ceases to have a value and reality of its own, because it must always be remembered that as we increasingly mortgage today and as we increasingly denigrate its value, we thereby correspondingly mortgage and denigrate our body. As I have said a number of times before, with enough mortgaging and denigrating of the body, we stifle it to death.

The body is the premise of human existence. This is very much like the arboreal premise of the species. While a great deal serves to mask the arboreal premise so that it is hard to see in modern man, it is nevertheless present and observable, provided one knows where to look and what to look beyond. The same is true of the body premise. But one must often look penetratingly and deeply to see beyond the impedimenta that pose as the essence. The great inversion of human thought concerns this very problem. Eastern philosophy, and to a large extent that of the West, provides man with a different premise, that of the spirit. On this spirit premise is constructed a philosophy that seeks to conform the body to the needs of the spirit. Consequently, asceticism is one of the highest virtues. At the same time, since the body is not an asset but a liability, little attention is paid it. As a result, matters relating to the body, such as poverty and disease, are largely ignored. One does not seek to remove these afflictions; one seeks to remove the body by transcending them. Indeed, the highest good is to escape from the body in order to attain total existence.

The great weakness of the spirit premise is that it is an unprovable explanation, not a self-revealing demonstration. It comes, even if one does not seek to be pejorative, from a physical entity that by this premise seeks to explain itself away. It is one thing for a body to disclaim spirit; it is another for the body to disclaim itself. It simply can't be done. The body is present. It exists. And it is from this body that the pronouncement is made that there is a spiritual world far more important and eternal than the small and transient world of things. If this is true, then why in the world did spirit involve itself with such corrupt and corruptible fixtures as the flesh? I don't think the spirit can provide us with an answer —without the aid of the body which does its talking and thinking for it. However, I believe that there is a more pertinent criticism of the spirit premise. It is an attitude toward the body, not an expression of the body. It is the mind's confessing its inability to serve as guide for the body. It is the ultimate form of despair, because it abandons the body in its great need.

Whereas other systems of thought employ the conscious mind to pull at the body, in this direction or that, depending on the particular philosophy, it seems to me that the mind should pull at the elements of terrestrial living so that they might be brought to the body, thereby serving the needs of the body. Mortar should serve the body; the body should not be a slave to mortar. The unit of utilitarianism should be mortar, not the individual. Man should not construct a social system according to the needs of mortar; he should construct a system of mortar based on the needs of the species.

The kernel of modern man's difficulties can be found in the ancient hunt era which, as I have pointed out earlier, was an interregnum between the arboreal and the neo-arboreal periods. It was a long and devastating time in which man had to fashion a highly structured existence in support of the hunt. But it wasn't the hunt itself that lay at the root of the problem. Man constructed a system of mortar around the hunt that had counter-lethality as one of its key elements. It was a defensive system, composed completely of psychic mortar, to protect man against the onslaught of natural predators. Every time man contemplated the hunt, he had to contemplate the counter-hunt of predators. In the making of a hunter, every adult male at the same time had to prepare the young male for counterattack. Thus every hunter was also a warrior and a defender of the species, and every hunting ground was a potential battleground. Because of this situation, mortar was designed not only to support the hunt but to protect the species against predators. Man not only had to rise up to the occasion of killing, he had also to rise up to the occasion of being threatened with death. For this purpose he built up within his organism a network of systemic responses to this constantly recurring danger. He also constructed a social system to reinforce mortar that was both offensive and defensive in nature.

The end of the hunt era, however, did not put an end to the psychic mortar laboriously compiled over hundreds of thousands of years. Man continued to function as if he were still living in the hunt era. He continues to do so today.

The single most significant fact about the Neolithic Revolution was not that it signaled the end of the hunt, but that it signaled the end of man's vulnerability to natural predators. Ever since the beginnings of settled life man has continued to kill animals for food, but he has not done so as a hunter. He has done so as a husbandman: a raiser of animals for food. In this capacity he does not have to face the problem of the counter-hunt. In other words, man is no longer menaced by predators. He can provide the results of the hunt without the dangers of the hunt.

Yet his psychic mortar continues to exist as if he were still menaced by predators. As was pointed out in "The Warrior," man views threats from other men as if they were from natural predators. As a result, he responds precisely as if he were faced by a natural predator, rather than by another arboreal primate. And because the ordinary individual no longer has the weapons of the hunter/warrior, he lives in a society that provides the warrior whose function it is to respond to threats, real or imagined, as if they originated from predators.

Because man continues to function as if he were still menaced by predators, he continues to construct psychic mortar containing large counter-lethal elements. This is a defensive system that is itself lethal. But it is not restricted to such overt systems as the military establishment; it incorporates subsidiary systems such as social, economic, and psychological violence. None of these subsidiary systems would be necessary were it not for the defensive mortar they support. The corollary is also true: Without them, the prime defense system could not exist. It is an integrated system that permeates every aspect of human existence, and it is a system that binds the individual to it so that he serves mortar. Mortar does not serve man.

A famous manifestation of this principle was provided by John F. Kennedy during his inauguration in 1961 when he said, "Ask not what your country can do for you; ask what you can do for your country." This polished epigram was not a twist in national policy but a restatement of policy that had endured from the earliest days of the ancient labyrinth. What it really says is that the state does not exist for man; man exists for the state. That is, man exists for mortar. And what makes it work is the psychic mortar that binds the individual to the system.

As a consequence of man's existing for mortar, man's body exists for mortar, and it is for mortar that it is pulled in every direction.

Historically there have been two principal forms of psychic mortar: religion and the state. Religion pulled the body one way, the state another. But, as we have seen, in the modern era there is no further need of religion, man being on the rim of neo-arborea. Therefore, the compelling force of religion is considerably diminished.

The danger to man today is the state, the most extensive form of mortar ever created by man. Significantly, the state is very much like the corporation. It has an existence independent of human control and commands a loyalty that is frequently at odds with the essential interests of the individual. And because it commands the loyalty of the warrior group, it has all the attributes of a deadly predator. Unfortunately, the individual has no protective mortar. All he can do is acceed to the demands of the state—or pay a severe penalty. What makes this so remarkable a situation, again like that of the corporation, is the fact that man has created the state and now has lost control of it. But then, man actually wishes to lose control of the state. He would very much prefer that the state exhibit the sovereignty of nature, thus absolving man from responsibility that is not natural to him.

Just as nature projects an environment profile to which a creature must conform, so too the state projects a profile to which the individual must conform. Whereas that of nature is physical, that of the state is psychic. And a major sector of the state's psychic profile is the lethal assumption, something that exists because of the terrestrial nature of the state.

In opposition is the arboreal nature of man's body; hence, the conflict. The state proceeds on terrestrial assumptions, while man's body proceeds on arboreal assumptions. Theoretically, the role of mortar is to reconcile the two, but it doesn't work out that way. The state is the conduit to the satisfaction of body needs and thereby holds the key to survival. Thus the state can make almost any demands on the body and still be obeyed, for to deny the state its demands is to destroy the conduit to the satisfaction of body needs. In this way the body is bent to the needs of mortar; mortar is not bent to the needs of man.

Th essential consequence of this state of affairs is extreme time-anxiety and body stress. Increasingly, strain is placed on the entire organism. Life becomes more and more contingent. Dependencies expand, to the point of filling every dimension of existence. One proceeds through life, not in blind faith, but in blind hope that somehow before death some sort of equanimity may be achieved.

The practice of bending man and his body around mortar must be stopped. Somehow, mortar must be bent around man. By this I mean that mortar must begin to serve man. Only this way can man enter into the state of existence. And he must be led by his body.

Where in the cycle of life may existence begin? One is tempted to start with birth, but a glance at our culture makes it clear that in many instances the moment of birth is too late. By that time the infant has already spent its entire lifetime in quivering mortar, its mother—with inimical results.

Perhaps conception would be better. But the moment of conception may be wrapped up in sharp apprehensions about sex. Maybe the mother doesn't like sex—or even her sexual partner. Still, the cycle of life must be broken into, so we will begin with the infant's first living moment: when its presence is first known to its newborn mother.

The first decision the woman must make is whether she wants the child. In all likelihood, being subjected to the pressures of society, she will proceed with the pregnancy whether she actually wants the child or not. If this is the way she goes about producing a child, the odds are heavily against the future well-being of the child, since whatever she produces will be not hers but society's. If she carries the child to please or placate her husband, then the child is her husband's. Only if *she* wants the child will it be hers. This is not a matter of nice distinctions. If she has anyone's child but her own, she will be having it and raising it for others and because of others. Thus there will not be the natural and necessary bond between mother and child. She will be a biological means to another's end which is not her end. Also, in such a case the baby becomes a means by which the mother maintains her psychic contact either with society or her husband. In this way, then, the baby is born with a utilitarian value and price. Should the baby not reflect the utilitarian value or meet the price set on it, it will have to pay up the difference by neglect, disinterest, or something else equally destructive.

If the newborn mother decides she wants the baby, then she must decide why she wants it. If she decides that she wants a boy more than a girl, she has already decided that she doesn't want a baby, she wants an economic unit of some sort. If she wants a girl, she may actually be more concerned with social consequences than anything else. In either event, she has placed a utilitarian value on the life within her and will most likely treat the baby accordingly from its birth on.

It is only when a woman follows her instinct to give birth to the life within her that the infant she bears will have a good prospect of being born into existence. Unfortunately, the considerations and inhibitions of the neo-cortex place conditions on that instinctive urge, thereby interfering with its natural tendencies.

In the modern era it is almost impossible for a newborn mother to feel simply and directly the life within her. Society persists in asserting its claim on maternity, for reasons discussed earlier. Every newborn baby—even girls, today—is a potential contributor to mortar. It must be added that most recently, as a reflection of man's awareness of the proximity of neo-arborea, the stigma once attached to abortions is diminished. However, the residual effect of history is still powerful and has an inhibitory effect on a woman's choices in this area. Also, of course, there is the way she was raised, most often in a social system in which she was socially and sexually subordinate to the male.

I mention these few considerations to show how difficult it is for a woman to give birth to the life within her and not to some preconceived notion of what that life should be. But we live in the midst of time and cannot start the clock running again, so we must begin with what we have: the newborn mother. Hopefully, she will become a full-term mother and give birth to the life within her.

The birth of a baby is the birth of life, and the core of that life is the baby's body. The subject of child development, from arboreal infant to terrestrial adult, has been gone into quite thoroughly in "The Cradle," so there is no need here to retrace those steps. What I want to emphasize here is the importance of the now of the baby. It is because it is, and not because someone else, including mother and father, wants what is there. If parents allow the baby to live in the now, rather than rush it through weaning, toilet training, walking, talking, and so on, the baby will go through all the necessary developmental processes, because it was designed by nature to do just that.

There is a most critical element here. We might think of the parents, especially the mother, as being the mortar that promotes the survival of the infant. The question is, will parental mortar form around the infant for the infant's sake, or must the infant be shaped around parental mortar?

This is undoubtedly the most important consideration in child-rearing. Being totally arboreal at birth and completely helpless, the newborn infant requires the unyielding and unremitting support and assistance of its mother during this critical period of its life. Because the infant is unable in any way to remedy a bad situation such as inadequate mothering, the deficient mother can cause great harm to the infant without anything occurring to let her know that something is wrong. Unlike the abused puppy that can slink away, the baby must remain wherever the mother puts it—and in any condition in which the mother leaves it. It is because of this helplessness and inability to respond adequately that the infant can be manipulated by the mother to fit her needs and not those of the baby, without anyone at the time being aware of the problem.

The newborn baby's needs are those of its body. These must be met, and met as they appear, or the infant runs the risk of permanent psychic and/or physical damage. The baby will remain almost pure body until such time as the cerebral cortex begins to function, something that doesn't ordinarily occur until the end of the first year. It is futile and dangerous to attempt to force or bribe the baby into a course of behavior. All you can do is meet its needs, and they are almost entirely body needs. (I qualify this point as I do because it may well be that soft sounds and sights have other than physical effects on the young infant.)

But every child must be taken down out of its tree. It cannot remain an arboreal primate while growing up in the terrestrial mode. It must, at the appropriate time, begin its descent to the ground, holding the guiding hand of its mother at all times as it descends the staircase to terrestria. The mother must allow the child to set its own pace. The child may dawdle or it may gallop. The timing is unimportant. It is the total descent that the child must make. If she seeks to alter the child's natural pace, or if she abandons the child on a landing, the child may never make it to the bottom. Or if it does, it may well become a crash victim.

The mother must understand that this descent from arborea is for the child's benefit, not hers. The descent does not take place so that when completed the mother might be free of the child; it takes place so that when completed the child may be free of the mother. It is in order that the child may survive that it progresses from an arboreal infant to a terrestrial adult. It does not do this simply to please its mother. For the mother to fret over weaning, toilet training, or other steps on the descending staircase, is to entangle her time with the child's timelessness. Too often any variance from the timetable established by pediatricians, child "authorities," or the mother herself is viewed as a failing of the child. Such "failings" all too often are considered reflections on the mother, and to correct her self-image or the image presented to others, she sets about to put the child on a schedule. By doing this she inserts her child into a time machine, thereby introducing the child's body to body stress and, as the child's cerebral cortex begins to function, to time-anxiety.

The mother is always in a difficult situation. She is essentially a terrestrial creature seeking to meet the needs of an arboreal infant. As the infant develops, she seeks to terrestrialize it. This is a particularly acute problem in modern society, which has for so long emphasized terrestrial virtues such as efficiency, promptness, order, and obedience. During the latter half of the nineteenth century and the first half of the twentieth, when society was girding itself for the final assault on arborea, the relative arboreality of mothers was stripped from them by excessively terrestrial men who in their specialties as pediatricians, child "authorities," and child psychologists, made it clear to mothers that they mustn't indulge their babies. The whole thrust of infant care in that century was toward the rapid terrestrialization of infants.

The modern mother is caught between two worlds: the timeless world of the infant, who lives in the constant now, and the clock world of the terrestrial adult, who lives in the inconstant future. The result is conflict, epitomized by the conflict between the needs of the infant and the frequently competing demands of the husband. The dilemma is pronounced. Every maternal force drives the mother toward her baby, yet the social-sexual dependency status of women also pulls her away from her baby and towards her husband who, because of his dominant economic position, is the conduit between both mother and infant and the satisfaction of their body needs.

The father lives in time; the baby doesn't. The father's time taken by the baby is time the father will lose forever, and time is precious to him. There is only so much of it, and it must be used to advantage. In this state, the father worries so much about time past and time future that he cannot exist in time present. In contrast, the baby knows nothing of time. It is hungry now, it cries now; it is wet now, it cries now. Its perceptions are jangled by a demanding time-conscious father and a time-fearing mother, and it cries—now.

The cry of a baby makes a demand on most men they cannot meet—cease being terrestrial, even if only for a moment, and become arboreal, where time is suspended and everyone exists in the now. Then a cry would not interfere with the father's time. Instead it would be a request for action to which even he might respond.[3]

It is because the baby lives in the constant now that any effort to put it on an adult-made time-schedule is so futile. The only time the baby knows is body time, and it functions according to the needs of the body. Therefore, if the mother wants as healthy and contented a baby as possible, she will raise it according to the baby's body clock.

At this point in history it is almost unnecessary to encourage

---

3. In addition, it must be remembered that the male has no paternal instinct to assist it in relating to an infant's needs.

a mother to take her lead from the baby in the matter of time. Still, only a few years ago it was taught by pediatricians, child "authorities," and child psychologists that a schedule should be established as soon as possible, primarily to have the baby fit into the family and its way of life as quickly as possible. The scheduled approach to child-rearing has been largely discarded, because it did not work. Without understanding the arboreal nature of the child, those prescribing for new mothers nevertheless took the lead from the baby, whose body system simply wouldn't fit into the social system of the parents. In other words, mortar had to bend around the baby, rather than the other way.

Other attempts have been made in recent years to accommodate mortar to the needs of the infant. More and more mothers are beginning to nurse their babies; they are having them sleep in the bed with them and their husbands; they are carrying them on their bodies as they go about; they are responding to crying when it occurs, and in other ways they are creating as arboreal a profile to the infant as possible. Quite simply, they have ignored their terrestrial pediatricians and other advisors, and have listened to their own bodies and those of their babies. Mother and baby are made for each other, not as part of mortar, but as part of nature. Anything that interferes with that symbiotic union imperils the baby—and can have serious psychological effects on the mother. Only when instinct had shown the way did pediatricians and others come along and stamp their imprimatur on the new method of mothering. They had to, or close down their offices as more and more women declined their advice.

The newest development, that of more women having their babies at home, is meeting opposition from many doctors because it is a threat to their entrenched position in baby production. The fact is that in the United States, 94% of all deliveries can safely take place in the home. Only 6% need the facilities of a hospital in case of complication. The medical profession opposes the new tendency because the new naturalness of childbirth is a threat to their mortar. This is so, notwithstanding their protests on grounds of baby and mother well-being. The fact is, increasing numbers of doctors are supporting this new drive in the direction of naturalness. And, as if to shame American doctors, most births all over the world take place at home, in most cases with better results than those obtained in American baby factories [4] where upon birth mother and baby are separated and separately mistreated by a hospital system that functions much less for the welfare of its patients than for the convenience of its staff—and the profit of the doctors. I do not intend this as an unduly sharp criticism of hospitals and doctors, but it must be remembered that while babies are natural to mothers, they are the mortar on which doctors and others depend for survival. The baby is their hunt.

If a woman wants a baby she should have it on as natural terms as possible. Mortar, such as medical supervision and assistance when necessary, should exist for the baby and the mother. However, whenever possible mortar should comprise no more than an ambience in which natural processes can take place. This is true at the birth of a baby and also during its critical first period. The reason for this is simple. The baby is an arboreal infant and mortar is a terrestrial invention. Only an arboreal mother can present a profile necessary to support the life of her arboreal infant. I am convinced that if the mother will present as arboreal a profile as possible to her baby for the first year, nothing short of a total catastrophe afterwards can amend the child's natural development. Such being the case, it can be said that the child has been born into existence and that that existence has been preserved by mother love which, as was defined earlier, means meeting the needs of the infant.

Finally, there is the matter of letting go of the child. Mothers don't like this moment, so often symbolized by the child going off to school for the first time. They let them go, but too often reluctantly.

Perhaps it might be best to remember that the human child

---

4. Studies show that the United States ranks about eleventh in infant mortality. See *Immaculate Deception*, Suzanne Arms (San Francisco Book Co./Houghton Mifflin, 1975), for details of the problem.

is an arboreal primate that once lived on its mother literally by clinging to it during its extreme dependency period. When the infant was ready to leave its mother-tree it did so, simply by ceasing to cling to the mother's coat. The only difference between that infant and the modern infant is that the latter has no mother's coat to cling to. And yet, when it is ready to be on its own, it will stop clinging to its mother. It is not the mother's decison, it is the child's. It knows when to let loose. The best thing the mother can do is to not clutch at her child; nature never intended that she should.

Of necessity, everyone must descend to the ground. We know that no one can continually live in arborea unless, of course, all needs of the body are met by mortar provided by someone else. Since this is a rare occurrence, enjoyed only by endowed arborealists, almost everyone faces the prospect of terrestrialization which, in essence, means being trained for participation in the production of mortar.

Man is thereby faced with two prime considerations. The first is the need for mortar, which obliges everyone to become, to varying extents, future-oriented. The second consideration, that for which the first functions, is the need of the body to exist, and it can only exist in the constant now. The conflict between these two considerations is clear, something mentioned several times earlier. Yet, notwithstanding this inevitable conflict, a *modus vivendi* must be established between body and mortar, in default of which the individual will suffer from underterrestrialization or overterrestrialization. Which one it is, will be determined by the special value system in which the individual is raised and, most important, by the journey down the terrestrialization staircase on which the child is taken. Too many children are abandoned on some intermediate landing, while others are carried down into the basement where they face life confined in a grim terrestrial dungeon. As for those left on a landing, they end up barely able to survive, never having reached the ground where life must be lived.

They remain suspended above terrestria; their opposite numbers are buried in it.

Because of the development of man's unique cerebral cortex, modern man is fully capable of adjusting to the demands of mortar. The question is: What sort of content goes into the vast reservoir of brain potential? If it is such as to frighten the child away from mortar or if it is such as to make the child compulsive about mortar, serious problems arise. The arborealist will do rather well living in the constant now, but will fail miserably in functioning with mortar. The terrestrialist will function well with mortar, but fail miserably in living in any situation divorced from mortar. What is needed is a reconciliation between the two extremes. The question is: How?

Actually, the problem of reconciliation is not that of the individual struggling to connect with mortar. Reconciliation begins with the mother, who in her raising of children must reconcile adult terrestrial time with infant arboreal timelessness. Reconciliation, then, must be effected between mortar and body. And since it is the mother who must prepare the child's body for mortar, it is the mother's function to reconcile body and mortar.

There are two starting points in this matter: the body, or mortar. The greatest obstacle to existence in the modern industrial society is the primacy of mortar. It has become the starting point for virtually all human considerations, and its primacy is constantly on the minds of parents. It begins with little things such as the choice of blue for boys and pink for girls. Boys are raised to be aggressive, competitive, stoical, and unemotional. Girls are raised to be submissive, conciliatory, and emotional. Each child born is unconsciously compared with a cultural ideal (or the neighbor's child), so that a boy with a frail body or protruding ears, or a girl with thick legs or acne, are considered to suffer from disabilities that must be compensated for, in order that someday the boy might be more effective in making mortar and the girl more effective in marrying mortar. It is so insidious a matter that giant corporations make millions out of selling mouthwashes and other poultices to anxious parents and teenage children. Under this system of priorities the individual is obliged to conform to mortar or run the risk of not surviving. If he or she should physically survive, it is either as a deep neurotic or as a ward of mortar.

The dilemma that has plagued modern man, even when he has not been aware of it consciously, has been the relation between body and mortar. While his conscious mind may not be aware of the dilemma, his body is, because it encounters the principle I have earlier enunciated: The greater the amount of mortar, the greater the body stress. The explanation offered—if it is ever thought of at all—is that the individual is sacrificing himself for his family, his business, his country or some other estimable cause. Body stress under these conditions becomes a silent badge of courage. Unfortunately, it is very much like awarding someone a medal for bravery—posthumously.

Dedication to mortar at the expense of the body is putting man on the road to extinction, because the greater the mortar, the greater the stifling of the body. Therefore, if man is to avoid extinction he must reorder his priorities, beginning with the starting point of all human considerations, the human body.

Unfortunately, the human body is often not even fit for polite conversation, to say nothing of serious consideration. The first thing that most children in western society are taught —subtlely, so very subtlely—is that the body should be covered. Elimination is accomplished in the diaper or on the toilet seat and, despite its importance, is never spoken of except in code: "Baby went potty," "John go wet-wet," "Mary has to go to the ladies' room," "I've got to see a man about a dog." The child develops accordingly.

Then comes the awkward matter of sex. Boys are quietly told not to "play with themselves"; girls are prepared for "the curse" of menstruation, usually by a series of frightening looks, cryptic warnings, and averted eyes. Masturbation becomes a parental crisis. Raised with a feeling that masturbation is a form of immorality, most parents can't face what they suspect their children may be doing and so, by evasive discourses, occasional hints, and suggestions that boys take a cold shower or run outdoors when they have a "funny feeling" in their "private" regions, they infect their children with their own morbid attitudes.

More mothers worry their pediatricians over feeding problems than all others combined. It is no wonder. Hardly is the baby home from the hospital than the mother wants to introduce it to baby foods such as applesauce, oatmeal, and strained carrots. This, combined with getting the baby on some sort of schedule (demand, yes, but within reason!), and rushing it through early weaning so as to be the first on the block, is enough to turn any infant's digestive system into a colicky vault. What compounds the offense, driving the mother to seek medical advice, is the emotional state of the mother. Impatience over feeding, worry over the lack of a morning bowel-movement, irritation over the baby's early waking, panic over long crying spells, competition with other mothers—all combine to create a jagged psychic profile that the infant can't possibly match. So the mother goes to the doctor and complains that something is wrong with her baby—it won't eat as it should.

Ideally, the body is encased in clothing and so disciplined as to become virtually invisible. For almost all our lives we see only the heads and hands of other people. Even sex is frequently experienced in darkness and with at least some garment on.

But the body betrays us. By sound and sight it reminds us of its presence. The reader need only recall hearing a loud fart in a public gathering, or a belch at a dinner party, to appreciate the horror of such grossness. Or the sight of one's employer picking his nose, or a judge rummaging around in his ear with his little finger and then judiciously staring at what he has brought out. Or the neighbor blowing his nose and then looking into his handkerchief to study what lies there. Or even something so meek as a gentle rumbling in the stomach. Or the smell of an actual body rather than a veiling perfume. The picking of teeth, the cleaning of nails, the loud coughing-up of phlegm, the undisguised odor of breath—all these natural actions betray our bodies to other people, and they embarrass us almost beyond endurance. We blush, thereby revealing our great sense of guilt. And when we don't blush and when no one responds visibly to the *faux pas*, everyone pretends that nothing has happened, that we are only heads and hands after all. And, as everyone knows, heads and hands are all that are necessary to produce mortar. Were they not, I am certain that they too would be obliged to disappear.

The body is where man lives; it is the residence of existence. Why, then, should it be the silent and invisible companion of our lives? Because the body is the missing link with our arboreal origins. It must, at all costs, be restrained by the terrestrial mind, lest it break loose and run away from its responsibility to produce mortar. The body, however, knows nothing of mortar. It knows only its needs and its functions. These must be provided for, and as much as possible on the body's terms, before man can begin to enter into existence.

What, then, is existence? To begin with, it is not the deification of the body. To deify the body, to make it the focal point of existence, is to create one more cult, thus producing one more perversion. Deification makes the body something it is not, the object of existence around which everything must revolve. The body is not the object of existence; it is the subject of existence.

It is when we reach this point in a discussion of man and existence that we confront the great question of ends. Metaphysics raises its crusty head and enters its dashing challenge: What is man's destiny? Or, if the metaphysician is not concerned with teleological matters, he becomes existential: What must man do with his life? Or, if he is a mere philosopher:

What is the meaning of such a life? To the first I would answer: Man's destiny is death. To the second: Live it. To the third: There is no meaning to existence; there is only existence.

No matter how we cast the issue, we must always come back to the three essential factors of existence: protection from predators, sustenance, and sex. There is absolutely nothing man can do in existence other than act upon these three matters. (Actually, now that man is no longer confronted by superior natural predators, he has only to act upon the matters of sustenance and sex.) Regardless of everything uttered by Zoroaster, Plato, Confucius, Buddha, Jesus, Mohammed, Thomas Aquinas, Luther, Marx, Freud, or the latest guru out of the hills of India, there is nothing but sustenance and sex, plus man's concern with each.

It has been man's ongoing concern with sustenance and sex that has prompted Zoroaster and all the others to contemplate the central concern of existence: suffering. In what ways does man suffer? From poverty, war, and oppression—plus his anxiety about the future in which poverty, war, and oppression may go on, as they have in the past and do in the present. And whence come these afflictions of man? From the mortar created by an arboreal primate seeking to survive in the terrestrial mode of existence. There is no poverty, war, or oppression arborea. These only occur in the life of man. They have been the hallmark of human existence from time immemorial, because man has been struggling since time immemorial to come to terms with mortar. And he has thus far failed in his efforts.

He has been continually confused between means and ends. At no time in his long terrestrial sojourn has he been able simply to exist. There has never been any natural and immediate way his body needs could be met. Mortar has been man's salvation, but it has also been his millstone. He can't go anywhere without it, just as the diabetic cannot move about without his insulin or the amputee without his prosthesis. But the diabetic who centers his life around his insulin, and the amputee who centers his life around his prosthesis, cannot be said to live, at best, each survives, but like someone clinging to a life-preserver in the middle of the ocean.

Man, however, is not in the middle of an ocean; he is on the shore of existence. While it is true that the original terrestrial hominids faced a monumental crisis that taxed their very limited capabilities—a pebble tool is extremely marginal mortar—so that survival was a clinging proposition, man today is not in that situation. It does not tax his enormous capabilities to produce the mortar necessary for survival. Indeed, survival mortar is among the least of his worries. What he is confronting now is life in neo-arborea, not life in primordial terrestria. Unfortunately, he confronts neo-arborea as if it were the original terrestrial moment, and as a result he clings desperately to every speck of mortar as if it were a life-saving pebble tool. In this mood man survives but he doesn't exist. Instead of being able to live in the midst of existence, he is constantly searching the ground ahead of him for another pebble tool.

How much mortar does a man need? Tolstoy once asked a similar question: How much land does a man need? In his story, the protagonist was given from sunup to sunset in which to stake out the land he needed. In his efforts to acquire as much land as possible, he overexerted himself and died. It turned out that all he actually needed was enough land for a grave.[5] When we examine man and his relation to mortar, we discover that the amount of mortar a man has bears no relation to his happiness. He can be miserable with a pebble tool or with the wealth of Croesus. And he has found it possible to be content with either. It is clear that it is not the quantity of mortar that determines man's well-being. What, then, of the quality of mortar?

Here, I believe, we face the essential issue. Man's terrestrial mind is a great receptacle that in the process of living and learning is filled with content required for survival in terrestria. It is, in brief, the mind of mortar. Whatever content goes into this mind, to a very large extent will determine what the in-

---

5. "How Much Land Does a Man Need?," *Leo Tolstoy, Short Stories*, ed. Ernest J. Simmons (New York: Modern Library, 1965), 2:183–199.

dividual gets out of life. This mind exerts a regulatory influence on the arboreal mind, the mind of man's body. Because of this, mortar considerations can, and do, have a strong influence on the body. Therefore, the type of content, much more than the amount of content, has an important effect on the body. If the body is to be allowed freedom to live in the now, it can only obtain this freedom on the basis of the content of the terrestrial mind, and the content of this mind is fed into it from external sources. It is not something a child is born with.

The body cannot function independently of the terrestrial mind, and the terrestrial mind can only function on the basis of what is put into it from external sources—principally the mother in the early period, society in the later periods. As can be seen, everything depends on the values of society that in one way or another are poured into the terrestrial mind, especially that of the young.

In America and in much of western society, the production-consumption process has become the dominant motif of life. For ease of analysis, this process might be considered acquisition mortar. The second most important motif is the military process which might be thought of as contention mortar. Both make intolerable demands on the body. Acquisition mortar, designed to construct a mortared existence, makes the body so future-oriented that it becomes decreasingly functional. Contention mortar, designed to protect acquisition mortar, places additional stress on the body by subjecting it to the lethality and counter-lethality hazards discussed earlier in this chapter. Man's life is structured around these two types of mortar. Unfortunately, they consume his life. There is no time left over for existence.

Mortared existence does something more. Acquisition mortar appeals to man's arboreal nature, while contention mortar appeals to his terrestrial fears. With both mortars functioning at the same time, the individual is caught in a conflict between aspiration and apprehension. Because immediate terrestrial survival has always been the first point in any set of conflicting considerations, contention mortar keeps man in a constant state of terrestrial apprehension, leading him at every juncture to decide in favor of terrestrial security, thereby unleashing the deflationary forces of the military process. This, in turn, serves to lessen the opportunity for the realization of arboreal aspirations, thus further heightening the hold of terrestrial forces on his life.

So much for life. What of existence?

All I can do here is seek to turn on a light that hopefully will chase shadows away and that will reveal some of the important elements in man's terrestrial predicament. It is my hope that once the light shines, man will begin to move around more freely in the lighted landscape. In this way I believe he will discover existence.

By far the most important shadow that must be dispelled is man's terrestrial premise. While he may accept the fact that his remote ancestor was an arboreal primate, he functions on the premise that *he* is a terrestrial creature. It has been my main purpose in presenting the Arboreal/Terrestrial Conflict Thesis to show that man's nature today remains the arboreal nature of his remote primate ancestor. The conflict, as I have attemped to show it, is between man's arboreal nature and his terrestrial circumstances. This is, I am convinced, the basis of man's existential difficulties. At almost every turn he is torn between the needs of his nature and the demands of his circumstances. One aspect of the conflict is manifested by his desire to reduce time-anxiety and body stress by reconstituting his terrestrial circumstances so that they might resemble arboreal conditions, while at the same time responding to sequential crises in such a way as to bury himself ever deeper in terrestria.

Man can only begin to solve his existential problems by proceeding from the arboreal premise. It is the only premise that will rid him of the shadows that plague his life.

The most important derivative of the arboreal premise is the fact that by nature man is nonlethal. Unfortunately, after hundreds of thousands of years of the hunt era in which all of man's terrestrial institutions and practices were established, he has continued to respond to threats from other nonlethal primates as if they were in fact from natural predators. It is for this reason that man has perpetuated war even though he lives in what might best be called the postwar era. We see a beginning breakdown of these anachronistic practices in the modern resurgence of man's original nonlethal nature as manifested by the world peace movement and the formal development of the philosophy of nonviolence. *It is not in the nature of man to kill, and in the modern era man is beginning to assert that fact.*

I must post a *caveat* at this point. It does no good to seek a solution to war merely by throwing military arms away. If everyone but one is without arms and that one has a big club, he can go a long way toward having what he wants. Armament can only be effectively done away with when man realizes there are no predators menacing him and when he recognizes within himself the nonlethal primate of long ago. However, this is not to say that there will be lasting amity among people and among nations. There is no lasting peace in arborea and there never has been. There will always be conflicts and differences. The integrity of the affinity group demands solidarity and noninterference by outsiders in order that it can function on its established terms and in order to assure the security of its food sources. Since there are no more predators for man to worry about, that problem need no longer concern him. However, man must not delude himself into thinking he is a peaceful, acquiescent creature. He is not. Like any arboreal primate, he can be quarrelsome, assertive, demanding, and sly. But he doesn't have to be lethal about it. He has a blustering nature, one of great display, that helps resolve relationships and rights. Besides all this, the long history of man has shown that lethality within the species hasn't worked. It has never solved a problem; it has only worsened the situation. Man has never really had a stomach for war. He wants what war may give him, but he has found in recent years that he can actually get more without it.

There will always be quarrels. They arise between lovers as

well as between nations, between friends as well as between neighbors. And they will be boisterous, clamorous, bristling affairs because man is an arboreal primate and primates are the masters of display. The proof? The proof is in you, the reader, and in your quarrels and angers, for you must remember that you are the missing link. And at this point, I suspect, you are beginning to realize it. Where, reader, are your lethal quarrels?

The second derivative from the arboreal premise, one that casts a long shadow, concerns the relationship between man and sustenance. By nature, man is a nonproducing, noncooperative, noncompetitive, direct consumer. Terrestrial circumstances have obliged him to become a producer of his own food, cooperate in its production and distribution, and engage in indirect transactions in order to consume what he has produced. Man's competitiveness is a holdover from the hunt era when he had to compete with natural predators—and sometimes with other men—for food.

This may appear to be a dreadful state of affairs in contrast to that of other arboreal primates, who merely have to "pluck the fruit from the trees," but it isn't at all. On the average, arboreal primates spend up to eight hours a day in the slow, inefficient process of eating. Man only requires a few minutes a day to eat. It is a revealing coincidence that western man today must spend an average of eight hours a day working in order to have enough money with which to meet his needs. So, in all, man and his fellow primates spend just about the same amount of time each day attending to sustenance and other needs.

The problem man faces is no longer that of consuming, something that once faced his original hominid ancestors with a monumental crisis. His problem is that of production and distribution (or food-sharing). He has no instinct for either. It would seem that this deficiency could be cured by basing production on consumption. But this isn't what has happened. Those who control the means of production are the ones who control consumption. This is a residual effect of the hunt era, when hunting leaders took command and determined the form and amount of the hunt. Industrial as well as political leaders set the pace of the hunt, as it were, and are followed by the consumers. Soviet Russia once sought to reverse this process, but failed. In the United States there is the fiction of democratic processes, but this is a veil behind which the ancient leadership principles still operate. (Nothing better exemplifies this than the current world energy crisis, created by the oil industry, abetted by various governments, and paid for by consumers.)

This is a formidable shadow and can only be dispelled by an understanding of the dynamic infusing it. It is a common practice among primates that in a food shortage the adult male leaders satisfy their needs first, the rest taking what is left. This is to assure the affinity group of the health of its dominant males, for both protective and reproductive purposes. When man's ancestors were forced into the terrestrial mode and thus into the hunt era, they lived for a very long time in an extreme emergency regarding sustenance. Not only were the best males needed to protect the group from predators, they were also the ones needed to lead the hunt. In this way a pattern established in the arboreal period was extended into the terrestrial period and continued as long as sustenance was a critical problem.

Once man domesticated his food sources, though, he no longer had to depend on those of nature. He possessed the ability to relate production to consumption, and on his own terms. This new condition should have solved his problems. There was no longer any competition for the limited supplies of nature, since man could produce what he needed, as little or as much as circumstances required. It could be said that by practicing farming and animal husbandry within the terrestrial confines of a state, man had begun to imitate the natural condition of arborea, in which an affinity group possessed a certain territory in which its food sources were supplied by nature

—except, of course, that man did the producing. Even so, this should have released him from the operation of the emergency principle. It is clear that it did not. Even today America, with its superabundance of food, has a food production and distribution system identical with that of starving India. It is clear that reality plays a far lesser role than does the ancient emergency principle which has followed man throughout his terrestrial career. We can only conclude that man continues to function as if he were still struggling for survival in the hunt era, in which the control of the hunt rested exclusively in the hands of the hunt leaders. Man is not responding to modern conditions; he is reacting to very ancient emergencies in which he had at best marginal control over obtaining food and none at all over the source of food.

The only substantive difference between the modern situation and that which existed in arborea is that now man is both producer and consumer. He has it within his power so to regulate food production and food consumption as to meet everyone's needs.

This is a reassuring fact that sems to fly in the face of rising population which threatens everything. The neo-Malthusians who predict catastrophe proceed from a faulty premise. As I have said earlier, human sexuality has existed not for normal reproductive purposes but to provide hunters and, more recently, workers in order that neo-arborea might be achieved. This is an emergency birth-rate system that will revert to its old rate once neo-arborea is approached. Every poor society has a high birth rate; every society on the rim of neo-arborea has a low birth rate. This is the fact that population experts must come to grips with.

The underlying dynamics of this situation are manifested in conscious action, in the same way that man's nonlethal nature manifests itself today in increasingly conscious activities. Not only does public policy in America favor limited births, but increasingly people are engaging in sexual activity that does not have reproduction as its object. This is occurring in

much of the West, as well as in such places as India. Yet, although it is successful in the West, it fails badly in India,
because in the West, by and large, great portions of the population are on the rim of neo-arborea, whereas in India the
emergency situation continues. Even though conscious efforts
in India seek to imitate the West, they are being contradicted
by the realities of the Indian situation, which is one of a
desperate food problem. Efforts at population control are failing because the emergency persists. India's population problem
will continue until such time as it solves its food production
and distribution problems. Then, the emergency over, the population will go down.

There is a final critical consideration relating to production.
It has to do with soiling the nest. Here we encounter not a
shadow but a dark curtain of smog.

There is no need to describe the situation. It exists everywhere industrial man nests on the earth. Everyone curses pollution; no one seems able to do anything about it. Minds have
come together over the problem and from these convocations
have issued the obvious solutions. They are, in fact, so obvious
that we can't help wondering why they have never been put
into effect.

The reason for the failure to end pollution of air, water, and
earth stems from the conflict between an instinct and a painfully and poorly acquired habit.

As an arboreal primate, man is born without an instinct
against soiling the nest. Ever since his entry into the terrestrial
mode, he has sought to remedy this deficiency. His failure is
excellent proof that the arboreal genes of the original primate
continue in modern man. Despite the urgency for not soiling
the nest in order to preserve health, man simply has never
gotten the hang of it. (Fortunately for archeologists he has
failed, for once man settled into caves, some of which were
occupied continuously for thousands of years, and once he established an early site such as Jericho, he stayed there. In the
caves, all the investigator has to do is dig down, and he will

come to every item dropped by its occupants, who never seemed to clean anything away, including tools, food remnants, and every sort of offal. As for cities, as one crumbled, another was built on top of it. To know the history of Catal Hüyük, all the archeologist has had to do is dig straight down. Each level discovered proves to be a "Fibber McGee closet," much to the pleasure of those digging.)

Man, driven by the instinct of consumption, produces by virtue of accumulated mortar, something that is not instinctual. As a result, there is a collision between his instinctive need to consume and his inadequate efforts at keeping his terrestrial nest clean.

Pollution is perpetrated by the refusal of those in the production process to curtail or significantly modify their methods or their products. This is their hunt on which their survival depends. If this soils the nest, that is a small price for their survival. No species with an instinct against soiling the nest would proceed in this manner. The instinct to consume and that against soiling the nest would clash, and either a nonsoiling method to arrive at consumption would be achieved or, immobilized, the species would become extinct. Man may do just that, not because of immobility but because of so soiling the nest as to destroy himself.

The question is, can man stop polluting his nest? I think not, until such time as an instinct, such as that of survival, is set up to counter that of consumption. In that event—and why must man wait for such an eventuality?—he will have to find nonpolluting methods of production to meet his consumption needs. Meanwhile he will continue to pollute. His mind tells him he is harming himself; his genes cut his mind's message off at the pass. As a result, the message never gets through. Soiling the nest continues to be an acceptable price to pay for consumption needs, and it will remain so until a survival crisis presents itself. We can only hope that it will not then be too late.

There is still the lingering shadow of sex, so distorted by

terrestrial demands. While it is all too clear that existence in the terrestrial mode has imposed an enormous set of burdens on man, there is one positive result that has been obtained from the situation: Unlike other forms of life, man can engage in sexual activity that is completely divorced from reproduction. Sexual activity is pleasurable; reproduction is utilitarian. They are separable activities.

Despite the fact that in the West man is on the rim of neo-arborea and no longer needs a high birth rate, the state, which has a strong propensity for conservatism in the midst of change, continues to think of sex as being related exclusively to reproduction. Therefore it outlaws as "crimes against nature" those acts that provide sexual pleasure without at the same time serving reproductive ends. The state, a terrestrial invention with a terrestrial bias, requires as many utilitarian units as possible, and in support of this need demands that all sexual activity relate specifically and exclusively to reproduction. It applies to this rule the situation in nature, where sexual activity is reserved solely for reproduction. When looked at that way there is a semblance of legitimacy to the state's position. But the state and the arbiters of sexual morality who support its position fail to take into account man's ability to control on a conscious level his reproductive processes, while at the same time experiencing instinctual sexual drives. Not every sexual drive has to be oriented toward reproductive ends. To make such a demand would be like insisting that no one might play—unless play can be found to have a utilitarian purpose. Must one ride a horse only to work? Must every walk in the country be an errand? Can't one sometimes play poker for the chips rather than the money they may represent? Why can't sex, like anything else that gives pleasure, be enjoyed without linking it to a utilitarian function?

This, I believe, brings us to the final shadow in man's life: that of utilitarianism. At best, play is considered a necessary concession to man's nature so as to enable him better to perform utilitarian functions. At worst, play is made a form of work. In recent years there has even developed a union of play and work. "Creative play" is utilitarian; it is not play. Then there is the saying that work can be fun. These are nothing but aids to utilitarianism. Play, in and of itself, has no value. It is in reality negative, because it does not contribute to mortar. Instead, it detracts from it.[6]

What is true of play, is true of all human activities that do not relate to mortar. Sex, as I have just suggested, must have a utilitarian function. It cannot be enjoyed solely for itself. The same thing is true of the individual. He cannot merely exist, he must perform some utilitarian role in the production of mortar.

While this may have been necessary during the early period when man was building up both mortar and his capacity to create more mortar, it is not necessary any more. Man is more than a utilitarian unit. Of necessity, he must have some utility value in order that mortar might be perpetuated. But the situation is very much like that of the modern primate which must spend up to one third of every day in eating. Similarly, man must spend a proportionate amount of time in securing his needs. But what of the rest of man's time? Surely, that should be his own. Unfortunately, the production-consumption process never ceases to invade the personal sector of life. One can't merely *exist*, one must do this or do that, either to improve oneself or to consume more fragments of mortar. Man is beginning to choke on those fragments, just as he is gagging on the increased violations of his personal integrity by the state and the controllers of the production-consumption process.

Mortar begets mortar, and that fact is beginning to engulf man. Even as his direct participation in the production of mortar is decreasing, his encasement in mortar grows, so that he can scarcely find a segment of his life where his actual nature can express itself. The encroachment is becoming so great that man himself is fast becoming mortar.

6. While play detracts from mortar, it has beneficial effects that help restore the union of body and mind, since play is a complete occupation of body and mind in the constant now.

The great myth of the western democracies, especially the United States, concerns the alleged dignity and merit of the individual. The truth is that the individual, as an individual, has no dignity or merit. The young are not delicately cared for except to preserve and develop them so that they might become "useful citizens." The mature who become ill are not helped back to health so that they might enjoy good health, but so that they might once more become "useful citizens." As for the elderly, except for a few humiliating and degrading touches of social cosmetics, they are allowed to fall away from life, their usefulness having been used up years earlier.

Democracy means the democratization of utilitarianism. As long as the individual has a use, he will be fitted into the scheme of things. The production-consumption process *demands* democracy in which all men are created equal parts of the process. The military process *demands* democracy in which all men are equal parts of a military machine. Democracy means that each individual is interchangeable with every other in both processes.

We need only look at those who lack utilitarian value to see how the system works. The young who are physically or mentally handicapped, in most instances, must be provided for by their families. The infant struggling for life or the retarded child struggling to comprehend even the simplest concepts has no value in the eyes of the state. Nor do the old, who are set aside to rot in lonely isolation in regimented and impersonal institutions. Within the social system, which wraps itself around mortar, it would be better to let such creatures die, but the system will not directly bring about their deaths. It does so indirectly by requiring families to provide for their special care out of their own marginal resources. The instant they go for help, they enter someone else's hunt, and they do so as the prey. Social organizations, hospitals, doctors, therapists, nursing homes, and all the rest who occupy themselves with the problems of the old and of the handicapped, do so by occupying a hunting preserve into which the old or handicapped and their families must enter. The greater the hunt,

the greater the care given, but the poorer the hunt, the poorer
the care. All one has to do is walk into facilities operating in
the poor regions of this country to verify this fact. The care,
with almost no exceptions, is totally dependent on how plentiful the hunt is for those rendering the care.

What is true of the handicapped child and the old person, is
true of all those who need help. At the very time when they
need the most care and are least able to provide for it or for
themselves, they are burdened with such enormous costs that
should they recover from a serious illness or accident they may
be bankrupted or in debt for years to come. Insurance companies, of course, have their own hunt, and they are infamous
for their concealed exclusions and limitations—and high cost.

America has rightly been characterized as being youth-
oriented. Some critics go so far as to claim that the American
system spoils the young. This is sheer sophistry. America is
a system in which the young are, like the lamb being led to
the slaughter, fattened up. They are given education—which
they cannot refuse—so that they can in the fullness of their
maturity become as competent producers of mortar as education and moral training (which is part of education) can make
them. This utilitarian view of the young is the great shadow
that spreads before them, and they know it. But they have no
choice. They must enter the shadow of utilitarianism knowing
that when they have used up their lives in making mortar,
they will be discarded, as their parents will soon be, and as
their grandparents are now.

Where is the sense of individual worth in such a system?
There is none. That is why modern life is so filled with shadows that obscure vision and fill life with numb despair. What
is so shocking about this state of affairs is that man is both
the victim and the perpetrator.

What is unique about man is that he gains his sustenance
through the medium of other men. Having spent 99 percent
of his terrestrial period as a hunter, he has been shaped into
an artificial creature who proceeds through the post-hunt era

as if he were still in the hunt era. As a result, he treats other men who are his medium of sustenance as if they were prey. As an artificial predator, man must cultivate all those practices that will assist him in his hunt for sustenance. Thus he is a scavenger, a trickster, a trapper, a stampeder, a plunderer, and a killer in his efforts to satisfy his basic needs. In the post-hunt era, the victim of all these devices has been other men. As a result, all other men function in two capacities: as an assisting instrumentality in gaining sustenance through other men, or as prey. In either event, other men have but a utilitarian function. In this way, then, all men are viewed as integral parts of the indirect transactions by which man maintains himself. Still, it must be pointed out that each individual is both hunter and prey. In seeking sustenance, the individual is a hunter. However, once he has received payment—say, for work done—and he seeks to use that money to acquire what he needs, he becomes the prey of the supplier who, in order to satisfy his own needs, seeks to gain possession of the other's money. It can be seen from this that money is the medium of the modern hunt, and it is money coming to the hunter or money going from the prey that controls interpersonal relationships. Of course, the paradox is that the same individual is both hunter and prey, depending on the direction his money is flowing.

This is really not an abstruse concept. Everyone knows how hard it is to earn a living. Jobs are often hard to find. Sometimes you have to be mendacious about your past experience, you may have to cut someone else out, maybe a reference isn't entirely gratuitous or truthful, and possibly a little boot-licking is necessary to get the job. Then, once you are working, there may be corners to be cut, expense accounts to be padded, a few minor deceptions played on customers, a kickback, a black-market transaction, a loss passed on to an insurance company, or an improper deduction on one's income taxes. But despite all the extra efforts required, a living is made. Thus, the successful hunt.

On the other hand, once the paycheck is deposited into a bank account, the hunt is on the other foot. Now, the individual guards what little he has, knowing that everyone else is out to get him, and he bitterly resents being victimized. Prices are too high, salesmen lie about their products, companies don't honor their warranties, and the products are obsolete before they are paid for. Alas, so much for the prey.

So between hunter and prey we have utilitarian man who lives all the days of his life, from birth to death, in an alternating set of transactional relationships. This deadly cycle can only be broken when men begin to realize that modern economic activity is not an extension of the ancient hunt, but instead, a process of exchange. It is not a case of an artificial predator pitting himself against natural prey that is faster, hears better, sees better, and that will escape if man the hunter doesn't in some way—by hook or by crook, by strength or by stealth, by trick or by trap—get possession of it. It is a case of equals (more equals in ineptitudes than anything else, since there is no instinct for sharing) seeking to assist each other in acquiring the means of sustenance. Man's situation today is not that of a "we-they" relationship that existed when it was deficient we $\longleftrightarrow$ superior they. By this I mean that man was deficient both in regard to obtaining prey and in protecting himself from predators. Today there are no predators and man controls the sources of "prey"—sustenance. It is not an imbalanced competition, it is a balanced cooperation that exists. Only it exists lost in the shadow of the hunt.

We see the growing efforts of man to emerge from this shadow. The European Economic Community is an example, as are the cooperative associations in this country that seek to reduce competition and increase cooperation. We see this also in the efforts of consumer organizations that are seeking to put limits on the predatory practices of the giant corporations. And we see it among some of the young who struggle with the concept of the commune.

Shadows, such as those I have enumerated here, are the

breeding places of time-anxiety and body stress, the two great obstacles to full existence. That is why the shadows must be dispelled. This is not an exercise in the power of positive thinking. What I have been describing are matters not of substance but of shadow. Man does not need them in order to live. Certainly he cannot have them and enter into existence.

The terrestrial premise is shadow, not substance. The substance of man's existence is the arboreal premise. Lethality and counter-lethality are both shadow. More than any other derivative of the terrestrial premise, they interfere with the substance of human existence, which has as its premise the nonlethal nature of man. The production-consumption process, incorporating as it does elements of lethality and counter-lethality, is shadow. The same process, founded in cooperation, is substance. Terrestrial sex in the post-hunt era is shadow, not substance. And, finally, utilitarianism based on the hunt ethic is shadow; the substance is limited utility exercised cooperatively among equals.

The substances I have set forth are not ideals, sought after in theory but unobtainable in reality. They are, in fact, continually emerging and taking increasingly recognizable form in modern life. They are the substances on which to base the future existence of man. But first, the shadows must be dispelled.

There will always be a conflict between man's arboreal nature and his terrestrial circumstances, because man is an arboreal primate obliged to exist in terrestria. Man has the capability, however, of so reconstituting the conditions of terrestrial life that they can be made to resemble those of arborea. The Arboreal/Terrestrial Conflict need not be debilitating. It is a fact of life, but it need not be the central fact of life. Once man reduces the Arboreal/Terrestrial Conflict within himself by constructing a way of life on substance rather than on shadow, then it can be said that he will have stepped across the final threshold and into existence.

BIBLIOGRAPHY

Acherly, S. Spafford. "A Case of Paranatal Bilateral Frontal Lobe Defect Observed for Thirty Years." In *Symposium on the Frontal Granular Cortex and Behavior*, edited by John N. Warren and K. Ahert. New York: McGraw-Hill, 1964.

Ardrey, Robert. *African Genesis*. New York: Atheneum, 1961.

Arms, Suzanne. *Immaculate Deception*. New York: A San Francisco Book Co./Houghton Mifflin, 1975.

Augustine (Bishop of Hippo). *The City of God*. New York: Modern Library, 1950.

Bardwick, Judith M., and Dowan, Elizabeth. "Ambivalence: The Socialization of Women." In *Woman in Sexist Society*, edited by Vivian Gornick and Barbara K. Moran. New York: Basic Books, 1971.

Bastian, Harmut. *And Then Came Man*. New York: Doubleday, 1966.

Beadle, Muriel. *A Child's Mind*. New York: Doubleday, 1970.

Beauvoir, Simone de. *The Second Sex*. New York: Alfred A. Knopf, 1952.

Blum, Richard. *Society and Drugs*. 2 vols. San Francisco: Jossey-Bass, 1969.

Bourne, Geoffrey. *The Ape People*. New York: G. P. Putnam's Sons, 1971.

Bowlby, John. *Maternal Care and Mental Health*. New York: Schocken Books, 1966.

Breger, Louis. *From Instinct to Identity*. Englewood Cliffs, N.J.: Prentice-Hall, 1974.

Breuil, Henri. *Four Hundred Centuries of Cave Art*. Translated by Mary E. Boyle. Montignoi, France: Centre d'études et de documentation préhistoriques, 1952.

Brody, Sylvia. *Patterns of Mothering*. New York: International Universities Press, 1956.

Bromberg, Walter. *Crime and the Mind*. New York: Macmillan, 1965.

Butzer, Karl W. *Environment and Archeology*. Chicago: Aldine, 1964.

Campbell, Bernard. *Human Evolution*. Chicago: Aldine, 1966.

Cannon, Walter B. *The Wisdom of the Body*. New York: W. W. Norton, 1932.

Claiborne, Robert. *Climate, Man, and History*. New York: W. W. Norton, 1970.

Claridge, Gordon. *Drugs and Human Behavior*. New York: Praeger, 1970.

Clark, Wilfred E. LeGros. *Antecedents of Man*. Chicago: Quadrangle, 1971.

Cohn, Norman. *The Pursuit of the Millennium*. New York: Harper & Row, 1957.

Cole, Sonia. *The Prehistory of Africa*. New York: Macmillan, 1963.

Conze, Edward. *Buddhism: Its Essence and Development*. New York: Harper & Row, 1959.

Cottrell, Leonard. *Life under the Phaorahs*. New York: Holt, Rinehart and Winston, 1960.

Däniken, Erich von. *Chariots of the Gods?* New York: G. P. Putnam's Sons, 1970.

Dart, Raymond. *Adventures with the Missing Link*. New York: Harper & Row, 1959.

Denzen, Norman K. "Children and Their Caretakers." *Trans-Action* (now *Society*) (July–August, 1971): Vol. 8, No. 9/10 (Whole No. 69).

Deutsch, Helene. *The Psychology of Women*. New York: Grune & Stratton, 1945.

DeVore, Irven et al. *Primate Behavior*. New York: Holt, Rinehart and Winston, 1965.

Diamond, A. S. *The History and Origins of Language*. New York: Philosophical Society, 1959.

Dobzhansky, Theodosius. "Genetic Entities and Hominid Evolution." In *Classification and Human Evolution*, edited by Sherwood Washburn. Chicago: Aldine, 1963.

―――. *Mankind Evolving*. New Haven: Yale University Press, 1962.

Dodds, Elisabeth D. *Marriage to a Difficult Man*. Philadelphia: Westminster Press, 1971.

Edwards, Jonathan. *The Works of Jonathan Edwards*. 2 vols. London: Ball, Arnold and Co., 1840.

Eliade, Mircea. *Images and Symbols*. New York: Sheed & Ward, 1961.

―――. *Myths, Dreams, and Mysteries*. New York: Harper & Row, 1960.

Ericson, David B., and Wollin, Gosta. *The Deep and the Past*. New York: Alfred A. Knopf, 1964.

Figes, Eva. *Patriarchal Attitudes.* London: Faber & Faber, 1970.

Freeman, Walter, and Robinson, Mary Frances. *Psychosurgery and the Self.* New York: Grune & Stratton, 1954.

————, and Watts, James W. *Psychosurgery in the Treatment of Mental Disorders and Intractable Pain.* 2d ed. Springfield, Ill.: Charles C. Thomas, 1950.

Freud, Sigmund. *A General Introduction to Psychoanalysis.* New York: Boni and Liveright, 1920.

————. *The Interpretation of Dreams.* New York: Modern Library, 1950.

————. *The Sexual Enlightenment of Children.* New York: Collier Books, 1963.

————. "The Taboo of Virginity." In *Selected Works.* London: Hogarth Press, 1953–66.

Fromm, Erich. *The Forgotten Language.* New York: Rinehart, 1951.

Goodall, Jane van Lawick. *In the Shadow of Man.* Boston: Houghton Mifflin, 1971.

————. *My Friends the Wild Chimpanzees.* Washington, D.C.: National Geographic Society, 1967.

Gornick, Vivian. "Woman as Outsider." In *Woman in Sexist Society,* edited by Vivian Gornick and Barbara K. Moran. New York: Basic Books, 1971.

————, and Moran, Barbara K., eds. *Woman in Sexist Society.* New York: Basic Books, 1971.

Halliday, James L. *Psychosocial Medicine.* New York: W. W. Norton, 1948.

Hamberg, David, and Washburn, Sherwood. "Aggressive Behavior in Old World Monkeys and Apes." In *Primates: Studies in Adaptation and Variability,* edited by Phyllis Jay. New York: Holt, Rinehart and Winston, 1968.

Harding, R. S., and Washburn, Sherwood. "Evolution of Primate Behavior." (*The Neurosciences: Second Study Program,* F. O. Schmitt, editor-in-chief) New York: Rockefeller University Press, 1970.

Harrison, G. A. *Human Biology.* New York: Oxford University Press, 1964.

Hawkes, Jacquetta, and Woolley, Leonard. *Prehistory and the Beginnings of Civilization.* New York: Harper & Row, 1963.

Hobbs, Lisa. *Love and Liberation.* New York: McGraw-Hill, 1970.

Hogg, Garry. *Cannibalism and Human Sacrifice.* New York: Citadel Press, 1966.

Holt, L. Emmett. *The Care and Feeding of Children.* New York: Appleton-Century-Crofts, 1907.

Huber, Richard M. *The American Idea of Success.* New York: McGraw-Hill, 1971.

Jameson, Marshall C. *Helping Your Child Succeed in Elementary School.* New York: G. P. Putnam's Sons, 1962.

Jung, Carl Gustav. *The Structure and Dynamics of the Psyche.* New York: Pantheon Books, 1960.
———— et al. *Man and His Symbols.* New York: Doubleday, 1964.
Kramer, Samuel Noah. *From the Tablets of Sumer.* Indian Wells, Colo.: Falcon's Wing Press, 1956.
————. *The Sumerians.* Chicago: University of Chicago Press, 1963.
Kurtin, Björn. *Not from the Apes.* New York: Random House, 1972.
Lancaster, C. S., and Washburn, Sherwood. "The Evolution of Hunting." In *Man the Hunter,* edited by Richard B. Lee and Irven DeVore. Chicago: Aldine, 1968.
Lancaster, Jane. "On the Evolution of Tool-Using Behavior." In *Background for Man,* edited by Phyllis Dolhinov and Vincent Sarich. Boston: Little, Brown, 1971.
Leakey, Louis S. B. *Adam's Ancestors.* New York: Harper & Row, 1960.
Lorenz, Konrad. *On Aggression.* New York: Harcourt Brace Jovanovich, 1966.
Malinowski, Bronislaw. *Sex and Repression in Savage Society.* New York: Harcourt Brace and Co., 1927.
Marais, Eugene. *The Soul of the Ape.* New York: Atheneum, 1969.
Marshall, S. L. A. *Men against Fire.* New York: William Morrow, 1947.
Mason, William A. "The Social Development of Monkeys and Apes." In *Primate Behavior,* edited by Irvin DeVore et al., New York: Holt, Rinehart and Winston, 1965.
Mead, Margaret. *Coming of Age in Samoa.* London: Penguin Books, 1954.
————. *Sex and Temperament in Three Primitive Societies.* New York: William Morrow, 1935.
Mever, Adolphe E. *An Educational History of the Western World.* New York: McGraw-Hill, 1965.
Montagu, Ashley. *Introduction to Physical Anthropology.* Springfield, Ill.: Charles C Thomas, 1960.
————. *Touching: The Human Significance of the Skin.* New York: Columbia University Press, 1971.
Morgan, Elaine. *The Descent of Woman.* New York: Stein and Day, 1972.
Morris, Desmond. *The Naked Ape.* New York: McGraw-Hill, 1967.
Paine, Lauran. *The Hierarchy of Hell.* New York: Hippocrene, 1972.
Peiper, Albrecht. *Cerebral Function in Infancy and Childhood.* New York: Cônsultant's Bureau, 1963.
Pfeiffer, John E. *The Emergence of Man.* New York: Harper & Row, 1964.

Robinson, Bryan W. "Vocalization Evoked from Forebrain in Macaca Mulatta." *In Physiology and Behavior* (1967) vol. 2, pp. 345–354.

Robinson, Mary Frances, and Freeman, Walter. *Psychosurgery and the Self*. New York: Grune & Stratton, 1954.

Sarich, Vincent. "A Molecular Approach to the Question of Human Origins." In *Background for Man*, edited by Phyllis Dolhinov and Vincent Sarich. Boston: Little, Brown, 1971.

Scarne, John. *Scarne's Complete Guide to Gambling*. New York: Simon & Schuster, 1961.

Shew, Joel. *Children: Their Hydropathic Management in Health and Disease*. New York: Fowler and Wells, 1852.

Shulman, Alix. "Organs and Orgasms." In *Woman in Sexist Society*, edited by Vivian Gornick and Barbara K. Moran. New York: Basic Books, 1971.

Skinner, B. F. *Science and Human Behavior*. New York: Macmillan, 1953.

Southwick, Charles H. *Aggression among Non-Human Primates*. Reading, Mass.: Addison-Wesley, 1972.

Storr, Anthony. *Human Aggression*. New York: Atheneum, 1968.

Stouffer, Samuel A. *The American Soldier: Adjustment during Army Life*. 2 vols. Princeton: Princeton University Press, 1949.

Tec, Nechama. *Gambling in Sweden*. Totowa, N.J.: The Bedminster Press, 1964.

Terhune, William B. *The Safe Way to Drink: How to Prevent Alcohol Problems Before They Start*. New York: William Morrow, 1968.

Thompson, Clara. *Psychoanalysis: Evolution and Development*. New York: Hermitage House, 1950.

Tooze, Ruth. *Storytelling*. Englewood Cliffs, N.J.: Prentice-Hall, 1959.

Torok, Maria. "The Significance of Penis Envy in Women." In *Female Sexuality*, edited by Janine Chasseguet-Smirgel. Ann Arbor: University of Michigan Press, 1970.

Toynbee, Arnold. *War and Civilization*. New York: Oxford University Press, 1950.

Wagner, Walter. *To Gamble or Not to Gamble*. New York: World, 1972.

Washburn, Sherwood. "Behavior and the Origin of Man." In *Rockefeller University Review*. Vol. 6, no. 1, pp. 10–19. New York: Rockefeller University Press, 1968.

———, and Shirek, Judith. "Human Evolution." In *Behavior-Genetic Analysis*, edited by Jerry Hirsch. New York: McGraw-Hill, 1967, pp. 10–21.

———. "Speculations on the Problem of Man's Coming to the Ground." In *Changing Perspectives of Man*, edited by Ben Rothblatt. Chicago: University of Chicago Press, 1968.

————, and Hamburg, David. "Aggressive Behavior in Old World Monkeys and Apes." In *Primates: Studies in Adaptation and Variability*, edited by Phyllis Jay. New York: Holt, Rinehart and Winston, 1968.

————, and Harding, R. S. "Evolution of Primate Behavior." (*The Neurosciences: Second Study Program*, F. O. Schmitt, editor-in-chief) New York: Rockefeller University Press, 1970.

————, and Lancaster, C. S. "The Evolution of Hunting." In *Man the Hunter*, edited by Richard B. Lee and Irven DeVore. Chicago: Aldine, 1968.

Watts, James W., and Freeman, Walter. *Psychosurgery in the Treatment of Mental Disorders and Intractable Pain*. 2d ed. Springfield, Ill.: Charles C Thomas, 1950.

Wollin, Gosta, and Ericson, David B. *The Deep and the Past*. New York: Alfred A. Knopf, 1964.

Woolley, Leonard, and Hawkes, Jacquetta. *Prehistory and the Beginnings of Civilization*. New York: Harper & Row, 1963.

Woolridge, Dean E. *The Machinery of the Brain*, New York: McGraw-Hill, 1963.

INDEX

Aborigine, 314
Abraham, 315, 316–17
Acherly, S. Spafford, 296–300
Acquatic mammals, 58
Adaptive aggression, 27
Advertising industry, 399–400, 402, 404, 445, 447
Affinity groups, 24–25, 163, 188, 191, 195–96, 199–200, 212–13, 242, 330, 331, 332, 422
Africa, 399
Aggression; See Adaptive aggression; Display of aggression; Human aggression; Primate aggression; Lethality; War
Albrecht, Helmut, 66
Alcohol, 261–63, 264–66, 267
Anti-Darwinism, See Darwinism
Antidepressants, 269
Anxiety, 300–31. See also time-anxiety
Ape People, The (Bourne), 10
Apes, The (Reynolds), 138
Arborea: as paradise, 421–22; return to, 86, 134, 213, 246, 306–7, 311–13, 320–21, 323, 327, 328, 329, 338, 342, 352, 357
Arboreal brain, 151–52

Arboreal class, 376
Arboreal man, 367–69
Arboreal mind/terrestrial body, 303, 305, 307, 440, 441, 442–43
Arboreal primates, 11, 12; life-style of, 20–22, 26, 28, 446; social organization of, 24–27, 97–104
Arboreal reflex, 137–40
Arboreal/terrestrial conflict thesis, 13–16, 137–40, 170, 171, 281–84, 303, 305, 307, 349–50, 394–95, 417, 419, 420, 444–46, 457
Ardrey, Robert, 42, 259
Art, 128–29
Artist, social role of, 383
Asia, 48–49
Augustine, Saint, 219
Australopithecus africanus, 52–54, 60, 72–73, 80, 83–84, 96, 192, 204

Baboon, 74–75, 82, 188–89, 260, 261–62
Backward perspective, weakness of, 213, 275–76, 305
Bardwick, Judith M., 212
Bastian, Harmut, 90
Beadle, Muriel, 146

Birth, 7, 428–29
Bison, 133–34
Blum, Richard, 267–68, 270
Body hair, loss of, 81–82
Body stress, 284, 290, 292, 293, 363, 371, 418, 421, 422, 428; cure for, 400, reduction in, 401, 444; release from, 327
Bourne, Geoffrey H., 10, 236
Brachiation, 165
Brain development, 22, 53, 79–80, 84, 95–96, 99, 100, 109–11, 133–34, 151–52, 265, 276–81, 293, 305. *See also* Gage, Phineas; J. P.
Breasts, 240–42
Breger, Louis, 186
Breuil, Henri, 128, 129, 131–32
Brody, Sylvia, 218–19, 220
Bromberg, Walter, 250
Broom, Robert, 53–54
Buddhism, 321, 322, 324, 337
Butzer, Karl W., 50

Calvin, John, 355
Campbell, Bernard, 43
Canaan, 316, 317
Cannibalism, 70–72, 92, 204–6
Cannon, Walter B., 68
Capitalism. *See* Mortar, self-generation of
Care and Feeding of Children, The (Holt), 149
Carnivorousness, 37
Çatal Hüyük, 450
Cave paintings, 117, 119, 127–28, 129–33, 304, 350
Cercocebus, 47
Cercopithecinae, 48
Cercopithecus, 47
Cerebral Function in Infancy and Childhood (Peiper), 143
Chariots of the Gods (von Däniken), 420
Childhood. *See* Infants

Child rearing, 429–35, 438; in primitive societies, 146–47; mortar in, 435; mother's role in, 141–47, 150; theories of, 147–49. *See also* Infants
Children: Their Hydropathic Management in Health and Disease (Shew), 147
Child's Mind, A (Beadle), 146
Chiliasm, 335–37
Chimpanzee, 138, 250, 281
Choukoutien caves, 92, 115
Christianity, 321–26, 328–29, 330–32, 335
City of God, The (St. Augustine), 219
Clark, Wilfred LeGros, 54
Cleanliness. *See* Soiling the nest
Cohn, Norman, 204
Cole, Sonia, 55
Colobinae, 48
Coming of Age in Samoa (Mead), 176
Communication, 38, 164; painting as, 130
Conscious mind, 279–83, 287–89, 303, 304, 327
Consumer credit, 401–2
Consumerism, 403–5
Corporations, 395–97, 404–5, 413
Credit. *See* Consumer credit
Crime, 249–52, 381
Crime and the Mind (Bromberg), 250
Cro-Magnon man, 204

Däniken, Erich von, 420
Dart, Raymond, 52–54, 192
Darwinism, 4–5, 273–74, 325
Death, 311–12, 313–14, 325–26, 419–20, 422, 423, 441
Denzin, Norman K., 170
Dependency, 101; of infants, 24; of females, 36, 210–11,

Dependency (*continued*)
227, 230. *See also* Women,
subordination of
Descartes, René, 3, 8
Descent from arborea, 41–73
Deutero-Isiah, 324
Deutsch, Helene, 233–34, 235
Dewey, John, 170
Diamond, A. S., 113, 114–15
Diet, 21, 26, 51, 91, 92, 93
Direct transactions, 87
Display of aggression, 188, 191,
417; systematization of, 69–
70, 71–72
Dobzhansky, Theodosius, 83
Domestication of animals and
grain, 120, 122, 206, 330,
405, 447
Dominance system. *See* Male
dominance; Dependence
Dostoevsky, Fyodor, 256
Douvan, Elizabeth, 212
Drugs, 269–70, 304, 350
Dunnett, Sinclair, 66

Education, 163–67, 168–71,
361–62, 382, 388–89; in
Sumer, 164, 168
Edwards, Jonathan, 354–56
Eliade, Mircea, 307, 308, 309,
310
Emergent I, 409
Energy crisis, 447
Environment and Archeology
(Butzer), 50
Essential genes, 86–87, 107, 164
Europe, 353
Eve, 209
*Evolutionary Biology of the
Primates* (Osman Hill), 11n
Existence, essential factors of,
441
Extinction, danger of, 185, 395

Fall of man, 319–20, 333
Family, 33–34, 174, 385–86

Fantasy. *See* Success fantasy;
Salvation fantasy
Fat, 82
Fatherhood, 103–4, 172, 174–
76, 181
Felines, 11
Female sex roles, 26–27, 29–30,
33–35, 85, 100–104, 105–6,
164, 166–67, 199, 210–44,
330, 340, 371, 379, 382, 429;
in Sumer, 33. *See also* Child
rearing; Dependency; Infants,
terrestrialization of; Women,
subordination of
Female Sexuality (Torok), 230
Feminism. *See* Liberation
movements
Figes, Eva, 209
Fire, 91–94, 108–9, 134
Food. *See* Diet
Ford, Henry, 376
Forelimbs, 64, 97; artificial
extension of, 72, 88, 104,
134, 152, 192, 194, 195, 196,
361, 373, 405. *See also* Tools
Forests, aridaridation of, 30;
reduction of, 49
Forward perspective, need for,
110
*Four Hundred Centuries of
Cave Art* (Breuil), 128n
Freeman, Walter, 294–95
Freud, Sigmund, 172–73, 175,
178–80, 213–35 *passim*, 256,
260, 272, 273, 274–75, 286–
87, 289–90, 302; on women,
213–24
From the Tablets of Sumer
(Kramer), 33
Fuel, 9–10

Gage, Phineas, 293–94
Gamblers Anonymous, 257
Gambling, 252–58
Gambling in Sweden (Tec),
254

Garden of Eden, 209, 421
Genesis, 209
Gestation periods, 100
Gibbon, 48, 189
Gilgamesh, 323
Gods, 311, 313–18
Goodall, James, 61, 64–65, 66, 67, 69
Gornick, Vivian, 226–27, 238
Guilt, 319–20
Gunz Glacial, 89–90

Halliday, James L., 143, 144
Hallucinogens, 269–70
Hamburg, David, 187
Hammurabi, 250
Harran, 315
Hawkes, Jacquetta, 127
Heaven, 326–27, 329, 331, 335–37, 347, 421
Heaven on earth. *See* Neo-arborea
Hierarchical society, 342–43, 346, 353
Hell, 333
Helping Your Child in Elementary School (Jameson), 165
Hinduism, 321, 322, 324
History and Origin of Language, The (Diamond), 113
Hitler, Adolf, 207–8
Hobbs, Lisa, 220, 221, 222
Hogg, Garry, 205n, 206
Holt, L. Emmett, 148, 149
Hominid, 75–78; in arborea, 56–57; changes in mores of, 98, 101–7; migration of, 91; predation by, 62–64; terrestrialization of, 57–58, 75–78, 193–94
Homo erectus, 83–84, 93–94, 99, 118. *See also* Peking man
Homo sapiens, 81, 82, 99, 118, 129, 194
Human aggression, 185–87, 189–91, 194–97, 409–10

Human Aggression (Storr), 190
Human Evolution (Campbell), 43n
Human psychology, theories of, 274–76
Hunting, 84–86, 96–97, 98–102, 112, 114, 117–18, 129, 166, 167, 179, 180, 190, 191–93, 196, 197–98, 206, 212–13, 215–16, 224–25; era of, 211, 425, 426, 445, 447
Hypnotics, 269

Images and Symbols (Eliade), 309
In the Shadow of Man (Goodall), 64
Indirect transactions, 78, 247, 414
Industrial Revolution, 227, 353, 362–63
Infant sexuality. *See* Oedipus complex, myth
Infants, arboreal nature of, 137–45, 430–36; reflexes of, 137–40, 143; terrestrialization of, 110, 137, 140–50, 152–71, 172, 179–81, 429–30, 431–32; nursery rhymes, 153–7; stories, 158–59, 161–63
Inferior primates, 50–51
Insectivores, 21, 23
Instinct, 9, 11, 12, 15, 449
Interpretation of Dreams, The (Freud), 173
Intoxicants, 261–63
Introduction to Physical Anthropology (Montagu), 43
Involuted evolution, 78–80, 82

Jameson, Marshall C., 165, 166
Jesus Christ, 323–24
Jews, persecution of, 207
John, the Apostle, 326
J.P., 296–300
Judaism, 315–18, 321, 322, 335

Jung, Carl Gustav, 272–75,
  290–91, 308
Kennedy, John F., 427
Killer "instinct" 9, 37, 62–63
Knuckle-walking, 44, 46, 47–
  48, 49, 50
Kramer, Samuel Noah, 32, 33–
  34, 168, 314
Kurtin, Björn, 42–43

Lactantius, 335–37
Lancaster, C. S., 96–97, 99
Lancaster, Jane B., 60
Law, 248–50
Leakey, Louis S. B., 49, 54, 105,
  192
Leakey, Mary, 55, 105
Lethality, 29, 190–94, 197–204,
  409–14, 445; miscalculation
  concerning, 409–11, 412–13;
  in twentieth century, 390–2;
  becomes neo-lethality, 395,
  409
Liberation movements, 377–79,
  380–81, 382
Lilith, 209
Limb functions, 20–21. See also
  Forelimbs
Locomotion, 56
Lorenz, Conrad, 186
Love and Liberation (Hobbs),
  220

Macaque, 48–49
McLuhan, Marshall, 400
Male dominance, 188–89, 210–
  14, 216–17, 222–23, 225,
  227–44, 433, 447
Male sex roles, 26–27, 29–30,
  33–35, 100–104, 105–6, 164,
  166, 172, 199, 210–44, 330,
  332, 340, 379, 382, 422, 425,
  428
Malinowski, Bronislaw, 173,
  174, 175, 176

Man, 7, 14, 15; arboreal nature
  of, 87; terrestrial conflict in,
  134, 137, 367; and lethality,
  87, 180, 201–4, 361, 362,
  389–95, 413, 445; self-
  destruction of, 407
Man-beast symbiosis, 131–33,
  200
Marais, Eugene, 259–61, 262
Marshall, S. L. A., 202–3
Marx, Karl, 374–75
Mason, William A., 139
Mather, Cotton, 359, 372
Matriarchal society, 174
Mead, Margaret, 176
Meat-eating. See Hominids,
  predation by
Melman, Seymour, 415
Meyer, Adolphe E., 169
Militarism, 199–204, 395, 411–
  15, 443–44, 445
Military economy, 415–17
Mindel Glacial, 89–90
Miocene, 47
Missing link, bison as, 134;
  body as, 440
Moltke, Hellmuth von, 199
Monkey, 45–49
Monogamy, 34
Montagu, Ashley, 43–44
Moon God. See Nannar
More, Thomas, 347
Morris, Desmond, 43, 81, 226,
  240, 241
Mortar, 77–87, 91, 97, 108–10,
  414, 428, 438; as basis for
  terrestrialization, 151, 246–
  48; as compensation for
  genetic deficiencies, 77, 86–
  87, 140–45, 228, 406–7;
  credit as, 401–2; excess of,
  417; exhaustion of, 395, 406–
  7; hunting as, 98–99; inability
  to produce, 141–42; man as,
  452; militarism as, 163–64;
  need for, 76–77, 103–4, 107,

Mortar (*continued*)
140, 145, 304, 402, 404, 406,
417, 422, 436; preservation
of, 371, 416; production of,
211, 214–15, 258, 406;
production-consumption
process as, 443; purpose of,
227; rejection of, 214, 387;
self-generation of, 373–74,
375–76, 384–85, 389, 452;
tools as, 93–94, 411, 416,
425–27, 442; training in
creation of, 163–64, 436;
writing as, 164. *See also*
Psychic mortar; Subsistence
mortar.
Moses, 322
Motherhood, 147–50. *See also*
Infants, terrestrialization of;
Women
*My Friends the Wild Chim-
panzees* (Goodall), 65
Myth, 307–11. *See also* Religion

Nader, Ralph, 403
Naked Ape, The (Morris), 43,
236, 240
Nannar, 315–16, 317
Nazis, 207–8
Neanderthal man, 204
Neo-arborea, 15–16, 213, 222,
225, 243, 321, 346, 348, 352,
357–58, 363–64, 369, 370,
374, 384, 401, 411, 418, 421,
430; destruction of, 407, 417;
and mortar, 417; rim of, 388,
392–93, 394, 406
Neo-lethality, 395, 408, 409,
414
Neolithic Revolution, 120–24,
426
Neo-terrestria, 394-95, 417
Nests, 27
New World, 347, 348–49, 352,
353
Nicea, Council of, 325

Nostalgia, 309–11
Not From the Apes (Kurtin),
42
Nursery rhymes, 153–57
Oedipus complex, myth of,
172–73, 175, 176, 177–81
Olduvai Gorge, 105
On Aggression (Lorenz), 186n
Orangutan, 48
Osman Hill, W. C., 11n
Outline of Psychoanalysis, An
(Freud), 289

Pain, 259–60, 263
Paine, Lauran, 334
Paleolithic Crisis, 120–24
Papio, 47
Paradisaical past, 308–9, 327
Patriarchal Attitudes (Figes),
209
Patriarchal society, 175, 176.
See also Male dominance
Paul, the Apostle, 141, 327,
328, 331–32, 341–42, 359–60
Peking man, 92, 96, 115, 204
Peiper, Albrecht, 143, 144
Penis envy, 217–21, 230–33
Personal property, 35
Phyletic memory, 131, 277–81,
307–8
Piltdown man, 53
Play. *See* Infants, terrestrializa-
tion of
Pleistocene Epoch, 89–92, 99,
109, 134
Pliocene, 50
Pollution, 10, 398, 449–50
Post-hunt era, 165, 185, 193–
94, 196–200, 243, 410, 417
Predation. *See* Man and
lethality
Predators, 21, 38, 71, 188–89,
193, 200, 422–23, 426. *See
also* Male sex roles
Prehensile feet, 56

Prehistory and the Beginnings of Civilization (Hawkes and Woolley), 128n
Primate aggression, 185–89, 195
Primate sexuality, 236, 242–44
Primates, toilet training of, 11
Primate vocalization, 111–16
Production-consumption process, 371–76, 395, 397–405, 413, 414, 415, 417–18, 443; uncontrollability of, 395–400; present state of, 402–5
Production Revolution, 225
Prostitute, social role of, 383–84
Protestant Ethic, 359, 401
Protestantism, 346, 361
Psychic mortar, 425–26, 427
Psychotherapy, 283, 286–87, 289–92, 302–3, 305; for women, 229–30
Pursuit of the Millennium, The (Cohn), 204

Racism. *See* Liberation movements
Ramapithecus, 47
Rape, 228–29, 236–37, 238
Reflex. *See* Arboreal reflex
Religion, 306–8, 311–38, 388, 419–20, 427
Religionists, 4, 420
Reproduction, 22–23
Responsibility for self, 351–52
Reynolds, Vernon, 66, 138
Riss Glacial, 89–90
Robinson, Bryan W., 111
Robinson, Mary Frances, 294
Roman Catholic Church, 344, 345–46, 388

Salvation fantasy, 357–62, 394
Samoans, 176–78
Scarne, John, 253
Sedatives, 269
Self-awareness, 84

Self-continuity, 295–96, 300
Sermon on the Mount, 328–29
Sex roles. *See* Female sex roles; Male sex roles
Sexual mores, 34–35, 175–76, 210–44, 379–80, 450–51
Sexual promiscuity, 29, 87, 106, 152, 249, 265, 383–84, 386–87, 400
Sexual signals, 238–43
Shew, Joel, 147, 149
Shulman, Alix, 232
Skinner, B. F., 291
Slavery, 205–6
Sleep, 267–69
Socialism, 247, 374, 375, 403
Society and Drugs (Blum), 267–8, 270
Soiling the nest, 27, 152, 449–50
Soul of the Ape, The (Marais), 259
Southwick, Charles H., 187
Species/environment equation, 88–89, 117, 120, 189–90, 227–28, 249, 277, 279
Species profile, 76, 83, 145, 151, 227, 395, 428; arboreal/terrestrial dichotomy of, 140–1; and fire, 92; of hominids, 76, 77, 108
Speech, 110–16
State, 451, 452; as psychic mortar, 427–28
Storr, Anthony, 190, 193, 194–95
Storytelling, 158–61, 161–63
Stouffer, Samuel A., 202
Subsistence mortar, 387–88
Success fantasy, 357–62, 394
Sumer, 31–38, 95, 122, 130, 164, 192, 198, 205, 211, 313–14, 316, 323, 340
Sumerians, The (Kramer), 32, 168

Survival crises. *See* Terrestrial crises
Sustenance, 35–37, 422
Tec, Nechama, 254–55
Ten Commandments, 248–49
Terhune, William B., 263–64, 265, 266
Terrestrial/arboreal conflict. *See* Arboreal/terrestrial conflict
Terrestrial brain, 151–52
Terrestrial crises, 129–30, 134, 140, 193–94, 212, 304, 305, 306, 307, 406–7
Terrestrialist, 370–71, 388, 431
Terrestrialization process, 51–52, 57–58, 78–81, 95–9, 108–10, 117
Terrestrial mind. *See* Conscious mind
Terrestrial stress. 15. *See also* Body Stress.
Thompson, Clara, 178
Time-anxiety, 84–86, 106–7, 124, 159, 169, 283, 284, 290, 292, 422, 428; cure for, 400; reduction of, 401; release from, 327, 361
To Gamble or Not to Gamble (Wagner), 253
Toilet training, 11, 148
Tools, 55–62, 88, 361, 362–63, 405. *See also* Forelimbs
Tooze, Ruth, 158, 160
Torok, Maria, 230, 231, 233
Tranquilizers, 269, 302, 304
Trobriand Islanders, 173–6, 177
Twilight melancholia, 260–63

Unconscious mind, *See* Arboreal brain
United States of America, 352–54, 369–70, 453
Ur, 314, 315, 316–17, 322
Utilitarianism, 266–67, 451, 454
Utopia (More), 347

Violence. *See* Hunting; Lethality; War
Visual acuity, 21–22
Voice From the Congo, A (Ward), 206

Wagner, Walter, 253, 256, 257
War, 191–92, 193–94, 196–97, 198–204, 206, 207–8, 411–12, 414–15, 416
Ward, Herbert, 206
Washburn, Sherwood, 44, 45–47, 48, 83, 96–97, 99, 187
Watts, James W., 294–95
Wesley, John, 360
Wisdom of the Body, The (Cannon), 68
Woman in Sexist Society (Bardwick and Douvan), 212, 232
Women, subordinate status of, 209–44
Woolley, Leonard, 128n, 314, 315
Work ethic, 370–72
Würm Glacial, 89–90, 119

Zoroaster, 324, 351

Edward M. Keating

Edward M. Keating, the author of *Free Huey!* and *The Scandal of Silence,* has practiced law, taught at the University of Santa Clara, and is the founder of *Ramparts* magazine. He lives in Sunnyvale, California.